# DRAWN FROM MEMORY

Moffett Studio

JTM

# DRAWN FROM MEMORY

BY

*John T. McCutcheon*

*Containing Many of the Author's
Famous Cartoons
and Sketches*

## THE BOBBS-MERRILL COMPANY, INC.
*Publishers*

INDIANAPOLIS                    NEW YORK

# FOREWORD

~

JOHN MCCUTCHEON could remember me when I wasn't much more than a wide grin. He had, therefore, the advantage of me, because my first clear memory of him is on a June week end in 1902 when I hung over his shoulder while he drew pictures of me in assorted attitudes and riding on various animals. I was growing rather lanky by that time and he did not fail to record the fact.

Whenever he was a guest at my parents' table, at Ragdale, I crept part-way down the stairs in my nightgown to peek into the dining room where I could watch him happily.

Sometimes the whole family sat by the fire while he told tale after tale of his adventures. Especially I liked the one about the Sultan of Sulu.

Later, at my urgent insistence after we were married, he began dictating these adventures to me. Gradually, over the years, the *Opus*, as he called it, developed and expanded.

But always there was something to hinder progress—some other deadline to meet, some other dream to be fulfilled. So it came about that the completion of the *Opus* was deferred too long.

Since, during thirty-two years, I had the happiness of being his secretary as well as his wife, it became my privilege, if also my responsibility, to make the final revision, to fill in the remaining gaps from his letters and speeches, and from my own Boswellian notebook.

It is my hope that I have done this in such a way that he would be pleased, and the reader not too conscious of the difference; in such a way that the shining through of his personality has not been dimmed— his gentleness, his insight, above all, the sweetness of his disposition and of his smile.

All that is good in the chronicle is John's; anything that could be better is mine.

EVELYN SHAW MCCUTCHEON

# INTRODUCTION

~

IN STARTING to write an autobiography, the writer confronts a major problem of psychology and ethics at the very outset. There is no getting around it. It is there and must be met. How modest shall he be?

If, for the sake of argument, he follows his natural inclination and is 100 per cent modest, that's the end of his autobiography, for no self-portrait in words can get very far without the appearance of the capital *I*. The hero of the book is himself—he is the Hamlet of the play.

Neither can one use the editorial *we* in an autobiography. It would sound absurd, not to say abandoned, to write, "We proposed to a charming young lady, and in time we married her."

Once I wrote a book about African hunting. A friend confessed to me his disappointment. It didn't provide as many goose-flesh thrills as other hunting books had given him. What I think I did was to write the first book that had a slightly debunking or deflationary effect on two thirds of the dangers of African hunting. But perhaps I was too modest. An autobiography is only a continuation of hunting trips and other things, and perhaps making oneself heroic is what helps to make the book more enjoyable.

One way of getting around this difficulty is to let someone else do the work and call it a biography. He can lie about you all he likes, and you will not only be thus glorified but will escape the suspicion of blowing your own horn.

However, other people have got away with it—so here goes.

J. T. McC.

# CONTENTS

## I. On the Banks of the Wabash

## II. Drawn to Chicago

## III. On the Toss of a Coin

## IV. Restless Roving

# CONTENTS—*Continued*

## V. Treasure Trove

## VI. Drawing to a Close

# ILLUSTRATIONS

# ILLUSTRATIONS—Continued

# ~I~

# ON THE BANKS OF THE WABASH

*The Harvest Home Party in Mrs. Riley Withersby's Barn*

# ~ 1 ~

## Across from the Yellow Barn

THE farmhouse where I was born was on a gentle hilltop on the Romney road a few miles south of Lafayette, Indiana. From its modest height I looked out over field after field of corn, east toward the Ashbys, west to the old Mintonye Church, north to the Wea (pronounced We-aw) Creek and south along the Crawfordsville pike, all within the intimate, friendly bounds of the Wea Plains, named for the Indian tribe formerly occupying the region. A Shawnee mound was near by. Eight or ten miles away was the site of Ouiatenon, one of the larger villages on the old Tecumseh Trail leading from Vincennes up to Lake Erie. Northward a few miles, near the Wabash River, lay the battlefield of Tippecanoe, where General Harrison defeated Tecumseh's warriors under the Prophet, thereby winning the Presidency of the United States.

The grownups around me were continually discussing Indian campaigns still being waged throughout the West. From time to time news filtered through of encounters with the Sioux or other tribes on the warpath. I must have listened popeyed to reports of the Custer massacre, for soon afterward I rushed into the kitchen screaming, "Ma! The Indians chased me!" as I retired to a new line of defense where I knew I was always safe. To arms! To arms! was my slogan in times of danger. I claimed to have escaped the onslaught of a presumably superior force unscathed except for a slight crisis of the

nerves. This was probably my first experience as a war correspondent.

There was, in fact, little on my young horizon in the middle seventies beyond corn and Indian traditions. Thirty years later, while groping in the early fall for an idea, it required only a small effort of imagination to see spears and tossing feathers in the tasseled stalks, tepees through the smoky haze; and I evolved *Injun Summer*.

Certainly this cartoon of mine about which I have heard most goes back to my earliest childhood, long before I even knew what a cartoon was.

Many other times when I sat at my drawing board, gazing blankly at the paper, with not an idea in my head, the deadline for tomorrow's front page creeping implacably nearer, nerves getting tauter with each tick of the clock, out of the past leaped an idea. By what cerebral path it came, by what association evoked I did not know, yet there it was, unsought, unbidden, but oh, so welcome!

Perhaps an explanation may be found among these rambling memorabilia in which I plan to tell all or nearly all. For it is likely that the images and impressions, conscious and unconscious, accumulated on my way through three quarters of a century and a large part of the world filled the hopper from which my cartoon ideas were drawn.

When the grownups were not talking of Indians, they were exchanging Civil War reminiscences. Our house was a rendezvous for all the men who served with my father. Rebels were still on everyone's mind. Even one of the farmhands was suspected. Thus my early ideas were incubated in an atmosphere of adventure. Undoubtedly this affected—but how differently—both my own life and my brother George Barr's. Unlike me, he cared nothing for the lure of danger except vicariously; nevertheless his later absorbing romances must have had their roots in this stimulating environment.

Across the road from our house was the Yellow Barn, a notable landmark at that time. Ninety feet long and nearly fifty wide, it was more familiar to the west-bound emigrants than the town of Lafayette itself. In it I suffered an early disaster. My brother George's legs had the advantage of four years' growth over mine. In following him across some open joists I failed to bridge a gap by a couple of inches. I fell and broke my nose, thereby detracting still further from an already minus quantity of pulchritude which had previously occasioned some concern in the family. The story goes that soon after my birth, my uncle George sought to console my mother: "Now don't you mind what they say, Clara. He'll look all right after a while!"

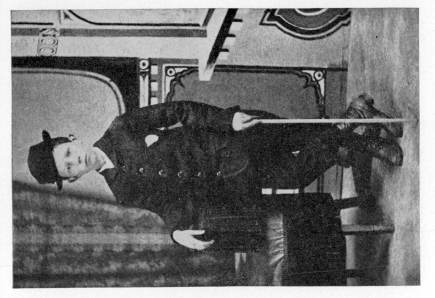

EIGHT YEARS OLD

MY BROTHER GEORGE AND I

MY BIRTHPLACE

DIPHTHERIA VICTIMS

The author is at lower left.

I suppose I was much like any other small boy growing up on a farm, unless down there in Indiana we wore more freckles and less shoes. Dressing in our little bare cold room was not a hardship, because we knew nothing different.

Up the crossroad beyond the tollgate at our corner was my paternal grandfather's house, the first brick one built in Tippecanoe County. It was occupied, when I knew it, by my Uncle George and Aunt Kate.

To my youthful fancy it seemed vast and impressive with its queer gables and diamond-shaped windowpanes, surrounded by somber cedar trees. Whenever I stayed there, owls hooted in those trees, branches rasped against the roof, and the overwhelming silences between caused me to scrooch down farther and farther into the billowy featherbed. Once I disgraced myself and had to walk home alone the long mile under the walnut trees planted by my grandfather, very uncomfortable as to my lower half, and vaguely rebellious against something or other! How firmly that sticks in my mind when I have forgotten so many more important things.

My maternal grandfather passed his later years visiting from one to another of his children. He liked to stay with my parents, perhaps because theirs was a happy household. He was a good-natured old man who loved to take a lunch in his pocket and be gone all day down along the creek, returning at sundown, very much pleased, with six little sunfish as long as his finger. I was always begging to go fishing with him.

My taste for big-game hunting may have germinated when somebody in Benton County, next west from ours, reported having seen a lion! Families in both counties were at once deeply stirred. We children were terrified. Armed parties combed the country and all ordinary work was suspended. As far as I am concerned the mystery of what became of the lion, or whether, indeed, there ever was one, remains unsolved.

It was always exciting to venture past the "Yaller Barn" as far as Jean La Pelle's house, silent and deserted and believed to be haunted. Something had happened there—another mystery! It bore a gruesome brand and was avoided by everyone. Up that same road plodded the local bogeyman, Thorntown Cyrus. He had become harmlessly demented at the death of his wife and now traveled through the country dragging a little wagon and a large doll. Thorntown Cyrus exercised such a hold on my imagination that whenever his name was invoked I was always careful to behave.

There were not many amusements in those days, and such as there were—cornhuskings, barn-raisings, spelling bees, weddings and funerals—were carried on slightly beyond my range of personal recollection. All the children for miles around attended their first theatrical performance when a traveling troupe came to Romney and gave *Ten Nights in a Barroom*. The show was likewise attended by a lively measles germ, and the ensuing epidemic was exhaustive. What happened in a barroom became of minor importance compared to what happened at home. I had to lie in bed with nothing to do except listen to the kildeers calling across the misty bottom lands down by the creek. Later in the darkness, if the wind were right, the sound of an accordion came up from a neighbor's farm playing "Do you love me, Mollie darling?" "Listen to the mockingbird" and "The Year of Jubilo."

Our parents often took us with them when they drove to Lafayette in the surrey. Our father would enliven the long eight miles with recitations such as that about the gallant fight between Roderick Dhu and James Fitz-James, or "Rainy Lake, Lake of the Woods, Bay of Campeche," a jingle by which we learned geography. Certainly George's subsequent skill in colorful narration was inherited from our father, a rare raconteur who thrilled us then as I have seldom been thrilled since.

Sometimes he would stop the horses, get out and be gone for a few mysterious moments. Upon his return our eager voices arose, clamorous for information. "What's the matter, Pa? What d'you get out for, Pa? Where'd you go, Pa?" This rapid-fire quiz always brought the same answer, "Thought I saw a prairie chicken." Further cross-examination always disclosed his failure to catch the prairie chicken. Often in later years I found this a handy euphemism, with enthusiastic co-operation on the part of my own small sons.

Once as we were driving up the hill toward home, the back seat of the surrey became detached and threw my brother and me to the road in a graceful back somersault.

A few years ago I revisited the old farm. Our house had been painted and much beporched, though the front gable was graced by the same rounded triple window. The trees were big and spreading; I could not recognize the one that had been struck by lightning as I sat in my mother's lap in a window close by.

The tollgate was gone, the Yellow Barn had been moved away. The line of walnut trees no longer sheltered the country road, and the old brick house had long ago burned and been replaced.

Only when I swung the gate into the little Mintonye burying ground could I recapture a link with the past. Those who lay beneath the handful of weather-beaten monuments, whatever their lives, had at last attained literally the coveted bed of roses, for the old-fashioned thousand-leaf blossoms had been allowed to spread deep over the graves. They were climbing higher and higher toward the pair of stone doves above the inscribed names of my grandparents, John McCutchen and his wife Kesiah Ritchie.

## Forebears

THIS John McCutchen was the son of a still earlier John McCutchen and his wife Suzanna Caldwell. The path of his immediate ancestors led from Fairfax County, Virginia, through Kentucky to Ohio. He had five children: Margaret and Martha, John Barr, Joseph and

George. The eldest son, my father, was born in 1828 in Fairfax Township, Ross County, Ohio.

The great western trek was then under way, so when my father was about five years old, my grandfather moved into Indiana where he built the brick house I have mentioned, developed a fine stock farm and accumulated considerable land. I have the government documents, signed for Andrew Jackson and Martin Van Buren, relating to deeds and transfers, all written longhand and sprinkled with stamps and seals. My grandfather died when I was a year old. Being his namesake I have also his gold watch, his gold-headed cane and an oil painting of him. It shows a clean-shaven, clearcut face of strength and intelligence.

Back in Wigtownshire, Scotland, and in the north of Ireland are doubtless many of our name who spell it with an *en*, an *an* or an *eon*. These puzzling differences come from carelessness or ignorance; or the spelling was changed for appearance or euphony, or to conform to a simpler pronunciation. When the Middle West was being settled, folks didn't spell very well and didn't attach much importance to unanimity in the way a name was passed along. My father used the spelling as it appears on the Mintonye tombstone, but my Uncle George adopted *eon*. When I was twelve or thirteen, in one of those crusading spirits that always spurred me in some direction or other at that time, I too began signing my name with the *o*. Gradually the rest of the family followed suit.

My mother's family was originally established in Lancaster, Pennsylvania, by one Valentine Gramlach who landed in America from Germany in 1749 or thereabouts. The name had somehow become Crumley by the time my grandmother married Benjamin Glick. Like other pioneers, they had a large family, three daughters and five sons: Sarah, Clarissa, Mary, Elias, Daniel, Rufus and Monroe. Only one child, Richard, died early. With a group of Pennsylvania Lutherans, they came west and founded Lancaster, Ohio. It was there that my mother, Clarissa, was born in 1841. Soon afterward the family moved farther westward to the rich grainlands of Tippecanoe County and settled only three or four miles from my other grandfather.

Will Wilgus was an old friend of the family. I remember him well. His wooden leg fascinated me, as did the story of how he came to need it. As a boy he had been chased by a sow, and before he could get out of reach over a fence, she mangled his leg so badly it had to be cut off. For some reason, I never knew why, he recorded details concerning the sort of life my forebears lived just before the Civil War:

The Glick farm fronted nearly a mile on the main-traveled road leading from Crawfordsville to Lafayette. The road had lately been planked with boards two inches thick and twelve feet long and in 1850 the surface was true and level.

The Glicks were good livers and were a very hospitable family. The poor and destitute coming into the county were always directed to Glicks', and they always received kind treatment, everybody being welcomed and everybody being treated as an equal.

In the middle fifties, Clarissa was just coming into womanhood. She was possessed of a beautiful face and form, was an expert in all kinds of housework, was a fine horsewoman, had a fine alto voice, was charitable and friendly to everybody and was universally loved. Along about 1855 her mother died and the management and much of the work of the large establishment was thrown upon her young but willing shoulders.

The Glick homestead was headquarters for the meetings of the young people for miles about, and nearly always there was excitement of some kind. Bees would swarm and tin pans and horns were brought into service to induce them to settle down. Seining parties were formed and wagonloads of fish were caught. Hounds were kept for coon hunting. The country abounded in wild geese, wild duck, wild turkey, pigeons and quail. Parties to hunt wild plums, wild grapes and other berries and nuts came home laden. At no time did less than twenty people eat at the Glick table, and this number often swelled upward toward a hundred [*sic!*]. It can be imagined what a task this put on the women of the household, but meals were always served promptly and the food was well-prepared and abundant.

The Glicks were all Democrats but in spite of the intense feeling elsewhere on politics, the neighbors around the Glick homestead were all friendly and tolerant. The Democratic Rangers and the Republican Wideawakes each helped to swell the others' ranks when prizes were offered by the political parties for well-filled rallies. This tolerance and good will was brought about mainly by the friendships formed at the Glick meetings, where there was little intoxication and no quarreling or fighting, although such things were common at other gatherings in the county. The Glick boys formed themselves into a band. Rufus was the fifer, Monroe played the tenor drum, and Dan performed on the bass drum. They played mostly for the Democrats, but when not otherwise engaged, their services were in demand by the Republicans.

At the age of nineteen my father had become a drover. He took his cattle through to Pennsylvania over the mountains, and his business increased until he was shipping in very large droves. Then, in 1857, he failed because of a financial panic. In the historic year of 1861 he organized a company recruited from his friends and neighbors in Tippecanoe County and went to war commissioned as captain of Company K, 15th Indiana Volunteers. During the first year, while serving in Virginia, he received a wound at the battle of Greenbrier River, a fragment of shell behind his right ear. He fought in the battles of Shiloh, Inka Springs, Perryville and Stone River. After about three years, the wound never having healed, he was invalided home from Murfreesboro, and he resumed the cattle business.

My father was always known by his middle name of Barr. He seems to have been a gay citizen, with a military beard, a broad-brimmed campaign hat and a jovial sense of humor. I have talked to many old ladies, belles of an earlier day, whose eyes have lighted up at the mention of "Captain Barr." Evidently he made love to all the girls in and around Lafayette until he met Clara Glick and his affections ceased to wander.

Will Wilgus had the following to say about this:

> Captain Barr returned to peaceful pursuits followed by the love and devotion of his whole command. He returned unmarried and heart-whole. Clarissa Glick, or Clara as she was called by her friends, had many suitors, but the man had not yet appeared who could win her away from her duty to her father and her home. The dashing Captain Barr soon became an active and persistent suitor. Her family unselfishly advised her to accept him, and their advice and the ardor of the captain's wooing gained the day.

They were married in October 1865. Her father gave her, as a wedding present, two farms. On one of these, a little way north of the Glick homestead on the Romney road, my brother George Barr was born in 1866. Not long afterward they moved to the less pretentious one across from the Yellow Barn, where I came along on May 6, 1870.

## 3

## Interval

WHEN I was six years old the prolonged depression which started in '73 was still afflicting the nation. Yet our family life, I remember, was always cheerful. A third little boy, Ben, arrived in '75.

My father's continued activities as drover had been widespread and profitable; his droves were encountered on almost every road; he shipped as far east as Baltimore, and north to Chicago. He never complained when markets went against him and often paid a bonus when they didn't. Farmers would hold their stock, year after year, for Captain Barr.

But he was too kindhearted. He would give whenever he had. It was not the code of a money-maker. Friends and neighbors soon discovered this convenient weakness. His generosity was greatly admired but often abused. His failure in the panic of '57 had been due to going on the note of a friend when he lost $60,000, a lot of money even today. After the war, there was never an end of old soldiers coming to him. By the early '70s he had regained a considerable fortune, which he once more lost.

In 1876, when he was forty-eight years old, conditions became so bad that my father was forced to abandon his life as a drover. Since he had never been a practical farmer, he gave up any idea of farming and became associated with Purdue University. My horizon then broadened beyond the green and yellow cornfields.

Purdue was only a little older than I. Its fame had hardly crossed the state line. The few buildings were crudely new; trees and vines had not yet started to soften a general baldness of the campus. Less than one hundred students were in attendance. The list of alumni numbered one—an imposing uniqueness.

We lived there for about a year, in the west end of the Ladies' Hall, and my father managed the commissariat, which is only a euphemistic way of saying he ran the place where the students ate, an occupation for which he was conspicuously unfitted.

I remember only two things about those days. One was the tremendous excitement when the first electric light was shown in front of the chemical laboratory. The other was the sound of the Chauncey School bell which summoned me to my first school. It filled me with a sickish foreboding. I hated the school with an intensity that was devastating. Today when I hear a bell of the same flat metallic tone, regardless of my surroundings the same old "gone" feeling sweeps over me.

Many people have sung the power of sounds and smells, the power of certain fragrances, or certain music, to turn the memory back from now to then. I know many such, not all with such gloomy association as the Chauncey School bell.

There is the clucking of a hen, moving earnestly about as she in-

structs her brood in the technique of finding food. This is a sound
of springtime. The pounding of a hammer in measured crescendo, the
clang of the blacksmith's anvil, the far-carrying cries of children at
play, the lazy flapping of curtains in early warm days—these are all

cheerful reminders of my boyhood down along the Wabash. I couldn't
forget any of them, though I seldom hear many of them now.

No matter where I might be, the refrain of "Sweet Heather Bells"
would transport me instantly back to the purple long ago when I was
a student at Purdue, full of romantic ideas involving moonlight and
organdies.

In the Philippines during the Spanish-American War I collected
many sense impressions: the sudden sharp, echoless pop of a Mauser
rifle operated by somebody hidden in the bamboos ahead; the sound
of distant artillery, like slamming of heavy doors; and the clank of
cavalry equipment along a lonely bamboo-fringed road in Luzon when
a troop was making a surprise night march. In the dark stillness,
whenever the sudden barking of a dog is taken up by other dogs far
and near, I am again with General Funston's shadowy scouts, falling
flat on my face while the air hums with bullets from the aroused insurgent earthworks across the Rio Grande.

Then there are the cries of the ricksha men who propelled me along
the road to Kampala in Uganda—a sort of haunting chant, once heard,
never forgotten.

Whoever has traveled in China can hear in his mind the liquid eerie music of the pigeons that fly over Peking at sunset with whistles of balsa wood fastened under their wings.

Once I spent a happy winter in Tucson. We rented a house which had a victrola. Two records were particular favorites of our ten-year-old son, Shaw—"Moonlight on the River Colorado" and "Hobo Bill's Last Ride." Endlessly he vibrated between the victrola and the piano, picking out the chords. They became inseparably associated with Arizona. No matter where we are, if one of us hums a snatch of either song, instantly we are transported to the cactus-covered desert in its ring of mountains, and a pleasant nostalgia comes over us.

And smells. Some smells are odors, aromas, perfumes, fragrances; others, confidentially, are not! Like sounds, they can call to mind, unexpectedly, some person or place.

Any schoolboy of the last century can easily invoke the smell of an old slate rag, musty and sour. Or a new Noah's Ark. Or the inside of a circus tent.

When I first came to Chicago I used to celebrate momentous events, such as a two-dollar raise, by buying a cake of odoriferous French soap, from which you got a maximum of result. When I approached, my friends knew at once that I was celebrating something.

Then there's the "odorous church where the organ swells," and the jasmine of yesterday, full of Victorian sentiment and oomph. And how about sizzling bacon after a day of hunting?

Sounds and smells can be like magic passwords that lift us out of the crowded hours of today and transport us back to the glamorous past when there was nothing much more exciting than our first pair of long pants—ours or our sons'. I have found cartoon material in many such memories.

After a year at Purdue my father was in a frame of mind distinctly receptive to any change. This came in the summer of 1877. A friend, James Baird, had been elected sheriff of Tippecanoe County. He was a bachelor and offered my father the position of deputy sheriff on condition that he occupy the sheriff's residence adjoining the jail and take care of the prisoners.

In August our family moved into it, and thereafter for two years I lived in close and friendly relations with various criminals and malefactors, male and female, who were domiciled behind the sturdy walls and bars of the county calaboose. It was not perhaps a refining influence for a boy from seven to nine, yet, I found many likable qualities among the inmates.

The only crime directly affecting me was on the outside. My uncle, Dr. Glick, lived near by with his hostler, who necessarily learned from time to time something of the layout of our house and the habits of our family. Upon a certain occasion this groom saw my parents depart for an evening at the local theater. He then crept in and secreted himself under the bed in which my brother George and I were peacefully asleep. He lay there quietly until the family had returned and retired; then he absconded with my father's pocketbook, containing about $100, and my small bank full of my entire fortune—$6.00, mostly in pennies! The following day a search revealed my bank smashed and rifled. Suspicion soon narrowed down to the culprit, who was arrested and confessed. The $100 was recovered, but my pile was gone.

When in the vicissitudes of local politics a new sheriff was elected, my father resumed his life as a drover, and after a time we moved to the little village of Elston, two miles out from Lafayette on the familiar Romney road.

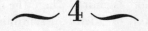

# Elston

Go SOUTH from Lafayette, turn down the old Plank Road; then with the Wabash River on your right, cross the road at the Man Trap, climb the hill past the old Lafayette Junction and go on two miles farther. You will now arrive at the outskirts of Elston. If you are in a car, you will slide through it so quickly you are hardly aware it is a settlement.

But in that distant day in 1880 of which I write there were no cars or even bicycles. Your horse-drawn vehicle would plod along, pass an occasional house, reach a little tollgate no longer in use, and then perhaps draw up at a watering trough in front of a two-story brick store, flanked by a one-story frame saloon. Across the road you'd see another little combination store and saloon; near by were a couple of blacksmith shops and a grain elevator, which dominated the village. From this simple nucleus which constituted the business district, twenty or thirty unpretentious dwellings were strung out for a mile or so along the two diverging roads, the southern one to Romney and Crawfordsville, the western one to West Point and Shawnee Mound.

In the blazing sun of a summer day you could not find a sleepier setting of uneventfulness in all the land, yet it was the glamorous background for absorbing activities. A belief I've had for a long time is that it doesn't matter where one is, it's wholly a matter of what one does while there that makes life interesting. Imagination is the handmaiden of adventure, and when aided by enterprise, no life can be wholly dull.

I was ten years old when my family, after two colorful and quite delightful years in the sheriff's residence, a brief few months on Sixth Street where my sister Jessie was born, and another briefer stop in Linnwood, moved out to Elston. We occupied a two-story brick house near the corner, which belonged to a cousin. When she married, we moved next door into a smaller frame cottage.

My father resumed his work as a drover. Nearly every day saw him faring forth in his buckboard to dicker for hogs. In the summer I went with him to help drive them, thereby acquiring a lot of information about their habits that was later to be useful in my cartoon work. If you've never driven hogs, you will be interested to know that it is almost as dusty a job as working on the tail end of a threshing machine. After a long summer day spent trudging in the wake of a drove of hogs it was difficult to distinguish between the driver and the driven.

These many trips gave me a chance to know my genial father. He talked and hummed a lot. He had a vast fund of reminiscences covering the war and his life as a drover which he told with keen humor. Nearly always, in the corner of his mouth was a much-chewed cigar, usually unlighted. His beard and his longish hair still had much of the jauntiness that made him such a romantic figure in Lafayette society before the shadow of the 1873 depression fell across the land.

Men and women along the way, in wagons or in farm yards, would call out "Hello, Barr," and my father would wave his whip in answer or else stop and talk. Wherever he went he was greeted with "Hello, Barr." It was never "Mr. McCutcheon," rarely "Captain." In all the greetings you could sense the affection behind them. He was very popular. I doubt if there was another man in Tippecanoe County who knew more of its inhabitants or had more real friends. Perhaps that was why later, running as a Democrat, he overcame the 1,500 Republican majority in Tippecanoe County and was elected sheriff, and still later overcame the same majority to be elected treasurer of Lafayette.

He had two horses—Dolly, a nice little mare, and Sam, an ex-racing trotter, who could burst into limited amounts of speed when flicked with the whip. As my father drove along the country roads, almost devoid of traffic, his two associates, Julius Vellinger, my number one Elston chum, and I, sat in the back of the buckboard with our feet swinging in the dust, and in low tones discussed matters of deep concern. We would drive far out—ten or twelve miles—then Julius and I would drive a bunch of hogs back to town.

At first I attended a country school half a mile from home, called the Red Eye School. Forty or fifty children of all grades went there. After a year, when I had advanced beyond its curriculum, my parents sent me to the Ford High School in Lafayette. Of all the wretched, unhappy days of my life those at the Ford were the most poignant. Torn from the easy yoke of the Red Eye, dropped among strangers, I was so acutely miserable that my parents, taking pity, withdrew me, and arranged with the teacher at Red Eye, Pierce Arnold, a patient elderly man of scholarly attainments, to provide an additional class to fit me and a very fat and pleasant young lady named Jennie Geyer.

Soon after arriving at Elston I established a Sunday paper route. To thirty or forty widely scattered farmhouses and residences I delivered the papers, arising at four every Sunday, sometimes in below-zero cold or winter darkness, jogging the two wind-swept miles to Lafayette, then returning to the subscribers—a total of eight or ten miles in the buckboard—before I could get home for breakfast around eight o'clock.

In addition to my Sunday paper route, Julius and I formed the sign, house, and carriage-painting firm of McCutcheon and Vellinger. The field was not large and we soon dominated it. Elston people no longer went to Lafayette for their painting. We painted several houses, two or three coats each. We painted two phaetons, one of which never dried, and for years it caught most of the vagrant dust and chaff in its vicinity. We painted all the signs and even ventured on gilt ones, only instead of gold leaf we used gilt paint which in time took on a faded greenish hue.

Regardless of the quality of our work, I feel that the people were amused by our serious efforts and good-naturedly wanted to help us out, even though art suffered in the attempt.

In later life Julius became the foremost sign painter in Lafayette, and excelled in the gold-leaf designs which still adorn most of the leading stores and office fronts. I often called on him when I went back there.

"Funny," he used to say, "how we both turned out to be artists."

Of literature, in those days, I had an oddly assorted background. I was devoted to *The Boys and Girls of New York* and the *New York Weekly*, both adventure publications full of exciting sea stories, pirate tales, trapping and Indian fights and some detective yarns. As a strange neighbor beside *Ups and Downs of a Donkey's Life* and *Adventures of a Three Guinea Watch*, I kept a boy's version of the *Iliad* which I loved. I never read any Henty, but *Golden Days* supplied much of my mental pabulum—a clean, wholesome publication that had legions of devoted readers. Even now the names of Frank Converse, Oliver Optic, Horatio Alger and Roger Starbuck awaken the eager thrill their serial stories used to give me. Castleman's *Frank on a Gun Boat* and all the other "Frank" stories always delighted me.

This type of reading undoubtedly quickened my imagination and stirred an intense desire to do things. If a boy's family life is normal, and his parents are not unkind or unjust, the books he reads in the formative period of his boyhood are likely to be important character-makers.

The social life of Elston, as far as the menfolk were concerned, was carried on in Johnston's store. In the winter the huge red-hot stove was surrounded by raconteurs, smoking and chewing tobacco. Many times I was on the shadowy outskirts of this masculine circle, smoking a cigar and absorbing much wisdom embellished in male phraseology which would raise an eyebrow in more refined circles.

One night a citizen of the village drove up, and, together with a blast of wintry wind, entered the store. He was tall and handsome in a mid-Victorian mustachioed, sardonic way, and possibly for this reason had always seemed to us a man of mystery. Imagine how that part of my being which had been fed on detective stories thrilled when the bill he tendered in payment for something was held up to the light and closely inspected by Fred Johnston and then handed back to him. The tall man exhibited obvious signs of annoyance, pocketed the bill and without a word stalked out of the store. After he had gone there was much talk about counterfeiters. Nothing was said derogatory to the tall man who bore an unsullied name and reputation, but the implication was that there was too damned much counterfeiting going on, and the government ought to do something about it. The incident resulted in the firm of McCutcheon and Vellinger—Detectives.

From that night on, two determined sleuths shadowed the unsuspecting citizen whenever he was in town, and at night crouched in the bushes near his house endeavoring to observe some activity in support of their suspicions. This continued until the incidents surrounding the Elston and Plank Road gang war presented newer and more explosive possibilities.

For years there had been bad blood between the boys and young men of the Plank Road, Irish boys somewhat given to rowdyism under the leadership of Caleb Maher, and the young men and boys of Elston under Bill Koepsel, a blacksmith of tremendous strength and pugnacity. Julius and I became attached to the Elston gang but being much younger were mere privates. We had our meeting place and our "call"—a shrill whistle keyed in minor notes not to be mistaken anywhere. The sound of this signal coming into a quiet kitchen or parlor in the evening would send a boy flying from the room.

The older boys carried .32 caliber revolvers. Julius and I never got beyond the .22 stage, and for a year or more we were never without these weapons, partly because they helped us entertain the illusion that we were detectives, and partly because, with them in our pockets, we felt we were really members of the gang.

A favorite meeting place was the Red Eye schoolyard. It was out of the center of town, if Elston could be said to have a center, and there were only three or four small cottages within half a mile. Here the gang mobilized, and when the Plank Roaders sent word they were coming out the following week to attend a big Irish picnic in Elston, this taunting challenge called for action.

There was much target practice against the back of the little schoolhouse. The .32's drilled through the frame weatherboards and shattered sections of the blackboard within. The little .22's did not go through the blackboard and so, when the county superintendent had the whole gang arrested for this vandalism, the punishment fell mostly on the older boys who carried the heavy artillery.

The fight between the two gangs which took place near McCrea's grocery store late in the evening after the Irish picnic was a real battle of pistols and stones. In the thick of it I secured momentary safety behind the horse trough in front of the store, while the bullets rattled against the framework of the windmill above.

When I was knocked down by a big stone, my recollection is that this foul attack only added wings to my flying feet as I departed from the area of acute combat.

About that time I decided to dramatize a story called "The Blunders of a Bashful Man," and, like the Bandarlog, we dropped everything else and became absorbed in this theatrical enterprise.

In the loft of our barn I established my first studio and here were painted the two scenes and the roll curtain that seemed necessary for a proper production of the new play, *The Blunders of a Bashful Dude*. The word *dude* was in its prime at that time. Yards and yards of unbleached muslin were sewed together, stretched tightly on frames and then sized with a glue sizing. The painting was done thereon. The curtain really rolled up and down, not smoothly, but at least its purpose was evident and it got there gradually. I've forgotten what this first curtain bore in the way of a picture, for it was so completely eclipsed by the splendor of a second one.

The actors were Julius Vellinger, John Haffner, George Munn and I. There were no girls. We took the female parts as well as the male.

We secured permission to give our show in the Red Eye school-house and were allowed two nights.

When you remember there were no movies or radio or any other attractions in the community, you may understand why on both nights the schoolhouse was packed to standing room. I think everybody came to kid the actors, but we didn't know that. We gave a conscientious show, with printed programs—printed on my hand press. With these and the roller curtain and peanuts and candy to be bought from the usher (my little brother Ben) the first success of this play led to its being repeated in the Lehman Church with a larger crowd.

Then I produced another dramatic effort called *Grimes Country Grocery.* Our attention to make-up was increasing, and Julius, as old Mr. Grimes, was really excellent. I played the part of the hero, such as he was, and John Haffner, the blacksmith's son, played Elvira de Schimmerhorn. She turned out to be a maiden of Wagnerian bulk. One scene represented the front of the grocery store, another showed a parlor interior; the curtain, having a magnificent representation of Venice on its shiny face, was the artistic sensation of the event. It was the only picture of Venice I know of that had a mountain in it.

Again the crowds came and jammed the house to admire or to scoff. At the time we thought it was to admire. Now I am less certain. They paid real money to do it, whatever it was.

In these Elston days I was still under the spell of *Tom Sawyer.* The idea of buried treasure was always in the background of my thoughts. It is therefore not surprising that our attentions should presently be withdrawn from the stage and turned into the most fascinating as well as the least remunerative of all human efforts, the search for buried treasure. There are hardly two other words in the language that have such potency and pull.

Back of the Red Eye School was a fairly good-sized wood. In one part we came across an odd cluster of stones, odd not alone for its shape but for the fact that there were no other stones in the neighborhood. They were arranged in a rough boxlike formation and we had every reason to believe they had been so arranged by human hands.

Carefully we unearthed the ground around them and within the wall of rock we found heaps of smaller stones sparkling with the glint of what looked like gold. At once our precautions were doubled. While one dug, the other paced in a hundred-foot circle around the cache, his trusty .22 clutched in his hand, his eyes peering sharply in all directions. Never before had that peaceful grove sheltered such intense purpose as now surged under its leafy tranquillity.

When twilight came we had a heap of thin gold-bearing ore stacked up, and now while one stood guard the other hastened home to secure a toy express wagon. The treasure was carefully placed in this and under cover of darkness dragged to the office of the grain elevator which we found locked. Cad Bell, the amiable manager, was in conference on the porch of the corner grocery where the affairs of the nation were undergoing a searching examination. I edged into the circle and mysteriously whispered to Mr. Bell to come to his little office. Here Julius was guarding the express wagon loaded with ore.

"We want to put this wagonload into your office where it can be locked up," I whispered to Mr. Bell.

"What's in it?" he asked, looking tremendously impressed.

"Gold!"

He picked up a piece of the treasure, lighted a match and looked carefully at it. Then in a stage whisper to correspond to my own, he said he would guard it very carefully. He unlocked the door and we shoved the heavy wagon in. Mr. Bell, still speaking in stage whispers, left us to rejoin his fellow philosophers on the porch.

The next day Fred Johnston, who had lived in Placerville, California, and presumably knew gold ore, examined the find and confidentially reported to Mr. Bell that it was mica. To me he suggested sending samples to the assay office. Various matters combined to delay this, and in a few days our attention was diverted to more important things.

In winter months we had spelling bees at the Red Eye School. In summer we walked miles along the dusty lanes to swim in the Wea or in the millrace at Bayle's mill. In the fall we combed the woods for hickory nuts, or gathered the wild grapes that made such savory tart jelly.

Occasionally Cad Bell would send me to Lafayette to bring out cash during a busy day at the grain elevator. Riding my father's horse, with an envelope containing $1,500 cash in my pocket, I made that return trip seem like all the daring rides in history rolled into one. Every passer-by became a potential enemy, every casual glance a sinister and designing look, baleful in character. I finished the ride in a quick dash through the surprised street of Elston, dismounted with a flourish and delivered the precious envelope at its destination.

I had begun to draw a little. In the back of my schoolbooks there were always pictures of schooners and calla lilies. Why the latter, I've never fathomed, but there was a reason for the former. In all my pirate and sea literature "the low rakish craft in the offing" was always a schooner. No good sea story could get along without one.

While in this seafaring mood I did one of the characteristically foolish things that lie plentifully sprinkled throughout my life. Joe McCrea owned a skiff. He occasionally fished in it on the Wabash but as age and weather impaired its seaworthiness, he brought it up from its natural element and put it out in his back yard. Here I came upon it one day and was at once eager to buy it. Mr. McCrea was easily convinced, and for five dollars, representing the profits of many weeks of newspaper delivering, I owned the boat.

Even though it was not a schooner, it gave me what H. T. Webster calls the thrill of a lifetime. I left it in Mr. McCrea's barn for a while, paying frequent visits to it. I named it the *Fanchon* and painted the name across its stern. Later the craft was transported to the old Wabash and Erie Canal and hitched to the bank near where the Main Street Bridge crosses the canal. Here during my four college years I could look over and see "my own boat." I have no recollection of ever having gone out in it. Gradually it disintegrated and was no more.

During my last two years in Elston I wrote a weekly column of local news which was printed in the *Lafayette Call*. A postmortem of this material reveals that it contained more or less poetry as well as a strong ingredient of public-works propaganda. The gunsmiths of Lafayette kept their explosives in three little square brick powder magazines in Elston. I began an intensive campaign to have these removed, and pictured them a deadly menace to the safety of the community. The Lafayette readers of the *Call* must have thought, after several weeks of this crusade, that the good people of Elston were lying awake nights with indignation. As a matter of fact I never heard any Elstonite express the slightest concern about the "deadly menace."

In this column, too, I named all the streets in the vicinity: Shawnee Avenue, Romney Road, Wea Highway and so on, fancy names for drowsy country roads.

The nearest approach to my later professional activities, in my Elston days, was the publication of the *Elston News*, a hand-printed and hand-illustrated newspaper containing advertisements, editorials, news items, political leaders and cartoons of the Cleveland-Blaine campaign in which I took an absorbed and intensely partisan part. People down in Indiana took their politics very seriously in the

eighties, and when you favored one side or the other, you favored it
100 per cent.

Perhaps because my father was a Democrat, I felt a trend in that
direction. I found myself a hungry reader of the political news and
more and more an admirer of this young Cleveland who had shot up
to national fame so quickly. The few cartoons to be found then,
mainly in the weeklies, were bitterly personal and full of venom. I
too drew cartoons highly unfavorable to the Plumed Knight with the
tattooed spots, with pointed allusions to the Mulligan letters, the
Star Route scandal and other black marks that his enemies had pinned
on Blaine. His public record was long and hence more vulnerable
than Cleveland's. I don't think I really understood what all those

revelations were about, but in my paper I used them with telling effect on its circulation of one.

As this did not provide a sufficient safety valve for my emotions, I enrolled in the Elston "Cleveland and Hendricks Drum Corps." By the end of the campaign I could beat a long roll and do fancy alternations on the rim of the snare drum.

With my drum corps, my *Elston News,* my weekly column for the *Lafayette Call,* my painting business, my Sunday newspaper route, my schoolwork and one thing and another, I was the busiest thing you ever saw. Yet all this went on in a tiny village which the casual traveler, on passing through, would consider the dullest, most unstimulating spot in the country, if indeed he noticed it at all.

## ～ 5 ～

## The Jail

WHEN I outgrew the little red schoolhouse in Elston, I entered the preparatory class at Purdue—a supplementary year offered at that time in addition to the regular four-year course. This meant a five-mile drive in an open buckboard. Sun, rain or blizzard, I rose in the early dark and was picked up by Jim MacBeth, also a student at Purdue, who was paid by my father to drive me the long way in and out. The classroom doors opened at eight o'clock. It sounds heroic to me now, but carrying the Sunday morning newspaper route made the daily drive seem by comparison a leisurely performance.

Exactly one year to a day before I was born, on May 6, 1869, the Indiana General Assembly had accepted a gift of $200,000 and 100 acres of land from John Purdue and others for the establishment of a university. On September 16, 1874, the first official academic year opened with an enrollment of six persons. When I entered as a "prep" in September of 1884, about 300 students were registered. The school consisted of a three-story main building, a three-story men's dormitory, a chemical laboratory, an engine house, a wooden gymnasium and the Ladies' Hall, where we ate—the same building in which I had lived for a year as a small boy.

The chapel bell punctuated our days. It called us to classes and to chapel, where daily attendance was compulsory and where Professor Craig led the hymns and side-whiskered President Smart looked out at us over his spectacles with twinkling eyes.

Down in front among the higher classmen I very early noted a delicately modeled face, strangely clean-cut and refined among its more rugged and corn-fed neighbors. I found myself fascinated by this cameo profile. Its owner, I eventually learned, was named George Ade. But in those lowly days I could only admire from afar. How could I have presumed to dream that there might come a time when "Ade and McCutcheon" had as natural a connection as "ham and eggs"?

Most of the students were country boys like me, but there were a few men marked with the unmistakable stamp of the city—the first I had ever seen. I was plunged at once into worshipful admiration and an acute inferiority complex. There were the aristocratic clothes and manner of blond Carl von Kimball from Chicago; and the easy good-fellowship and self-confidence of Morris Levistein; Harry Garden, who had been to Europe; George Floyd, handsome and debonair, playing "A Wandering Minstrel I" on his cornet in the dorm.

I was shy and scared and appeared to myself in comparison hopelessly green and awkward, like a puppy who has been taken into a family and doesn't yet know if he is to be kept, ready to like everybody but too timid to make friends. The fact that I was the next to youngest in my class did not help. To this day I envy *savoir-faire*, a gay insouciant manner.

My abysmal shyness, my hero worship, my crushing sense of youthful greenness are etched in my memory. I remember my feeling of not being in the current of college life and my long rides to and from Elston. Beyond these tenuous, fragmentary impressions, the prep year at Purdue (except for the Elston Drum Corps activities in the Cleveland-Blaine campaign) is pretty much of a blank.

By the beginning of freshman year—1885—my father had been elected sheriff of Tippecanoe County and we had moved back to the familiar sheriff's residence connected with the jail where we had lived before (the two years of 1877 to 1879), and a new and fascinating phase of life opened before me.

It was an imposing house with four huge rooms on each of two floors. Wide hallways separated the rooms. In the basement were the kitchen, laundry and service quarters, and backed up against this residence was the jail surrounded by a high brick wall.

Adjoining our house was the office, reached by stone steps leading from the street. A large, cheerful prisoners' dining room came next, flanked by the women's cell house. The women prisoners were permitted the use of this room when the men were not at meals; at those times the women were locked in their quarters behind a steel slab door. Beyond the dining room, and separated from it by another solid steel slab door and also a circular barred door which locked and unlocked by a lever operated from the outside, was the men's cell house, a two-story tier of cells, perhaps eighty in all. Half were for the "State" cases, the more serious crimes; the other half for milder offenses—vags, drunks and drunk-and-disorderlies.

A broad stone hallway faced these two strongly barred divisions from which an iron stairway led up to the hospital. It was here that Ike Baker, charged with bigamy, played insane for two weeks, during which time he never relaxed day or night his pose of stupid, vacant-eyed insanity. Only after his trial and conviction did his eyes again light with reason and humor as he discussed his long and heroic if unavailing bit of acting.

In a little enclosed corner of the office slept the jailer, ready to leap up at any hour of the night when a prisoner was brought in. After I was fifteen, there were many occasions when I acted as turnkey during the absence of the jailer. After attending Purdue by day, I often slept in the jailer's bed at night, and many and exciting were the interruptions to my repose.

One night I was aroused by what seemed to be a national uprising. I unbarred the door and a whirling mass of struggling figures surged in, made up mostly of police clubs and violent curses. Finally the huge, well-dressed form of Dan Scribner, the notorious confidence man, emerged panting and exhausted. I had to search him, place all his possessions, properly listed, in the jail safe; then take him—this time with police help—to a cell.

Whenever Stell Davis, Moll James or any other "ladies" resident in the rather few Lafayette houses of ill fame were brought in, it was a noisy and memorable night. I'm not sure what a welkin is, but they made it ring.

One day when I was on duty a gentleman called. It was Matt Pinkerton, one of the great detective family. He presented his credentials and said he wished to talk with one of the prisoners. I locked them in the dining room during this conference and felt a noteworthy thrill at turning the key on a Pinkerton!

Once a crazy woman swallowed two or three feet of hat ribbon before I could stop her. It may have been she I took to the State Asylum at Indianapolis. Another time, alone, with a revolver, I escorted a handcuffed convict, John Ott, ninety miles to the Michigan City Pen. You may imagine how I dramatized this far-from-daring accomplishment.

Unavoidably during these years I became convinced that much of the disorder and wickedness of the world is due to drink. Take Nell Nash for example. It used to take two or three policemen to get her into the office, cursing, screaming, tearing at them like a demon. After a day or two to sober up, she became one of the quietest, best-hearted women you could want to meet. With a strong, beautiful voice, she sang most of the day. A single bar of "Beautiful Pond Lilies" or "The Sh-ip that Nev-er Returned!" will transport me instantly back to the Tippecanoe County Jail and Nell. Everybody liked her, particularly the children of our family.

The same applied to most of the others who came in crazy-drunk, fighting and blaspheming. It was easy to understand how they could commit almost any crime while in this irresponsible state. Then after a period of rest and sleep they would emerge likable, decent men who spent the day playing the French harp or cards or pacing back and forth in the shadowy coolness of the immaculately clean cell house, over which hung the faint odor of disinfectant. I came to associate the smell of iodoform with syphilis.

The disagreeable prisoners with bad dispositions were a small minority. Most of them had qualities one could like. Bill Relander, an accomplished crook who specialized in very illegal acquisitive work, was a good deal of a gentleman. Paddy James, a frequent guest, was agreeable and pleasant. Henry Stone was a noisy old drunk who would swear and scream until, subdued by a few gallons of good clean cold city water applied externally, he would résume his normal role—that of a quiet elderly man smoking a pipe.

Possibly my most noteworthy experience in helping my father in the jail was the time I was directing the transfer of about twenty prisoners from the dining room through the stone passage to the cells. One prisoner, a horse thief named Douglass Kramer, stood behind the heavy steel door, and when I returned from locking, by the lever, the circular grating door, he upset me, slammed the door to the office and escaped to the street. I locked the slab door as quickly as I could—which he had fortunately failed to do—grabbed a revolver from the desk drawer and went in pursuit. I shouted, "Halt!" as he rounded the front of the building, but when I reached the corner he was running down Fourth Street. I went after him, firing as I ran. One bullet grazed him and he dodged across the street into a brewery yard. I doubled on him around the brewery, and was fortunate enough to corner him and march him back to the jail. By this time quite a crowd was gathering, and I got a fine write-up in the Lafayette papers.

HE RAN BUT JOHNNY MCCUTCHEN OUTLIMBED AND OUTWINDED HIM were the headlines of the *Evening Call* of March 27, 1886, followed by a sensational account: "Douglass Kramer, one of the Cass County thieves, made a bold attempt for liberty this morning, which would have proved successful had it not been for the bravery and intrepidity of a fifteen-year-old boy."

The *Evening Courier* also played up the story with a scarehead.

BREAK FOR LIBERTY
A HORSE THIEF ATTEMPTS ESCAPE

Douglass Kramer makes his way out of the County Jail. He is closely followed by Sheriff McCutcheon's son who fires several shots at him.

These accounts are of further interest to me, illustrating as they do how the spelling of our name was in the confusing throes of evolution, the "eon" gradually supplementing the "en" which my father and grandfather had used.

Our own household life, meanwhile, proceeded quietly on the other side of the jail wall. It always seemed busy and entertaining. We never knew how many there would be for dinner. Old retainers, old soldiers—my father couldn't turn them down—neighbors, everybody apparently felt welcome to drop in. My mother had a couple of girls to help her at this period and nothing seemed to ruffle her. She had a most gentle, patient disposition, calm and philosophical, with a delightful sense of humor and a character of gold.

Even when the entire family came down with diphtheria she seems to have retained enough presence of mind and fun to have us all photographed—all eleven of us: four children, two hired girls, the nurse, McCutcheon Gregory and Harry Glick—cousins—Ben Taylor a boarder, and herself. There we all are with rags around our throats, some looking much more doleful than others.

# 6

# Purdue

For some reason which I have now forgotten, I did not enter Purdue until three weeks after the rest of my class. From that day to this, more than half a century later, I have never caught up. I have always been three weeks behind in algebra, a sort of guessing contest where one said, "Let $x$ equal so and so, and something else equal $y$," the mystery of what conditioned one's choice never revealing itself to me. This was unfortunate, for I had started in the mechanical engineering course which is beset with mathematics of a most virulent type. Part way through freshman year I began showing acute signs of distress. One day a friend asked me why and I explained the lack of affinity between myself and algebra.

"Your heart isn't set on being a mechanical engineer, is it?" he asked.

"No," I answered quickly. "I'd prefer to graduate."

He advised me to switch to a course less infested with math. I thereupon switched to the industrial arts course which was much more humane. There were only two boys taking this course. All the rest were girls. But that was not the reason I took it, as I have explained.

This detour enabled me to graduate, probably also switching my destiny from one road to another. So far as I know, however, the mechanical engineering field has never suffered any sense of loss.

The other boy in the art class was Bert Rogers. He was well-built, fair-haired and blue-eyed, and you at once liked and respected him. Years later, as Bruce Rogers the leading typographer and book designer of the world, he was selected in England to do that monumental work, the Oxford Lectern Bible. To know him—then and now—is to understand why he made nineteen layouts for the title page before he was satisfied. Others with less exacting ideals might have stopped at the fifth, saying, "I guess that'll be good enough."

I graduated in 1889, Bruce in 1890. He went to Indianapolis, I to Chicago, where, in my groping efforts to find an individual style, I was trying to combine a Joseph Pennell architectural technique with the figure treatment of F. Opper, Charles Howard Johnson and C. Jay Taylor. Naturally this kept me very busy. While I often went back to Purdue, it so happened that Bruce never attended the same reunions I did. He was climbing up his ladder step by step, and when he joined the Riverside Press in 1895 he had arrived in his preordained niche. Since then he has been accorded great honors by America and England. At intervals I heard of him and followed his mounting success. And yet, from the day I graduated in 1889 until May 1938, we never once saw each other! A lapse of almost fifty years! It is incredible—and quite disgraceful.

We both lived in Lafayette and had to reach the university, three miles away, by eight o'clock. This meant a long walk to the bridge over the Wabash, a march up across a wind-swept half mile of levee, a climb up Chauncey Hill and then another half mile to the campus. It was not nearly so hard as coming in from Elston. In fact it seemed quite simple. We either walked or drove in a buggy or else did part of the trip in a herdic—a kind of horse-drawn bus that held twelve or so shivering students pitting their bodily warmth against the wintry blasts that whistled through every crack.

The art course was directed at first by a tall, thin professor with a silky beard, mild blue eyes and a sedate frock coat. He looked rather

like a modern rendering of one of those early English kings, say
Ethelred the Unready as portrayed by John Leech. The keystone of
his teaching was the phrase: "Learning to draw is learning to see."
I'm sure we progressed because there was no other direction open to
us. Later on, this professor was succeeded by a young New Yorker,
Ernest Knaufft, who was more abreast of the facts of art. He had been
art critic on the *New York Graphic* for nine years.

In my scrapbook I find a clipping dated January 1, 1887, under the
caption: A RISING YOUNG ARTIST.

Young John T. McCutcheon, son of the Sheriff, a student of Purdue
University, is developing a wonderful talent in portrait making.
With an ordinary lead pencil or pen he has a faculty of making a
correct likeness of anyone who chances to come within his vision.
In the Sheriff's office is a portrait of President Smart [of Purdue]
and of Deputy Sheriff John Kennedy. They are as clean and clear
as though made by a first-class crayon artist.

However, I am quite sure I had no serious intentions toward art. I
still thought of artists in the current terms of crayon portraits and
precarious living. If the agricultural course had had still less math, I
might have taken that.

In the eighties there were only two big fraternities at Purdue, Sigma
Chi and Kappa Sigma. The former was the pioneer there, and because
President White had been opposed to fraternities, the Sigs for a time
were obliged to meet *sub rosa*. They carried the fight to the legislature
and finally succeeded in establishing themselves openly. The history
of this fight has a large place in the annals of fraternities in the United

States. While I was in college, there was the most intense feeling not only between the two rival fraternities, but between the Greeks and the barbarians as well.

Along in my sophomore year one of the Sigs was delegated by his chapter to look me over. It was that same youth whose cameo profile I had been admiring from afar and whose name turned out to be George Ade.

Evidently George's report on me was favorable because I was presently invited to become a Sig. From that day began a relationship which has remained one of the most valued throughout my life. I can point to many times when my membership in Sigma Chi has been a powerful influence in determining the course of my career. I have been helped and entertained by Sigs the world over—in Honolulu, Tokyo, Peking. The American Ambassador to Belgium, Brother Brand Whitlock, helped me in the troublesome days of August 1914.

The greatest asset Sigma Chi gave me, however, if one may speak of such a thing selfishly, was the friendship of George Ade.

He was thin and tall and wore a sedate blue suit with tight spring-bottomed trousers that flared out at the ankle. And he had three outstanding characteristics which made him an inviting subject for caricature: an unusual expanse of head behind the ears, a sweep of strongly marked eyebrows and a striking lack of abdominal fullness, described by realists as slab belly.

It is customary when a man becomes great for his early friends to claim that they knew away back when that he was bound to succeed. In this case even my undeveloped instinct told me that here was an exceptional person. In his class, in the old Irving Literary Society, in the Sig chapter, indeed in all student activities he gravitated to leadership with easy inevitability.

When he first showed signs of embarking in literary work, his father, who was a prosperous banker in the old home town of Kentland, and his brothers, who were well-to-do landowners, predicted a future for him that would contain very little money. When his *Fables in Slang* were syndicated and the royalties began rolling in in huge streams to his father's bank, the home folks were mystified and amazed. His brother began buying choice land for him until he owned 2,000 acres in the rich heart of the corn belt.

According to a well-known story, a girl once remarked to him: "It is amazing how many bright men come from Indiana."

"Yes," George was reported to have answered, "and the brighter they are, the quicker they come."

The line is clever enough to have been delivered by him, but, when reported in Indiana, it created such a terrific furor that, in order to prove to the state that he never said it, he moved back and made his permanent home on Hazeldon Farm near Brook. The friendly house, the swimming pool, the golf course and small clubhouse soon became famous. He shared them with characteristic generosity. During the Taft campaign in 1908 he entertained the candidate there, and about 25,000 people attended the party. The Sigma Chis, the Purdue Alumni, the Indiana Society of Chicago and many other organizations have often been feted there.

There was a time in Lafayette when his attention seemed centered on the most beautiful girl in town. Suddenly he ceased his visits. The estrangement was reported due to the fact that her mother wished him to join the Methodist Church. If he had other affairs in later life, he successfully concealed them from me.

He had the most extraordinary memory. His experiences, his endless assortment of humorous stories, the words of songs and quotations—his grip on all these always astonished me. He remembered vividly common experiences we had in 1895 in Europe and elsewhere— people we met and what they said—things that have faded completely from my less flexible memory. As a raconteur, he was unrivaled.

So far as I can remember, George Ade never complimented me to my face for anything I ever did. But I have had so many evidences from what he said to others, or what he wrote, that I am sure he was not indifferent to my work. It seemed to embarrass him to bestow compliments face to face, but indirectly he was most generous in his approval.

For more than ten years, through the Purdue days and through all of our early Chicago newspaper work up to the time I started around the world, our paths lay intimately together. We were inseparable and people began to associate our names in a Damon and Pythias relationship.

He graduated two years before I did, in 1887, one of a class of eight, and at once got a job on a Lafayette paper at $6.00 a week. Another economy of the editor was to use old envelopes, split open, as copy paper.

When the demands of the Fourth Estate relaxed in the late afternoon he and I used to go calling together on the young ladies who, at various times, wore our fraternity pins. Perhaps he found it safer. At any rate, to enhance our social gifts, I wrote in a little book the names of all the songs we knew—in whole or in part—and numbered them.

To entertain the ladies we would ask them to select any number from one to 165 inclusive, and then we would sing it. Perhaps that is how George got the idea for "The Fable of the Two Mandolin Players," neither of whom ever married the girl. I still have the little red book, but I doubt if I could now sing more than 150 of the songs.

Summers were the dull times. The brothers were scattered far and wide. Many were at work. At such times Charley Pifer and I would occasionally go up into the empty, dusty Sig hall at the corner of Fourth and Main streets and reminisce over the good old days a few weeks before. Sometimes we even got a bottle of port wine and a bag of cream puffs and were men of the world for a while.

Yet all was not lighthearted and gay. There were serious times that drew us close together. One in particular I recall.

The Wabash was in high flood. It spread far out over the bottoms, and its angry, sullen current, carrying branches, logs and other flotsam, was fearsome to look upon. I don't know why we thought this would be a good time to go boating, but George Ade, Jasper Dresser and I rowed up the old Erie Canal and then, some miles up, portaged the boat over into the Wabash and started down with the current, a mad rush homeward. Darkness came on. We shot under the Brown Street Bridge and then through the gloom we saw we were headed for one of the stone piers of the Main Street Bridge. Frantically we used our oars and barely cleared it, but unfortunately we did not see the tree that jutted out from the tangled mass lodged against the pier and overhanging the swirling waters by only a couple of feet. We ducked and tried to ward it off with our hands, but the swift current yanked the boat out from under us. We were left dangling from the tree, our legs in the rushing water.

We yelled and yelled. Jap said he couldn't hang on any longer, but we begged him to because we couldn't help him. Finally somebody crossing the bridge heard us, and after a long time, just as Jap's hands were slipping, old Joker Hill came and rescued us. Joker Hill was the boatman at the end of the bridge, and we had chartered our craft from him. Later it transpired that he had first rescued his boat, thus detracting somewhat from the nobility of his heroic deed.

I went home sopping wet, and in my nervous excitement accidentally set fire to my bedroom curtains and nearly burned the house down. It was, on the whole, a memorable evening, and the world very nearly lost a lot of funny fables and a promising attorney as well as several thousand cartoons.

In 1888 I came up to Chicago for the first time—it was in fact the first time I had ever been outside of Indiana, and it provided also my first glimpse of a President of the United States. When Cleveland appeared on a balcony of the Palmer House, the crowd in the street was so dense I thought I would be suffocated. During his campaign for re-election I joined the Old Roman Marching Club and wore a silver toga and carried a kerosene torch, but alas, all those torches failed to light Mr. Cleveland and his Old Roman, an elderly gentleman named Allen Thurman, to victory!

In the summer of my junior year, July 22, 1888, my father died after an illness of three weeks. The piece of shell which had lodged behind his right ear in the Civil War had been extracted but the wound had never healed. For more than twenty-two years it had to be dressed every day. A doctor in Lafayette finally succeeded in healing it with some powerful drug, and blood poisoning set in at once.

The funeral cortege was reported one of the largest ever seen in Lafayette. The obituaries praised his integrity, affability and generosity. "As a soldier he was brave and patriotic; as an officer he was considerate, watchful and prompt. His men almost worshipped him, and his superior officers were proud to know him."

As I think back about my father, he seems by force of economic unkindness to have been out of place in his daily activities. You thought of him as riding up on a spirited horse, sweeping his broad-brimmed hat in salutation to ladies of the old school. That *was* his life in his younger days. I don't remember ever seeing him fixing anything about the place. He seemed too elegant for anything like that. There always seemed to be other hands around even when depression hung heaviest. He was never really a farmer, and even in his days as drover his only chore was the care of a horse or two.

Our family life was full of glow and warmth with no jarring note. I cannot recall a single quarrel between my father and mother. Our table talk was always gay. Although we children had perfectly convenient names, he gave us others which in the past had been worn by people he had known. George was called Tyler, and sometimes Eph. I was called Simeon P. Jack, but who my prototype was I never had the faintest idea. My younger brother Ben was "Medders," probably a corruption of Meadows.

"Another cup of your delicious coffee, Mrs. Warner, *if* you please," my father would say to my mother. "Clara" was reserved for more informal occasions.

It sometimes happens in the grim self-revealing biographies of these days that a writer will confess that he hated his father; sometimes, even, that he couldn't get on with his mother. These are confessions of a loss too great ever to be repaired, no matter what successes may have followed. I rejoice that my childhood recollections—and those of my own children—do not have to carry the memory of bickerings, naggings, ill temper and possibly the shifting of parents through divorce interchanges. There are many cartoon suggestions in those modern relationships, but somehow they seem so poignant and cutting that I cannot help thinking cartoons exploiting them would hurt a lot of children.

My father's death occurred in the middle of his term as city treasurer of Lafayette. Part of his salary of $3,600 was paid to my mother for the rest of the term, while my brother George acted as deputy treasurer.

Two or three weeks after my father's funeral my friend Sam Shortle and I found the summer vacation hanging heavy on our hands and decided to go tramping. I was curious to find out how far we could get on our wits. So about eleven o'clock one warm August morning we put on our oldest clothes, took a dollar apiece in case of emergency and sallied forth across the old wooden Brown Street Bridge. Then we left the road and struck off northwest through the fields.

Our trip might have been a commonplace affair but for one thing. An hour or so after we had crossed the bridge, two other youths about our age murdered Dippy Ellsworth on that same bridge and fled westward. The police sent telegrams to all neighboring towns asking that a sharp lookout be kept for two boys wanted for murder. Police squads were rushed out in an effort to pick up the trail. But of all this we knew nothing.

We were not a very reputable-looking pair—we did not intend to be—but no one seeing Sam's velvety brown eyes and long lashes would have taken him for a dangerous character and I hope I did not have such an appearance either. Some miles west of the Wabash we came by an orchard and asked a farmer if we might have some apples. With his consent we filled our pockets and went on.

Late afternoon found us resting by the side of the Big Four tracks near Montmorenci. After four or five hours of hiking in the broiling sun along the oily ties we just collapsed on a pile of them, too weary to seek a softer or shadier refuge. Presently, far down the tracks in the direction from which we came, we descried a small white object which

EDITORIAL BOARD OF THE *DEBRIS*, 1889
The author is at extreme right.

A SIGMA CHI PARTY ON THE CAMPUS
The author is at left in the middle row.

PROFESSOR CRAIG

delivers an address while Dean Goss (left) and

GEORGE ADE

has apparently just heard the dinner bell at the

slowly evolved itself into a man in shirt sleeves. As he drew near, another man came up from the west. Then one suddenly popped out from the cornfield on our right and a fourth from the woods on our left. We were surrounded.

They were all old friends of mine on the Lafayette police force, and their faces registered unflattering disappointment as they recognized me. Hot, tired, dusty and mad, the four of them glared at us.

"What the hell are you doing here?" growled Officer Yelm.

"What's wrong?" I asked.

"Did you get some apples from a man a couple of miles back?"

"Yes, we did."

"Did you pull a gun on him?"

"Of course not. We have no gun."

They looked even more disappointed.

"Why? What *is* the matter?" I demanded again. They told us about the murder on the bridge. As they retraced their steps to look for more clues, Sam and I resumed our westward way with something new to talk about. How many trails of justice have been confused by would-be helpful people telling what they think you want to hear!

That night we won grudging permission from a farmer to sleep on his parlor floor. Very early we stepped over him, where he lay across the threshold, and struck the tracks again. As day broke a locomotive came bearing down on us from ahead, but instead of hurtling past, it screeched to a stop and Officer Yelm jumped off. He let out an angry oath and jumped back into the engine cab while we grinned.

Everywhere we went we were eyed with suspicion. People stared and whispered. We traveled by gravel train and freight train, once by handcar, but mostly on foot. Part way we rode a boxcar in the company of Bill Sexton, formerly a jailbird in Lafayette, consequently an old acquaintance. The brakeman took most of our remaining cash, then shoved us off. At Medaryville we asked for Lafayette papers before starting to walk the eight-mile stretch to San Pierre.

At that moment hasty telegrams went to Lafayette. Marshal Ed Cunningham hopped the first train. At last here was a hot tip. As we approached San Pierre via the tracks we saw quite a crowd gathered at the station. Sam suggested that, looking as tough as we undoubtedly did, we had better make a detour and enter the town by some other route. But this seemed a lot of trouble, so we came along the tracks. Thirty or forty people on the platform all gazed at us; others were looking at us out of windows. Startled children stared at

us. Sam saw a barber pole and made for the shop, the wide-eyed
crowd parting as we passed. Sam seated himself in the barber chair;
somebody handed me a paper with another story of the murder which
I read avidly. The shop soon filled with people.

We had been there perhaps ten minutes when the Lafayette train
thundered in and the marshal leaped from the single car of the little
branch line.

"Here they are! We've got 'em!" There was a great rush of feet
in our direction.

The marshal's eye fell on me and he burst into a string of profanity.
"You again! Blankety blank blank blank! You get home now as
quick as you can!"

It was Saturday afternoon and there was not another train south
until Monday. He had either to stay in San Pierre or hire a buggy to
drive him to another railroad fifteen or twenty miles away. Sam and
I left him very disgruntled. We walked the twenty-three miles to
Monon and boarded a train from Chicago to Lafayette and Cincinnati. We were the only passengers who got on, and we very carefully
took the seats farthest away from where we had seen the conductor, to
be certain that the train would be under full headway when he reached
us. Then we threw ourselves on his mercy, told him our names,
and that we would leave the fare at the Monon ticket office next
day. Apparently he believed us. We arrived in Lafayette long
after midnight and slept soundly on the billiard table in the Sigma
Chi room.

Next day we dutifully left our fares at the office and had the fun of
seeing our adventures written up very dramatically in the *Journal* by
one of the local editors. The real murderers were later caught and con-
victed.

## ∼ 7 ∼

# The Class of '89

IN A MOMENT of poetic frenzy, I composed the class song which
ranks high among the worst poems in history.

> She's the flower of the College,
>   The Class of '89.
> Purdue has not another class
>   That is one half so fine;
> So fill up your beakers
>   With nectar pure as wine,
> And drink her to the health
>   Of the Class of '89!

Only the members of '89 discovered merit in this perfectly idiotic ditty composed by McCutcheon. The tune was a desecration of an old-time Methodist hymn. There never had been and never could be such a thing as "nectar pure as wine," and besides, neither beakers nor nectar should be referred to as "her." But they scoffed at critics and sang their foolish song at the slightest provocation.

So wrote George Ade, and elsewhere he went on to explain the Class of '89.

Several influences combined to make '89 a hurrah organization. It came upon the scene just as the University was emerging from the fog of uncertainty into the sunlight of an assured future.

In 1883, when James H. Smart came up from Indianapolis to be President, Purdue was at a low ebb. It was struggling along on borrowed capital, and there were not enough students to make the campus look inhabited.

Two years later, when the Class of '89 mustered in as Freshmen, the quagmires were behind and the whole student body was marching confidently under an inspired leadership. The class of '89 was assembled as a result of an active and intelligent campaign to secure desirables, and it had the courage of numbers from the very start.

It was about the first class in Purdue that persistently did things. The day was counted lost whose low-descending sun saw not some deed performed for the glorification of '89. It was closely organized both for offense and defense. It was constantly animated by an eager desire to make things today somewhat different from yesterday. Sometimes the outcome was a laudable enterprise; often enough it was plain deviltry.

It was during the '89 era that the high school atmosphere was dispelled from the campus and the "Purdue Spirit" began to be generated.

Along with the advent of our class, President Smart established, in 1886, the Agricultural Experimental Station. This was destined to develop into one of the pioneer agricultural schools of the country, accomplishing a vast program of help to agriculture generally. But what it calls to my mind especially is the new building that was put up, and its nice, newly shingled tower. Day after day I observed this inviting expanse until I could resist it no longer. At risk of imminent disaster I climbed up and painted the numerals " '89" where all the

world could see. Soon afterward those numerals were suddenly and foully changed to " '88." They were quickly changed back again. This was the beginning of the nationally famous Purdue Tank Scraps, for years regular battles between freshmen and sophomores to get their numerals first on the newer Water Tower Tank. Many boys were hurt, finally a couple were killed, and the scraps were suppressed.

Having been the Elston correspondent for the *Lafayette Call* at thirteen and fourteen, I naturally continued as special Purdue reporter. In my old scrapbooks are many clippings.

On last Friday the students thus far enrolled were 338.

The number of Cadets in the Military Academy is 68.

The debaters for the Carlyle Society were Wells, Waters, and Rainy. It was anything but a dry discussion.

On last Saturday morning a crowd of Purdue students sailed away from the Lafayette Main in a couple of Gregory's barks, steering for Tecumseh's Trail. The only breaker they struck was the tollgate, which totally broke two of the voyagers.

Occasionally I struck a poetic note:

> The golden sun had long since sunk
> Beneath the hills from sight
> When at the tryst two students sighed:
> Where are our girls tonight?

They promised that they'd both be here
While we both vowed the same.
'Tis sad to think the maidens that
We longed for never came!

I don't remember just when I got over my painful bashfulness and
began to enjoy parties. I still have a most extraordinary account of the
first time I asked a young lady to go to a social event. There was a
class custom in those days of making a list of girls, on which each
boy marked the one he would escort to the party. On this occasion, a
Carlyle picnic, I marked Mary Cooper, but as I didn't know her very
well, I asked Ben Taylor to go with me to her house to invite her. I
could not have been more awkward and embarrassed if I had been
proposing to her. We sat around all evening while I tried to get up
my nerve. Finally, in order to get home, Ben had to break the stale-
mate.

"Weren't you going to ask Miss Cooper something, John?"

And then I asked her, she thanked me and accepted and it all ended
happily. Afterward I wrote it up, discussing every phase of the episode
to the tune of at least 10,000 words, if anyone should ever care to do
any research.

Also among my archives, along with my *Journal* correspondence, are
all the dance programs, as well as souvenirs of various literary and
other society picnics and banquets, to which we often used to ask
Queen Victoria, Queen Liliuokalani and other distinguished guests.
It seems I have never thrown anything away.

Old souvenirs in musty attics recall a recitation George Ade and I
used to give when sufficiently urged. I spoke the words with my hands
clasped behind my back, while he, stooping behind me with his arms
through mine, made all the requisite gestures, such as pulling out my
watch, blowing my nose, picking my teeth and any others which might
occur to him. By means of this collaboration, according to several
existing reports, we seem to have "brought down the house." One of
the things we recited, author unknown, concerned a lock of hair, tied
with faded ribbon. After much sorrowful sentiment, the last stanza
ran:

Strange how such things affect us—
  Make our spirits sadly droop—
But how MAD that hair would make us
  If we found it in our soup!

Judging from the following clipping, I must have done a lot of reciting:

> The declamation, "Bill's Return," by J. T. McCutcheon was next in order. It was a dialect rhyme and was rendered in a remarkable, realistic and touching manner. During the recitation, the close attention paid Mr. McCutcheon was proof of the interest the audience manifested in his delivery. This gentleman has few superiors as a declaimer.

Perhaps I missed my true vocation!

Concerning our class I wrote for the papers at the beginning of senior year:

> The present Senior Class numbers 28. This class numbered 97 in the Preparatory School, 76 Freshmen, 49 Sophomores, 31 Juniors, and now 28 are graduating.
>
> The average age of the class is 22, nine of whom wear beards, six wear pompadours; the majority affiliate with the Republican party, some incline toward Prohibition, while one or two are suspected of leaning toward Belva Lockwoodism.

Our senior year was a period of activity on all fronts. Some memories are poignant. For instance, I try not to think of the time I took Fanny McGrath to an evening reception at the Ladies' Hall. We drove over from Lafayette behind the family white horse, which I hitched to a post near the hall. When we came out, some three hours later, the horse was still hitched to the post, but the buggy had been removed by certain fiends in human form to the remote recesses of some place at the time unknown. This turned out to be a neighboring cornfield, but I didn't discover that for several days.

I had to take Fanny on one arm and lead the horse with the other all the way back to town, a most unromantic pilgrimage. To make matters worse, the white horse shed all over my best suit, and some unfeeling wretch wrote a poem about the whole thing for the papers.

The senior uniform which we wore at all times was a frock coat and silk hat! We even went to picnics in this august garb and nobody seemed to think it funny. Furthermore, our class colors were salmon pink, seashell green and sky blue! Indeed our class of '89 was particularly full of zest. And the members of the class were not the only ones who thought so.

Forty years later George Ade once more expressed an unbiased opinion:

Another Commencement is here and I shall endeavor to be on the campus, if for no other reason than to meet again some of the members of '89 which was a great class. It did more than any preceding class to make Purdue aware of itself, and stir up campus activities, establish traditions, and raise Cain generally. It wrote the first songs which really belonged to the school, and published the first "Debris."

The *Debris* which George mentions was the first annual issued at Purdue. Our class got it out as a memorial. The name was my suggestion. I didn't know French but I had an idea that "debris" meant "mess of stuff." Bruce Rogers and I did the illustrations for it, the first of our work ever to be reproduced. My efforts were mostly along humorous lines where my technical limitations were not so evident. Bruce designed the title page, headings and other drawings.

It was an excellent training field. Bruce's drawing "Toiling toward Light"—the Class Motto—shows members of '89 pushing the Earth up toward a benign Sun. If you ever care to try it, you will realize what difficulties he overcame. His design for Field Sports is good enough to be a collector's item today. It has an interest for historians also. The bicycle was a high-wheel job of the eighties, the tennis player wore a striped blazer, and the football star was jaunty in the headgear of the period—a peaked tam-o'-shanter with a long tassel!

For our illustrations we were thanked in the foreword of the *Debris*: "Both these gentlemen have added no small amount of interest to our work"—a dignified and restrained acknowledgment, not calculated to turn our heads.

Even after we left college, we continued to do work for the succeeding annuals. In the '91 *Debris* may be noted a third artist—Mr. Booth Tarkington, a newcomer at Purdue and also in the art world. Had he continued in this promising field, he would have made a great name for himself, but he got sidetracked and took to writing.

I have taken great pride and pleasure in watching Purdue's victory parade from those dim beginnings in the seventies up to the present unchallenged position in the forefront of America's technological and engineering universities.

# ~ II ~

# DRAWN TO CHICAGO

## ～8～

## A Job in Chicago

WELL over a half century ago I was called a "grave and reverend senior." Whether I am still grave and reverend may be debatable, but a certain newspaper clipping may be considered somewhat startling. It appeared in the *Miami Herald* the day after I had passed through town in 1938, and it contained a slight error.

> Mr. McCutcheon still does a weekly cartoon for the Sunday papers, and although 88, he is as active as ever. His island is probably the most beautiful in the Bahamas, and has a blue lagoon in its center.

*one of my Bosses*

Tiffany Blake, leading editorial writer for the *Tribune*, saw this item and sent it to me with a letter.

Dear John,
A mutual friend has forwarded a sensational news report from the well-informed correspondent of the *Miami Herald*.
Needless to say, we are all shocked to learn that you have been aging so fast since you left.
I don't wonder that even the lagoon is blue.
You often tell me how much better I look when I am working, and urge me to take shorter vacations—if any. But I never expected that this rule would be demonstrated in your case—at any rate so excessively.
Come home at once before you are a hundred!

When a man looks back over fifty or sixty years—any kind of years— he has certainly acquired a lot of perspective, if nothing else. He sees the mistakes he has made and the lucky breaks he may have had. The entire trend of his life in the early formative period has hinged upon certain decisions he has taken, good or bad.

A few months before I graduated from Purdue, I received two offers from Lafayette newspapers. The *Journal* offered me a job as telegraph editor. The *Courier* offered me the city editorship. Both papers wanted a man at once.

I declined these offers, preferring to get my degree. After commencement both positions had been filled. I have often wondered what might have happened to me had I chosen otherwise at this crossroads.

At any rate, when commencement came, Dr. Frank Gunsaulus delivered the baccalaureate; Governor Hovey came over to lend his august presence to the occasion and, among other speakers, I delivered an oration entitled—curiously enough—"Caricature in Art." I couldn't have known a very great deal about it, but I felt reasonably certain, I remember, that whatever I might say could not be questioned by anyone down in front.

I spoke pontifically as follows:

Every age is marked by the culmination of some great power. We have had the age of oratory. The age when books exerted their greatest influence is waning, and in their stead has gradually appeared first, the plain printed newspaper, and later its evolution into a sheet enhanced by the skill of the illustrator. It is this age that will pass down as an age eminently utilitarian and practical, and it is here that caricature and comic art first come into common application and use. . . .

When I wrote the callow and complicated wisdom that followed this opening, I am quite sure I had never considered art—and certainly not caricature—as a profession.

My father had some wish that I might be a lawyer, but his death put an end to any such notion. I am lucky never to have embarked on a profession for which I was so unfitted. One who showed such ineptitude at figuring out the intricacies of a simple equation would have done a lot of floundering around in the mazes of courtroom forensics.

I think I must always have intended to be a writer of sorts. I remember showing my father a story I had written. It was called "A Horrible Metempsychosis." It was horrible all right, but whether it promised a literary career he never said. Some of it was pretty good—a description of dark and creepy nights that I had copied from *Tom Sawyer*.

I had also written a burlesque for the Class Day Exercises called "Gates of Heaven."

But now I was told by someone that "art" paid better than writing, so I appear to have changed my spots without any trouble and left literature flat on its back. I spent a couple of months sizing up the drawings in Chicago papers and sketching a number of samples to show.

Then I came up to Chicago in the late summer of 1889, with $17 in my pocket and not a friend in the city. Up to that time I had been outside of Indiana only twice in my life. Both were hasty trips to Chicago with Purdue pals.

Bob Jaques, who kept the corner bookstore in Lafayette, gave me a letter to Horace Taylor, an artist on the *Chicago Herald* and a Sigma Chi brother. Taylor inspected my samples and advised me to practice some more.

Perhaps I should add that Brother Taylor gave further advice. He suggested that I leave my hotel, the Windsor, which stood near where the old *Tribune* building now stands at the corner of Dearborn and Madison streets, and look for a boardinghouse to conserve my capital. So I rented a basement room at $6.00 a week for board and lodging, in a fairly decent place down on South Wabash Avenue. All day I practiced drawing in that room and went up only for meals. One of the young lady boarders, a Miss Martin, was sympathetic, knowing—as who didn't?—that I was young and green. Then there was a shooting scrape upstairs and a police raid, and it dawned on me that all was not well, so I departed.

One Vernie Ruggles, a Lafayette girl much older than I, who lived far down on the South Side, took pity on me and invited me out a couple of times; but mostly when I was not drawing, I walked up and down Michigan Avenue looking at the long, converging rows of gas lamps, and was very lonesome and homesick. My greatest excitement was lunching off ten cents' worth of Tokay grapes, which were new and unusual then and considered very grand.

After about a month in the city I went back to Lafayette, but only for three weeks. At the end of October I returned with more samples. This time the friendly Mr. Taylor took me across the street to the office of the old morning edition of the *Daily News*. The time was propitious. I was taken on at once on two weeks' probation.

The head of the art department—practically the entire department —was William Schmedtgen. He was covering the Cronin trial, a historic murder case, and had to spend much of his time in the courtroom. Perhaps for this reason a helper was required.

If I ever became an artist it was largely due to the kindness of this gentleman, whose wise council guided me through those early years. Either he took a liking to me or took pity on me, because from the very start he did everything to help me along. With endless patience he drilled me in the rudiments of the profession. After only college publication experience, I doubt if I would have weathered the first few weeks had it not been for his unfailing help.

On the side he was mayor of West Ridge, and a great duck hunter and fisherman. His paintings of these avocations are among the best of the kind in the country. Once he suffered a nervous breakdown. One of his best friends was a member of a duck and fishing club on the Illinois River. Schmedtgen asked for a job as caretaker and common laborer at this club. His friend at once offered financial assistance, but Schmetty assured him it wasn't money, it was that kind of work he wanted. He went down and worked there, living on the simplest fare and doing hard manual labor out in the wet and cold, and in six months he was entirely well.

I was best man at his wedding. Our close business relations were interrupted later when I went to the *Tribune,* but our friendship continued unbroken until his death.

Many prominent men in the art world today were given their first opportunity under Schmedtgen's guidance. At intervals during the years from 1890 to 1898 I went away. In my place Schmedtgen once put Charles Sarka; at another time, C. D. Williams. Both became well-known illustrators. An office boy named Stanley Adamson was working in the business end. We brought him up to the art department. Later, under the name of Penryn Stanlaws, he became widely known as a portrait painter and magazine-cover artist of exceptional delicacy and refinement.

Carl Emil Schultze also worked for Schmedtgen. He was distinguished in those days only by a front of imposing grandeur. He was an exceedingly nice fellow with one dominant desire. He loved to be well-dressed. He was tall and wore a little pointed beard that made him look like a grand duke. Whenever he came into the office there was a hush. He carried a cane and a stranger would have assumed he was the owner of the paper or a foreign ambassador slumming in Chicago.

Early in his career on the *News* he met Mr. Grimm, the tailor, who made him a suit to be paid for at the rate of $2.50 a week. This news spread like wildfire in the office. In a short time most of the staff were

wearing Grimm suits, and there was hardly a day when you could not look furtively around and see the collector leaning against something waiting for his $2.50 which was always due or overdue from some one of us.

Schultze, though regal in appearance, was simple and friendly by nature. He worked a good deal for the *Budget,* an illustrated story paper the *News* published for a while. Then he went to New York, and presently we heard of "Foxy Grandpa," one of the earliest and most widely known features in the newly developing comic-strip world. He must have made good money but he died practically penniless.

Schmedtgen himself was one of the first of newspaper illustrators and helped to introduce photoengraving into the *Daily News.*

The *Morning* and *Evening News* shared editorial offices in one of the dingiest buildings in town, an old firetrap on the corner of Madison and Wells streets. At first our office was merely a cubbyhole five feet by eight with one end window and a chute for sending copy to the composing room below. Copy boys kept rushing in to send or get stuff from this chute. There were continuous clatter and scurrying, all very distracting. But Schmetty and I seem to have worked along undisturbed.

Eugene Field had a similar cubbyhole for a time and turned out much of his best work there. The office of the managing editor was in a partitioned corner of the same floor. When the editor, Butch White, strode out, looking over his glasses and barking his orders, there was general terror on the floor. He had formerly been a horse reporter and retained his interest in horsy affairs.

Eugene Field was a practical joker. Once he started down at the corner of Madison and Fifth Avenue and chalked hoofprints of a horse on the sidewalk, turning in at the narrow, dark stairway of the *Daily News*, going up two flights of grimy steps and into Butch White's office.

Another time he felt that Mr. Victor Lawson, the publisher of the paper, should raise his salary, so he began appearing in a convict's suit. It attracted much attention which Mr. Lawson considered undesirable. He called in Field, who assured him that, on his salary, this was the only kind of clothes he could afford. Mr. Lawson gave him a raise.

Still later he appeared in his oldest clothes, accompanied by ten or twelve ragged children he had picked up en route, introduced them to Mr. Lawson as his own and begged an increase in pay in order to clothe and feed them better. Again he was successful. But the raises must have been small, for I understand his salary never exceeded $50 a week.

One of his most amusing doings occurred on a streetcar. He got on the back platform, and after the car had passed out of the Loop, the conductor started through after the fares. This was before the days of paying as you enter. Field hailed the conductor and paid the fare of everybody in the car. Then he instructed him to walk through without collecting any fares. The passengers mechanically held out nickels which the conductor appeared not to notice. A few minutes later Field sent him through again. This time the nickels were held out but not quite so conspicuously. The third time he passed, every passenger was hidden behind his newspaper.

Field was a versatile genius. The old ladies who loved his tender, beautiful children's poems did not dream that the same pen could have produced "French Crisis" or "Socratic Love." Collectors have to keep these in asbestos containers.

My first picture for the *News* was a one-column cut for Hallowe'en. I worked constantly on sketches. After two weeks Schmedtgen introduced me to Mr. Lawson, who took me on at $16 a week with a promise of a raise to $20 if I improved by the end of the month. Tremendous excitement! I was bursting with pride. Friends at home were getting $9.00 at most!

My job was to draw all day long. Most of my newspaper work for the first five years was illustration for news events. The weekly *Budget* also used some of my pictures. Before George Ade came up to Chicago, my social activities were limited to meeting with a group of

Sigma Chis in the preparation of a fraternity directory. Here I came to know many of the foremost men in the city.

In December 1889 the Auditorium was finished and I was assigned to draw the details of the interior. This was the first outside work I had done. I began writing up "Artistic Doorways" and illustrating my own column; also views like the Pullman Tower against the moon and scenes at the stockyards. A series called "Scraps of Conversation in Different Hotels" was, as indicated, just snatches to illustrate the types of people who frequented each: commercial travelers at the Palmer House; the stylish element at the Richelieu; something else at the Grand Pacific and the Sherman. "Captain Potts from Salem Town," a column-length poem, was another illustrated contribution.

Doing all these things without having to, or being told to, showed industry and ingenuity in getting up feature stuff, and the editors were pleased.

Back on the farm, sometime before I was six, I became enamored of Miss Lydia Jones, a pretty young schoolteacher whose parents were old friends of my father and mother. It was love at first sight, and to the surprise of all it persisted until it became a matter of family interest. Years later this tendency of little boys to fall in love with older young ladies provided cartoon material of the human-interest sort. I used it as one of the earlier heart interests in the series "Boy in Springtime."

Lydia married a man named Charles Lang and lived at 3113 South Michigan Avenue. Oddly enough, through my mother, I now found myself living at their house. As there were six children, the atmosphere was homelike and nice, if somewhat crowded, and dampening to the last remnants of those early embers.

The five-column front-page cartoon at that time was done by Schmedtgen, but it so happened that Dr. Reilly, then managing editor, was not overly friendly to the chief artist, or to his cartoon style, and wanted to work me into his place. Once when Schmetty was away I was ordered to draw a half-page cartoon. This was in December 1889, long before I had given up realism. The subject was political. The paper was supporting a reform candidate for mayor, a highly reputable businessman named Washburn, who was something of an amateur in politics. The next day they wanted another. These were drawn and printed—by far the largest drawings ever seen in a Chicago paper up to that time. What was my astonishment when on top of such unusual prominence, I was called in and detailed to draw a full-page one!

The caption was to be "We Are the People," and it was to represent a great horde of aroused voters of all classes pouring through a triumphal arch on the way to the polls to elect the reform candidate. It was the first as well as the last of this size I ever did, although in later years several of my cartoons have been given full-page repeat printings in color.

I was so impressed with my responsibility that I worked all night, and the cartoon created something of a sensation. Mr. Lawson gave orders that copies of it, printed on calendered paper, should be presented to every employee of the *Daily News*, and the matrix, gilded all over, was framed and hung in Mr. Lawson's office for many years.

Perhaps in being selected to draw these conspicuous campaign cartoons, I was the unintentional beneficiary of the feud between the managing editor and the chief artist, who was at that time my very best friend. It might be called a piece of luck which was the outgrowth of conditions I had no part in forming.

## ~ 9 ~

## Hall-Bedroom Days

MEANWHILE George Ade was still in Indiana.

During my last two years at Purdue he had been working, first on Judge Haggard's morning paper at $6.00 a week, then for $10 on another paper which soon went broke. Then he did publicity work for a patent-medicine concern selling a tobacco cure. This company guaranteed to cure the most persistent tobacco habit if the patient followed directions. The first direction was: "Discontinue the use of tobacco." Harry L. Kramer, who headed the concern, was one of the early promoters. He established Mudlavia, a health resort near Attica, Indiana; he got out Cascarets, the things that "work while you sleep," and he issued the *Lafayette City Directory*. One of my own first gainful employments had been collecting from the subscribers to this directory.

I'm sure George found these outlets for his genius far from exhilarating. He was so ripe for a change that when I wrote him letters about glamorous life in the big city, my propaganda fell on fertile soil.

At any rate, the following June, after I had been with the paper about seven months, George came up and was presented to the editorial powers at the *Morning News* office, where he was given a tryout doing the weather at $12 a week.

Of course their chances of holding him down to this humble niche were absolutely nil, as I could have told them, only somehow they always like to make such a discovery themselves.

Perhaps I played a part in getting George to Chicago. I should be proud to think I contributed even so little to his start along the brilliant trail he subsequently followed. But as a cold matter of fact, I know perfectly well that he would have succeeded no matter where or how handicapped the start.

George's chance came one night when he was pretty much alone in the office. This was the moment the steamer *Tioga* chose to blow up in the river. In despair the editor had to send the cub weather reporter to do the best he could with this whale of a story.

The rest is history. Of all accounts appearing next morning, Ade's was far and away the best. It was a gem of reporting. His star had risen—or rather shot up. From that moment he became not *a*, but *the*, star reporter. Thereafter he covered assignments of nationwide interest like the famous Homestead strike and the Sullivan-Corbett fight when the invincible John L. was dethroned.

George's advent in Chicago, pleasantly trivial as it may have seemed at the time, was also to be a major factor in shaping my own particular destiny.

He joined me first at the Langs'. But that was too far away. The "owl cars" were slow coming up from the office at night!

So we got a room in a three-story annex just south of the old Bucklin Building at the corner of Michigan Avenue and Peck Court. As late as 1922 you could still see where this annex had been attached. Here we established ourselves.

The room, a little third-floor back-hall bedroom, extended in sweeping perspective twelve feet in one direction and ten in the other. You had to take careful aim to walk between the bed and the sofa. There was no closet, and no bathroom on that floor. Across the corner hung a curtain behind which we draped our wardrobe on a row of hooks— a row of two hooks. The single window looked out over a back area filled with discarded packing cases, bottles and other rubbish. In the distance was the magnificent uplift of the Polk Street Station.

We shared the one double bed. The rickety sofa opened, and on the ridge down the middle of it we entertained visiting Sigs up from Purdue to enjoy life in the metropolis. One loyal Sig liked it so well he stayed three weeks, but unfortunately his collars wouldn't fit either of us.

The furnishings also included a washbasin, a plush-covered armchair and two paintings. One of these represented a forest of asparagus in the foreground, a lake in the middle distance, and a range of the Himalayas shooting violently upward from its edge. The other portrayed a large pink watermelon. To give the place a literary aspect we scattered newspapers on the floor, and to impart a jolly Bohemian atmosphere we threw the remains of our cigars all over.

We paid $5 a week for this abode which we christened "The Oaks" in honor of a couple of stunted, half-dead trees in the yard below. And there we stayed three years—probably three of the most important years of our lives.

We stayed because we couldn't bear to tell the landlady we were going. She had a tubercular daughter and we knew how much she depended on our rent.

We thought of ourselves as men-about-town, and in fact we were. We were about town much more than we were about our little radiator. We never went home as long as there was anything more interesting to see or any place more inviting to go, and in consequence we saw nearly everything and every place in Chicago. Also, in consequence of a contracted currency system and the high cost of living, we lived on a high moral plane.

One of George's most humorous and delightful series of newspaper stories revolved about the doings of three young men—Jim (representing George himself), Barney and Mac.

"Barney" was Barney Dorner, up from Lafayette to try a fling at newspaper work. He was the one who slept on our lounge for three weeks, and he groaned every time he turned over.

Evidence accumulated which convinced the editors that Barney was in no conceivable respect ordained to be a reporter. For example, one night he was sent down to a large dance hall, an incorrigible offender against all laws. He was told the police expected to "pull" it, which might cause a riot. Barney took up his vigil, but the police did not come. However, for some other cause, a full-fledged riot occurred, shots were fired, one or two men were badly wounded. The affair quickly became a major newspaper sensation. But Barney didn't hustle back to the paper to write his scarehead story. He had been told to wait till the police came, and that was what he proposed to do.

Barney was also a member of a glee club that met at Kinsley's Restaurant on Adams Street. They put him at the head table where wine flowed freely, and he didn't get back to the office till four in the morning. The paper had gone to press two hours before. George and I had an awful time saving him. We couldn't do it more than two or three times. His sojourn in Chicago was brief.

George and I were hard up all the time. Every week I pawned an opal ring set with thirteen little diamond chips, given me by a cousin, and George pawned a watch he had drawn in a lottery. On payday we redeemed them till the next week. They were our gold reserve. We ate anywhere we happened to be, each of us busy with his own work.

We were full of the joy of life and loved our work. Each day was an adventure, never a drudgery.

The city was still a novelty. It was a tough town with a good deal of crime. Peck Court led from the old levee district—cheap lodging-houses and cheaper saloons. The riffraff drifted back and forth from sleeping in the park. One night George stepped on a fellow asleep in the hall; one morning there was a crowd in what is now Grant Park where a fellow had been murdered. There was often shooting in the alley and policemen chasing someone. We used to walk home down the middle of the cobbled streets.

One night I stopped in the Auditorium drugstore. It had huge plate-glass windows down to the sidewalk. I bought something and, in doing so, displayed a very modest roll. It was late. Congress Street was silent and deserted. Of course there were no automobiles then. Even the street-walker traffic indigenous to Wabash Avenue had called it a day.

I turned south on Michigan. That was empty too. Presently I heard a man's footsteps behind me. I slowed down to let him pass, and noted with definite concern that he also slowed down. I scanned the street ahead for some reassuring signs of life. There was not a soul in sight. I walked faster, and the footsteps quickened their pace. There was no doubt I was being followed.

Suddenly the steps quickened to catch up with me. A cold chill went down my back. It looked like a holdup, and I felt the moment had arrived. So, just as suddenly, I stepped off the sidewalk and turned to face him.

He stopped before me and asked for something to help him out. He said he was broke and hungry and had no place to sleep. I stepped back farther out of range before putting my hand in my pocket. I gave him something—not enough to show how nervous I was, but still enough to get him a meal and a bed for the night. Then I asked him something about himself. We stood there talking for some minutes. I said good night. He thanked me and started west on Peck Court toward South State Street, the haven of the derelicts and criminals. I'm sure he was desperate. He might have reached a point where he was ready to do anything. But I had a feeling he was not a real crook. He struck me as a country boy up against a run of hard luck.

I went on across Peck Court, unlocked the door, climbed up the stairs to our room and into the double bed.

Half a century after this happened, the Indiana Society held a banquet in the grand ballroom of the Stevens Hotel. It was in honor of my seventieth year. There were some 1,250 guests. In my speech I told the foregoing story. Then I went on:

"Gentlemen, I have told this rather long story for a definite reason. That bed stood almost exactly in front of where I am now standing. If it were here now, just where it was then, George Ade would be lying just where that fourth table stands. He might even be asking what kept me out so late."

Along in the early part of 1892 I was doing sketches out where the World's Columbian Exposition was under construction. There was feverish activity. Dozens of noted sculptors were modeling the clay into the tremendous sculptural designs which later were to contribute so greatly to the beauty of the fair. Everything was in a chaotic state, and it was hard to realize that completion could come within a year.

Most of my drawings were sketches on the spot; some were made from photographs of involved and intricate detail. I used what was called a silver print. You inked in the picture on the print and then bleached out the print in a chemical bath, and there was your completed drawing ready for the engraver. It was a tremendous timesaver.

Evidently my sketches attracted attention because one day Charles Higgins, assistant passenger traffic manager of the Santa Fe Railroad, asked if I would illustrate a small booklet called "The Land of Sunshine." I was delighted and soon completed the drawings. The little advertising booklet was so successful that it was followed by a more elaborate one. This was to be a book covering the whole Santa Fe system, called *To California and Back*. The plan required that Mr. Higgins and I both make the trip; he to write, I to draw.

I had never been outside of Indiana and Illinois. California seemed as far as India, and in my opinion the opportunity seemed gigantic. I was almost prepared to resign from the paper if necessary, but they let me go. Even now I can feel something of the heart-stirring thrill at the prospect of my first real trip.

Near Manitou, on the way from Colorado Springs to Cripple Creek, I was standing on the back platform of the poky little three-car train admiring the scenery, of which there was an abundance, when we stopped with a jerk. After a time I grew curious about the cause of the delay and looked ahead. The engine was overturned in a ditch, the tender likewise; the baggage car was away off the track and the car just ahead of mine partly off. Nobody was hurt, and nobody, apparently, much scared. This was the only railway wreck in which I ever took part.

We continued our way by stagecoach and I sat with the driver. When I heard that he had been driving coaches in all parts of the West for many years, including the Black Hills, I licked my chops. Now for some firsthand stories of redskins, road agents and runaways! I worked hopefully for several hours, but as nearly as I could discover by painstaking cross-examination, nothing in the world had ever happened to him—not even a busted trace or surcingle! And that was in the bad old days. Cripple Creek was wide open day and night, with saloons, gambling and ladies of doubtful virtue, although I don't think there was a reasonable doubt about it. Anyhow, they were lending a woman's touch to a place that was a movie producer's dream of a mining town, only nobody in those pre-Hollywood days knew what a good "Western" was.

I used to sketch on the back platform, and a pretty girl used to look over my shoulder. The art of picking up was not so prevalent then.

When I got off at Flagstaff, however, we waved good-by to each other. For several years I kept her in my mind's eye and wove a sort of dream romance about her, always looking for her face wherever I went, especially at the World's Fair. Four or five years later I was writing a letter in the Press Club. Herbert Jones, a newspaper acquaintance, sat at the opposite side of the desk also writing—to a girl in Coronado. "A fine girl!" he said, and he exhibited her picture. It was the same girl! She was a Miss Babcock from Indiana whose father ran the great hotel at Coronado Beach. Jones married her and I finally met her on a tug party on Lake Michigan. She remembered clearly the circumstances of the exchanged look and wave—or at least politely said she did.

Just before I left Los Angeles, a stranger spoke to me, walked with me to a park and on to a saloon. At first I refused a drink, but then accepted and we shook for it. Then we shook a couple of times for a quarter. A fellow dressed like a miner came in and pulled out some gold pieces.

"Shall we play him together?" whispered my companion. Vaguely I began to suspect something.

"No—no—no! Good-by!" I cried and beat a hasty retreat. It was, of course, the old game to trim the stranger—me—and then divide.

On returning to Chicago, I went right back to my *News* job. But up in the room on Peck Court at night I did what now would easily have been $10,000 worth of work on a hundred most elaborate drawings, although I received only the trip itself, a fine time, the companionship of a fine man, a tremendous lot of practice and a certain measure of fame. All these at twenty-two made me feel amply repaid. I still think I was. Even today the book, with some modernizing of its contents, is in use. In 1893 a number of those drawings were in an exhibition at the Art Institute. One was reproduced in the catalogue, but they tempered my pleasure by giving me an *F* instead of a *T* as a middle initial.

I recall the Democratic Convention that nominated Cleveland in 1892. It was held in the old Wigwam on the lake front, a temporary wooden structure. The drumming of the rain on the roof roared above the rest of the din, streams of water leaked through on the delegates, scores of umbrellas were raised. For nearly two hours Bourke Cochran used every argument, every oratorical device, every trick which his great ability and experience could muster, to checkmate the Cleveland supporters' strategy of not adjourning until their candidate was nominated. This was the high-water mark of the Hill effort, but it was not enough. The Cochran shock troops failed to break the Cleveland hollow square. After the nomination, when I left the Wigwam, Michigan Avenue was in full daylight.

I cast my first vote that fall for Cleveland. In my eyes he personified clean government, anti-spoils politics, civil service and great courage in administration. After many years I still feel that this hero of my boyhood lived up, to a notable degree, to what was expected of him. He couldn't do it entirely because, being the first Democratic President since the fifties, he was plagued by hordes of Democratic office seekers who had been waiting hungrily all their lives.

Not long after his election the Pullman strike came along and turned Chicago into an armed camp. Tents of the National Guard lined the lake front; trains were burned, transportation disrupted, while news extras fanned the passions of an inflamed populace. It was real war on a minor scale. Only Cleveland's courageous stand quelled a drift toward nationwide disorder. This was doubtless one of the earlier symptoms of resentment over the way the rewards of industry were being apportioned.

Out of that grim strike came a pleasing breath of comedy. The valiant reporters and artists who served at the front—the lake front and the stockyards—organized themselves into a Brigade of War Correspondents, the purpose being to have an occasional banquet and fight over the battles of '94. The first dinner was held the following fall at the Victoria Hotel, where a song written for us by Frank Finnegan was sung in many keys and hics:

> War correspondents bold are we
> And our trade is grim and gory.
> Peace and quiet suit us not—
> We want war and we want it hot!

This is doubtless where I first got the habit—an insidious one.

My first real cartoon for the *News*, a two-column cut appearing a few weeks after I started work, emphasized Chicago's claim to be the site of the fair scheduled for 1893.

I sometimes think that the World's Columbian Exposition was the most splendid thing I have ever seen. Nearly everything architectural or spectacular since then has had the edge taken off it. Of course I had never seen *anything* before—more impressive than the big silver dollars in the floor of the Palmer House barbershop.

I spent a full year working exclusively at the fair—six months during the construction period before the opening, watching it grow from wasteland of scrub and brushwood into a vision of loveliness, and six months during the operation of the fair.

For that whole year I covered nothing but the fair—sketches, architectural detail, anything. Instead of getting used to it, my wonder grew steadily. George Ade tells me that when I first saw Venice, all I could say was "Gosh!" The same comment would apply to me during the months I spent in the midst of this incomparable spectacle.

Ben surely must see this! I thought.

Ben, my younger brother, was now eighteen years old and still living down in Lafayette. He had never traveled anywhere, even to Chicago. I could think of no greater pleasure than that which I would get from showing these breath-taking wonders to Ben. No one could behold them without a catch in his throat.

I fairly glowed when I thought what a treat lay in store for Ben, and how much I would enjoy his enjoyment.

I sent for him and he arrived. He was strangely quiet. First I showed him the skyscrapers, one of which was the world's first steel giant. Here I expected openmouthed and popeyed amazement. There was none. He glanced up at the building and said nothing. I asked him pointedly and he answered indifferently.

I began to sense what was in his mind. He was not going to act like a jay. He wasn't going to gape and exclaim! Come what might, he'd be darned if he'd show any countrified excitement. And he didn't. Although the highest thing he had ever seen was the Tippecanoe County Courthouse, and no doubt underneath he was literally spellbound, he never showed it by the flicker of an eye.

Wait till he sees the fair! I thought. He can't hold this pose then. And to the fair we went—where the buildings were mirrored in the broad lagoons, transcendent with the soft light of millions of bulbs.

But he could—and did—even better. I don't see how he held it in. Here was I slinging adjectives around and gaping till my hat nearly fell off, but there was never a break in Ben's restraint.

Mr. Higinbotham, president of the fair, gave me a medal for distinguished service. This medal was stolen several years later from my room in the Granada Hotel. It had my name on it and was of absolutely no value to anyone else. Fifteen or twenty years later a man returned it with the story of a friend who found it in the snow. He did not explain why it took so long to find my name on the back.

The most vivid memory of that year spent so closely in contact with the great exhibition was the tragic burning of the cold-storage warehouse. The building had a tower ninety feet high above its flat roof, and while some of the firemen were up there fire broke out between them and the roof below. They slid down the hose till it burst. Then they jumped the ninety feet to the roof, their bodies turning over and over in the fall. I saw nineteen of those trapped firemen plunge to certain death. In the bright sunlight of a lovely day a hundred thousand spectators looked on, helpless and horrified. As each man jumped, a groan welled up from the crowd. The last poor fellow hung by his hands till the tower crashed down with him. This most agonizing experience haunted me for months.

The newspaper veterans of the fair met again in 1933 at the Century of Progress Exposition in Chicago and had a tremendously good time recalling the old days. Some of us creaked slightly; others had been kindly treated by time.

Perhaps the most important aspect of the earlier fair for me was the opportunity it gave me to become acquainted with many of the people who contributed to the later interest of my life.

Mr. and Mrs. Hobart Chatfield-Taylor entertained officially for the Infanta Eulalie and her escort, the most distinguished visitors to the fair, and all Chicago stood about and gawked. I went over to the Spanish building, myself, to gape at royalty, and for the first time Rose Chatfield-Taylor, one of the nation's great beauties, became more than a name to me. There were ten busy years ahead before I was destined to meet her.

Of most immediate and lasting importance, however, among those chance encounters at the fair, was that with a chubby-faced young reporter from Kansas working for the *Chicago Tribune*. His name was Edward Harden.

When the fair closed, he got a commission in 1894 to write up a new extension of the Burlington Railway, cutting across from Sheridan to the Northern Pacific, and invited me to go along. I went. I seemed always ready to go somewhere.

Harden and I inspected the Crow Indian Agency and the Custer Battlefield, and then we ran out of money and had the humiliation of having to borrow $30 from a rancher we met, oddly enough named Hardin. We rode across the terrible stretch of alkali plains in a buckboard. From Huntley, Montana, we had to hire a handcar to take us to Billings, where we finally arrived at 4:00 A.M. with every saloon wide open and the life of the town running at high tide.

The trip culminated in a three-day tour of Yellowstone Park. We drove in a surrey piloted by a tobacco-chewing gentleman who wore whiskers. His name was Dave Johnson. He swore all the time. Not unpleasantly. It just rolled out naturally without the slightest effort. One day while going up a steep slope the horses were languidly turning their heads from side to side and showing a noticeable lack of interest in their work.

Dave rebuked them gently. "Giddap there, you goddam, ornery, pisellum, scenery-lovin' sons o' bitches!"

The phrase struck us as being quite an artistic bit of word painting. So when we got home, we had a silver medal made at Spaulding's. On one side was engraved "To Dave Johnson, Champion Cusser of the Pacific Slope." On the other were our two names under the chaste phrase: "From his admiring friends." The medal hung by a ribbon from a silver bar, on which was inscribed—in shorthand—the colorful if slightly salty expression I have quoted.

We sent the medal to him. There was no response. Years passed, fifteen at least. Then one day E. O. McCormick, an official of the Union Pacific, stopped me.

"I was reminded of you recently," he said. "Our driver in the Yellowstone wore a medal with your name on it. I asked him what the shorthand meant. He said, 'Oh, jest ornyment, I reckon.'"

But McCormick wasn't content with that. It seems he took it to several hotel stenographers who hesitated and professed to be unable to read it. Then he found a male clerk to whom the language was more familiar, and who read it off without hesitation, but not without considerable surprise.

That was my first trip with Ed Harden. I don't suppose he invented my love of travel, but he has certainly been responsible for many of my most interesting experiences.

In 1897 Ed suggested a trip to New Orleans, and I couldn't seem to refuse. In those days everything presented itself as an "opportunity" which shouldn't be let slip.

We took a steamer to Tampa, where Ed got off to see his mother. I went on to Havana. I was the only passenger, but on board also were 165 mules for General Weyler. This was about a year before the Spanish-American War, and as relations were already rather tense, I was allowed to land only for the day. Before sunset that night I sailed for home on the same boat. A bad storm came up, and the little *Aransas*, being absolutely empty, practically rolled over. This was the first of my several terrifying nights at sea.

I changed at Key West to a side-wheel steamer, *City of Richmond*, and went to Miami where the Royal Palm Hotel had just been built in almost virgin jungle, then on to Palm Beach.

I felt rather important dallying thus idly at a winter resort, sketching a pretty girl—until my money gave out. Stone-broke, I arrived at Waycross, Georgia, where I was to meet Harden. To my consternation Harden turned up also stone-broke. We managed to get one berth as far as Washington. There I borrowed enough from Frank Vanderlip to return home, where I worked until August.

In 1903 Ed Harden married Vanderlip's sister Ruth. When they became engaged, I gave him an unstamped gold-disk Transvaal sovereign out of which her engagement ring was made. I was best man at their wedding, and my wedding present seems to have created amusement. I wanted something adequate to the importance of the occasion and picked out a beautiful silver fish dish with appropriate tools to go with it. I thought it was all right, up to the last minute, and then it didn't seem quite enough, so I had two of them sent.

# ～ 10 ～

## Stories of the Streets

AFTER the fair the paper—as well as the city—seemed dull and dead. Mr. Charles H. Dennis, the managing editor, joyfully received George's suggestion of a story department, atmospheric bits about the Chicago of those days—"Stories of the Streets and of the Town." This feature occupied two columns on the editorial page and continued for several years.

The first installment appeared on November 20, 1893, and from that day on the space was George's to do with as he liked. In later years he could have sold these single stories for a couple of thousand each, instead of the small $25 weekly salary he was getting for six of them. I mention this without bitterness. Those were very happy days, and money meant little to us except as a medium of barter for food and lodging.

After the feature had been running for less than a year, a selected number appeared in book form, and thereafter succeeding books appeared every few months.

From the beginning I illustrated this feature with several drawings each day—five or six half-column and one-column inserts, with occasionally a two-column cut accompanied by smaller ones.

During those years George and I learned more about Chicago than we have ever known since. We went all over, writing up people and neighborhoods and events. We got to know the police stations, the jails, the hospitals, schools and universities; in fact, nearly every department of human life and activity in Chicago during the nineties was material for us.

We didn't suspect that we were painting the portrait of a special decade that was to go down through history as "the Gay Nineties." But certainly the collection of these stories and pictures published by the Caxton Club would give a future historian useful information on that period, its life and customs.

This limited edition of 500 copies was launched in 1941 at a big luncheon. Inasmuch as Mr. Dennis, George Ade, Carl Werntz—one of the artists who drew the pictures when I was away—and I were all present in a reminiscent mood, the occasion had a good deal of the old flavor of the days when the feature was first appearing, forty-eight years before.

In January 1894 a group of Chicago newspapermen were invited to go to San Francisco to the Midwinter Fair as an advertising stunt.

All expenses were to be paid, and George and I felt flattered to be included on this junket. In addition to the fair, the lot of us—I think there were thirteen—were taken on a tour of Chinatown and its offshoot, the Barbary Coast. Did we see everything? Oh, gosh, yes! We saw everything the police permitted, and that was just about everything. For a couple of boys from the farm lands, we had our eyes well opened.

Some time after this, George and I finally decided to leave Peck Court. Our sympathy for Chuck, the consumptive girl, and her mother was at last outweighed by our dislike of the dangerous and undesirable part of town in which they lived.

Since we had for quite a while been able to afford better quarters, we joined up with another newspaper friend, Charlie Rhodes, and moved to a room on LaSalle Avenue. Rhodes was sincere and likable, a droll character with noticeably wide jawbones. George called him Octonomichosis Rhodes.

Then as we became still more affluent, we progressed to Chestnut Street, near Clark, where we had a sitting room but ate out. Often there were as many as five of us living there at once. One was Herbert Carleton Wright from Kansas City. He was distinctly the swell of the crowd. He had attended an Eastern college. He got into the financial end of the paper, and met people on Wall Street for whom he shortly deserted us. Another was Billy Etten, up from Purdue, who later went to Grand Rapids and was editor of the *News* there for many years. Still another was Albert C. Wilkie, the music critic. James O'Donnell Bennett lived upstairs.

We called this place "The Commune" and it became quite a literary center, with dutch-treat suppers of considerable style. George and I reveled in our "interesting life." I guess they thought I was too young to be a member of the Whitechapel Club. Sometimes I went on assignments with George when he interviewed theatrical people. I made a sketch of Joseph Jefferson and also of Viola Allen. She was enough older than I to realize that I was head over heels in love with her.

After that George and I lived for a couple of years at the old Granada across from the Virginia Hotel on Ohio Street. We had a room on the seventh floor.

Once, long after midnight, we were suddenly awakened. Our beds were shaking. The gas fixture was swinging and jingling.

"Did you feel that?"

"Yes. What was it, an explosion?"

"Do you suppose it could have been an earthquake?"

Full of excitement, we dressed hastily and went down to the main

JTM, 1902

GEORGE BARR

Photographed by the firm of Homrig and McCutcheon, in which he was a partner.

TWELFTH NIGHT AT ROSWELL FIELD'S IN THE MID-NINETIES

Among those present: George Ade (rear center), Franklin Head, Elia W. Peattie, Roswell Field,

floor. The night clerk, dozing over his paper, was surprised to see us coming down at that hour.

"What's the matter?" he asked.

"The earthquake. Didn't you feel it?" We both spoke at once. He looked at us sharply.

"Didn't you feel the building shake?" we insisted.

"Oh, now, you boys better get back to bed," he said.

"But everything in our room jiggled," we assured him.

"You must have been dreaming. It's all right now. You boys go on back to bed and get a good rest." And he waved us away and went on with his reading. Puzzled, we returned upstairs.

We had a lot of fun over his astonishment in the morning when he saw the bold headlines in the papers: EARTHQUAKE SHAKES CITY.

Our ability, inch by inch, to improve our standard of living depended entirely on our employer Victor Lawson.

Mr. Lawson paid relatively small salaries, but the man who did his work conscientiously was certain of his job as long as he wanted to stay, and was also certain of excellent treatment in case of illness or misfortune. Many men stayed in his employ who could have got larger salaries elsewhere.

Mr. Lawson always seemed a man apart from the rest of the world. He dressed unlike anybody else. His office costume was a long gray Prince Albert suit. His everyday hat was a flat-topped black derby, doubtless made from an individual mold, because only in the pictures of J. Pierpont Morgan, Sr., and Winston Churchill did you ever see its prototype. He wore also a carefully trimmed pointed beard. He had few social contacts. I have an idea he felt he could retain his journalistic independence only by avoiding too friendly relations with powerful citizens who might have favors to ask.

When he left his rather modest home on LaSalle Avenue, he built a magnificent house on the Lake Shore Drive. There were many stories of the beauty of its interior. I say stories because, as far as I know, very few people ever got inside. I know of only three or four—Hope Rogers, Walter Strong, probably Mr. Dennis. Mr. Edward Blair lived next door, and when Mr. Lawson moved in, Mr. Blair called and invited Mr. Lawson to tea. Mr. Lawson went, stayed a good while, seemed to have a splendid time, but that was the last Mr. Blair ever heard from him. I think Mr. Lawson wasn't familiar with common social customs. So far as I know there were no informal friendly relations between Mr. Lawson and the members of his staff, many of whom had been with him for years. Soon after his death the house built to stand a hundred years was razed to make way for a towering apartment.

Once when George Ade was crossing to England—I think it was in 1899 when he was sent to Turkey and the Near East to engage foreign correspondents for the new foreign service the *Record* was starting— Mr. Lawson happened to be on the same steamer. In Chicago their relations of employer and employee had been friendly but formal. Yet when they arrived in London, George took him on a comprehensive tour of all the popular music halls. Mr. Lawson enjoyed himself enormously. It was a phase of life which he had probably never seen before.

Long after I left his employ he and I became members of the same small monthly dinner club, the Wayfarers. He came regularly, and it was evident that he relished these contacts. Once we sat together and the talk turned on retirement from business.

"I know of only one man who retired successfully," he said, "A. M. Day. He was senior partner of his firm. He retired at fifty."

"But," I said, "Mr. Day took over the presidency of the Presbyterian Hospital and worked harder than ever."

Mr. Lawson smiled. "Perhaps that is why his retirement was successful."

My own interviews with him during the early days were comparatively few. I have told how I was taken on the paper by Schmedtgen, and given a two weeks' trial at $16. It was my understanding that Mr. Lawson said that if I improved at the end of that time, this salary should be raised to $20. No increase came during the first month, and my first interview with Mr. Lawson was to remind him of the agreement. Mr. Schmedtgen had assured me that my work *had* improved. My salary was raised to $18.

After George came up, every time one of us struck for a raise the other did too. Mr. Lawson finally put us on equal salaries and raised us together. By 1894 we were receiving $25 a week. This had necessitated six or eight personal calls on Mr. Lawson, each eliciting at most a two-dollar increase. Mr. Lawson didn't believe in spoiling young men by raising their wages too fast!

After the story department had well established its popularity, numerous offers began to come in. When the Carter Harrisons took over the *Chicago Times*, they offered us $60 a week to leave the *Record*. Then we each received an offer from Hearst of $80 a week to come to New York. Thirty years later we both did stories and illustrations for Hearst-owned magazines. But in 1895, though we were dazzled, we never thought of accepting any of these offers. I don't think we even informed Mr. Lawson of them. We had lofty ideals of what a newspaper should be, and we were very loyal to our paper.

We had, however, a keen desire, and that was to visit Europe. When we finally got an impressive ten-dollar raise to $35 a week, George said: "Let's pretend we didn't get that raise. Let's put away ten dollars a week, and when we get five hundred dollars, we'll go abroad."

For fifty weeks, then, we never missed one. By the spring of '95 we had our $500 apiece.

We were determined to go, and we had no intention of asking favors of the paper. We decided we'd have to tell the editor we were resigning in order to travel. It never occurred to us we could go away and still connect with the weekly pay roll! We expected it might cost us our jobs. So we simply walked up and told Mr. Lawson we were going to Europe for four months, and waited with bated breath.

"Well, that'll be a nice trip," said Mr. Lawson. "Send home two illustrated stories a week, and I'll keep on with your salaries."

These stories afterward came out in pamphlet form called "What a Man Sees Who Goes Away from Home."

We sailed on the old *Etruria* on April 27. Carroll Kent went along, too, an old friend from Kentland, Indiana. His father had founded the town.

Frank Vanderlip, then doing markets and finance on the *Chicago Tribune*, or it may still have been just Board of Trade news, knew the Cunard manager and secured for us the minimum rate of $110 apiece, round trip.

But in New York we ran into our first high prices—$5.00 a day for two and no food! We nearly came home.

On board the *Etruria* on that trip were the Honorable George Curzon and his Chicago wife, Mary Leiter, on their honeymoon. He was chairman of the ship's concert and enrolled the services of several grand-opera stars. He also asked if I would favor the occasion by drawing a few caricatures, which I was glad to do.

This was probably my first formal recognition among strangers. I had been signing my work from the start. But George, to his suppressed resentment, had not yet been permitted to sign, and was therefore little known outside the office.

We landed at Liverpool and took a train to London. After all those days at sea rural England with its hedges and stone walls and big luscious trees, its clean, neatly built villages and its damp haze seemed a close approximation to Heaven. In London we stayed at the Victoria Hotel. On arrival, on my twenty-fifth birthday, I bought myself a stick and I have carried one ever since.

Our next visit was to the Bow Street Police Court to see the morning grist of trials. To our astonishment one of our fellow passengers on the *Etruria* was brought in under arrest, a lady who used to walk the deck with her dog while her husband played cards. She had been fighting with another woman. As we came out of the station, we mentioned this to a man who happened to be connected with Scotland Yard, together with the fact that we had just caught sight of her husband standing opposite, apparently hesitating to cross over.

"Have you talked with them around here this morning?" asked the detective, eying us sharply.

"No. We haven't seen them since we landed."

"Well, don't. That's one of the best-known con men in England. Anyone seen with him is being shadowed."

Then he took us into a corridor of the gaol where ten or twelve men were lined up, and stood the three of us alongside them. It seemed that one of these men was a criminal and was about to be identified. Presently several French bankers and detectives came in and inspected the whole line, pausing before each one of us with keen scrutiny. I remember most earnestly hoping I did not resemble the culprit. Unerringly they picked out the right man.

After that, we took in a prize fight on High Holborn. Ted Pritchard was fighting Jem Smith, heavyweights. The seats were one, five and ten shillings, and the crowd was all in the cheaper rows, but moved up unceremoniously as the fight progressed. It was an awful one. One man was knocked clean over the ropes. The crowd, uncontrollable, jumped in and a regular free-for-all ensued. The referee couldn't clear the ring and the affair broke up in disorder.

Then we went on a special expedition to Whitechapel where Jack the Ripper was at large. This engaging personality spent much of his time murdering women, and always left his victim ripped wide open. The people I saw and the places in Whitechapel were so unbelievably awful that I went back and got my old-fashioned box camera and returned alone to get some good effects. I went into narrow alleys of the most noisome slums. I picked out the most vicious and villainous-looking characters and snapped them as they glowered with blazing eyes at the impertinence. I felt I might be risking my life getting those shots. At last when I got back to the safety of Trafalgar Square and went in to leave the films to be developed, the man took the camera, looked at it a moment, and then remarked mildly, "But you haven't pulled ont the slide."

Thirty-five years later I went again to Whitechapel, this time with Tiffany Blake. Our wives were at that very moment being presented to King George and Queen Mary in Buckingham Palace. Whitechapel was quite different. The only gruesome amusement we got out of this visit was when Tiffany barely escaped being run down by a taxicab as we came out of a bar, and we began picturing the headlines in the morning papers:

TIFFANY BLAKE INJURED IN WHITECHAPEL SLUMS
LAST NIGHT

opposite to:

MRS. TIFFANY BLAKE PRESENTED AT COURT LAST NIGHT

To Holland, Belgium, up the Rhine to Switzerland, Italy, France, and so back to England and Ireland we went. London and Paris each got three weeks. We heard Albert Chevalier and his coster songs in one, and Yvette Guilbert in the other. Everywhere we traveled third-class.

Conscientiously we sent back our two stories a week to the paper, and it was just as well we did. We would never have got home otherwise. Our $500 gave out in Paris and I cabled to Mr. Schmedtgen for an advance. The total cost of the trip was $800 apiece. I suppose that George and I may each have spent at least as much in a single week in New York in later years, but we never had so much for our money again.

We took the *Lucania* home. She was then Queen of the Seas. It was very rough and nearly everyone was ill. One day a woman, frowsily dressed, collapsed on a bench beside me.

"Isn't it dreadful!" she moaned, and told me it was her first voyage, and that she was going to Newport for a few weeks. She had reddish hair and she looked terrible. Like a jay of jays, I feared my position might be compromised, and I shied away assiduously on all subsequent occasions lest she might try to resume the acquaintance.

On the night of the ship's concert the name of a princess appeared on the program. Out she came, red hair and all, beautifully gowned and blazing with jewels. She sang wonderfully, and showed absolutely no sign of remembering a certain young man, overcome in the background.

We got home dead-broke and owing $100.

## ～11～

## I Draw a Dog

By this time the old *Morning News* had gone through various phases. It had become the *News-Record*, and now it was the *Chicago Record*. Still later it became the *Record-Herald*. During these early days of the *Record* it became a sparkling competitor of the *New York Sun*, then considered the most brilliantly edited paper in the country. Mr. Dennis had those qualities which drew able men around him and inspired them to do their best. Brand Whitlock, Ray Stannard Baker, John E. Wilkie, Kirke La Shelle and Will Payne are among those I remember.

The character of our department, also, had been changing gradually from skits and anecdotes to longer stories, then to continued ones.

George Ade found himself the center of ever-expanding fame as one of the earliest and most successful column conductors. *Artie* was his first serial, and appeared much as Dickens' first stories were run in London newspapers and magazines. It made an instant hit.

*Pink Marsh* followed it to equal popularity, a series of stories in perfect city-darky dialect, as different as possible from *Artie*, but alike in humor and charm. Some time ago there came to light a letter from Mark Twain to William Dean Howells thanking Howells for introducing *Pink Marsh* to him. It includes the most gratifying bit of praise I have ever received about my illustrations.

George also had charge of the dramatic column, as well as "Letters from the People," an early form of Vox Pop.

As for me, in addition to illustrating George's stuff—five or six pictures a day—and doing a news picture, I began drawing a regular five-column front-page cartoon.

And I leaned heavily on George for ideas.

Except for this I don't know where I might have landed as a cartoonist. Up to that time I had been a realist. Now I had to be made over into something requiring whimsy and, if possible, humor. In this transition George helped materially. He provided the excellent suggestions that gave my early cartoons whatever distinction they had.

At the beginning of the summer of 1896 I went to St. Louis to cover the Republican National Convention, where, after a bitter fight, the gold plank was adopted. Then occurred one of the purple moments of convention history. Senator Teller of Colorado, grown old in service of the Republicans, followed by the senators from the other silver states, arose from their seats and in a tense silence walked out of the hall and out of the party.

June 22-1896

As soon as McKinley was nominated, I took the first train for Canton, Ohio. For several days I watched the cohorts come in swarms to trample his lawns, jostle through his modest brick house and litter up the neighborhood with the debris of the campaign. Since I was one of the first arrivals, he had the time and graciously gave it while I made my first sketch of him.

In Canton I met another young reporter from the *Omaha Times-*

*Herald,* sent down on much the same mission as I. His black hair was swept back from a fine brow. I remembered seeing him in the press section at the convention.

A few weeks later 20,000 people sweltered in the stifling heat of the old Coliseum at Sixty-third Street and spent days trying to nominate a Democrat to run against McKinley. The crowd was noisy and restless. Nobody could hear the speakers, and as time went on, nobody wanted to hear them. Governor Altgeld, Governor Hill, Senator Vilas all tried without success. The voice of Governor Russell of Massachusetts, who ordinarily would have been granted a courteous hearing, was lost in the steadily rising din of inattention and boredom. A girl in the gallery started a boom for Boies of Iowa but it soon died out.

I was sitting on the platform, the better to draw the various speakers. The last one was announced. An alternate from Nebraska elbowed his way down the aisle amid the pandemonium and mounted the platform. It was the broad-browed young man in a black alpaca coat whom I recognized as the Omaha reporter that I had met in Canton. A lady in the row ahead of me leaned forward—his wife.

Then a miracle happened. A clarion voice stilled the crowd. Less than half a minute after William Jennings Bryan began to speak, the huge hall was hushed. It was so silent it seemed as if everyone was holding his breath. The words of the famous Cross of Gold speech, delivered by that voice of uncommon beauty, swelled through the hall and were heard to its uttermost ends. Each sentence rang out to a crash of thunderous applause.

The speaker's youth, his unusual face, his impressive brow compelled attention; but it was the voice, rising to each climax with a cadence almost like a trumpet, that you could feel up and down your back. Topping all was a speech he had worked on, word by word, period by period, climax by climax, testing it out before minor audiences throughout the preceding months, and now flung in all its studied mastery to a crowd who had been praying through hot tired noisy hours for something worth listening to.

Thus Bryan threw down the challenge to the Republicans. The issue of "16 to 1" was raised against the gold standard. It was what most of the delegates were waiting to hear.

When he sat down, the convention went wild, the huge building rocked and rocked again with the storms of cheers. The name of Bryan was taken up by the stamping processions which surged to a frenzied crescendo. One could see the enthusiasm visibly grow until

nothing in the world could have prevented his nomination for President.

We who watched saw a man march relatively unknown to the platform, and march down again the leader of a national party.

As I went back to the office, after this emotional upheaval, I was still under the spell of the voice, the setting, the splendid periods of the speech. I knew it was the greatest one I was ever likely to hear—one can expect only one such in a lifetime—and yet there lurked beneath the surface a conviction that it might not stand searching analysis after the blood had cooled. When I read it next morning, it was still great, but it lacked the thunderclaps that had exploded in the hearts of those who heard his silver-tongued eloquence on the stuffy history-making afternoon before.

During the ensuing battle my cartoons favored the gold platform of McKinley, popularly symbolizing sound money as against what was called fiat money. But it is a curious fact that although I always opposed Mr. Bryan in my work, he apparently bore me no ill will. Many times he sent me cartoon ideas which I was able to use, with due credit. He always got in touch with me when he passed through town, and often in after years, when my wife and I were en route to Treasure Island, we stopped to see him and his family in Miami.

The free-silver campaign was rich in material for George Ade's keenness and wit, and he kept strengthening me with ideas for my cartoons until I was able to stand alone.

Under such conditions I got off to a propitious start.

As I look back, I feel sure I could not have effected the change by myself. Through his persistence I gradually acquired the knack of looking at things with the eye and technique of a cartoonist. George was the pillar I leaned against until 1897 when I was given leave of absence to go around the world on the *McCulloch,* scheduled to take six months. I did not return to Chicago for nearly three years.

Then I had to resume my cartoon work without George's help. He had originated his first Fable in Slang, and had stepped from $60 a week into big money.

By that time I had got the hang of it—at least sufficiently to hold my job on the *Tribune* for more than forty years.

About the middle of the campaign I had a cartoon ready for the paper which had some space left untouched in a lower corner. I might have put in a bush or a fence post, but without any purpose except to fill the space I finally drew a little dog—not a valuable one, just a harmless-looking little dog whose architectural lines were more friendly than good.

The next day a similar condition arose, and I again drew a small dog. Quite by chance he bore a faint family resemblance to the first one.

Four people wrote in, demanding to know the significance of the dog.

On the third day—and this time intentionally—I drew the same dog, and there were twelve letters!

Thereafter the dog always appeared in the cartoon. Sometimes he would be with McKinley, sometimes with Bryan, so that you couldn't tell whether he was a Democratic dog or a Republican—he was always very well-behaved and respectful. Sometimes he looked surprised or incredulous; often he wore a look of deep concern or maybe of exuberant glee. As the days went by, the number of letters increased. Everybody wanted to know "what the odd-looking dog in the *Record* political cartoons means." "Kindly state in your columns what the cheerful little square-nosed pup represents." There were guesses, suggestions and poems.

The whole office was amazed by the interest this homely little dog created.

One day I drew Mr. Cleveland accidentally rocking on its tail. By early afternoon I was already receiving hundreds of letters suggesting remedies—all very facetious in such an extremity. Next day when the dog appeared with no visible sign of damage beyond a neat bandage, there was general rejoicing.

By election time the reporters around our particular paper felt that the campaign had been completely blanketed by the dog. The issue appeared to be, not the free coinage of silver, but "Why is the dog?"

Whenever I was introduced to a person, the first thing he would say was "You aren't the fellow who draws the dog, are you?"

People never referred to the cartoons or to anything else that I thought might be creditable; they always spoke about the dog. It amused me at first, but by and by I resolved to get rid of him. I drew a cartoon in which a tail was shown disappearing off the side from which floated a little banner saying, "Farewell forever."

But in vain. All those alert eyes which had spotted the dog, even if only the tip of his tail was visible sticking out from behind a haystack, weren't sharp enough to see this farewell notice. Letters poured in, literally by the thousands.

Kindly let us know what has become of the flop-eared dough-faced hound who has so assiduously followed the fortunes of the campaign just past. We feel real lonesome without him.

There is a feeling of goneness. Where, oh where has the little dog gone? Doggerel is not good enough for that dog; he was a howling success! . . .

Schmedtgen tried to help me out in this crisis by drowning the dog in a cartoon representing conditions after the political cyclone, but there was an avalanche of disapproval.

In self-defense I had to bring him back for a time.

In the course of several months I found myself in the Philippines. I had stood it as long as I could. One day I happened to sit down under a tree—a bamboo tree I think it was—beside a tired American soldier. We got to talking about what they called out there "God's country, the U.S.A." When I got up to go, we exchanged names. His eye lighted up and he exclaimed, "You're not the fellow that draws the dog, are you?"

# ~ III ~

## ON THE TOSS OF A COIN

*Switzerland, the Asylum of Kings*

## ～ 12 ～

## A Momentous Invitation

MEANWHILE Frank Vanderlip, erstwhile financial editor of the *Tribune*, had been appointed Assistant Secretary of the Treasury under Lyman Gage in McKinley's Cabinet.

In August I received a momentous letter from Ed Harden. It seems he had been on board a revenue cutter with Vanderlip when Captain Shoemaker, Chief of the Service, brought out blueprints of a new cutter, the *McCulloch*. She was about to be launched from Cramp's Yard and sent around for service on the Pacific Coast.

"Why wouldn't that be a good trip for you to take?" asked Vanderlip.

"I was just on the point of asking if I could go," Harden answered.

"Is there anyone you'd like to have with you?"

"John McCutcheon," replied Harden promptly.

In consequence Vanderlip arranged for us to be invited.

At first I was frantic with joy—but of course the thing was impossible! I sat down and composed eight closely written pages explaining how I had no money, how I had just returned from a self-elected vacation, how it was quite inconceivable that the paper would let me go again so soon, and how I most certainly could not think of it—and ended by saying that I would do everything in my power to arrange it!

Then I wrote to Mr. Lawson, who was at the time in Switzerland, and who proved as usual most obliging.

"It is too great an opportunity for you to miss," he wrote me. "By all means go. But remember we have a mortgage on you. You must come back to us when you return."

There was some question whether the *McCulloch* should go around Cape Horn or around the world. This was about ten years before the Panama Canal was built. The cost of coal in South America made the expense practically equal. Harden and I expressed a preference for circling the globe, and through Vanderlip's influence it was so arranged. We expected to start in December.

But the sailing date kept being postponed. There were farewell ban-

quets over and over again. They became somewhat embarrassing, so
on December 18 I went to Washington anyhow.

From there I went to Indianapolis. I was at that time flirting rather
indefinitely with the idea of matrimony. I had not progressed so far
as the ring stage. Now it became advisable to remain a free lance; the
opportunity of a private warship was too stupendous to forego! Fortunately I had no sooner reached Indianapolis than a message came to
hurry back. But there was then another delay.

A second flying visit to Indianapolis was interrupted at once by
another telegram. I departed hastily for Baltimore, whence we sailed
on January 8, 1898.

The *McCulloch* had been built in Philadelphia. She sailed up
Chesapeake Bay to Baltimore, all white and tan and new and shiny.
But we stopped at Norfolk for more coal. Being intended only for
coastwise service, she had to carry ninety extra tons on the bright new
orlop deck, where it was heaped six or eight feet high in big sacks.

On the twelfth of January Captain Shoemaker came to say a final
good-by. Then, escorted from Hampton Roads by two other cutters
with guns firing "Farewell" and "Good Luck," with bands playing and
sailors lined up at attention, we sailed through the Virginia capes into
open ocean.

The *McCulloch* was the first revenue cutter to go even to Europe,
let alone around the world.

We had left a printed itinerary with our friends, with the latest date
for letters to be sent around the world the opposite way to meet us.
We fully expected to be home within five months.

Harden and I were guests of the Treasury Department. Captain
Daniel B. Hodgsdon, aged sixty-two and in the service for many years,
had also invited two guests—Colonel George A. Loud from Au Sable,
Michigan, who had been appointed paymaster and so wore a uniform;
and Ralph Phelps of Detroit, six and a half feet tall, who wore
whiskers.

The five of us lived in the captain's quarters. Phelps and Harden
had the two staterooms, the captain slept on a transom, and Colonel
Loud and I had swinging beds put up every night in the dining saloon.
There were two cabin boys, Claude Long and Archie Forbis. Nine or
ten other officers bunked below, among them Foley, the executive
officer; Chief Engineer Randall; Lieutenant Ridgely of Annapolis; W.
W. Joynes, navigating officer, also from Annapolis and very polished;
and Dr. Joseph Greene, a Southerner, later of Asheville. There was a
crew of 100.

The first leg of this cruise, to Madeira, was to be the first test of this 1,000-ton cutter in ocean voyaging. In addition to the ninety tons of coal on deck, there was a steam launch hung up in front. One could not get from forward to the captain's quarters aft without climbing over the coal. The ship was narrow and built for speed. There was no bilge keel or other device to prevent rolling. She had a new type of construction and nobody knew how she was going to act.

The faults of that construction were so very serious that she nearly went down the first twenty-four hours out.

That first evening we had a jolly dinner, all unsuspecting what lay ahead. Soon after turning in we struck the Gulf Stream which was being lashed by the tail of a storm. Our swinging beds plunged from side to side, almost hitting the ceiling. It seemed as if we *must* roll over. Next morning the sea was worse. The center of gravity of the ship appeared to be too high. With the launch and the huge cross boom and all that coal, she was hopelessly top-heavy. A sail was hoisted to steady her. We could not *walk* around, we had to crawl. We formed the Coal Bag Club. Colonel Loud read aloud *The Man without a Country* as we perched on top of the sacks.

During the afternoon we ran into an unusually heavy sea and the ship turned on her side. A lot of coal fell off and the cabins were flooded. She didn't right! Another great sea came on board, and tons and tons of water rolled into the wardroom. A third wave like that would probably have sunk the ship. The scuppers, aside from being too small, were completely stopped up by the coal. The spar of the sail was in the water. Fortunately the next few waves were small, and slowly, slowly, the *McCulloch* came up to position. Everyone was scared stiff. Then her steering gear jammed and there was more genuine terror.

From that time on nobody had any confidence in the ship, and practically at the outset the pleasures of the cruise were enormously lessened. We were pursued by storms. We had to keep her nose in the wind whether we turned toward Brazil or Newfoundland, just to avoid getting in the trough of the sea. We had to "wear ship" twice, that terrifying process of swinging her on her heel into the trough of the seas and praying the impetus of the swing would carry her on until she took the big seas on her stern instead of her bow—a feat often performed with sailing craft but seldom with steamships. We were all given warning and braced ourselves. Everything else crashed about and smashed in the dizzy whirling.

Fourteen days of constant storm brought us to Ponta Delgada in the Azores. Not enough coal had been saved to reach Madeira. My recollection is that we had less than twenty-five tons left. There was, of course, no wireless in those days. Port seemed like Heaven to our group of shaken adventurers. Captain Hodgsdon and I alone, of all on board, had not been seasick. Phelps had lost twenty pounds!

We stayed six days in an effort to make some slight improvements in the ship, especially in the scuppers. Very much later she was reconstructed, her faults were entirely eliminated, and she continued in service until 1917 when she was sunk in a collision on the Pacific Coast. It was the *McCulloch* that rescued the Borden Arctic party from the barren island on which they had lived for two weeks after their ship struck an uncharted rock and went down near the Aleutian Islands.

At Gibraltar things began to look up. Salutes were fired by shore guns. It was etiquette in the various ports of call for the captain in full dress to call on whoever was in authority, or on the admiral of a fleet if there happened to be one. These officers would return the call. We were then entertained everywhere. These ceremonials and courtesies offered unusual opportunities for sight-seeing. We crossed the border into Spain. We visited Tangier and Morocco. By night we toured the underworld of dancing girls and sensual music.

Malta was the next port, with Governor Freemantle's ball and the magnificent spectacle of a costume ball given by the Bourse.

At a secondhand store I bought a ring, a Maltese Cross and Crown worn by the old Knights of Malta hundreds of years before, which I have worn ever since.

At Malta Captain Hodgsdon received a short dispatch telling of the sinking of the *Maine* in Havana Harbor with 265 lives lost. The cause appeared unknown. Was it accident or the Spaniards? In any case it seemed a very remote occurrence. I did not even record it in my diary, although from then on the thought of war hovered in the offing.

After still other alterations to make the ship more seaworthy, on February 22 we left Malta for Port Said. While she coaled we went to Heliopolis, the Pyramids, Cairo and the famous fish market. One morning while eating breakfast in Shepheard's Hotel, we heard a band far down the street. One after another, people left the dining room. We followed. The band preceded a long file of British soldiers. Everyone cheered. It was evidently no ordinary parade. On inquiry it transpired that they were going to join Kitchener in Khartoum and were later in the Battle of Omdurman. This was the first time I had seen men marching to real war, and even after my father's Civil War stories and the old soldiers who frequented our house during my childhood, I found it unexpectedly impressive.

We rejoined the *McCulloch* at Suez and started down the Red Sea. Soon we encountered another storm, but with our previous experience still in mind we craftily got behind a rock—Gebel Tier, about a mile long—and as it was too deep to anchor, we spent two days just steaming back and forth in its protection. At Aden the American consul was very cordial. He provided a carriage for a drive to the oasis of Sheik Othman, ten or twelve miles out. Nevertheless Aden, with not a leaf nor a drop of water except in reservoirs, was at best a depressing place to spend the six days we were held in port on account of a sick sailor!

Although it was in the change of monsoons, when rough seas might be expected, our Indian Ocean crossing was unbelievably smooth, even glassy at times so that a pencil set on end would not fall over. On those quiet nights I used to climb up to the foreyard, far above the deck, and ride for hours in the comfortable perch, whence I had the exquisite pleasure of watching a full-rigged ship cross the rising moon. I used also to stand the middle watch, twelve to four, up on the bridge with Lieutenant Joynes, the navigating officer. It was he who introduced me to the books of Louis Becke and filled my avid ears with tales of South Sea atolls, kindling a desire that was to grow more intense with the years until at last—but that is another chapter.

Colombo was very hot, so while the ship was delayed, we went up to Kandy and still farther, to Nuwara Eliya where it was cooler.

Then I came to a crossroads in my life. Harden and I were eager to see more of India, it was so tantalizingly near. The French ship *Dupleix* was about to sail for Bombay. We could take her, see a lot of India and catch up with the *McCulloch* in Japan. Not to do so seemed to us a terrific loss of opportunity. On the other hand, what if war with Spain should be declared? Perhaps there would be time for the one before the other broke. The debate seemed endless. Finally we tossed a coin—a momentous coin! If I had waited to go with the *Dupleix*, I would have missed the Battle of Manila and all its subsequent ramifications, which would have been a major calamity as I look back on it. I might have come home and perhaps married at once. Not getting my blood full of adventure and war might have made all the difference in the world in my career, possibly in my character.

As it was, the coin said no. We sailed for Singapore with the *McCulloch,* and that night the *Dupleix* burned at her dock!

Six days later, at Raffles Hotel, the American consul, Mr. Pratt, had a message for Captain Hodgsdon. The *McCulloch* had been transferred from the Treasury to the Navy Department, with orders to proceed at once to Hong Kong. Hodgsdon was cautioned to avoid Spanish ports and Spanish ships. War was not yet, but was inevitable.

## ～ 13 ～

## With the Asiatic Squadron

IT WAS in the Spanish-American War that I came to realize the real intensity of war fever. From the time we received news in Malta of the destruction of the battleship *Maine,* the imminence of war was constantly in mind. We didn't know at what moment the *McCulloch* might be recalled to America. There was no radio. From port to port we proceeded—Port Said, Suez, Aden, Colombo, Singapore. We sailed slowly as long as we were in sight of signal masts. No recall came, but at each succeeding port the news dispatches grew graver and more inflamed. It was like reading a suspenseful weekly serial.

At Singapore the *McCulloch* received the official orders transferring her to the Navy and ordering her to report to Commodore Dewey at Hong Kong. At last we were on the heels of war! The peaceful round-the-world cruise supposed to take five months was to be interrupted. I was to be in the throes of war experiences for the better part of three years, the virus working gaily all the time! Many unusual experiences, by-products of war, made life interesting.

While the *McCulloch* coaled in Singapore, Harden and I went up to Johore. We did not hunt any tigers; there was time only for a little gambling. Meanwhile the big Spanish transport *Mindanao* left the harbor for Manila. Then, while we steamed for five days up the China Sea, the men practiced with sabers. Should war be declared, it would be easy for the Spanish fleet to cut off our single ship, and the American fleet might already have left Hong Kong. The uncertainty of it all was thrilling.

But on April 17 we sighted the squadron, still in white, with awnings spread, and we knew that we were in time.

Our captain called on the commodore, who presently returned the call. Since the *McCulloch* had been transferred to the Navy, there was a good chance that Harden and I might not be allowed to go on.

Nervously we awaited an opportunity to speak to Dewey. He said that in any other circumstances he would have had to say no, but inasmuch as we were guests of the Treasury we could proceed. Of course we were jubilant. Colonel Loud also was to go on. But Ralph Phelps, for business reasons, decided not to take the risk and left the ship.

It seemed probable that as soon as war *was* declared, the squadron would go to Manila to engage the Spanish fleet. For this it was necessary to await the cruiser *Baltimore* with supplies.

With the help of the American consul general, Rounseville Wildman, Harden made arrangements to act as *New York World* correspondent. Joseph Stickney, who had been naval editor of the *New York Herald,* was on hand. I cabled the *Record* for instructions and was told to send all the stuff I could. So there were three of us.

I wrote and mailed three long letters describing preparations, giving the current talk. In a straightaway fight between the two forces it was thought that the Americans were vastly superior in strength and equipment, though not in numbers. The Spaniards had four good ships and a great number of small gunboats. They were known to be rapidly removing from Manila all valuables and church treasures, more in anticipation of the fury of the rebels than of any pillage by the Americans. Great numbers of Spanish and foreign residents were leaving the islands and it was doubtful if any but natives and the Spanish fighting forces would be there when the fleet arrived.

It was thought that the land batteries would open up on us, and that the Spanish vessels would remain inside the harbor behind the protection of a torpedo-filled strip of water and the highlands flanking the bay. In this way a short decisive action would be impossible, and it might be necessary to reduce the forts and force an entrance to the harbor in spite of torpedoes. It was important that these maneuvers be accomplished as quickly as possible, because during the bombardment the fleet would have to lie in open sea, and a typhoon would be of little help. Supplies and coal were also a consideration in a long siege. It was prophesied that while this naval conflict was going on in the bay the rebels would attack the city.

For us it seemed a good deal like going into the jaws of a dragon. No one had ever heard of a naval battle in which less than a quarter of the participants were killed. We all wrote farewell letters home, and packed everything we did not really need in big camphorwood chests and sent them to a comprador on shore. In Hong Kong harbor, wash girls visited the ships in their own boats to solicit laundry for their respective agencies. I became well acquainted with little Ah Soo, a witty, intelligent girl. When she found we were going off to battle, she brought out her small sampan filled with flowers—even roses in April—and decorated all our quarters.

One night Harden and I spent in Canton. Coming down next day in a storm, with sampans blowing about in distress and bodies of Chinese floating down the river with us, we found that the *Baltimore* had arrived. Governor Blake of Hong Kong gave notice he considered that a state of war existed, and his neutrality required that he allow us forty-eight hours to get out of the harbor. British feeling being friendly, it had been figured out that all painting and important preparations could be completed by that time. Forthwith the *Baltimore* was put in dry dock, scraped and painted. In addition to the four six-pounders already on the *McCulloch*, two three-inch army guns were lashed on. The *Nanshan* and the *Zafiro* were purchased as supply ships.

Inasmuch as the Chinese had no way of protecting their neutrality, a sheltered cove thirty-five miles north of Hong Kong had been selected as a rendezvous. The *McCulloch*, the *Boston*, the *Concord* and the *Petrel* went up on Sunday afternoon; the *Olympia*, *Baltimore* and *Raleigh* followed on Monday morning. I obtained permission to make this short trip on the *Olympia*. The British sailors all cheered as we went out.

Mirs Bay was a lonesome spot. There were high forbidding mountains on three sides. Only a few Chinese shacks were visible on shore, a few scattered sampans on the water. There was a tense feeling of expectancy in the air. War was inevitable, and yet, as is the way with wars, there was always a chance it might be staved off. At six o'clock on that first evening as we lay at anchor a small smudge of smoke was seen away out at sea. An hour later a ship drew alongside the *Olympia* and delivered a cipher dispatch to Dewey. In fifteen minutes the signal was flashed through the night from the ardoise lights on the foremast that war had been declared.

Amid the ensuing excitement there was a shifting of ammunition and supplies, and then the Asiatic Squadron was ready to start at a moment's notice. Dewey's orders from Washington were to proceed to the Philippines to capture or destroy the Spanish fleet. The commodore now waited only the arrival of the American consul, Williams, from Manila with information about the strength and position of the Spanish ships. Every day lost gave time for preparation in Manila and added to the general uneasiness aboard our ships. Early one morning the consul arrived by tug, having come up to Hong Kong on the *Esmeralda*. Dewey called a conference of commanders; the formation of ships was arranged and orders were given to sail. At two o'clock on the afternoon of April 27 the *Olympia* raised her anchor, the marines were drawn up on the quarter-deck and the bands struck up the inspiring march from *El Capitan*. The rest of the vessels followed according to plan. There were two columns: the first, led by the *Olympia*, was composed of the *Baltimore*, the *Raleigh*, the *Petrel*, the *Concord* and the *Boston*; the second consisted of the *McCulloch*, the *Nanshan* and the *Zafiro*.

It was a cheerless, bleak, unfriendly kind of day. A heavy mist lay over the bay. Only a few junks were on hand to see us off. And, without radio, we knew that from this moment on we would be cut off from touch with the world. The *McCulloch's* crew, which had been reduced to seventy, were lined up to hear Lieutenant Elliott read aloud the Spanish proclamation of war as issued by authorities at Manila. It was an inflammatory cry to the people of the Philippines to unite against the sacrilegious vandals who were coming to loot their churches and insult their women. It was an appeal to the ignorant passions of an unlettered people. At the conclusion of the reading, which contained a number of other uncomplimentary things about American seamen as well as Uncle Sam, there was a second of silence. Then the crew broke into three ringing cheers for the American flag.

Three days it took to cross the China Sea, and they were filled with signal drills, musket drills, cutlass drills. All useless articles such as woodwork and doors were thrown overboard. Masts were bound with anchor chains; the rigging was "snaked" with zigzag rope to keep the heavy wire stays from falling on deck; shot plugs were made for stopping shell holes in the hull; lifeboats were wrapped with canvas to prevent flying splinters; the after lifeboats were lowered halfway in case of emergency. As our crew was comparatively small, even the three civilians, including me, were assigned positions with the gun and ammunition squads. A sick bay was arranged, with an operating table on the berth deck, and four men were assigned to assist the surgeon. A stretcher was built—most unpleasantly suggestive. Life preservers and buoyant cushions were heaped about. The decks were cleared for action.

At night we moved in absolute darkness except for the masthead lights ahead. It was the lonesomest trip in the world—with the conviction in everyone's mind that in a very few days a lot of us would be killed.

## ∼ 14 ∼

## The Battle of Manila

EARLY in the morning of that thirtieth of April so many years ago we sighted land, Cape Bolinao, almost straight north of Manila Bay 110 miles. Thence we turned southward. We stopped some Spanish fishing schooners but they had no information about anything. Subig Bay, about thirty miles north of Manila, was known to be partly fortified, and there was a chance the Spaniards might have gone in there. The *Concord* and the *Boston* were sent ahead to search, the *Baltimore* following to support them if necessary, but nothing was found. The squadron came to a full stop and the captains were signaled to another conference.

A few minutes after six o'clock the gigs left the flagship's side. A very grave Captain Hodgsdon and Lieutenant Elliott came back. They told us we were to run the forts that night in order to attack the Spanish fleet inside Manila Bay in the morning. The ships were to sail in single column with every light extinguished save only a small one at the stern as guide. There was to be no talking, not even a whisper. The battle ports were put up; the chartroom was sealed. Each of us strapped ten or fifteen gold pieces around his waist in case

*Ships in Subig Bay*

he was cast ashore. The groups of sailors on deck and officers on the bridge looked shadowy and vague. With all the hurry of final preparation there was hardly a sound.

Slowly we steamed south, timing the trip so as to reach the entrance to the bay at midnight. Shortly after sunset a remarkable cloud formation was observed on the western horizon. It represented absolutely and without imaginative aid the gun deck and turret of a warship, with gun protruding, black and vivid. A marvelous portent, but for whom?

The night was a good one for running the forts. Masses of cloud hid the half-moon. There was lightning in the southwest. During the last hour the men stretched out on mattresses on deck to try to get some rest, their loaded revolvers and cutlasses within easy reach. There was one hectic moment when a life buoy equipped with Greek fire fell off one of the forward ships. The queer, unearthly blaze darting and dancing on the face of the water gave an ominous effect.

About eleven-thirty two dark headlands loomed against the shifting clouds. In the space between, a smaller mass showed where Corregidor lay with its dreaded Krupp guns.

We were moving forward noiselessly; only the dim gleam of the stern lights on the ships ahead was visible. The *Nanshan* and the *Zafiro* were quite lost in the blackness behind. The *Olympia* turned in and steered directly for the center of the southern and wider channel. Consul Williams had advised this channel, the Boca Grande, in spite of scattered rocks, as the Boca Chica, through which he had but lately come by a very devious route, was probably mined. The *Baltimore* followed, then the other ships, gliding slowly and silently, separated from one another by 400 yards. We strained our eyes to catch the slightest sign on the somber shores.

Just at that moment the soot in the *McCulloch's* funnel caught fire and flamed up like a rolling mill! A faint light flashed up and down, up and down, on shore. A rocket leaped from Corregidor. Discovered! We ground our teeth. But nothing further came, so we kept on. And then the funnel flared again!

The head of the column was well into the bay. The *Boston* was about 200 yards ahead of us. The *McCulloch* was almost directly between the two forts. Suddenly there was a flash to the south, a white puff of smoke curled out, and for the first time in the lives of nearly all on board, we heard the scream of a cannon ball, *not* from Corregidor but from a near-by rock called El Fraile! Just a single pinnacle nobody had realized was large enough for a battery. The shell seemed to go between the masts of the *McCulloch*. Lieutenant Elliott of the Navy, who represented Dewey, gave orders to man the aft six-pounders and fire, but countermanded the order in the lull that followed. However, the *Boston* sent an eight-inch shell like a crash of thunder. This was the first shot fired by the Americans. The *McCulloch* fired the next three. Then the column continued, the Spaniards still firing into the darkness.

Meanwhile the chief engineer on the *McCulloch* died of heart failure. Mr. Randall was a stout, thick-necked man who had been pretty excited and obviously nervous. The others had joked him about it a good deal and he had been drinking rather heavily in consequence. When we started into the bay, I was leaning on the rail in the dark. Mr. Randall came up and stood by me for a moment. With all the ports closed, below decks was like a furnace. I think I was the last to see him alive. Soon after his body was discovered, the *McCulloch* signaled to the flagship for another doctor. The *Olympia* signaled back: "Impossible."

The forts were passed at seventeen minutes past midnight. Another twenty minutes took us out of range of the batteries at the mouth of the harbor. Manila lay twenty miles ahead, and, not wishing to arrive before daybreak, we slowed to four knots an hour. The hazard over, everyone lay down where he was, but nobody slept much. Randall's body, sewed in canvas and wrapped in a flag, was carried up to a bier on the quarter-deck, to be buried at sea later in the day. This initial tragedy appeared completely overshadowed by the prospect ahead. Earlier that night at dinner the three of us civilians remarked that surely some were there who might not be at dinner the next night.

On the morning of the first of May the bay was like glass. All were up and ready, and when the sky showed the first faint tint of gray the domes and spires of Manila were silhouetted spectrally. To each side was revealed the position of the enemy.

Off Cavite, seven miles nearer than Manila, lay the Spanish fleet. The flagship, *Reina Cristina,* showed up in front, black and fierce. Nearly abreast of her lay the *Castilla,* protected by large barges which made it impossible for shells to penetrate below the water line. The *Don Antonio de Ulloa* was a little behind, and in the naval anchorage in Bacoor Bay were the *Don Juan de Austria,* the *Isla de Luzon* and the other vessels. Small protected cruisers and torpedo boats steamed back and forth or retreated behind the walls of the arsenal.

The Spaniards started firing when we were still four miles distant. At the sound the *Olympia* wheeled and started straight for them, grim and determined, without answering fire. From every mast and peak of the American squadron floated a flag, an inspiring sight which aroused tremendous enthusiasm.

The *Nanshan* and the *Zafiro* were ordered to the middle of the bay. The *McCulloch* was to lie behind the battle line, about two miles from the Spanish fleet and forts, to protect the transports and to pull

*Captain Gridley of the Olympia*

out disabled ships. The captain appointed Harden and me in charge of the first ammunition magazine to keep the guns supplied in case the *McCulloch* went into action.

The Spaniards had started firing at 5:10 A.M. Thirteen minutes later Dewey gave the historic order: "You may fire when you are ready, Gridley."

The plan of action was for the American ships, headed by the *Olympia*, to proceed in single file, firing all the port batteries; then to turn in a great ellipse and steam back, firing the stern and starboard batteries. The roar of guns became continuous, and the flashes and flames, the geysers of water and the clouds of smoke. At times, when one of our ships disappeared in smoke, we'd say "She's gone!" but then there would emerge from the haze, one after another, the battle flags of each separate mast and peak. In the intensity of his excitement Lieutenant Elliott edged the *McCulloch* nearer and nearer. At the times when the American ships passed between us and the Spaniards, we were in the direct line of the enemy's fire, and shots screamed through the rigging and fell around us.

The Spaniards were courageous and daring. Once the *Reina Cristina* started out alone at full speed, in the face of combined American fire, to run down the *Olympia*. For long minutes she came on, but the shelling was too heavy. As she swung around, an eight-inch shell from the *Olympia* struck her in the stern, ripped right through her and set her afire. Later we learned that this shell killed her captain and forty men and wounded the admiral. Yet at the time she kept right on throwing shells. It seemed as if she must go down, but half an hour later we saw her through the smoke, belching flame, her pennant still waving bravely at her main peak.

Two little torpedo boats started out in a desperate effort but were turned back at 800 yards, one diving headlong into the sea. A gunboat slipped out and headed for the *McCulloch*, hoping by this bold move to destroy the transports, but it too was forced to retreat. Throughout the storm of shells Commodore Dewey, with Flag Captain Lamberton, stood on the bridge of the *Olympia*, completely exposed.

My running commentary on the battle continues:

Now there are two vessels burning, the *Reina Cristina* and the *Castilla*, although both have their flags flying. Whenever hope arises that they are completely disabled, they seem to renew firing with increased vigor. It is impossible to determine what damage is being

done to either side. Three times the American fleet makes its deadly round, passing five times before the Spanish forces, drawing in closer and closer. Now the *Olympia* has ceased firing; it is said her after turret is damaged. She withdraws, followed by the rest of the squadron. The Spanish keep on firing with almost as much vigor as ever. It is 7:45. The fight has lasted two and a half hours. There has been incessant firing, the whole sky is hazy with smoke. The tremendous resistance and striking courage of the Spanish is a revelation.

A feeling of profound gloom comes over us as the American fleet withdraws for conference. How much damage has been done? Are their decks swimming in blood, their cabins choked with wounded and dead, their guns battered? These things cannot be determined until the commanders return from the conference. There comes a long hard wait. At last, after feverish anxiety, the marvelous news comes that not a single life has been lost, not a single man seriously hurt! And hardly a scrap of rigging has been cut through.

We were forthwith ordered to eat breakfast. The reason for the withdrawal, it transpired, was a misunderstanding about the amount of ammunition left, and a desire to let the smoke clear away.

Soon the *Baltimore* was sent in to silence the shore batteries, and the *Petrel* to clean up the rest of the ships. But only masts and battered funnels and parts of shattered decks were above water. The

Spaniards themselves had deserted them, pulled out the sea plugs and sunk them on their own account. When night fell the shore line was bright with burning ships. The *Reina Cristina* and the *Castilla* were mere skeletons, flames silhouetting their black bones against the white heat. Fearful explosions came from Cavite—magazines of ships or ammunition stores. Back in the hills curling columns of smoke lifted lazily to the sky, marking where the insurgents were applying the torch to complete what the Americans had left undone. From Manila came the sound of cathedral bells.

The Battle of Manila was, of course, the peak of my war experiences. In its historic significance it was the greatest single event of my life.

I passed the time of battle trying to sketch and to photograph, but it was too early and too far, although from our position we could see the whole panorama of the battle better than anyone else. The next afternoon I took a dinghy and went among the wrecks. The only live thing I saw was a chicken perched on a bow stanchion of the *Reina Cristina*, once the proudest of them all.

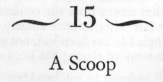

# A Scoop

WE WERE naturally very anxious to get ashore as soon as possible, but the *McCulloch* people had no opportunity on the afternoon of May 1, although we were very near land.

Captain Lamberton of the *Olympia* was sent to see what conditions ashore were. He found that our shells had damaged the arsenal, and that the hospitals were full of Spanish wounded. Their dead were estimated at 400; the wounded at 600. Six or eight Americans had been hurt but not seriously; and Engineer Randall's death turned out to be our only fatality.

Toward evening the *McCulloch* was ordered to lie across the mouth of the Pasig River, which runs through Manila. She was to intercept any torpedo boats that might attempt an attack. She took up her position about a mile from the mouth, in the heart of the dangerously mined area. All night she lay there, only a few hundred feet from the big Krupp shore battery, still undamaged, which could have blown the little cutter out of the water. But the commodore had sent word that if they fired on his ships he would destroy the city.

About 2:00 A.M. general quarters were sounded. Everyone leaped to his post as a small boat was observed coming from the Pasig. It proved to be a launch which we covered with searchlights and guns as it drew alongside. It carried a Spaniard named Bertrand de Lis, who wished to go out to the flagship to arrange for the surrender of the forts on Corregidor. These, of course, still remained intact and might have prevented our ships from leaving the bay. The launch was allowed to proceed and the commodore received this emissary, but with skepticism. De Lis promised that if they would land him at Corregidor, he would arrange for the surrender and dismantling of the guns. He was warned that if any false move was made he would be killed instantly. All went smoothly.

It was learned that the wires between Corregidor and Cavite had been cut by the insurgents before the entrance of our fleet on Saturday night. That was why the Spanish fleet was not aware until dawn that the Americans had entered the bay.

Next morning the *McCulloch* was sent back to Cavite, and later we were landed with a party. We were met at the landing and treated by the Spanish civilians with the utmost courtesy. The soldiers had all fled to Manila. The Filipinos greeted us with enthusiasm. We visited the arsenals and hospitals, and were offered all sorts of souvenirs. I took a flag from the *Isla de Luzon* and one of its smaller guns. This ship was later raised and ended its career, curiously enough, in Lake Michigan.

On our return to the ship Dewey sent word to go out and cut the cable to the outside world. With grappling hooks we picked it up,

laid it over a small boat and took out a hundred-foot section, which we divided among ourselves. The cable was two and one-half inches in diameter.

There still remained the battery at Manila to reduce. Dewey sent Mr. Williams, recently our consul there, to the English sailing ship *Buccleuch,* with the object of establishing communication with the Spanish captain general through the British consul. His intention was to give forty-eight hours for the surrender of all the stores, supplies and war materials before shelling the city. But as by May 4 he had not yet heard from the captain general, he decided to accomplish by blockade what he might otherwise have had to do by bombardment, thus avoiding loss of life and property.

Of course the three of us, Harden, Stickney and I, were eager to know how soon we could get dispatches off to our papers, but until Thursday the fifth there was no sign of anyone's going to Hong Kong, the nearest station, 640 miles away. On that morning the *McCulloch* was ordered to go ahead. Flag Lieutenant Brumby was sent with the commodore's dispatches, and one or two other officers from the flagship came along. The run to Hong Kong was made under forced draft in two days. We arrived there Saturday noon.

We had all given our word that the commodore's dispatch was to be filed first. After that it was a free race to the cable office. Each of us had his dispatch ready.

I sent mine of 600 words at press rates, 60 cents a word. I noticed that Harden was sending a brief thirty-word message.

"What's the short one?" I inquired.

"Just a bulletin for the *World,*" he answered.

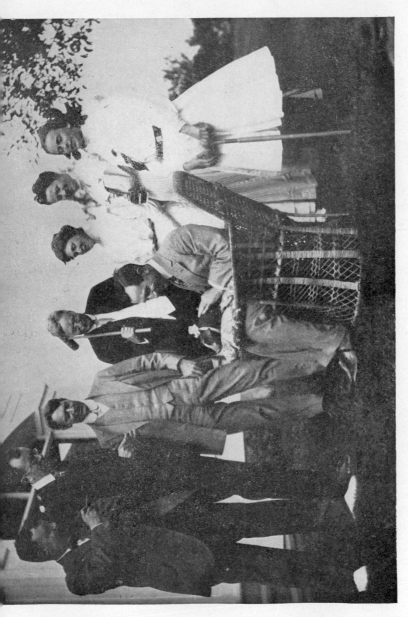

A CHRISTENING AT JIM KEELEY'S FARM AT WHEATON

Left to right: Jim Keeley, Dick Little, Albert Beveridge, Judge Calhoun, Mrs. Keeley, Mrs. Beveridge, Dorothy Keeley. The pig is sitting on the author's lap.

A YAKBACK TRIP THROUGH THE KIPCHAK COUNTRY, 1906

So I filed a sixty-word bulletin for the *Record* at the regular commercial rate of $1.80 which took precedence over press dispatches.

But Harden had failed to mention that he was sending his bulletin "Urgent." Wildman, the American consul, had tipped him off to send a few words this way. It took precedence over everything else but cost $9.90 a word!

Harden's message got to the *New York World* at about five-thirty Saturday morning, too late for the regular edition. There were no plans for an extra, so it was sent on to the *Chicago Tribune*, which used the *World's* news. Jim Keeley, then editor of the *Tribune*, had kept his office open for several nights with everyone on hand for just this news. It was five days since the battle; nobody knew anything and there was intense anxiety.

The *Tribune*, then, receiving it in Chicago at four-thirty Central Time, was able to use it and scored a tremendous "beat," one of the most conspicuous in American journalism.

Jim Keeley wrote me about it in a letter:

Murphy was our correspondent in New York in the *World* office. The last edition of the *World* had gone to press and a few of the dogwatch men were staying around playing Poker. Murphy, who didn't get "30" [his night's dismissal] until about half past four Chicago time, was in the game.

The telephone rang. Every guy around the table had what he thought was a good hand except Murphy who chucked his in, and somebody said:

"Murphy, you're out. Answer that damned telephone!"

He did. It was the cable operator announcing the receipt of Harden's "Urgent" message. Murphy took it over the telephone, then hopped to our open wire with it. When he had done that little trick, he turned it over to the *World* people.

Then a *World* row started as to whether the *Morning World*, which had gone to press, was entitled to it, or the *Evening World* which was getting its first edition ready. They got in such a jolly jam that the *Evening Journal*, I believe, beat them on the street, because Bob Peattie, who was Hearst correspondent in the *Chicago Tribune* office, shot it back to New York before the *World* squabble was settled.

Fifteen minutes' delay for us in the *Tribune* office would have made it impossible to get our entire city circulation, and that might have happened if Murphy had held aces up or three deuces.

Keeley, always an enterprising fellow, telephoned the news to the White House. The night watchman was patrolling the corridor outside the bedrooms when the telephone rang. It was down the hall, an old-fashioned wall telephone.

"The *Chicago Tribune* speaking. I have news for the President. May I speak with him?"

"The President is asleep. I can't disturb him."

"You'll lose your job if you don't call him. I've got news from Manila."

The watchman debated and finally knocked on the President's door to report the conversation. It was a warm night, so, barefoot and in his nightshirt, McKinley ambled down the hall to hear from Jim Keeley the news of the Battle of Manila in the words of Ed Harden's dispatch.

Some months later, on Harden's return, the President sent for him. Doubtless he wanted to find out about Admiral Dewey, who was being spoken of as his opponent at the next election. The President then described to Harden how he had heard the news that night.

My inexperience in handling cable material had put me at this disadvantage. At the time, of course, I was sorry, but now so long afterward, I think I'm really glad poetic justice was served. If it hadn't been for Harden, I wouldn't have been there at all. I had a job. My career, except for the acclaim, would hardly have been altered. He had no definite job and needed a boost. To have scooped him in addition would have been a pretty serious blow. At the same time—I didn't know about "Urgent" dispatches!

The fate of my own dispatch, however, is one of the sorest points in my life. The editor of the *Record,* Mr. Dennis, was not so alert as Mr. Keeley. In fact he was asleep out in Buena Park when my commercial dispatch began coming in. There was no one on hand except a night police reporter and he didn't know what to do with it. Mr. Dennis had no telephone—they were scarce in those days—and it would have taken a couple of hours or more to drive out to his house and back in a carriage. Even so, they could have had an extra only an hour later than the *Tribune,* with their own correspondent's story in it. They should have done this at any hour.

Then later Saturday morning my longer dispatch began coming in, but as there was no Sunday *Record,* it could not be used until Monday! There was at that time an ironclad rule that the *Evening News* could not use the *Morning Record's* stuff. Mr. Lawson was journeying up the Nile. There was nobody at home with authority to break the rule. They cabled Lawson, but either he did not realize the importance of the situation, or the terms of the Associated Press agreement may have prevented. In any case he refused.

However, the *New York Journal*, a Hearst paper, knowing I was over there, telegraphed the *Record* asking if they could use my dispatch.

"Yes, if you wait until the *Record* prints it Monday morning."

They promised, and then Creelman rewrote it into a 3,500-word story and used it Sunday morning, and the *Chicago Tribune* got that and published it too! Thus my own paper was the very last to make use of the tremendous opportunity. It *had* been an unusual opportunity, with only three correspondents in all the world on hand.

I never asked Mr. Dennis for the details of this miserable business. I was afraid it might imply dissatisfaction on my part. The *Record* was always generous and considerate about our mistakes, but it was doubtless touchy about its own. I felt, too, a little bitter over not receiving special word from my paper about my sixty word message, and wondered what had happened to it. It was many months before I learned, and then I *was* disappointed.

However, they cabled me in Hong Kong, "File without limit" and "Details in full." And Hearst cabled, "Will you accept position on *New York Journal*? Name your own salary."

As the neutrality laws permitted only a twenty-four-hour stay in port, I sat up all night to write another full dispatch from my very complete diary. Cutting out all unnecessary words, I skeletonized it down to 4,500 words and sent it press rates at a cost of $2,700. George Ade received this one and filled it out to 6,000 words. It was printed along with my two earlier dispatches on Monday morning.

So the *Record* did, after all, get the first long complete story, which was reprinted all over the country.

Little Ah Soo came out to the ship, but we were all too busy with our dispatches to say more than how-d'ye-do to her. Within the allotted time the *McCulloch* left Hong Kong, and we returned to Manila about the tenth of May.

Six weeks later the home papers began arriving in the Far East, revealing the tension of public interest at home. I found my story horribly garbled, especially in the Hearst version. It made me ashamed to talk to the Navy officers. This, coming on top of Harden's scoop, was very depressing.

## ∽ 16 ∽

## Blockade

ON MY return to Manila I found the blockade in full force. The *McCulloch* was assigned to patrol duty. She had always to be under steam, ready at the first faint smudge of smoke in the Boca Chica, seventeen miles away, to intercept any vessel entering the bay.

Sometimes I moved on board the *Zafiro* to be nearer the fleet and the shore. On the morning of May 12, while I was breakfasting off quantities of the best rice cakes in the world drowned in thick golden drip molasses, I heard heavy guns and rushed on deck to find the *Raleigh* and another ship steaming down the bay, firing simultaneously on an incoming vessel which finally pulled down its Spanish flag in some perplexity. It was the *Callao*, one of the smaller Spanish gun-boats, which had been on duty for sixteen months in the Caroline Islands. With no cable and no mail, her people had heard no syllable of any sort of war news and had come back to Manila licking their chops at the thought of shore leave.

During the three months of the blockade I had the fun of witnessing the gathering of the clans—the men who were drawn irresistibly to the focal points of international trouble, wherever they might be. John Bass, James Creelman, Frederick Palmer, Dick Little, Ed Keene, Poultney Bigelow, Jack Dunning, Bob Collins, Will Levington Comfort—they came tramping in, some of them veterans of the Greek and Balkan conflicts, others tasting for the first time the delectable fruit of war. Martin Egan, a clever, sunny-dispositioned fellow, appeared for the *Frisco Chronicle*; Oscar King Davis for the *New York Sun* arrived with one of the first big convoys; John Barrett, who had been American minister to Siam, came to represent Hearst and the *New York Journal*. Kirk Brice arrived in June. Just out of Harvard, genial and companionable, with an inquiring student type of mind, he had been traveling around the world with Charles Flandrau. His father, Senator Brice of Ohio, had secured for him a commission as lieutenant of engineers. Thus Kirk became the first representative of the United States Army, either officer or soldier, on the scene.

Then as time went on there came the adventurers—gentlemen adventurers, soldiers of fortune, wanderers, remittance men, rolling stones who would rather lead the life of adventure, precarious though it might be, than endure the comfortable monotony of an orderly existence catching the eight-o'clock train every morning.

Life on board at this time was a very enjoyable experience. At dawn the sea was as smooth as glass. From every ship came the domestic cackle of chickens. Reveille at five o'clock was followed by the shrill whistle of the bosun. The companionways became lively with white figures putting away folded hammocks. After coffee at five-thirty came the sound of scraping brushes and bare feet splashing water. By the time the bugle sounded "Mess" at seven-twenty, everything was shipshape for the day. The crew ate and rested. At eight o'clock, at the inspiring call of "Colors," the flag of every ship was run up, and the bands of the *Olympia* and the *Baltimore* played "The Star-Spangled Banner" with every soul on deck at rigid attention. Then a launchload of marines pushed off for twenty-four-hour guard duty at the arsenal at Cavite.

During the morning there was a sense of absolute peacefulness and tranquillity about the bay. Flocks of native outriggers crowded up to the gangway ladders offering for sale big yellow mangoes, boxes of Manila cigars, wicker crates of chickens, baskets of eggs and bunches of delicious bananas. There was nothing to indicate that the lazy ships and calm waters had so lately been the scene of a great naval battle.

By afternoon the sea would roughen up. We went ashore every day. We had a special boat for the correspondents with Filipinos in uniform and an American flag flying so the other ships would not fire. But boating in small craft was hazardous because of sudden violent squalls incident to the southwest monsoon.

Evening was the most enjoyable time of the day. Down the bay, behind the high peaks of Mariveles across from Corregidor, the sun set in a veritable explosion of color. The *Olympia* band concert began at six. Colors came down at seven. Lights began to twinkle along the shore, ships were darkened, and as the searchlights started traveling across the water, the easy chairs on the quarter-deck filled with white-clad shadowy figures, and curling smoke from many cigars floated off into the night.

It was a time for gossip and speculation. The arrival of the *Charleston* and other troopships from San Francisco was expected daily.

What would become of the insurgent cause if America decided to hold the Philippines? We could hear the cannonading and musket fire of skirmishing between the Spaniards and the insurgents around the bay.

Beyond Manila to the north were the foreign warships and merchant vessels with Manila refugees on board. There were over twenty ships by this time, and they lay there waiting, like spectators at a circus, for something to happen.

Whenever a ship left for Hong Kong it carried a regular series of my sketches for the *Record*, with stories and cablegrams. Once the *McCulloch* was sent back with the dispatches—we moved to the *Zafiro* meanwhile—and when she returned she brought nineteen Filipino revolutionaries headed by young Aguinaldo. They had agreed with the Spaniards to leave the islands for a certain sum of money, but on the advice of Consuls Pratt and Williams they were now returning to resume their activity for independence from Spain. They at once began organizing the Filipino armies. I used to go ashore to

*Aguinaldo's Headquarters*

visit them at their headquarters in Cavite, and often smoked a friendly cigar with Aguinaldo's mother. Dewey gave them permission to retrieve several million rounds of ammunition thrown into the bay by the Spaniards. Thus the riffraff of Luzon came to be armed, and they had surprising success. They recovered town after town, and brought in many Spanish prisoners. At that time no one knew what America's course concerning the Philippines would be. It was generally supposed we were helping them to fight for their independence, after which we would withdraw.

Coal was something of a problem for us. To avoid neutrality rules, British ships would allow themselves to be captured and their coal seized—for thirty dollars a ton.

The British and Japanese were regarded as friendly to us, the Germans and French opposed. In looking back on those pregnant days which contained so much chess play between the British and the Germans, I realize how very innocent I was. I could comprehend the things on the surface, but I could not understand the subtleties of *Weltpolitik* which lay underneath. Also, I think very few of us suspected then that the United States had become a world power on May 1.

The first warship to come into the bay after the Battle of Manila was the British ship *Linnet*. She arrived the second of May. On the sixth came the German gunboat *Cormoran*; on the eighth, the big British cruiser *Immortalité* commanded by Captain Chichester; and on the ninth, the German cruiser *Irene*. On June 12 Vice-Admiral von Diederichs arrived on board the first-class cruiser *Kaiserin Augusta*. This gave the Germans the advantage of one ship. By that time the whole American personnel was buzzing with speculation as to why the Germans were arriving in such force. The matter became such an engrossing one that it blanketed our own Spanish War.

As time went on the tension increased between Dewey and the German ships, and there was a great scurrying about to determine exactly what were the rules governing blockades, and all the established precedents in a blockaded port to which nonbelligerent warships were coming. When the German ships went out, in practice operations, an American boarding officer had to board them each time they left or re-entered the bay. This irked the Germans. They had searchlight drills at night without asking permission, and in other ways, through ignorance, indifference or arrogance, they frequently violated blockade rules.

By June 20 the Germans had five ships, more than they could possibly need to protect German interests there. They seemed a more imminent menace than the Spanish fleet reported approaching through Suez. Dewey anxiously awaited our big armored monitors.

I was on board the *McCulloch* near Corregidor on June 27 when she

signaled the *Irene* to stop. The German cruiser was insolently slow
in complying and our boarding officer, Ridgely, had a long row in a
small boat to catch up to her. When the *Irene* returned into the bay
it was necessary to signal her again. This time she did not stop and
the *McCulloch* caught up and crossed her bow, a significant naval
maneuver which in some way reached the outside world in a highly
provocative form. It was reported that the *McCulloch* had stopped
her with a shot.

This was the last straw. In anger Von Diederichs sent his flag
lieutenant to complain to Dewey.

Dewey stormed. "I want to know this," he shouted: "Is Germany
at war with the United States? If she is, she can have it here and now.
If not, she'll have to conform to the blockade!"

This straight-from-the-shoulder talk ended the German incident.

In the light of events as I see them now, I am convinced the Germans came to Manila ready to take action in case of certain eventuali-
ties. The United States had publicly announced it was fighting to
free Cuba, and would retire from Cuba when the Spaniards were overcome. I think the Germans said to themselves—or the Kaiser said, "If
the Americans are going to get out of the Philippines also, after licking the Spaniards, we want to be there to pick up those islands, and
we must get there before the British grab them." This seems to me
a reasonable explanation of the German activity. Von Diederichs'
immediate cessation of disturbing tactics after Dewey's plain talk in-
dicates that his instructions certainly did not envisage war with the
United States; but if America was going to sail away, Germany wanted
to be on the spot. She had at the time practically no colonies.

On the morning of the taking of Manila, August 13, the British
ships *Immortalité* and *Powerful* came over and took up a position
directly between the American fleet and the German flagship, which
subsequently shifted its position. This incident also was enormously
magnified. I doubt if either Chichester or Von Diederichs had any
sinister purpose in mind other than to get a less obstructed view of
the fight. However, it is significant that the attitude of Great Britain
during this whole time did much to overcome whatever anti-British
feeling there may have been in our country. It was a major diplomatic
victory and, in my opinion, was so regarded by the Germans. In a
couple of years they countered by sending Prince Henry on a good-
will visit to the United States.

Finally the American troops began arriving, five or six shiploads at
a time, on Pacific passenger steamers put into transport service.

Twenty-five hundred men were encamped at Cavite. After the handful of marines who had been quartered there, they made things tremendously lively. The insurgents crowded around and watched wonderingly and listened to the bands. The great difference in size between the American and Filipino soldiers was pronounced.

In all these weeks I had slept only one night ashore. Brice and I went over to Parañaque, about a mile behind the American lines on the outskirts of Manila. A typhoon came up and the sea was far too heavy for us to return to the ship. We went into a native house, where there were two nice daughters and a piano, and were put up for the night on mats on the floor. The rain and the sea thundered. But above both, at midnight, I was awakened by firing. It soon became like the steady roll of a drum.

I roused Brice. "The Americans are in it! We must get back!"

But Brice was reluctant—the prospect was definitely not inviting—and we ended by staying. Early in the morning we went back, knee-deep in mud, with Spanish bullets falling here and there. This was the first clash between the Americans and the Filipinos. The story was that each thought the other began firing, and it developed into quite a battle without anyone's knowing what it was all about. Worst of all, two companies of Americans fought each other in the storm and several men were killed. Dewey had hoped to avoid or prevent such premature engagements.

News reached us only occasionally. Early in July we heard of a defeat suffered by the Americans in Cuba. There followed an anxious two weeks of absolute silence. On July 17 a Japanese ship brought news of the battle of Santiago and the destruction of the Spanish fleet. Everyone celebrated by getting drunk.

Early in August Dewey was ready to move on Manila. By this time the pennant of a commodore had been hauled down, and a rear admiral's flag flew from the *Olympia*. Every mail brought new evidence of the popular enthusiasm that had sprung up all over America. Through all this bombardment of compliments the admiral changed not a bit and never indicated by his manner that the tremendous hit he had made was affecting him other than pleasantly.

Dewey was a man you could admire greatly, but with whom you couldn't feel companionable. I never ceased to be afraid of him. I was always in a hurry to get my business over before I had outstripped his patience. Everybody in the fleet felt the same. Nobody out there had a chatty relationship with him.

Back on the *Olympia* on that day in 1898—August 13, it was—

Dewey surveyed the scene before him. Our fleet was in formation before the 300-year-old walls of the city. An ultimatum had been sent to the governor general through the medium of M. Edouard André, the Belgian consul, and Dewey flew the international signal, "Do you surrender?" The ultimatum had been to the effect that if the city were not given up peacefully within forty-eight hours, it might be bombarded. Ten or twelve merchant ships filled with refugees stood down the bay; all the foreign vessels had moved out of range. Through the kindness of Dewey and Lamberton, Harden, Barrett and I had been permitted to watch the operations from the flagship. The time was up, and the *Olympia* began dropping a few shells around Fort de San Antonio Abad and Malate, south of the city. I took a photograph of Dewey. After snapping it I hastily skipped out of sight.

To save the face of the governor general it had been arranged to fire these few rounds, and then he was to hoist a white flag. The rounds were fired—but no white flag appeared. More rounds. Still no white flag.

The admiral's testy temper was getting away from him. His language became correspondingly snappy. Harden and I were near by, but had sense enough to keep out of the way. Whenever he approached on one of his rumbling rambles, we got behind a ventilator. Just then John Barrett came up. He had only recently arrived. He went up to Dewey. "Er—Admiral," he said, "what are your plans?"

What the admiral said to him would have blown up the whole town.

Early in the afternoon the Belgian consul's launch came alongside and Lieutenant Brumby climbed up the sea ladder. "They've surrendered all right."

"Why don't they haul down that flag?" stormed Dewey.

"They'll do it as soon as General Merritt gets six or seven hundred men in there to protect them."

"Well, go over and tell Merritt I agree to anything."

Some troops were landed on the Pasig River, others came by land to occupy the city. From our vantage point on the *Olympia* we could see the taking of the forts. At 5:45 the Spanish flag was seen slowly coming down, and a minute later an enormous American flag was hoisted over the city. At that moment the sun burst through clouds as opportunely as the spotlight in the theater falls on an entering star. In the next ten minutes 189 saluting charges were fired, twenty-one guns from each ship. Then came relaxation and a riot of gaiety.

General Merritt established himself in the Malacañan, the governor's palace on the Pasig, and all during the night the Spaniards surrendered their arms.

## ～ 17 ～

## At Home in Manila

ON THE fourteenth of August four of us went ashore and set up housekeeping.

All the beautiful houses on the outskirts of the walled town had been left vacant by the fleeing Spaniards, who were anxious to have them occupied by American officers rather than Filipinos.

At first we took one in the Calle Marina, with balconies over the sea, in the fashionable suburb of Ermita. But soon after settling there, we discovered a better house—Calle San Luis No. 21. It was a double house, each side having its own spacious courtyard. The windows looked over the great parade ground where the regiments drilled every afternoon and, beyond that, to the walled city with its domes and spires. To the left, the Luneta skirted the edge of the sea. Here bands played, and all the fashionables of Manila drove at sunset—the most stupendously gorgeous sunsets ever seen, against which were silhouetted the sails of small boats, the American fleet, Corregidor in the distance, and the entrance to the bay. It was one of the most desirable locations in the city for seeing things and we moved there at once.

Each of us had his own room, Martin Egan, O. K. Davis, Colonel Jewett—who was a judge advocate of the Army, and had an amazing fund of anecdotes—and I. There were more rooms for Harden, Brice and Barrett until they left for home, and for others who joined us off and on. We engaged a staff of eleven servants, including a laundress and a florist. In those days wages were six or seven dollars a month. Cervera, my personal attendant, had been a member of the crew on our press boat.

The rich Spaniards were selling out in order to get back to Spain, so we procured horses and carriages. I had a *carromata* and a stunning horse and my own driver. Davis had a Victoria and pair. We decorated the living room with flags and swords, and the table was always set for two extra, whether they came or not.

We called our establishment the Casa de Todas—the House Where Everything Goes.

From the middle of August until after Christmas was one of the most delightful periods of my life. It was perpetually interesting. Against a background of insurgent fighting in the hills, and an ever-increasing friction between the Americans and the Filipinos, we carried on in superb style. Everything was cheap. There were constant luncheons and dinner parties. Women correspondents had begun arriving. There were many nurses. The Filipino girls were friendly. And in the other half of our double house lived two beautiful Spanish girls. The younger was named Luz Rubio. At a Manila Day dinner in Chicago in 1928, to my astonishment I met her again. She had married an American and lived in Indiana!

On one occasion, and one only, our house was robbed. On my return to my room after a bath one morning, I discovered that my Sigma Chi pin, a purse with some money and my gold watch—the one my mother had given me on my graduation from Purdue—had all disappeared. At once I notified Jewett, Davis and Harden, who found that they too had been robbed. All the houseboys protested innocence. Cervera was considered absolutely honest, as was Gregorio, one of the coachmen who had access to the house. But Davis' boy, Rufino, and Colonel Jewett's little José were not entirely trusted. We decided to adopt a third-degree method and staged a very impressive performance. That evening Major Burke, who spoke Spanish, arrived at the house with a squad of soldiers. They marched up the steps into the big living room, spurs and rifles clanking. They cross-examined each man separately, but still all maintained innocence. Rufino and José were taken to prison. Little José cried and Rufino was sullenly obstinate. They were sent to separate cells in the hope that one or the other would weaken, but nothing happened. So after a few hours we released them. We never found out who stole the things but we never lost anything else.

The story has a sequel. After my serious illness in 1900, my death was announced and obituaries were printed in the Manila papers. Some time later a letter from the Manila Police Department came to Mr. Dennis at the *Record* office stating that a watch with my name on it had been found on a Filipino arrested on Christmas Day, 1901. Having heard that I was dead, they were inquiring the name of my nearest surviving relative in order to return the watch. I answered this letter personally, and in April 1902 a police official from Manila, back on leave, restored my watch to me. The Filipinos had had it for over three years. The crystal was gone but it still worked, and I used it for many more years. I have often wondered who is wearing my Sigma Chi pin.

From my window in the Casa de Todas I could look across our carriage court with its sweet-smelling ilang-ilang tree, into the windows of Commander de la Concha, lately in command of the Spanish cruiser *Don Juan de Austria*. As the Spaniards and Filipinos were still fighting, his safety lay in remaining under the protection of the Americans. However, he had a great desire to revisit the scene of the battle three months before, and I had a great desire to take him. I wanted to hear what he had to say of the battle from the Spanish point of view. To get from Cavite to Sangley Point where the ships lay, it was necessary to pass through Filipino-held territory, so we hired a closed carriage, drew the curtains and succeeded in making the round trip without discovery. A guard gave a desultory glance inside but seemed reassured at sight of an American. The captain was deeply affected at seeing his old ship, which had been raised and was in dry dock; he pointed out the spot where his native servant had brought him coffee during the battle.

In early October John Bass and Abba—she always accompanied her husband on his assignments wherever possible—and I went down to Iloilo on the southern island of Panay, which was still in possession of the Spaniards. No American had been there and it seemed like promising newspaper copy. After much delay we were permitted ashore and regarded with suspicious interest as specimens of a nation with which they had recently been at war.

When I returned to Manila, since nobody knew anything about the other outlying islands, I decided it would be pleasant to make a more extensive exploration. To do this I found a brigantine with a native crew, the *Dos Hermanos*, but by the time the *Record* had O.K.'d the project and its authorization reached me, the feeling between the Americans and Filipinos had become so tense and threatening it was imprudent to venture so far away.

The Filipinos had been armed and organized with our acquiescence, if nothing more; but in evident contradiction to our supposed intention of freeing them from Spanish oppression and then departing, American soldiers were stationed in all the outskirts of Manila and the Filipinos had been forbidden the city, in which there was martial law. It was a sort of armed truce; the chief topic of conversation was how soon an outbreak would occur which would precipitate war.

The Casa de Todas regime seemed about to be dispersed, but it was nice while it lasted.

~ 18 ~

## Broke in Bombay

TOWARD the end of 1898 I was given another assignment. The *Record* wrote that it was establishing a world-wide system of cable correspondents and asked me to visit different countries in the Far East to pick out and appoint men as *Record* representatives. It supplied me with instructions but left to my judgment which countries and cities I should choose. They sent George Ade to do the same work in southern Europe and the Balkans.

I laid out my plans with the idea of returning to Chicago immediately after the trip. Harden had left Manila some weeks before. Brice, Egan and Barrett also had gone so that O. K. Davis and I were the only remaining members of our original group. On December 26 we both departed, after visiting all the ships of the fleet. On each and every one we were plied with farewell refreshments so that by the time we got away we had only the haziest notion of where we'd been. We sailed for Hong Kong thinking we'd said good-by forever to the Philippines.

After appointing correspondents in Hong Kong, Saïgon, Singapore and Ceylon, I took ship for Bombay. On board I made two acquaintances which I have always valued: Barber Lathrop and David Fairchild, who represented the Bureau of Agriculture and was even then finding the world his garden. I met also a Britisher, Captain Todd, stationed on the Afghanistan frontier. He invited me to visit him at Peshawar.

Needing funds when we reached Colombo, I cabled the *Record* to send £200 in care of the Hong Kong and Shanghai Bank in Bombay, expecting to find it on arrival within a day or two.

In Bombay the bubonic plague was raging. Deaths amounted to

some 600 a day; several people had died of it even in Watson's Esplanade Hotel where I took lodgings. My British friend left as soon as possible, and I hurried to the bank to see if my money had arrived. It had not. I put in a day or two sight-seeing. Each morning I went first to the bank. A week passed. The cruiser *Raleigh* came in, homeward-bound. There was much gaiety and entertainment. The American consul gave a big luncheon at a fine club. I had a grand time with the officers and used up most of my remaining funds.

By this time I was getting worried and cabled the *Record* that the money had not come. It answered that a draft had been sent on a certain date. I showed the cable to the bank and they telegraphed their various branches. Then I cabled again to say that the money could not be traced. The *Record* answered that it was sending a duplicate amount. But there was no sign of that! It took practically my last cent to cable, "Please investigate." And they sent back the details all over again. From the amount I spent on cables it was obvious that I was not trying to cheat the bank. They were polite, but they would not advance a penny.

I was in despair. My hotel bill had grown to 119 rupees. Each day I had told the native servant, whom I had engaged for traveling through India, to pack up and be ready, and each day I had to postpone departure. I decided to try to borrow some money to send one final message. The American consul was sympathetic. I showed him all the cables and told him I had been to the two other leading banks to see if there had been a mistake. He gave me fifty rupees, thirty-seven of which I spent at once in a last despairing cry: "Am broke. Money unarrived. Cannot explain. Investigate immediately. Shall cable no more."

Then I stayed in my hotel room with my thirteen remaining rupees. The plague-infested streets were too hot for walking, and I could not hire a gharry. After eight or nine more days my servant got nervous and resolved to test me. His pay was not due, but he said he wanted to leave some money with his wife. Casually I drew a ten-rupee note from my pocket and handed it to him. This satisfied him but left me with three rupees. They were worth about thirty-three cents each.

After that I couldn't even buy magazines! I became unbelievably depressed. It seemed incredible that both remittances could have gone wrong. I feared I would have to take any sort of work I could get there in Bombay. The chances were not too good. In all my life I was never so low in my mind.

On the eleventh day I walked to the bank and received the usual stereotyped answer, "No, nothing has arrived." I went back to the hotel and was sitting gloomily in my room when there came a knock at the door. One of the bank messengers, very imposing-looking in a red sash and fez, handed me a note saying they had just received to my credit 5,900 rupees, the equivalent of £400.

I dashed to the bank. They said it had been sent over to them from the very small French Comptoir Bank where it had been all the time! At the French bank, where I hurried for an explanation, they said Chicago had cabled it to their bank in London saying, "Pay Fallway to credit of John T. McCutcheon £200." The second cable was the same. "Fallway" should have meant the Hong Kong and Shanghai Bank in Bombay. But either the French banker in Bombay or his London agent had made a mistake in the code, so they had simply held it! I showed him all the cables and receipts for money that had been spent because of his mistake. He just shrugged his shoulders.

That night we left for Agra, the courier and I. We spent a couple of days sight-seeing; then, late on a bitterly cold night, we boarded another train for Delhi.

Early in my stay in Bombay, before my funds gave out, I had made a trip to the Caves of Elephanta. Our launch was supposed to leave the Apolla Bandar at eleven, but we did not stir. It seemed that we had to wait for some notable, and we were all much annoyed. Presently a dapper little man with a Russian cut of beard came down the steps. He was eminently distinguished-looking, obviously a person of consequence, and he proved also very affable and friendly. We visited the caves together, said farewell on our return to Bombay, and I supposed I had seen the last of him. But there on the platform at Agra, all bundled up in a Russian greatcoat, was my friend. He inquired my destination, and when I told him the Khyber Pass to Afghanistan he became at once tremendously excited and expressed a great eagerness to go with me. I explained that there was no hotel accommodation, that I was going as the guest of a British officer. In ordinary circumstances my impulse would have been to suggest that he come along, but I realized that England and Russia were almost at the point of war and that both nations had their eyes on the northwest of India and the regions beyond. A Russian, therefore, would be singularly unwelcome up along the frontier.

In Kipling's India a pilgrimage to Lahore was a necessity. My courier, as usual, got the tickets and took care of the baggage. Once

I got on a wrong train and thought I had lost him and everything forever. I still recall my relief when he apeared and rescued me. I went to the offices of the *Civil and Military Gazette*, where Kipling first made his reputation, almost as one would go to a shrine. When I met the editor, Stevenson, and expressed to him my glowing enthusiasm and mentioned the wide renown Kipling had achieved in America, he seemed vastly surprised. To him and to the other men here, Kipling was still merely a former associate who had made some success

as a writer. They took me into the room where he had written many of his early stories and showed me the old files. Then we went out to the pressroom in an adjacent building which had been part of the background for "The Man Who Would Be King."

An Oxfordshire soldier showed me through the old fort mentioned in *Soldiers Three.*

"So this is where Mulvaney and Ortheris and Learoyd used to live," I said. He said nothing, so I tried again. "Kipling has written a lot of his stories about this place."

He said, "Oh, there's lots of writers that comes 'ere."

"You know about Kipling, of course?"

"I don't know the names o' them old Johnnies as lived 'ere, but yonder's the tomb o' one of 'em." He pointed out the grave of the Maharaja Ranjit Singh. It struck me with crushing force that this British Tommy had never even heard of the man who had practically put him on the map, although living right here amid the scenes rendered famous by the stories hardly a dozen years before.

At that time Peshawar was completely off the beaten track. It was a great native town, walled in, the refuge of all the rough characters to be found on such a border. Among the Afghans, Afridis and other wild tribesmen, white people were far from safe, and the British had placed cannon on the walls to sweep the streets in case of an uprising. There was a dak bungalow where a wayfarer might stay, but he had to supply his own bedding and attendants. I lived with Captain Todd at the Army cantonment a mile or two away. It was very pretty out there with the broad low-lying Indian residences, the trees and compounds. It was a little world of its own, with races, gymkhana and falconry.

The mess halls were high-ceilinged and imposing, the walls ornamented with hunting trophies and English sporting pictures. Saturday nights were guest nights. All the fifteen or twenty officers wore evening dress—red mess jacket and black trousers. They surrounded a great table loaded with ponderous regimental silver—trophies gained through long years of service. The regiment was the Princess of Wales' Own, Lieutenant Colonel Bowles in command. Native Hindu attendants in long white coats, red sashes and turbans moved noiselessly. Huge logs crackled in the fireplace, and over the brilliant table the high-beamed ceiling was lost in shadow.

At the end of dinner the president of the mess rose and lifted his glass. "Mr. Vice, the Queen Empress!"

The regimental band in the billiard room struck up "God Save the Queen," and simultaneously everyone at the long table rose. At the farther end the vice-president repeated the toast: "The Queen Empress!" It was drunk in silence.

A few minutes later the president again stood up. "Mr. Vice, the Princess of Wales!" The words were repeated, the bright row of red mess jackets and gleaming shirt fronts rose and the band swung into the Danish national air.

Somehow the whole scene seemed to embody, to crystallize vividly, all the impressions I had ever formed of British army life and India, and I thought how similar the situation would have been to that of Kipling's "Man Who Was," had I brought my mysterious Russian friend.

The Khyber Pass was open only two days a week. There was genuine danger in following this trail through its fifteen or twenty miles of gorges, for there was always much unrest among the natives, and armed guards were posted at intervals for protection. Naturally I was eager to make this trip, and secured the necessary permission. A small party was made up which included Swan Perker, Gervaise Lyon and me. I kept thinking: along here Kamal rode with the colonel's son hot upon his heels. Beyond the fort of Ali Masjid the roadway hugged the steep cliffs of the great solemn gorges. Once we heard a rifle shot up among the rocks. But we saw nothing, and never knew whether it was fired at us.

And I kept on thinking: Alexander the Great came through here when he invaded India; down through here swept the hordes of Central Asia to establish Mohammedan supremacy in India. Few places are more historically interesting. From Landi Kotal on the Afghan side we climbed the Suffolk Hill and looked curiously ahead to where stretched the caravan trail to Jalalabad, and on to Kabul. The shaggy Afghan natives eyed us sullenly. There was no friendliness in their attitude, and it was not possible to go any farther.

Although early February was not the season for Simla, I arranged to make a detour on Kipling's account. Up into the Himalayas I drove in a tonga, a sort of Persian chariot with two stout wheels and two horses and many relays. Recklessly we dashed past the strings of bullock carts and camel trains, and the creak of the tonga bar remains in my ears. Simla was deserted by fashionable life. There was snow on the hills, and the Great Mall was as quiet as a country village. But the elaborate Government House was being brushed up in anticipation of the first viceregal arrival of Lord Curzon and his American wife, Mary Leiter, who grew up on Prairie Avenue and played over their joint back fence with my wife's father. Here I was greeted by newspaper dispatches announcing that an outbreak had occurred in Manila. The long-expected clash had come. I determined to hurry back; so after brief stops in Lucknow and Benares I sailed from Calcutta on the British-Indian steamer *Palamcotta*. When she stopped at Rangoon for three days, the spell of Kipling was still so heavily upon me that I took a train up to Mandalay, even though I had to turn and come right back.

To my great surprise one of my fellow passengers on the ship to Singapore was the Russian gentleman! I sat by him at the long dining table and we became well acquainted. During the daytime I worked on India stories, and often he sat by me while I drew. In connection with the Khyber Pass story I had occasion to draw a camel. My friend looked at my drawing and made the polite suggestion that a camel's head is always held in a horizontal position. With a few strokes he indicated perfectly the exact way, showing a sureness of line quite professional. He drew on the back of a place card, and the name on the other side was *M. Kologrivoff*. Each of my long talks with him those quiet evenings on deck stimulated my curiosity more and more. He spoke with the greatest familiarity of the Czar, and mentioned casually an invitation to visit the King of Siam. He had known General Sheridan in the United States. While in California, he had longed to be held up by Western highwaymen—had, in fact, gone alone into the Yosemite and done all he could to invite an attack by road agents. He *was* accosted by a rough-looking fellow who fell in with him and took him to his cabin, but who turned out to be merely a good-hearted mountaineer. That Russian had the keenest zest in life and an unusually observant mind, and his conversation was full of endless interest. No occasion offered itself to ask who and what he was, and he volunteered nothing.

We separated in Singapore, this time permanently. He asked if I would be good enough to deliver a present to the wife of the Russian minister in Bangkok for him, and he brought a sizable package to my hotel. I had some misgivings—some moments of wondering what sort of international intrigue I was becoming involved in—but the package proved, on presentation, to be filled with the choicest Russian cigarettes, and the enclosed card caused immense gratification.

Monsieur Kologrivoff, it seems, was the Russian Minister of Transportation. He had been sent as a delegate to the opening of a new railway system in South Africa, and was returning through India. He was one of the Privy Councilors of the Czar, and the fourth commoner of the Empire.

Bangkok was a bad cholera spot. At the American Legation, while John Barrett was serving as United States minister, eighteen of his twenty-three servants had died. Only the previous year the ship *Devawongse*, on the three or four-day run to Hong Kong, had lost sixty passengers and crew. She was constantly stopping to cast bodies over—stopping so as to avoid their being caught in the propellers.

Consequently, I had some misgivings when I found that the ship on which I was to sail for Hong Kong was that same *Devawongse*.

However, nothing untoward occurred, and I at once took passage on the *Esmeralda* for Manila.

# ～ 19 ～

## Filipino Warfare

THE war with the Filipino Insurrectos had a maximum of thrills with a minimum of danger. I campaigned as far north as Laoag in Luzon, and the Cordilleras of Bontoc, and as far south as Sulu. Nearly every phase of war experience was duly registered. Every day was a chapter of gay adventure.

The outbreak of hostilities had occurred on the fourth of February. The big Manila suburb of Binondo had been burned, with a number of Filipinos and some Americans killed. The day after I returned to Manila on the eighteenth of March, some minor fighting cleared the insurgents out of the district southeast of the city, along the Pasig River. So far no military operations of any consequence had taken place. The Filipinos, supposed to be 30,000 strong, armed with Mauser rifles, had drawn a strong cordon about the city. Our army was about to strike. I went to live with the Officers' Mess of the Twenty-third Regular Infantry at Fort Santiago. Colonel French was in command. Military circles were seething with excitement and impatience.

Our first major action began on March 25. It was directed toward the Filipino capital, Malolos, twenty-five miles to the north. American trenches ran inland in a long zigzag for several miles from the shore of Malolos Bay. Brigadier General MacArthur, father of General Mac-Arthur of current history, with his staff, was at the Church of La Loma. Its immense dome rose above a vast lonely plain, and its grave-yards were crowded with troops and artillery batteries.

Learning confidentially of the proposed action, I borrowed a horse from Colonel French and rode out to the lines at night. I rode alone through the burned, deserted suburbs and past the leper hospital. Finally the great dome of La Loma Church loomed spectrally, and with relief I found myself within its four walled acres, among the dark masses of our wagons and piles of equipment. The fires were covered. The soldiers were trying to get a little sleep before the surprise dawn attack.

It was still dark when I awakened, and I went over to a little block-house before which the plain stretched away for a mile or more. At the farther edge, hidden from view by a fringe of bamboos, was the first of the insurgent positions. Just before the sun rose the deep boom of our heavy guns was heard; then from the trenches, right and left, as far as I could see, khaki-clad soldiers climbed out and started across the dry fields, firing as they went. Instantly the whole line of trees ahead rocked with the crash of rifle volleys. Our skirmish line made no impetuous charge; the advance was slow but resolute. When the fearful volleys came from the hidden enemy, a dozen gaps would appear, but the line pushed on, neither faster nor slower, as implacably as before. Stretcher-bearers carried the casualties off the field. The whole action was on a pretty big scale for those days; the firing line actively engaged was over two miles long.

We rode out after the troops. James Creelman—the fellow who doctored my Battle of Manila story for the *New York Journal*—had his horse shot from under him.

When our soldiers had crossed the open fields and disappeared into the bamboo thickets, General MacArthur ordered a pause in the little clearing of Talipapa, to get telegraphic reports from his flanks and to straighten out the lines. It was ten o'clock in the morning and broiling hot. Frederick Palmer and I dismounted and sat down under a tree, where we were presently joined by Eugene Hale, son of Senator Hale of Maine, Adelbert Hay, son of John Hay, and Ensign McCauley from the *Olympia*, whose glaring white uniform struck us as being

very conspicuous. General MacArthur and his aide, Putnam Bradlee Strong, were walking up and down the road in the hot sun. Suddenly out of the woods, and apparently from within a couple of hundred yards, came a crash of Mauser reports. The bullets struck the dust around us, tearing through the leaves and whining past our ears. We threw ourselves flat. One cavalryman was hit. Several pieces of artillery were hastily called into action. But General MacArthur continued his walk up and down the road.

The Filipinos were firing from a dilapidated old church in the woods. When we advanced and drove them out, they resumed firing from a new position which we could not at first locate. The bullets seemed to come from nowhere. MacArthur detailed Major General Franklin Bell and twenty-four troopers to go out and silence them. Soon afterward the sounds of a fierce battle came back to us. It proved one of the most spectacular incidents of the day, and made a hero of every man engaged in it. A number were killed and wounded. Heavy artillery was rushed up, a flanking maneuver caused the Filipinos to flee, and we then crossed the river on an improvised army bridge and bivouacked for the night. The advance on Malolos for the next five days was mainly a matter of fighting an unseen enemy.

The most dramatic of my own experiences occurred during the ambush at Guiguintó on the fourth day. The advance regiments had reached the edge of the river there, and some were beginning to cross the bridge, which was only partially destroyed. It was jammed and masses of troops were waiting to follow. I had crossed among the first and was talking to General Hale.

"Are they going to let us march in without putting up any fight?"

I had barely uttered the words when there was a sudden devastating burst of Mauser fire. It ripped through the bushes and grass and plopped into the earth on every side. Major Strong, behind me, was grazed. The whole command broke and dived into the cuts beside the tracks. I hugged the ground tightly. A man near by said, "I'm hit!" I could hear the angry cursings of the officers trying to get their troops to cover, but the hundreds massed on the bridge were panic-stricken and helpless. Forty were hit. The firing continued for fifteen minutes. When it ceased, for the first and only time that I know of in the Philippines, the order was given to withdraw—back across the river. We had not actually been repulsed. The troops had advanced much faster than the supply wagons, and many had no rations for the evening.

Off to the left the town of Guiguintó was ablaze. John Bass and I had no food, and we hesitated to ask for any from the few soldiers who had. We resolved to search for something to eat in the burning town. The streets were either brilliantly illuminated or in the densest shadow, because of the flaring of the flames. We found a frightened pig. I ran after it through the debris. Suddenly I was terrified to find myself going down. I had fallen into a well! Fortunately it was dry and only eight or ten feet deep. Bass helped me out and we resumed the chase, but when we finally cornered the pig, it showed such a savage front that we decided to seek farther. We managed to catch a couple of young chickens barely larger than robins and cooked them on the side of a burning house. Without salt the meat was most unpalatable. On returning to the railroad we found that more units had come up, among them the Utah Battery, old friends who invited us to dinner. As they were well supplied, even to blackberry jam, we joined them joyfully.

On the first evening of the American attack it had been necessary for me to ride back to Manila with my dispatches, a matter of twelve miles through districts that had been rushed over by our troops during the day. Villages were still smoldering. Frequently along the little roads that led through the jungles my horse would shy away from the bodies of natives. To begin with, a country road in the Philippines at night is about the lonesomest place in the world! I lost my way and wandered into an unfamiliar section. I had a revolver, but couldn't tell whether the white-clothed forms lurking in the bamboo thickets behind the lines were true "amigos" or snipers disguised as innocent villagers. Finally my horse could go no farther, so I had to leave him and lose him. Eventually I reached the city and got my dispatches off, but I had no horse during the rest of the week's action.

The sixth morning found us on the outskirts of Malolos, our goal. We had learned that it was the Filipino custom to shoot like everything and then retreat, but we did expect a stand before their capital.

Our advance began. I went over to join the Kansas Battery with General Funston, the most picturesque and daring of all the Army leaders out there. I was with him when he decided to lead a scouting party into Malolos. He took seventeen men with him, and five correspondents, including me. This little party was the first to enter the town. Up where the street reached the big plaza, a heavy stone barricade had been thrown across it. We were feeling our way toward this when there came the dry echoless pop of a Mauser, then another and another.

General Funston ordered his troopers to shoot. "Give 'em hell, boys!" he cried as he spurred his horse forward.

A scene of confusion greeted us in the plaza. Aguinaldo's headquarters were burning fiercely. Smoke and firebrands filled the air. Hundreds of Chinese were scrambling out of the buildings, loaded with loot, exhorting us not to kill them and saying that the Filipinos had fled to the north. There was a continual popping of bursting bamboo, a roaring of flames and a crashing of roofs caving in, and above all sounded the cheers of the American soldiers as they streamed into the town.

When I stopped to make a sketch of the scene in the shelter of a building which had begun to sizzle, a Chinese rushed up and told me it contained explosives. I found another point of vantage.

Thus the birthplace of the Filipino republic had fallen without any severe resistance, but it was the culmination of six and a half days of very picturesque warfare and constituted the largest and most elaborate military movement in the whole war.

We hurried back to Manila to send our dispatches and get cleaned up. It was late March; good campaigning weather might last two or three months longer, but we knew there would be no immediate resumption of offensive. So O. K. Davis and I took a little native house on the Calle Isaak Peral. It was built of broad polished narra boards, and its thatched roof nestled under two banana trees. Upstairs the living quarters had sliding shell windows and great four-post beds draped with mosquito netting.

From this pleasant headquarters I sallied forth to join the various military movements as the American forces pressed continuously northward.

I was at the attack on the Bagbag River where Colonel Funston gained his reputation as a swimmer. The Filipinos had heavy earthworks along the north bank and had partially destroyed the railway bridge. The rails were intact, but the heavy timbers of one span near the opposite shore were missing. MacArthur planned a strong attack. He improvised an armored car out of a flatcar sheathed with half-inch steel plates, to carry a six-inch gun and other smaller pieces. Ammunition was piled into a wooden car just behind. There was no engine. The motive power was to be man power. Skirmish lines were to advance on each side of the cars. I elected to go with the car because it promised something new and unusual. About a dozen artillery soldiers were in the armored car. Five of us took positions in the other one to help pass the boxes of shells—Lieutenant Bridges; Major Shields, a medical officer; Paul Gompertz, hospital steward; Fred Palmer and I. As the cars advanced toward the river the clatter of insurgent bullets against the armor ahead made an impressively terrifying sound. The steel plates, being crudely arranged, left gaps through which one or two men were hit. In our car the bullets bored through the wooden sides above our heads. My camera hung up there. I had just risen to take back an empty shell box when there was a fierce crash. I ducked as a bullet broke through.

"That was a close call!" I said.

Behind me Gompertz was staring at the floor with a strange fixed look, and spurts of blood came from his neck. Major Shields tried to stay the flow, but Gompertz' face became paler and paler and his eyes more glassy, till he collapsed on the floor. He probably never knew what hit him.

When the car had been pushed up close to the steep riverbank, Funston took a handful of men and ventured out onto the bridge as far as the missing span. Here they slid down a girder into the water and swam to a farther girder. By the time they had climbed out and into the Filipino stronghold, the insurgents had been put to rout by our heavy gunfire.

One night I was again with Funston when General MacArthur gave him permission to try a plan to surprise a strong insurgent position across the Rio Grande. Here it was known that the Filipinos had artillery and thousands of rifles. Funston called for volunteers for what seemed like a pretty desperate mission. Everybody volunteered, and 100 men were selected. This time I was the only correspondent. At midnight, silently, like so many shadows, we marched down the south bank of the river which was at that point about 200 yards wide. Each clink of metal sounded in our nervous ears like a terrific clamor. We held our breath and went on. But barking dogs defeated this ruse. A single one started, then it seemed as if the whole countryside resounded with excited and clamorous dogs and the entire length of the Filipino position flashed with rifle fire. The element of surprise having been lost, Funston led us back to camp.

I returned to headquarters to see about getting my story in, and early next morning I made my way back along the track amid stray bullets, hoping to rejoin Funston. But I was too late. He had sent two men—by name, White and Trembly, believe it or not!—swimming across with a rope which they attached to the farther bank. Then, by means of a raft, the rest of the soldiers crossed, covered by fire from their own men above. After Funston and his band were over and the whole line had opened fire, the Filipinos realized their position had been flanked, and began retreating as usual. The rest of us crossed by the repaired bridge. This crossing of the Rio Grande at Calumpit proved one of the biggest single achievements in Filipino warfare.

It was incredibly hot. The water gave out. We advanced a few miles in the blistering heat, almost crazed with thirst. Arriving at a little town called Santo Tomas, with the insurgents entrenched on a stretch of rising ground ahead, someone called, "Here's a well!"

There was a stampede. No one thought of the bullets which were raining upon us. I never drank anything in my life with such gratitude. Later we discovered the Filipinos had dropped a dead Chinese down the well.

The Insurrectos set up another headquarters in San Fernando, a town of 30,000 inhabitants. And as at Malolos I was among the first to enter this new capital. With Major General Franklin Bell, at that time in charge of intelligence work, I crept through hundreds of yards of ditches right into the heart of town without being discovered. There were eleven of us this time. Then we hugged walls and dodged among the stilts, on which all native houses are built, until we were near the plaza and could see the big bridge strongly patrolled. Also, between the cracks, we could see insurgent soldiers, sometimes within only a few feet of us. Bell was a man of dash. It was his purpose to make a sudden charge, shooting and shouting, in the hope of stampeding the Filipinos out of town. But he didn't attempt it and I was glad. Such a small charge could not have succeeded, no matter how dashing. Instead, we worked our way back, and the city was finally captured after an attack in force.

I had another horse by this time. When the general attack began it was necessary to cross the river under fire. The water was four feet deep. Bullets splashed about, and my horse refused to go either forward or back! I think he was in the pay of the insurgents. I had to leap off and drag him into the protection of some trees.

As a variation from horseback riding and forced marches in the sweltering heat, I was on the clumsily armored ferryboat *Laguna de Bay* when General Lawton took Santa Cruz. While he landed part of his troops from barges some way down the shore, to surround the town, the insurgent sharpshooters were busily engaged trying to pick off the gunners on the *Laguna*. When they realized that they were surrounded, they tried to escape across the open field along the water front while our guns played on them like a garden hose. We could watch the lines crumble. Later I counted ninety dead and wounded, almost the entire garrison. Palmer, Bass and I hired a little launch to take us back to Manila. We all had army rifles although, as civilians, we were not supposed to use them. As we passed close to a coastal village, crowds on the water front appeared definitely unfriendly, so we opened fire at long range. Our bullets probably did not reach shore, but the sound and our clearly hostile intent cleared the streets with amazing suddenness. That was the only time I used a rifle against the enemy in the Philippines.

Along about this time I decided to hunt for some carrier pigeons. It was such a nuisance to get our dispatches in from the country. I found that the Compañia Tabacalera used them to get news from the tobacco plantations when the rivers were flooded and no other means of communication was possible. Bass, who spoke excellent French, gained their permission to use the pigeons and the pigeon cote. Thereafter, he, Dinwiddie and I carried large baskets of carrier pigeons. We had always to watch them carefully, because they were looked on with considerable disfavor by the other correspondents. We could get 300 or 400 words on a single sheet of cigarette paper. This, folded tightly, fitted into a metal capsule attached to the bird's ankle. The pigeon was then tossed up and after two or three sweeping circles, it would start unerringly in the direction of Manila, where Mrs. Bass was always at the cote at certain specified hours. She then took the messages to the censor and had them filed. Once one of my pigeons flew up, but instead of heading for home it settled on a telegraph pole, where a soldier shot and ate it. However, the messages usually went through quickly this way and saved infinite trouble. When printed, they were always marked "via carrier pigeon."

The censorship restrictions began to be felt acutely by the correspondents. We were not allowed to send an honest statement of the military situation. Real conditions in the Philippines were being concealed from the people at home. General Lawton and others said it would take 75,000 troops to quell the islands. General Otis refused to send for any more or to let any report get to the States that might alarm the country.

Under existing conditions the war might drag on for years with no decisive result. We correspondents believed in a quick settlement by force and no deception at home. We held a meeting and wrote out a round robin for all the newspapers simultaneously, making our complaint known. As senior correspondent in point of Philippine service, I signed my name first. Bass and Dinwiddie, both of the *New York Herald*, came farther down although I seem to remember that they were the prime movers in the protest. Eleven correspondents signed. But General Otis declined to let this letter go through, and threatened to put off the islands any man who signed it.

We all felt very gloomy after this stormy session with him. But we succeeded in arranging for a second interview at the Malacañan Palace, with General Bates present. It lasted three hours. The correspondents were represented by a committee of four, Bass, Dinwiddie, Davis and me. General Otis was determined to oppose us; we were equally determined to send the message. General Bates's attitude was sympathetic to us. We left with the understanding that *if* we sent the message, we *might* be subject to court-martial or expulsion, and we were definitely forbidden to send it from Manila.

Finally, via Hong Kong, it was circulated throughout the United States and created such a sensation that the Secretary of War, Russell Alger, was compelled to resign.

General Otis was ordered to appoint a new censor and to allow correspondents far greater liberty. As a direct result of our action, the government resolved to send more troops, and well over 75,000 were landed before the islands were pacified.

## ～ 20 ～

## The Sultan of Sulu

WORD went about Manila that General Bates was going to Sulu to make a treaty with the sultan. The trip promised great interest. John Bass and I secured permission to go along, and in view of the fact that we had just sent the round robin, it seemed an excellent time to leave Manila.

The Moros of Mindanao had bitterly opposed white men. In Sulu they had been even worse; the Spaniards had barely been able to go beyond the outskirts of Jolo without being murdered. The job of supervising them had not been popular among the Spaniards. We gathered that any aggressive officer who displeased the Spanish governor general was sent to the Sulu archipelago.

When the Americans took over the Philippines, two batteries of the Twenty-third Infantry under Captain Pratt were sent down to occupy Jolo. Their heads were full of how a sultan and his retinue had once come to pay a visit of state to a Spanish governor. When all were assembled, so the story went, the sultan presented to the governor a valuable gift, and as the governor bent over to admire it, the sultan whipped out his barong and sunk it from the top of the governor's head clear down to his chest. At this signal the Moros started slaughtering the Spanish garrison. The story is a good one, though unverified. It served to prepare our soldiers for any such diverting eventuality. However, things went on more or less comfortably for a time.

Then the sultan began to get a little worried about whether the Americans were going to continue his yearly allowance according to the terms of his agreement with the Spaniards. Nothing had been said about it, and he felt himself face to face with the prospect of having to cut down his harem and smoke several less pipes of opium each day. Weeks went by and the sultan noticed that the Americans were making no effort to occupy the enchanting little island of Siasi. He hurried down there with an army of twelve men, assumed formal possession, collected $8,000 Mex. in cash and hoisted his flag over the whitewashed ramparts of the mud fort.

This was the situation which induced General Otis to send
General Bates, a cool, levelheaded officer, to effect some sort of
definite agreement between the Moros and our government. Details
of the whole negotiation were left entirely to his good judgment and
discretion.

Hence it came about that General Bates, his staff, John Bass and
I set sail in July 1899 on a small Spanish steamer, the *Churruca*. For
two or three days we cruised among the most exquisite islands. Many
of them were uninhabited. Bass and I used to sit with our feet on
the rail, looking out across the smooth sea, and pick out islands on
which we might reign as neighboring kings.

At Jolo a huge castellated gateway led from the end of a stone pier
into the heavily walled city. The wall was about ten feet high with
scattered sentry towers and fancy blockhouses at the corners. The
streets were as clean as brooms could make them, for there were no
vehicles in Jolo, and horses were allowed in the village only by special
permission. Great trees arched over carefully kept gardens. All the
houses were ornate and gaily colored, and everything was on such a
tiny scale that you imagined yourself looking at some decorative stage
setting. In fifteen minutes you could walk through every street in
town.

It seems that Governor Arolas, whom the Spaniards had sent there
to get rid of, determined that if he had to stay, he would make things
as pleasant as possible. He was responsible for the layout of the town.
Tradition says he was just. Those who were square were treated well,
while those who imposed on him were promptly shot.

Occasionally a juramentado would come down from the hills and
do a little killing until finally Arolas became exasperated. He told the
sultan that he was getting tired of it and it must stop. The sultan responded that he would try to stop it, but it might sometimes be beyond
his power. However, he would promise to send Arolas word if he
heard of any of his subjects running amuck.

One day a few more zealots shaved off their eyebrows, put on their
white clothes, went before a hadji and took the oath to die killing
Christians. Then they came down to Jolo and left a crimson trail
behind them during their brief but exciting crusade.

The following day the governor received a note from the sultan
warning him that some of his subjects had run amuck and for him to
prepare for them.

Next day a Spanish gunboat and a battalion of soldiers started out and blew two or three Moro villages off the face of the earth, together with a considerable number of the sultan's subjects. The sultan was thunderstruck until he received a polite note from Arolas telling him that one Spanish gunboat and a battalion of infantry had run amuck and advising the sultan to prepare for them.

The remainder of Arolas' term of office, it was said, was without incident.

General Bates, his staff, Bass and I took up quarters ashore, and the general sent word over to the sultan in his palace in Maibun, inviting him over for a conference.

The sultan evaded this by many subterfuges. After some time had passed in more than the usual Oriental delay, Bass and I approached the general and asked permission to go over to Maibun.

The general was horrified. He considered it much too dangerous and was not disposed to grant permission. "If you go, you go at your own risk. We can do nothing to help you!"

We decided to try it, trusting that our unarmed appearance and the very boldness of the attempt might get us by. Of course, the sultan spoke only the native language, so we had to have an interpreter. A renegade Nubian from Busbus, just outside Jolo, was found who could speak a little English. A couple of guides, Bass and I and a young man named Pierce got all ready to start. Then we couldn't find the interpreter. We combed the town and finally located him cowering in hiding. He refused to go, saying the sultan would murder him, so we had to compel him at the point of our revolvers, which we then concealed.

No American had ever crossed the island before. As we left the sanctuary of the town behind and entered the hills, we began to remember all the tales that had been told of Moro treachery. The Moros might jump from behind the tall waving grass flanking the single trail, and attack with krises, barongs and *campilans*—an assortment of curved or double-headed knives and swords, specimens of which now adorn my studio in a much less harmful manner.

At last we emerged on the far side of the hills and came to the long causeway across the flooded coastal lowlands that led into Maibun. It had taken us about three hours of slow riding. We had seen not a single soul on the way. Now it became necessary to leave our horses and proceed on foot. This narrow causeway was the only way into or out of town. Once in Maibun, we knew that a hasty retreat would be impossible.

Immediately swarms of half-naked savages with krises surrounded us, their teeth black from betel nut. Such a vicious-looking mob there never was! At first they seemed more astonished than anything else. Since our attitude remained cool and we showed no signs of force or hostility, they remained curious rather than suspicious.

As we waited in the market place, however, they became more threatening, and we were relieved when we were taken to a little shack where Hadji Butu, the sultan's chief official, came to see us. We told him our desire to confer with the sultan, but he was unimpressed. He continued reluctant until we showed him a five-dollar gold piece. This, he indicated, he would like to show to the sultan. He took it away and we never saw it again.

After another interminable and nervous wait, with the hum of hostility rising from the market place, we were at last led to where the

sultan was living, a better type of native house with a galvanized iron roof, evidently the mark of royalty. His regular palace, it was explained, was farther out of town.

Hadji Butu motioned us to enter, and any anticipation of glamour or regality hastily evaporated. The sultan was sitting on an ordinary chair. He was a small man of about thirty with a pock-marked face and a little fringe of mustache. He wore a turban and a long, white, not overly clean robe. Several servants stood by with cuspidors which he used occasionally, and another held his bowl of betel-nut juice which gave his lips and teeth the usual dark, reddish-black, unpleasant effect. His mouth was open part of the time in a stupid expression of curiosity. His mother was supposed to be the real power, and he only the tool of the sultana's ambition. We did not see her, but suspected she was secreted behind the wooden partition before which we sat.

Our Nubian interpreter was instructed to say that we represented the great American people through the great American newspapers; that everyone was eager to know about the great sultan, and that we had come to carry greetings to him and to ask him to send a message back. As the interpreter used the word "newspaper," it is doubtful whether the sultan knew what he was talking about. The interview rambled on and on about the friendliness of all parties and lagged definitely in interest.

So I interrupted to ask if the sultan would go out in the sunlight to be photographed. He refused. Then I asked if I might sketch him.

Inasmuch as this involved no effort on his part, he consented. After that I asked for a signed statement that I could send back to the United States, and received the following:

I, Hadji Mohammed Jemalol Kiram, Sultan of Sulu, am like a brother to the Americans and hope they will treat me the same.

This bore the Mohammedan date of 1317 and his signature.

After a few other ceremonies we departed from the presence with considerable relief. His subjects, impressed by our having been received by the sultan, had quieted down and did not impede our getaway.

We were elated at the success of our enterprise, and we hurried to get back to Jolo before the gates were locked for the night.

Surprise, excitement and joy greeted our return. Nobody had had the least idea what the attitude of the sultan might be. Our friendly visit helped make the subsequent negotiations and peace treaty possible.

Ultimately the sultan did come to Jolo. He was surrounded by a dozen members of his court and sixty men-at-arms. The sunlight glinted on kris, barong and spear, and on the kaleidoscopic colors of their costumes. At the town gate this retinue was met by four companies and the band of the Twenty-third Regulars. It was a picturesque sight.

When General Bates finally left the islands, he also left many friends behind, among them the old sultana, who presented the general with one of the gaudy state uniforms of her late husband, with the message: "It is dear to me because it was made with my own hands and still contains the sweat of my husband." Court gossip hinted that she had poisoned him.

I wrote stories for the *Record* about the queer customs of Sulu, including those of marriage, which aroused so much interest at home that George Ade was moved to piece it all together into his first operetta, *The Sultan of Sulu.* I gave him native names and local color and designed all the costumes.

About this time the interisland steamboat *Churruca* went up to Borneo, so I went along. I seem always to have been willing to go anywhere at any time! Sandakan was like a civilized oasis in the midst of a wild, head-hunting population in the primitive jungles. A Mr. Cook was acting governor at the time and living in the governmental

palace, a huge seminative building. His wife owned a baby rhinoceros which had been captured in the interior and to which she fed fourteen bottles of milk a day. I presented her with a sketch of him.

For some reason I was moved to write from Sandakan an affectionate letter back home to "the girl I left behind me." I had been writing her off and on. I used to put a dollar's worth of colorful local stamps on the envelopes to make them look interesting. But as my own plans continued so uncertain, and I never knew where I would be next, I had finally notified the consuls at Shanghai and Yokohama to forward all my mail back to Manila. When I returned there in August I received mail that had been pursuing me for nearly a year.

The lady indicated her strong suspicion that I would rather stay out in the wilds than come back to her. I cabled at once with reply prepaid: "Is it too late if I return immediately?"

The answer came: "Too late. Was married July third."

And then she continued getting my letters, including the one from Borneo.

# ~ 21 ~

# Li Hung Chang

IT WAS the end of August. The rainy season was on. This was a good time to go up to appoint more correspondents for the *Record* in north China and Japan.

From Hong Kong I went to Amoy and Shanghai; thence I took a Chinese steamer to Weihaiwei and Chefoo and Tientsin. Here I encountered Dr. Louis Livingston Seaman, whom I had last seen in Sulu. Together we proceeded to Peking where relations between the Chinese and foreigners were becoming threatening. These were the first rumblings of the Boxer Rebellion which broke out the following summer, but they did not interfere with the usual three-day trip out to the Ming Tombs and the Great Wall. We traveled on mules and slept on native k'angs. I appointed Dr. Robert Coltman correspondent for the *Record*.

Li Hung Chang was still the greatest figure in China. Although no longer viceroy, he virtually conducted China's foreign policy and was supposed to be still the confidential adviser of the empress. His secretary was an American named Pethick, a keen, studious-looking man of about forty-five who had lived in China most of his life. Through him and Dr. Coltman, an interview was arranged for me and for Dr. Seaman, who had met Li before.

After a half hour's ricksha ride through the dust and bewildering din of the Tartar City, rocking back and forth over mountains of dirt and jolting down narrow alleys, we were whisked up to the heavy doors of a temple within the walls of which Li had his home. We entered the gateway and were escorted through courtyard after courtyard to the living quarters of the great Chinese.

We finally arrived at a room furnished in the most atrocious plush furniture, with garish rugs and a big Union Pacific advertisement on the wall. The European style was used as a concession to the West, and doubtless was considered very elegant. Five bulky upholstered easy chairs were ranged in a circle in the middle of the room, and beside each one was a small tea table.

We rose when we heard a shuffling of feet, and in came old Li, leaning heavily on the arm of a retainer, and carrying a stout cane in his left hand. He was bareheaded and was dressed in a common light-blue Chinese coat, white Chinese trousers and curious clumsy boots. Low on his nose rested a pair of big steel spectacles, and above them looked out the merry, lively eyes that had been made so familiar by his photographs. He shook hands all around and was assisted to his seat. Then we all sat down.

The twinkling eyes studied us slowly and deliberately. Then he asked endless personal questions—our ages, how much we were making, how much we were both worth.

He remembered clearly having met Dr. Seaman on his trip around the world a few years before. They had crossed the Atlantic together on the *St. Louis* when Li had become interested in two young American chorus girls. In New York he and his whole retinue had paid a formal visit of state to the modest apartment of the two sisters, creating much talk and amusement. It now appeared that they had made the most lasting impression of any of his American experiences.

"Are they married yet?" he asked through Mr. Pethick.

"No," answered Dr. Seaman.

"Are they rich?"

Dr. Seaman said he understood they were comfortably fixed.

"Pethick here is not married. Perhaps we could arrange to get one of them for him." His Excellency smiled broadly as he looked over his spectacles at that gentleman.

"Would you give me a dowry of half a million?" asked Pethick, and Li shook with laughter.

Dr. Seaman skillfully switched the subject to another channel. Li was curious to know what we were going to do about the Philippines.

"What do you think of the American occupation?" we asked.

"I consider it a great mistake," he answered at once. "When President Grant was here, he assured me that America was firmly committed to a policy of nonaggression toward weaker nations, but since this man McKinley has been President, America seems to have cast aside her traditional policy of honor, safety and riches and adopted the same land-grabbing policy as England, Germany and Russia. If Grant had lived," he continued decisively, "no such mistake would have been made. I think America should withdraw."

"And have the flag trailed in the dust by Aguinaldo?" exclaimed Seaman vigorously. "America could not retire now with honor. The islands were forced upon us by the result of battle. America did not deliberately go in to gain possession of them. Now we've got them, how could we get rid of them?"

"Isn't the Filipino chief Aguinaldo a man of ability and patriotism?"

"Patriotism! He sold his country once to Spain. He's probably waiting for another chance to be bought off!"

"Then why not buy him off?" asked Li calmly. "You have already begun buying the islands by paying Spain twenty million dollars for them. It seems to me that you might pay a little more to Aguinaldo and make the bargain complete. It's the same thing. You would then prevent further loss of American lives and avoid an endless pension roll that in the end will amount to many times what you would pay Aguinaldo."

Then he suggested that we sell the islands to Japan. We asked why China didn't buy them.

"China is too poor. She hasn't the money."

"Why don't you buy them yourself, Your Excellency?" The question tickled Li hugely. He liked to be joked about his wealth. He answered only by a long spell of laughing, punctuated by vigorous puffing at his pipe.

A native attendant stood behind his chair, filled the pipe with a pinch of tobacco, lighted it and, while Li was talking, steered the long, thin mouthpiece between his lips. Li would draw a puff or two, remove it, and soon the process would be repeated.

We had been told that we must not leave until he signaled. The signal was the raising of a glass of champagne. And the champagne was already poured out and stood beside us on the little tables, getting warmer and warmer as Li's interest continued for nearly two hours.

He confessed his age to be seventy-seven and seemed inordinately afraid of death. Dr. Seaman mentioned that his father had lived to be ninety-eight. Li asked quickly and eagerly how that great age had been achieved.

"By drinking and smoking moderately, taking plenty of exercise and always making it a rule to get up from the table still feeling a little hungry."

Old Li didn't care much for this sort of advice. He was a gluttonous eater.

We left the audience with the consciousness of having been in the presence of real greatness. Unlike our friend in Sulu, Li Hung Chang had an impressive personality.

Back in Chefoo, Dr. Seaman and I resolved to try to get into Port Arthur, the Russian naval base. There was already speculation on the date of war between Russia and Japan, over four years before it actually broke. We went over on the *Tzitsikar*, but were held up far outside because the ship had been in Newchwang where there was a bubonic plague. The Russians said we must wait in the roadstead until the full ten days' quarantine had expired. This was considered an ultimatum by the captain of our craft but not by Major Seaman. Perhaps you will understand the character of the major better when I tell you that he once threatened to clean out the English Club in Shanghai because one of its members made a slighting remark about the land of the free and the home of the brave. Later he was to be largely responsible for the reorganization of the medical department of the United States Army.

Now he indulged in a prodigious bit of verbal fireworks which the Russian health officer received with shrugs. Dr. Seaman became even more emphatic, this time waving a piece of paper. The Russian paused. A piece of paper is something that may be very important. He went into consultation with other officers. Seaman continued to brandish the paper, with such effect that the ship was allowed to proceed all the way in to the dock at once.

"What in the world was that?" I asked him afterward.

He held it out. It was a receipt from a tailor in Shanghai.

# 22

# The Hemp Deal

LIFE was running comfortably for me in the little house on Calle Isaak Peral. Davis and I were the only ones of the old guard who remained. We had a Chinese cook who had cooked for the Navy for twenty years. We had him bake us a fresh chocolate cake every day. We also had our own carriage or *carromata*. There was a certain amount of social life, and, ladies being very few, each one had an abundance of attention.

Since the outbreak of the Filipino insurrection, the great hemp ports in southern Luzon, Samar and Leyte, were almost completely cut off from the outside world. They were of course still in insurgent hands. Occasionally a little native schooner would escape the patrol of our gunboats and successfully land food supplies, but as weeks went by, the patrols became so effective and blockade-running so perilous that interisland traffic practically ceased.

The hemp demand was starved; prices rose 300 per cent over normal figures; importunities of Manila businessmen became urgent. Then a big corner in hemp in the United States aroused a general clamor from that direction, and in response to this an expedition was organized under General Kobbé to occupy several of the larger hemp towns in the south.

It is doubtful if there ever was an expedition so crowded with incident, grave and funny, tragic and *opéra bouffe*. Nine different towns were taken, and each town offered a distinctive reception, some with bolos, some with rifles, some with ancient guns and some with white flags. Detachments were left at each of the captured towns and the outfit returned to Manila after eighteen days.

By that time dozens of steamers of assorted nationalities were racing down the China Sea to get at the hemp. My letters to the *Record* recounted the opening of the hemp ports, but there was one story that I did not tell.

That was about my own flier in hemp.

As my *carromata* clattered out on the broad Plaza Calderón on my way to join the military expedition which was scheduled to sail at one o'clock, I happened to glance at the clock in the Binondo Church and saw that I was twenty minutes ahead of time.

If I had not glanced at that clock, I would never have become a Napoleon of Hemp. I did look up, however, and that made all the difference in the world.

I poked the *cochero* and pointed to a narrow street on which was located the office of an acquaintance who dealt in hemp. My intention was to get from him some pointers about the southern ports. He too had looked at the Binondo clock and was preparing for the rest that he had taken every day at this hour during twenty-five years of life in the tropics; he had heard the busy drone of traffic in the Plaza die away until only an occasional carriage rattled over its blazing cobblestones. The city was knocking off for its midday siesta. I pushed open the flapping screen doors and found him still at his desk, a punkah swishing lazily above his head. He looked up with a show of interest.

"Well, well, McCutcheon," he said, "what's the hurry?"

"I have only a couple of minutes," I answered. "I'm off with this expedition at one o'clock—two cruisers, a battery of artillery, a fleet of transports and four weeks' supplies. Lots of fighting expected."

"I hadn't heard," he said.

"No, it's more or less secret. I thought you might give me some information about these southern ports."

"What?" He sat up straight. "What ports? You don't mean . . ."

"That's right, the hemp ports. I want to know . . ."

"Great Scott! When did you say the expedition starts?"

"One o'clock. What's the matter?"

"Too late to send anybody," he muttered. Then he looked at me. "McCutcheon, why don't you buy some hemp down there?"

"Me buy hemp! Great guns, what in the world do I want with hemp? I couldn't use enough to make a clothesline!"

"Listen. I'll give you all the money you want. Don't you see? There's a world famine in hemp since those ports have been blockaded, but the people in the ports probably don't know it. They haven't had any outside news in months. Hemp's worth three times as much as it was; those storehouses are full, and the people need money. You'll be the first buyer on the spot. Don't you see? You can give twice what they've ever received and still make money! Will you do it for me?"

There seemed no good reason to refuse, so he hurriedly explained the procedure to me.

All hemp contracts were made on a basis of the first grade or "fair current." That is, the price paid for the fair current is stated in the contract, and the prices of the other three grades are in fixed proportion to that price. Assuming you offer $20 per picul for the first grade, it is unnecessary to mention in the contract the prices for the other grades, for it would be definitely understood that the second grade should be 25 per cent less than the first grade, the third grade should be 40 per cent less, and the fourth, or "ovillo," 50 per cent less.

My friend hastily wrote several cards of introduction, gave me some blank contracts and said I could safely give as much as $23.50 per picul, but that I ought to get the hemp much lower, perhaps for $18 or $19.

"How about the different grades?" I asked.

"Pay no attention to the grades. They will take care of themselves. Don't give more than $23.50 per picul."

"Well," I said as I hurried out, "I'll make a try at it, but remember, I don't know a darn thing about buying hemp!"

The small fleet sailed promptly. Black plumes of smoke curled from a dozen funnels. At night there was singing and band playing, and also an ominous oiling of Krag rifles and Colt revolvers. Going to war was getting to be an old story with me, but this thing of being a trader and financier was disturbingly strange and unnerving.

At dawn on the third day we reached the first of the hemp ports. Hundreds of soldiers were loaded into lifeboats and towed ashore by the ships' launches. With my camera and my contracts, I was in one of the first boats to land. Rifles in readiness, the soldiers rushed along the rickety piers, but there was no fight, for the garrison had fled. In half an hour the town was full of "amigos" and Spanish merchants who appeared as if by magic from stone cellars and from behind stone walls and from near-by jungles.

But although I spoke with several of them, my halting Spanish served only to mystify them and I got nowhere. That night I took a fellow correspondent named Martin, who spoke some Spanish, into my confidence, and he agreed to act as interpreter for me.

The taking of the second port was more of an event. For a time there was a deadly short-range duel between the transports and the earthworks on shore. Several hundred soldiers landed far down the beach and enfiladed, while the cruisers opened up with shrapnel. Thirty or forty insurgents were trapped in a stone warehouse, and as they fled across the open plaza, their only way of escape, they were shot down one by one like clay pigeons. Two great hemp warehouses or "godowns" were roaring with fire caused by exploding shells.

· Out of the white blanket of smoke that rested on the water, another boatload of soldiers left the transport and crept toward shore through a spatter of Mauser bullets. When the boat grounded in shallow water, I was among those who leaped out and splashed ashore. I joined the skirmish line and dashed across the plaza till I came to a slightly wounded insurgent. Then I stopped and showed him a letter addressed to "Sr. Rodriguez, Mercate de Abaca." He pointed down a side street. I beckoned to Martin.

Occasional bullets clipped the banana leaves that lined the street, a nipa hut near by was roaring in flames, and the bursting bamboo was popping loudly. But Sr. Rodriguez was not at home, and our efforts to find him were in vain. He must have departed to his country seat to wait until the shooting was over. The whole town was deserted and lay empty under the broiling sun. At dawn we sailed out of that harbor and headed farther south.

For the next few days conditions were unpropitious for calm business transactions. As soon as the fleet reached a port the merchants fled for their lives. Even by landing with the first boat's crew I was unable to arrest the swifter progress of the hemp merchants. A few twelve-pounders might have overtaken them but I couldn't. And what was worse, they ran so far in one day that they could not return in a week's hard walking. So my commercial venture languished.

Three ports remained. One was empty. The next was impossible for peaceful negotiations.

"There's lots of hemp here," Martin opined, "but how can we get men to talk business when the town's burning up and the air is full of shells?"

By the time the expedition reached Tacloban on the island of Leyte, it was reduced to one battalion, the Forty-third, because of the garrisons left in the other ports. When the *Nashville* and the *Mariveles* steamed into the bay, Chinese and British flags fluttered from the better buildings, indicating the neutrality of the occupants, and only a few insurgents could be seen along the earthworks on the water front. Under a flag of truce General Kobbé sent in a boat to confer with them. Their general, they said, was six or seven miles away, and they asked for a few hours' time in which to communicate with him. This General Kobbé granted.

At the expiration of the time they asked for still more "because the roads were so bad," but instead the general sent in a company of infantry.

For a few minutes the shore was oppressively silent. Three hundred yards, 200 yards, 100—and still nothing happened. Then boom! Crash! A shell screamed angrily above the landing party and struck the water behind them. They hurried ashore and advanced in open order, and from the bay the ships opened up, combing the bamboos that fringed the hills behind the town. And that was all there was to it.

Meanwhile I was fuming with impatience. Nobody but Martin knew of my business ashore and consequently nobody understood my hurry. As usual the shore was lined with hemp godowns, which were of course highly inflammable, and I was in an agony of suspense lest they go up in flames before I could transact my errand.

Finally I got ashore with my letter to a Tacloban Chinese and as soon as possible located him among a throng of his terrified countrymen who were seeking protection in the lower story of one of the stone godowns. Beyond them in the half-darkness were thousands of bales of hemp.

Our merchant, dressed with care in rich silks, nervously led us upstairs to a great room with polished floors and splendid furniture. Several others followed us with astonishment and curiosity. We three, the Chinese, Martin and I, entered a small office, each of us bowing with profuse politeness.

Martin introduced me as a great merchant. I made a desperate effort to look like one. My trousers were wet and bedraggled and I had several days' beard. My battered camera case swung from my shoulder. The Chinese looked at me with interest but not with awe. Then through Martin I gave him my credentials and offered him $18 dollars per picul for his hemp, of which he said he had 10,000 piculs. This offer was immediately refused. By some local grapevine the rise in hemp prices seemed to be known and he was already asking $22. Little by little I came up. When I reached $20 he still refused.

Following his eye, Martin and I simultaneously observed a small English steamer slowly warping to the dock. Already competitors were arriving! It made me even more nervous.

"How much will $20 a picul come to?" I asked Martin. Then Martin made a mistake. He produced a piece of paper and deliberately multiplied 10,000 by 20, the result of course being $200,000. This he allowed the Chinese to see, hoping the immense figure would close the deal.

The Chinese looked, looked again, then glanced sharply at me. His expression never changed but he seemed to take new interest in the negotiations.

"Twenty's all I'll give," I announced decisively.

"The English boat is at the wharf," said Martin.

"What had we better do? I can still go up a little and be safe."

"An Englishman is coming this way," said Martin.

I determined to make one more bid to avoid competition.

"The Señor Merchant says," interpreted Martin, "that he will give $21. This is final. You may take it or not."

Through the window we could see the Englishman, and I must confess I felt wildly excited although I tried to gaze disinterestedly out at the bay and appear indifferent to the trifling fact that I was offering a man a fortune for a little hemp.

"This money—$21 per picul—will be paid when our ship comes for the hemp," Martin said for me.

The Chinese bowed. "We will sell you our hemp," he said and produced pen and ink. Martin began to fill out the contract according to the model I had brought from Manila. The Chinese watched the formation of the words, his lean fingers working convulsively. Looking obliquely at me, he spoke a few words to Martin and indicated something on the paper with his long fingernail.

"He wants me to insert three words here," Martin said to me, " '*sin ninguna rebaja*'—without rebate. Shall I put them in?"

"What does he mean by that?" I asked.

"I have no idea," said Martin.

I could not ask further without betraying my ignorance to the Chinese. I could hear the Englishman's voice below. I nodded to Martin who added those three fatal words, "*sin ninguna rebaja*," each one of which was costing my Manila friend $10,000 although I didn't know it at the time. In fact I was elated, although in my conservative heart I wondered whether it was really possible that I was getting the best of a bargain with a Chinese, the shrewdest and craftiest of all traders.

When the contract was filled out, the Chinese hurried away with it and held long and excited conversation with other Chinese in the big room. The news spread and all the important merchants in town thronged up to look at the contract and to talk excitedly.

Occasionally from the corner of my eye I could see them looking wonderingly at the cool, deliberate figure sitting by the window, smoking as calmly as if he had not just made the most stupendous plunge in hemp ever recorded in Philippine history.

Why don't they hurry? Why doesn't he sign? I thought desperately. The agony of suspense was fearful, but I tried to show no sign of the deep agitation within me.

Nearly half an hour passed and then the Chinese came back and said he wished it stipulated in the contract that if a steamer did not call within fifteen days the contract would be void. I saw no objection to that because I knew that our steamer could reach Tacloban in much less time. In fact the clause seemed to have no particular bearing whatever. It had, however, as I subsequently learned, for that was what saved my friend in Manila and acted as a boomerang against the grasping Chinese. Why he ever insisted on this clause is a mystery to me, for that was where he woefully overstepped himself.

The contract was finally signed. The little Filipino notary who witnessed it kept repeating to me,

"*Muy caro! Muy caro, Señor!*"

What the devil does he want to butt in for? I thought nervously because I feared that he might start the Chinese on some new and delaying argument which might draw in the Englishman. Nothing so dreadful happened, however, and we walked out as nonchalantly as if it were an everyday matter to spend a few hundred thousand dollars. From all the windows in the neighborhood, wide-eyed and amazed Chinese peered at me, a Napoleon of finance that dazzled even their understanding.

You have probably figured out what I had done. Of the 10,000 piculs, there were only about 2,000 of the first grade, 3,600 of the second grade, 4,000 of the third grade, and 400 ovillo. I had given $21 for *all* this hemp, regardless of the customary rebate. Figuring afterward, I discovered that I had agreed to pay about $30 for the first grade, the others being calculated according to the fixed ratio. I had offered about $7.00 per picul more for the hemp than the maximum price arranged between the Manila merchant and me. To catch even, the price of hemp must advance nearly 25 per cent above the enormous price it had already reached.

Now here's where the funny part comes in.

It seems that two great Manila firms had contracted to deliver a gigantic shipment of hemp in London for May. Neither firm had all the hemp it needed and they were feverishly buying up all they could find. The Englishman who was on our heels in Tacloban was an agent for one of these firms.

The Chinese there had *not* heard how high the price of hemp had really gone, because of the effective blockade, but when I offered practically $30 per picul, they argued that hemp must have gone skyward, and when the Englishman tried to deal with them they laughed at him and asked $32. He was driven nearly crazy, for he couldn't buy a pound of hemp in the district. So he wrote back to Manila saying that a new dealer was buying at an unheard-of figure and that producers absolutely refused to sell for anything reasonable.

Then the Manila merchants who had to get the hemp if they had to pay its weight in gold were dumfounded. "Who is this mysterious operator? What does it mean? What is going on in the world? What sort of gigantic deal is being engineered?"

In desperation they began to advance their offers. Up jumped hemp two or three dollars at a clip. In three days it had reached nearly $30, and I began to see that possibly I could sell at a profit, for of course on my return to Manila I had discovered what a ghastly blunder I had made. For a time the price hung at a standstill near $30, a terrific price, equaled only once before in the hemp market. Then new ports were opened and the price began to fall, slowly at first—$27, $26.50, $25. There it stayed for a while but with a downward tendency.

In the meantime the Manila representative of the Tacloban Chinese had called on me several times. He finally began to realize that I had simply made a mistake and intended to take refuge behind the fifteen-day option, merely letting the contract die. Then was when he began to sweat blood. He saw the price fall day by day, and he came to me on his knees to ask that I annul the contract at once. He even offered to make it worth my while.

How my heart hardened! And how he groveled!

"Oh, no, really I couldn't think of it. That hemp is mine for fifteen days and if you dare to sell any of it I'll have you imprisoned!"

Down she went, dollar by dollar, until, when my option expired, the price was about $23. He had lessened his profits by about $6.00 per picul—$60,000 dollars—and if you ever saw a crazy Chinese, he was the man. But he could expect no mercy from one whom his Tacloban partner had so shamefully tried to cheat.

That was the end of my great hemp deal—a transaction that became famous in the Philippines. I had lots of fun out of it, for I stirred up trade and commerce out there as they had rarely been stirred before. Of course I had certain regrets. I could have bought that hemp at $22 without those three fatal words, and at that price I could have made about $15,000 Mex. But then I always knew I was an ill-fated speculator, so that I never allowed my dreams to dazzle my reason.

## ～ 23 ～

## On the Trail of Aguinaldo

THE American operations in the Philippines were coming to a head. Feeling the circle drawing in around him, Aguinaldo and his main body of troops slipped through a twenty-mile gap in our lines. His capital at Tarlac captured, his organization going to pieces, his men suffering defeats on all sides, his family scattered except for his wife who refused to leave him, he was a fugitive for his life. His whereabouts was the all-absorbing question.

Soon after my return to Manila I accompanied General Wheaton's expedition to San Fabian. When the gunboat *Samar*, in command of Ensign Henry C. Mustin, was sent up along the coast to communicate with our forces at San Fernando, I went with it. As I expected to be back in San Fabian that same evening, I took nothing at all with me, not even my precious cigars.

I never did get back. We were delayed at sea by a severe storm and when, three days later, I finally landed at San Fernando, I learned that Major Peyton C. March, with four companies of the famous Thirty-third, had started north hot on the trail of Aguinaldo.

Immediately I bought a horse and an old Spanish saddle and blanket. The horse was a vicious animal. I called him Julius the Ghost Horse or the Man-Eating Stallion in memory of one of that name in Chicago when I first came up from the country. With no further campaign equipment I set out under the gigantic royal palms of the *Camino Real* and trailed after the troops until I caught up with them at Namacpacán and joined the other correspondents, Dick Little, Ed Keane and John Dunning.

The Filipinos were just ahead. Up through La Union and Ilocos Sur provinces, they were pushing rapidly northward toward the Cordilleras, the sound of the clashes of their rear guards with the pursuers often reaching their ears.

These were hard times for the natives. Our advance was so swift, the good "amigo" had only a very few minutes in which to shift his allegiance and change his flag.

At Candon the Americans received information that Aguinaldo had taken a trusted bodyguard of 150 men under his good friend General Gregorio del Pilar, and had turned inland toward the mountain retreats of Lepanto Province where it would be difficult for us to follow.

March took a picked force of 300 men with their supplies on pack animals and struck off boldly in pursuit. For two days we made our way laboriously up the trail through giant gorges and jungles and half-savage Igorrote villages, crossing and recrossing icy torrents. The midday sun scorched and the night winds chilled us. Aguinaldo had passed this way five days before, entrenching or destroying the path but making no resistance. Evidently he had decided to make a stand nearer the top of the pass.

About seven in the morning of December 2, March's main column reached the plaza of the village of Lingay. Beyond the rice terraces, the last lap of the trail to Tilad Pass zigzagged dizzily up the mountainside. Ahead we could see the dark file of Company E already pushing up the first few hundred feet. Suddenly they were met by a vicious volley of Mauser shots and we saw them take cover in the crosscuts of the trail. They lay pinned down and helpless.

From the plaza the whole scene was as plainly visible as if on a stage. We could see the insurgents far above, a few at a time, raise their rifles to shoot, then pause to await another target. Sometimes there were eight or ten leaning over the rocks blazing away at the Americans as they ducked around exposed corners.

Major March studied the situation, then sent Company G under Captain Jenkinson to the side to make a flanking movement, but their advance was stopped with a dozen or more casualties. March led his two remaining companies forward and came under fire. It became evident that any sort of frontal attack was impossible. The insurgents commanded the steep ascent absolutely. Sergeant Major McDougall and ten sharpshooters made a stiff climb to a near-by peak on a level with the Filipinos, but the latter only shifted farther behind their protecting rocks.

The insurgents had not given an inch; they had inflicted greater loss than they had suffered. It appeared probable that they would be able to hold out until the 140 rounds of American ammunition were exhausted. Even with one company of our troops working up to a point scarcely a hundred feet from them, another pressing forward from the side, and Major March advancing from below with two more companies, they gave no indication of alarm. Their exhibition of cool, deliberate nerve was something I had not seen previously in the war.

March resorted to the only plan remaining. He ordered H Company, under Lieutenants Tompkins and True, to circle back up a small ravine and attempt to scale the steep cliffs at the right. If they could reach a position *above* the insurgents, they might be able to rout them by their own method of plunging fire.

Then came an interminable wait, as trying as active fighting. The rows of soldiers were huddled with their backs to the cut at the upper side of the narrow trail, chafing at the delay and wondering what it meant. For amusement the men would raise their hats on sticks above the ledge and have insurgent bullets put through them. The doctor was bandaging the wounded under a ledge; the dead lay stretched out with handkerchiefs over their faces. The sharpshooters on the neighboring peak and the insurgents were exchanging shot for shot. From the ledge where I lay to the next crosscut there was an exposed bend around which no one passed without being fired upon. Bullets clipped the long grass and spattered us with dirt.

At ten o'clock, after an hour and a half of waiting, the feeling grew that H Company could not make it, and that other insurgents might be using the time to cut us off from the rear. Major March himself went forward to the upper trail to reassure the men.

Clouds hung below us in the valley, and other rolling clouds, enveloping us as they passed, shut out the wild terrain above the pass. It might have been possible to make a charge while thus concealed but even this chance diminished as the sun grew warmer and the heat on the ledges became intense.

Down from the rocks above came the jeering laughter of the insurgents, and occasionally a big boulder.

For the hundredth time Major March paced up and down, looking from his watch anxiously upward to the heights. Another hour passed with no change in the situation. If Tompkins failed, it would be necessary either to storm the pass or to withdraw. Neither course was pleasing to consider.

At eleven-twenty, when the conviction of failure had descended on us all, we suddenly heard, far above us, the sound of rifle fire and cheering. With a wild rush the troops on the trail followed March up toward the insurgent position. For a time the quick popping of Mausers and the smashing reports of Krags mingled equally; then the Krags won out and our men scrambled over the insurgent barricades.

Tompkins' men had been compelled to discard their haversacks, blanket rolls and part of their canteens and ammunition in their perilous climb, where they needed every bit of strength to pull themselves up. After two hours and fifty minutes they had reached the little plateau more dead than alive, but they had effectively turned the tide.

The fleeing Filipinos were targets for these men and for McDougall's men, as well as for the throng hounding them from behind. Many fell or threw themselves over the edge of the precipice and went crashing down. Most of their casualties occurred during this hopeless flight toward a second barricade farther on.

How stubbornly they had fought may be seen from the fact that they had held back a battalion of Texans for five hours. How brave and loyal they were is shown by their coolness in the early hours of the battle and by the grim record of their casualties: fifty-two killed or wounded out of sixty.

General del Pilar was the last man to fall. A native was holding a horse for him and just as he was preparing to mount a bullet caught him in the neck. Only twenty-three years old, he had been through the whole campaign as a brigadier general. He wore silver spurs, shoulder straps of gold and three little gold lockets. In his pocket was a letter from his sweetheart Dolores, and an American twenty-dollar gold piece which he had shown me when he was in Manila some

months before. Of most interest, however, was his diary which covered the last ten days of his life and told of the wild flight he had made in the command of Aguinaldo's bodyguard. The final entry, written just before the battle, read, "I am holding a difficult position against desperate odds, but I will gladly die for my beloved country." Pilar was one of those Filipinos who were actuated by honestly patriotic motives and who fought because they believed their cause was right.

With the defeat of Pilar's men, the pass was open. Major March led his men forward and that night we camped in a large shelter hut at the summit. The fight above the clouds at Tilad Pass was in many respects a last stand, and although the numbers engaged were not great it might be called the crowning achievement of the war.

Officially the revolution was crushed. The big military operations had now practically ended, although desultory fighting continued for some months. The whereabouts of Aguinaldo remained wrapped in mystery which General Otis made no further effort to solve. Eventually he was captured by General Funston. As a sample of "The Changing World" which I have so often used as a cartoon caption, Aguinaldo's son went to West Point and was a classmate of the son of his father's captor.

Strange to realize that the Filipinos have at last received their longed-for independence. For my own part, I have felt all along that they should have got down on their knees every day of the year to thank God for American occupation. The benefits received from it far outweighed any fancied drawbacks.

## ～ 24 ～

## In the Transvaal

THE first two years of the American occupation of the Philippines, "days of the Empire" as we called them, were satisfyingly full of hiking and fighting, of rumors and alarums, of infinite romance and adventure.

When the Filipino insurrection petered out and the grim necessity of going home loomed ahead, it seemed to me highly desirable to go to Africa. The Boer War had been in progress for some time. A siege of Pretoria seemed likely. Anyhow I didn't want to go home at all, and was eager for any excuse to continue this fascinating sort of existence. I knew the *Record* had a man with the British forces, but none with the Boers; I suggested that they send me down.

The answer came: "If you think you can join the Boers, go ahead."

So, at the end of April 1900, I left the Philippines, this time for good. Our little bungalow never looked more cosy and charming; my ties in Manila were many and pleasant. There were many farewell dinners before I sailed for Hong Kong.

The *Prinz Heinrich* took me to Colombo; the *Ernest Simon* took me to Djibouti. During the daytime the French women coming home from Tonkin and Saïgon and the Dutch women from Sumatra and Java wore Mother Hubbards that hung sheer all around like the face of a cliff. In the evening they would appear radiant in silk and jewels. By day I used to hide in the smoking room.

At Aden the dispatches were full of the Boxer Rebellion in Peking. The eyes of the world were shifting back to the Orient. It would have been too complicated for me to return, but as I sailed south I realized that the tag end of the Boer War would be of fading interest.

At Djibouti I had to wait eleven days for the boat for Madagascar. It was miserably hot and there was nobody in town I could talk to except a Somali guide called Hadji Awat, who wanted to guide me to "Haybysheeny." It was some time before I realized that he was

speaking of Abyssinia. I was so lonesome I decided to go with him and made a week's brief hunting expedition on horseback beyond the end of the railway. On our return I was again so eager to get away from Djibouti that I had Hadji Awat sit on the pier all night with instructions to come and wake me the moment the steamer appeared.

The *Djemnah* took me to Madagascar. It was crowded to the rails with French officers. At first I was regarded with distrust as being possibly British, for the French were contemplating with jealousy and bitterness this English gathering-in of the richest part of Africa. My chief companion was a Dutchman from Antwerp named Savelkoul. He was going to Pretoria to sell overcoats to the Boers. He was a great admirer of President Kruger.

"England has tried in every way to fool him into some diplomatic trap, but he has always been too shrewd for them. The only way they could beat him was by force. Kruger had the ability to look far into the future. He knew what was coming and prepared for it. He is a great old man, and it's a pity he isn't twenty years younger. As long as he lives the spirit of independence will be kept alive."

"What sort of man is he personally?" I asked.

"Well, he is a plain, hardheaded old farmer. He has made his money and has settled down in his armchair before the fireplace. All the people in town come to ask his advice. He's that kind of old man. He lives very plainly—doesn't spend five hundred pounds on his living, although he's worth about two million."

The *Gironde* took me to Lourenço Marques. Much warlike paraphernalia, such as machine guns, was entering Delagoa Bay in the peaceful garb of piano crates and suchlike. Consequently a British cruiser sized us up with suspicious interest.

"Now," said my friend Savelkoul, "the minute the ship anchors, you'll be watched. Every other man you meet is apt to be either a British or a Boer spy, and every one of them will make it his business to find out all about you."

This looked interesting and I amused myself picking out the Sherlock Holmeses who snooped inquisitively around the customhouse. Philosophically I suffered my saddle and saddlebags to be detained until my departure from the country, also an ancient hippopotamus-hide shield and an Abyssinian knife. Evidently they figured that I might charge the British lines armed with a medieval shield and a ten-inch dirk.

The terrific red tape necessary to get my passport and permission to go on the railway into the Transvaal merited a special newspaper story, and I still have that hard-won Portuguese pass. Mr. Savelkoul and I went up together. Inasmuch as he wished to take up several coats as samples and was not allowed to, he asked me to wear one.

The train was filled with a jostling crowd from all corners of the earth. In our compartment were a mysterious Englishman, a German baron, a French recruit, a Boer commandant, an American Jewish contractor and the postmaster general of the Transvaal. After about fifty miles of climbing gradually upward through Portuguese territory we reached the well-guarded border. To north and south of that border town the Boers were ably assisted in their work of guarding by their natural allies, the lions.

Beyond Waterval Onder the scenery is the finest in Africa. Two engines with cog attachments hauled us up the steep ascent, crawling along the ledges cut in the solid rock, piercing huge granite spurs and hanging dizzily above the noisy Ellandspruit that roars over the boulders far below. Dozens of big baboons nearly as large as men played about the rocky shelves with no thought of danger. After half an hour more of slow toilsome climbing along the sides of battlemented mountains that shoot up almost vertically, we could hear the droning thunder of the great waterfall. After passing a group of armed Boers, the train plunged into the sulphurous opaqueness of a tunnel, then out through a deep cleft in the rock.

"Now," said the Hollander, "you are on the High Veldt."

A wind-swept rolling tableland stretched ahead of us, all the same brown color. No trees, no blue valleys, nothing but an endless swelling and dipping of smooth brown ridges.

Machadodorp was a straggling village of squatty buildings much like an American prairie town. After a few minutes' walk in any direction, you were either at the hotel or the railway station. Beyond, the veldt extended in long slopes of dry grass. The only warlike atmosphere was lent by an occasional horseman clattering into town, wearing a slouch hat and carrying a rifle.

There had been no siege of Pretoria. The capital had been given up with little resistance. In consequence of its proximity to the Lydenburg Mountains, Machadodorp was strategically the only place east of Pretoria which the Boers could occupy. Here President Kruger had established headquarters. The entire machinery of government was on wheels and calculated to be as mobile as the Boer cavalry, should occasion demand a hurried movement.

At the end of a siding stood the private car in which Kruger was making his home since leaving Pretoria. It was a handsome one, highly polished and decorated with the Transvaal coat of arms. He seldom left it, walking only a short distance each morning to take a bath in a hot sulphur spring. I had my first glimpse of him through a window of his car. There was no need to ask whether that heavy, stoop-shouldered old man with the massive features, the fringe of whiskers and the stovepipe hat pulled down over his ears was Oom Paul. His individuality was as striking as that of the Sphinx.

Other cars were loaded with guns and ammunition; and still others held most of the government offices. Secretary of State Reitz's office was a very small table between the seats of a compartment. His personal baggage was round about and in the racks overhead. The British papers were full of articles accusing him of every sort of political rascality. My impression was that he had been slandered, that he was an honest, patriotic, intelligent official who would stick to the ship. Switching easily from Dutch to English, he asked me with a smile, "How are things in the Philippines? Aren't you Americans trying to do about the same thing to the Filipinos that the British are doing to us down here?"

There was a certain underdog similarity. The "portable" capital of the Boers did indeed suggest the restless journeyings of Aguinaldo's seat of government.

A Kaffir boy shouldered my roll and led me to a little corrugated iron annex to the hotel. An overcoat thrown on the right-hand cot of Number Eleven showed me that I was to be only half of the inhabitants of that apartment.

Later in the evening I met my "bunkie." It was Du Plessis, the famous jailer of Pretoria, the man of all the Boers most despised and reviled by the *uitlanders* who supported the Jameson raiders, and by the prisoners confined just after the raid. I had often read of this notorious character and was quite prepared to find him a cruel-visaged tyrant.

Mr. Du Plessis turned out to be a fat, good-natured old man with scraggly red whiskers and velveteen pants. He came in at night very softly so as not to awaken me, and subsequently snored so loudly that he roused the whole neighborhood. In our little box of a room, Mr.

Du Plessis succeeded in shaking the walls. In the morning he said, "You're not a very good sleeper, are you? Every time I wakened, you were awake!"

I had often to allay suspicion about my nationality. "*Ich bin ein Amerikaner,*" I would say, and after a few more minutes of my German, during which they would wince every time I flatted an *a*, the Dutchmen would swing into excellent English. It was a matter of never-ending astonishment to me when some peaceful bewhiskered old burgher would break out into a flood of "ballies" and "bloodies." Oom Paul, however, would not speak English, refusing to make that concession to a people he so consistently and generously hated.

In general the reports of Boer courage and morale were good.

"The Boers have their own style of fighting," I was told. "Every man takes his own position and shoots whenever he sees anything to shoot at. If things get dull he goes home for a spell. But he comes back in a few days for another whirl. They always have their horses saddled and waiting in a protected spot during a fight, and when the time comes to leave, they're off. In ten minutes you'll hardly see a man, but next morning they'll all be assembled together.

"Occasionally the older men get homesick and tired and go home for a rest. But as soon as they've had it, their wives send them back."

One day 580 British prisoners arrived in charge of forty Boers. There were several members of the Black Watch, the Seaforth Highlanders and other famous British regiments, including some turbaned Hindus. They smoked and laughed as if they were not altogether displeased at the idea of escaping those unpleasant trips up the sides of Boer *kopjes* which had proved so disastrous to the Britishers. They walked in throngs with no pretense at order and were loaded onto flatcars. Several of the Boer guards were in danger of being left behind and rushed frantically along the sides of the moving train. One by one they were given a helping hand by their prisoners and yanked bodily over the sides of the cars. One fat Boer was jerked so enthusiastically that he disappeared with a great flourish of waving boots. The prisoners cheered, the guards cheered, and the train rolled out of sight down the steep grade toward the prison camp at Nooitgedacht.

Later I visited this camp where several thousand prisoners were enclosed in barbed wire. The Boers had had no time to prepare a suitable prison camp; in consequence it was a curious village of grass and brushwood huts, of extemporized shelters, burrows, caves, lean-tos of old iron roofing or piled-up bags of dirt.

Awnings made of bright-colored blankets made some of the huts look quite inviting. In the heat of the day the men lay under the awnings, and at night the awnings were taken down and lay on the men.

The Boer guards, I might add, were almost as poorly housed and rationed as the prisoners.

Strangers were apt to think of the Boers as not very well educated or intelligent. They struck me as much like men of our own country. Certainly they did not take such a broad-minded view as to believe in an open-door policy by which the whole world could come in and milk their country of its treasures and then leave. In other words, they took the position that as they had cleared the country of savages and some of the lions, the country was theirs to run as they liked, and those who didn't like it could go elsewhere.

The war had by then entered the guerrilla stage. Several noted Boer commanders such as De Wet and De la Rey were still raiding the country. Soon after I had arrived in Machadodorp, President Kruger and his staff moved down to take up their residence in Waterval Onder. When he left, he made a vigorous and stirring speech from the back platform. I made several sketches before the train left.

The big show was over and what was left was blanketed by the tense news from Peking. South Africa had lost its place on the front page, and the *Record* cabled me to get an interview with Oom Paul and then come home.

In Waterval Onder, Kruger had moved into a squatty, gabled cottage standing in a soldierly row of gum trees, a much pleasanter abode than a railway carriage. It had a warm, sunny porch and a beautiful view. Secretary Reitz arranged an interview for me in the tiny room which served as parlor and office.

Oom Paul sat at the farther end of a table in a large easy chair. His silk hat lay on the table. His thin hair was combed straight back from his forehead until it reached his neck. A little gold earring hung from each ear. His eyes were red and inflamed and he kept them closed most of the time.

His features were large and coarse, and I looked in vain for the fatherly, sympathetic expression of which I had heard so many of his admirers speak. It was not there. Every line was hard and severe. But

as if to make up for a lack of gentleness, there was tremendous power in the leonine head, the huge pear-shaped nose and the stern unsmiling mouth.

The big features, the massive shoulders, stooped and round, the head bent forward on his breast, his somber black clothes, stolid hands and heavy feet made a memorable picture.

He rose and shook hands with me when I was introduced, then settled back in the armchair, his eyes opening and closing as he looked me over. Mr. Reitz interpreted for me while I made notes, and Oom Paul emphasized his remarks by vigorous smashings on the table with his powerful fist. As he understood little if anything of what I said, there was nothing very responsive in our half or three-quarter-hour talk. Also he was in a far from cheerful mood.

In consequence of good scenery, good climate and good cooking, the prospect in ordinary circumstances might have been very pleasant. But, alas, for him the conditions were not ordinary!

For twenty years he had been president of a republic, one of the great figures of South Africa. Now he was a fugitive, beyond the consolation of scenery and good cooking. Moreover, he was an old man. His wife, Tanta Susanna, was sick in Pretoria and might die before he had an opportunity of seeing her again. He could not fight because he was too old.

Consquently he must sit out the evening of his life in his little mountain home or in Holland and contemplate the procession of bitter memories passing in endless review.

After my interview with Oom Paul, I filed my dispatch and left at once for the coast, still wearing my friend Savelkoul's sample overcoat which he had exhibited and then given to me. I wore it for years, and eventually, during an exceptionally cold spell, I gave it to an old man who used to come often to my studio and always looked half frozen.

## ~ 25 ~

# Reported Dead

UPON emerging from the Transvaal, I received word from my mother of my brother Ben's approaching wedding. My letter to her in response was preserved among the family archives:

> I'm sorry to miss the event, for marriages haven't been very common with us children.
> As for me, I'll probably get married some time when I get home, although I haven't arranged with any particular young lady. Perhaps I will be too ancient by that time to capture a young lady, but when one of them sees all the loot and souvenirs I've picked up, why, I don't see how she could resist, even if she didn't care for me myself.

From Lourenço Marques I sailed north on the German East African steamship *General,* stopping at Beira, Mozambique, Dar es Salaam and Zanzibar. Aden was closed to us on account of the plague. If I could have gone ashore I would undoubtedly have tried to catch a steamer back to China and the Boxer Rebellion. There was plague also at Suez and Port Said. We were not allowed to disembark until we reached Naples. That same morning all Italy was shocked by the assassination of King Humbert at his summer palace outside of Milan. I hurried up to Monza at once but was not permitted inside the palace, so I took a few pictures and sent a dispatch. After brief stops in Paris and London, I sailed for home at last on the *St. Louis.*

At each port along the African coast I had mailed a post card to my mother.

"Am homeward bound. Have the fried chicken ready." Fried chicken, country style, with cream gravy pleasantly mottled with particles of browned chicken, has always been a source of rapture to me.

"Don't forget the cream gravy."

"Be sure to have blackberry jam."

These and many more reached home only a little while before I did. I had been away nearly three years. My friends had planned a reception, but somehow I didn't want that. I took a train that arrived at seven o'clock in the morning and I didn't telegraph anybody.

Everyone was at home except George Barr. We all went down to Lafayette to see my other relatives and friends, and I had fried chicken with cream gravy and blackberry jam and all the other trimmings at every house at every meal!

My mother and my sister Jess came to live with me in a rented house on Bellevue Place but I was seldom at home. In fact I attended twenty-six banquets in a single month, some large and impressive, some small and informal, and many receptions. I had to speak at almost all of them. Soon afterward I was scheduled to speak at Purdue. There was not a moment to prepare this speech until the night before. I was worn out from the banquets and had been having frequent chills, but I knew Purdue had made special plans so I worked until four in the morning.

When I joined George Ade at the train he was worried by my appearance but said nothing.

A couple of nights later, on December 19, after a dinner given by C. K. G. Billings at the Chicago Athletic Club, I woke up feeling as if a sword had been run through my lung. The pain continued. We had no telephone. Jess went out in the snow to look for a doctor's sign. She found Dr. Keyes on North State Street. It was two in the morning and he didn't want to come, but she wouldn't leave without him.

That was only the beginning. I got worse and worse. I didn't know it was double pneumonia. At first it never occurred to me that I was seriously ill. I used to have my Mauser pistol put on the bed so I could admire the workmanship on the gun metal and live over the days it brought to mind. I expected to be out soon and kept making dates ahead. But on Christmas Eve they sent for my brother George, thinking I could not live through the night.

Dr. Frank Billings was called in and declared there was no hope. This gave rise to rumors of my death and notices went out, including the one reprinted in the Manila papers which I have mentioned before. However, Dr. Henry Favill said, "Serious, but there's a ghost of a chance if he can get south where there's better air." George Ade conferred with Mr. Lawson who arranged for a private car. An ambulance took me to the Polk Street Station and my stretcher was lifted through a car window. The engineer was cautioned to go slowly around curves.

The minute I began jolting along the tracks my spirits started to revive. Dr. Keyes, a nurse named Graham, Mother, Jess and John Bass went with me. Frank Holme was on the same train, but since he had tuberculosis he was not allowed to come into my car. George Ade had gone ahead to prepare the way in Asheville. No ambulance was available, but somehow they carried me to a pleasant house called "Oakholm" on Beaucatcher Mountain. Dr. Minor took Dr. Keyes's place.

I got better, then I got worse again. Various malarial bugs from the Orient put in an appearance. My heart became affected, then my kidneys. My only hope was an operation but my kidneys couldn't stand ether or my heart chloroform. The doctor said he would use ethyl chloride, a freezing mixture. Everyone joined him in jollying me until I thought it would be a mere incident—and all the time he was laying out about forty different implements.

And then he couldn't get the knife between my ribs! Two or three times he tried. My mother held my feet and I clutched the nurse. For half an hour he worked, cutting and prying. They were all too scared by that time to think of my feelings.

Finally the doctor forced the knife through and a hole was opened in my side big enough for drainage tubes. Improvement set in at once. Later I had vacuum treatments to expand the lung. One day, while the doctor was changing tubes, the pleura was damaged and it was touch and go for a while. But I got over that too. I weighed only eighty-five pounds.

As spring approached I began to take drives—six or eight of us in a high-seated sort of tallyho with four horses. Girl friends of Jess's came down. Kirk Brice came down. The nurse left. George Ade began writing *The Sultan of Sulu*. I took walks and then I climbed. It was May. Nothing to do, nothing to worry about, lots of people fussing over me—it was all extremely nice.

Then George Barr sent us his first book, called by the unprepossessing name of *Graustark*.

# ~IV~

## RESTLESS ROVING

# ~ 26 ~

## Brother George

ABOUT my brother George in those dimly remembered days when we lived on a farm, the things that were true are jumbled together with things I have imagined.

After we moved to Elston the picture becomes clearer. George became associated with cousin Charlie Homrig who conducted a photograph gallery in Lafayette. Every moment that George could escape from other duties found him up in the duskiness of the studio. He assisted the artist in many ways, such as running the newly printed photographs through the burnishing press. The family didn't realize that there was more in this than met the eye.

Charlie's soul was not in his art. He lived and dreamed and thought only of a theatrical career. No one, of course, excepting George, suspected Cousin Charlie of these aspirations. He lived a hermit among his tintypes and cabinet-size photographs, amid his plush, his papier-mâché rocks and his tawdry backgrounds of arched and pillared galleries overlooking Italian lakes, with a heavy smell of collodion and stale tobacco smoke overhanging it all.

We didn't suspect, either, that the spirit of high adventure was stirring in George, until, when he was about eighteen, we learned that a wagon road show financed by Cousin Charlie had fared forth on the unpredictable sea of the Drama.

A few days later we heard that a band of strolling players had opened in a little town a few miles to the west, in a play called *Linna*. Cousin Charlie had written the play, also the music, and had cast himself in the leading role. A lesser part was taken by one "GEORGE M. CLIFFORD, COMMEDIENNE," as his name appeared in bold letters on his cheap little trunk.

This imposing artist turned out to be my brother George. Whether he really sang in the part, we never knew. I know we always thought he had been taken into the Methodist Choir because they liked to have him around.

Occasionally the family would get brief letters from towns in southern Indiana and Kentucky. Always the note of cheerful optimism was sounded, until it became a stereotyped form. My mother was worried. "Let him alone," said my father. "He'll come back."

I shall never forget the day George came back. It was my sister's birthday. All the good things that went to make up an old-fashioned midday dinner were spread before us, and we were in the midst of the meal when a tired, dusty, forlorn figure came down the road and hesitatingly turned in at the gate.

It was George M. Clifford, late comedian. Failure was written in every inch of his travel-worn clothes, and there were gaunt lines of hunger in his face.

He was welcomed cheerfully. No word of comment or reproach was uttered, for even we younger children could sense something of the fearful blow his pride was suffering. Mother tried to pretend that all was well with him even though she could hardly keep back the tears.

"Just in time for dinner, George."

But no. George muttered huskily that he had had his dinner and wasn't hungry.

The meal proceeded under a mask of assumed naturalness, and the prodigal son looked on. At times he was proffered favorite dishes but he stolidly refused them. It was not until dinner was nearly over that Mother induced him to take a cup of coffee because it was Jessie's birthday.

The wall of resistance, once breached, crumbled away and from that moment I never saw a human being eat so ravenously. I'm sure he never ate so much again, although passing years and comfortable living gave him a rounded amplitude of form.

This was the end of his life as a professional actor, but once as an amateur he played the part of a soldier in *The German Volunteer*. The soldiers were in bivouac, hungry, tired and dying of thirst. George had only one line to speak. Many times he rehearsed it, gasping in the hoarse, hesitant whisper of a dying man, "Water! Water! For God's sake, water!"

On the night of the performance, with the Lafayette Opera House jammed, his moment came, and he shouted in a ringing voice: "WaterwaterforGod'ssakewater!"

George had by this time reached the girl stage. With his reputation as a real actor, and his enforced idleness in the field of drama, he embarked quite actively on a social career in Elston. He organized dancing parties at our house and attended many others at the neighbors'.

One night Jennie Defrees, half a mile down the Romney road, gave a party to which our entire family went. It must have been in the earlier days of George's emergence from the chrysalis to the butterfly, because he was still somewhat diffident when out in company. Or perhaps it was the presence of the family which cramped his style. At any rate, he was seated by the base-burner while the lap supper of cakes and apples was being passed. My father suddenly observed him and whispered a message to me. I went across to George and delivered it in a tense whisper audible to the whole room.

"George, Pa says for God's sake to pull up your socks."

It was a deflationary remark. In the midst of the laughter George glared at me.

But somewhere in his soul there was still something struggling for expression. He began to write plays. One of his first, called *The Old Dominion*, was sent to Minnie Maddern Fiske, who returned it with a kind comment. It could not be used, she wrote, because the first act would require two weeks to play.

When he was about twenty-two he went on the *Lafayette Daily Courier* as a reporter, and subsequently was made city editor. It was a monotonous routine, day after day, searching for news, but like our father, George had the ability to give a holding interest to such a thing as a stroll from the Big Four Depot back to the courthouse.

After his full day of filling the hungry columns of the *Courier* he would go home and write far into the night on stories or plays. He wrote reams of stories that rebounded with depressing inevitability. Months of application always wound up in the same way: a neat packet of manuscript—not typewritten in those days—returned with a stereotyped note of regret. We, the family, looked on with wonder that he could weather these discouragements without complete and crushing despair, and for fear of touching on a painful nerve, we hesitated to ask embarrassing questions about his literary activities.

Father died. I was working in Chicago. In the eyes of our Lafayette friends it was something to be employed on a great Chicago paper, and as time passed and George continued in his path of disappointment, people began to refer to him as "John's brother." When I came home on my occasional visits, I almost dreaded seeing him and having to tell of the fun I was having in Chicago.

On one occasion I suggested a plot to him and he sent me a version which I took to Herbert S. Stone and Company. This was his first contact with them. It was too long for a short story and not long enough for a book, so they declined it, causing me, I am sure, an even more poignant disappointment than George felt.

On my return in 1900 from the Far East, George greeted me with the news that Stone's had taken one of his books. I'm sorry to say I doubted it. I felt that he was trying to save his face, that he couldn't bear to confess that all these years of patient struggle had brought nothing of real accomplishment.

"That so?" said I enthusiastically. "What's its name?"

"*Graustark,*" replied George. My spirits sank.

What an awful name! I thought to myself. I was afraid to ask any more questions for fear the affair was not really settled.

To my amazement the book actually came to me while I was convalescing in Asheville. Dutifully I started out to read it as a measure of brotherly affection. After the first chapter I forgot where I was and who had written it—and didn't put down the book until I had reached, regretfully, the very end. I think he had asked George Ade's advice and George told him to accept $500 for the story, the sale of which has reached over half a million copies in several languages.

Some weeks after *Graustark* was issued, I returned to Chicago where George Barr came up to pay us a visit. Already the book had demonstrated its success. It was to be found on all newsstands. As he went to the Polk Street Depot to return to Lafayette, he stopped at a stand to get a book. The bookseller shoved forward a copy of *Graustark.* "It's a great book," he said. "Everybody's reading it."

George opened the book. A happy idea struck him and taking out his pen he wrote his name in bold characters across the flyleaf.

"Here, what are you doing?" exclaimed the perturbed salesman.

"I am the author of this book," said George proudly.

"But you've spoiled it!" cried the indignant bookseller and made George buy the copy.

The Stones took George's next book, *Castle Craneycrow,* the success of which was even greater. Then Dodd, Mead and Company asked him to write for them and sent him an advance-royalty check for $15,000 for his third book, *The Sherrods.* George didn't know there was so much money in the world!

His first publishers, however, also wanted a third story. George felt it would be unfair to Dodd, Mead to have another of his books on the market to compete with *The Sherrods.* But Stone's pleaded with him, and in gratitude for having given him his first chance, he agreed to write a story for them under an assumed name.

*Brewster's Millions* therefore came out under the name of Richard Greaves. The number of people who have read or seen this story on stage or screen must run into astronomical figures. A chance remark by our youngest brother Ben, "Why not write about a fella who spends a million dollars in a year?" caused George to give Ben one quarter of the royalties for fifteen years.

The curious thing is that Brother George traveled but little. He was booked to go abroad in 1912, but the sinking of the *Titanic* emphasized the peril of the sea and he gave up his reservations. Only once, later, did he screw up courage to undertake a trip to Europe. He gave all his adventurous spirit to his heroes. The Balkans, where the romantic land of Graustark is supposed to lie, remained terra incognita to him.

But he was "John's brother" no more. For many years I was the brother of the novelist, though many people haven't yet got us straight.

## ～ 27 ～

## Bird Center

THE first saving I did after coming to Chicago was to buy—on monthly installments—a lot near Purdue and build a house for my mother. It had many little porches and balconies, a round window here and there and a kind of turret in one corner. Regularly I paid my $20 a month until 1896 when I brought my mother and Jess up to keep house for George Ade and me. Then the payments lapsed and the property reverted to the party of the first part.

Now while I was recuperating in Asheville, the Northern Pacific panic wiped out everything else I had saved—a total perhaps of three or four thousand dollars.

Mr. Lawson sent my salary of about $60 a week and said I was to keep on drawing it as long as I needed it. I felt conscience-stricken and came home as soon as possible; but the doctor wouldn't allow me to work. Pretty soon I told Mr. Lawson to stop the pay.

George Ade and I got a little office on the eighth floor of the Fine Arts Building, where he finished writing *The Sultan of Sulu* and I designed the costumes for it.

Meanwhile the *Record* and the *Herald* had combined, and when I really started work again in earnest, in September 1901, it was for the *Record-Herald*.

Here was I, ten years older, broke again and starting out afresh, but with a very different setup.

Immediately requests began for the dog's return. Had I lost him on my travels?

I wondered if I might not create something new that would have the same appeal. I reflected that, next to a little dog, the most appealing thing in the world is a little boy, the barefooted kind with patches on his pants and a battered straw hat—the sort of boy that nearly every man in the Middle West used to be.

So, the following spring, I drew a picture of such a boy. I called the cartoon "A Boy in Springtime." I reflected also that if one dog was funny, perhaps five dogs would be five times as funny, so this boy was accompanied by five dogs, worth in the aggregate about a dollar and a quarter.

A number of people spoke of the cartoon. Perhaps it occasioned unusual comment because it was an unusual type of cartoon to appear on the front page—purely human interest rather than political or topical. A week later I repeated the type under the same title, showing another common activity of boyhood at that season.

The reaction was even more pronounced, and led to a series of these "Boy" cartoons running through all the seasons.

The visit of Prince Henry of Prussia to the United States in 1902 was a big event in the news of the day. Admiral Robley D. Evans was appointed to conduct him through the country and wherever he went there was tremendous curiosity and general acclaim.

The Prince had a likable manner and was exceedingly tactful and diplomatic. I drew a very elaborate cartoon of his reception in one of the first cities he visited, again with no intention of following it up; but Slason Thompson, on the staff of the *Record-Herald*, urged me to go on.

Frequently, then, during the course of the Prince's trip, I drew others, probably ten or twelve. I have seldom done so much detailed work as I put into that series. Hundreds of figures, great processions of people, buildings, characteristic features of different cities and scenes took a good deal of drawing. Six or eight hours of actual manual labor went into each cartoon.

Naturally I was delighted that they created favorable comment, so

MY STUDIO IN THE FINE ARTS BUILDING

First Flight, Simms Field, Dayton.

Air Race over Grant Park, Chicago, 1911.

EARLY FLYING

very favorable that the *Record-Herald* printed them in book form under a caption chosen by someone else, *The Cartoons That Made Prince Henry Famous.*

Prince Henry requested the originals and they were afterward hung in the billiard room in his castle at Kiel.

In a similar way the "Bird Center" series was an unintentional development from a single cartoon.

One very dull day, when ideas were scarcer than hen's teeth, I found myself in desperation for a subject for the following morning. As a final resort I drew a picture of a church social such as I had known in the early Indiana days. Church socials happened to be in season just then, but I am certain that I had no definite purpose in mind. I called it "Bird Center," a name George Ade had once used casually in a fable.

People commented and wrote in favorably, so a week later I drew a second cartoon and accompanied it with comments and items as if by the local editor. I introduced types I had known in real life in a country town and gave them definite names which the editor of the *Bird Center Argosy* used in his list of "among those present."

Certain characters began to take form: the minister, his wife and their numerous children; the local doctor; the judge; the town drunkard; Captain Fry, the Civil War veteran; Smiley Green, the popular undertaker; J. Milton Brown, the tintype artist—all types to be found in most smaller communities. In addition there was the *grande dame* of the place, the local rich matron whose name is always first of "those present." Then, there was the village Lothario and wag, who was a "great hand" with the girls. Nobody ever took him seriously except the visiting young lady. There were also the two young men who played the mandolins, whose dulcet strains "evoked many encomiums" at all social gatherings.

It may be said that these types are conventional and hackneyed, but if a defense were necessary, it would be supplied by the obvious fact that all small towns are conventional, and the adventures of the social set rather hackneyed.

After I drew several cartoons in which all of these characters appeared, it was natural that a slender plot should develop, and it was easy to introduce a consecutive interest in the series. There was never anything very dramatic, but there were little love affairs and little ambitions that were gradually unfolded as the series advanced.

Each drawing represented some small-town gaiety. One week the good people of Bird Center were observing the Fourth of July. The next week they were having a baby show. Then they were all picnicking in the woods. This series developed a rather ambitious plan. The activities of the town were described in the words of the editor of the *Bird Center Argosy*. The plot of the story was carried along in the various items he recorded. And the reader, reading between the lines, was able to follow the threads.

As it was found that people looked forward to the Monday morning issue which contained the Bird Center installment, I began inserting in the Sunday paper little half-column sketches here and there, to whet their curiosity—maybe a dozen or so.

I kept up the series after I shifted over to the *Tribune*. One time in 1903 I was invited to spend a week end at Lake Geneva at the home of Harry Gordon Selfridge, who later became the great merchant in London. Leaving my Saturday and Sunday cartoons at the office, I planned to do the Bird Center installment at Lake Geneva and send it down by special delivery on an evening train Saturday so that it would be in the office on Sunday in ample time for the Monday morning paper.

The ensuing incident was printed along with the cartoon:

## THRILLING TALE OF A LOST CARTOON, AN ANGRY EDITOR AND AN EXCITED ARTIST

### HOW THE DAY WAS SAVED BY A SPECIAL TRAIN, AN INTREPID HORSEMAN, AND THE MAZUMA OF H. G. SELFRIDGE

---

"The Lost Cartoon," a melodrama from real life in a prologue and three acts.
Time, the present.
The characters:
Harry G. Selfridge, the hero.
John T. McCutcheon, the artist in trouble.
Henry, the horseman, and McCutcheon's good angel.
Postmaster at Lake Geneva, the comedian.
Tribune Foreman, the low-browed villain.

---

#### PROLOGUE

*Scene*—Summer home of H. G. Selfridge, Lake Geneva, Saturday afternoon.
John T. McCutcheon to Henry—"My good man, here is a draw-

ing for a cartoon of Bird Center for the Tribune Monday. On it you will see a special-delivery stamp. Take it to Lake Geneva and mail it for the evening train to Chicago.

Harry G. Selfridge—And hurry, Henry. Be sure to hurry.

Henry—Aye, aye, sir.

McCutcheon—And now for a day of real pleasure. Away with melancholy and care.

## Act I.

*Scene 1*—The same. Time, late Sunday afternoon. (Henry, on horseback, has summoned Artist McCutcheon to the long-distance telephone.)

McCutcheon—Haven't got the cartoon? Searched the office and can't find it? Why, it was mailed last night by special delivery. You say you have searched the office and the post office and can find no trace of it? Zounds! We have been betrayed.

Mr. Selfridge (to Henry)—Take the horse in a hurry. Ride to Lake Geneva. Find the postmaster. We must save that cartoon!

*Scene 2*—The postoffice.

Lake Geneva postmaster (produces the cartoon, its special-delivery stamp yellowing with age)—Yes, here it is. I am waiting for the regular mail Monday morning. They ain't no mail frum here frum Saturday noon till Monday morning. But I'll take good keer of it.

Henry—No, we must have it now. (Grabs the cartoon and rushes back to the Selfridge home.)

## Act II.

*Scene 1*—The Selfridge home. Time, Sunday evening.

Harry G. Selfridge to Henry—My good man, it is now 7 o'clock. At 8:04 a fast train leaves Burlington, twelve miles away, for Chicago. Take the fastest horse we have and ride like the wind. That cartoon must be saved. Telephone me when you get there.

Henry (mounting the horse)—All right, sir. The cartoon will be saved. You can trust Henry the Horseman.

*Scene 2*—The same. 8:12 P.M.

Harry G. Selfridge (answering the telephone)—Henry? Yes, Henry. Did you get it on the train all right?

Henry—I regret to report, sir. The train was four minutes late, but I was three minutes later than the train. It's gone.

Mr. Selfridge—Foiled again!

McCutcheon—Zounds! Gadzooks, we are ruined. No cartoon from Bird Center tomorrow.

Act III.

*Scene 1*—Northwestern Depot, Lake Geneva, 10 p.m. Sunday.

Hero Selfridge—Now, my man, you've got my special train ready. Run as fast as steam will carry you to Chicago. Henry will be here in a minute. He is riding back from Burlington with the cartoon. He will go with you to Chicago and see the precious document safe in the arms of the Tribune foreman.

McCutcheon—And if you break the record for time I'll draw the picture of the man who does it and he shall have a plaster cast of "A Boy in Summertime."

*Scene 2*—Tribune Office, 11:30 p.m.

Foreman of Composing Room—That McCutcheon guy is still shy his cartoon. It's him to the hell box. We can't hold this paper all night. What's he doing at Lake Geneva, anyhow? Why ain't he here workin' like the rest of us? Huh? I give him just five minutes to get here. The first edition's gone down now without a cartoon, with a note telling the people the cartoon has been stolen from J. Oscar Fisher of the *Bird Center Argosy.*

Jimmy Durkin—Hist! There are footsteps approaching!

Henry the Horseman, bursting into the room—Is it too late? No! Thank God!

Hero Selfridge (five minutes later, over the telephone)—Saved! Saved! McCutcheon, wake up! Can't you speak? Fainted? We are saved. The cartoon is safe and sound in the etching room.

(curtain)

The Bird Center Series of cartoons gave me my widest professional reputation. The novelty of carrying a story along by means of newspaper clippings, wherein the reader reads between the lines, was sufficiently fresh and original to bring from Henry B. Fuller the opinion that in the Bird Center Series a new form of literature had been created.

Both the Boy and the Bird Center Series resulted in a vogue of ornaments, plates, sofa cushions and leather goods all marked with characters from them. There was a Bird Center card game patterned after the old game of Authors, which obtained temporary popularity.

All these things reflected on me a certain amount of limelight, which, combined with the publicity given my war correspondence, resulted in a good many social invitations. I found I liked frivoling around. My status as an unattached male, suitable for filling in, was doubtless responsible; nevertheless I was just about the busiest person you ever saw.

During this period I evolved a working relationship with drink. It was customary to serve one cocktail, sherry with the fish, champagne with the roast, then port and liqueurs. After some experimenting, I discovered that I could manage nicely on one cocktail, one glass of sherry, a glass and a half of champagne, and a small glass of Benedictine. This quantity gave me a pleasant sense of self-confidence. My bashfulness vanished to the extent that I said the funny things I thought of instead of regretting all next day that I had not, but my syllables were never mixed nor my voice raised. Whether or not I was really a sparkling dinner guest, the fact remains that after those drinks I thought I was—which helped immensely.

What with prohibition, then the wars and the income tax, not to mention my doctor's orders, this carefully acquired skill is of no further use to me.

As I wrote in the introduction to the published volume of the Bird Center cartoons, if the series had any definite purpose, it was to show how very cheerful and optimistic life may be in a small town. If it seemed to satirize some forms of gaiety in the smaller communities, or to poke a little good-natured fun at some of the ornate pretensions of society in larger communities, so much the better, for then the cartoons might be endowed with a mission. You will find Bird Centerites in large cities as well as in small ones, and it is to be regretted that there are not more of them. For they are all good, generous and genuine people, and their social circle is one to which anyone gifted with good instincts and decency may enter. The poor are as welcome as the rich, and the one who would share their pleasures is not required to show a luxuriant genealogical tree. There are no social feuds or jealousies, no false pretenses and no striving to be more than one really is. No one feels himself to be better than his neighbor, and the impulse of generosity and kindness is common to all.

If there was a "villain" in the piece, it was the old banker whose nearest approach to villainy lay in the fact that he believed a mortgage is no respecter of sentiment. With this single exception "there is not a cross word in the history of Bird Center," to quote one of the inhabitants.

The series ran for a year or more, although a few country newspapers resented it because they thought the text made fun of the country style of journalism.

Glen MacDonough dramatized it for the stage, and it was the inspiration for many amateur productions throughout the Middle West.

The Little Room, a club of literary and artistic people in Chicago, gave one of these performances with a notable cast.

George Ade wrote up the Bird Center material under the title *Cap Fry's Birthday Party*. George Barr McCutcheon was Cap Fry; Franklin Head was Mort Peters, "ye host"; and a rising young architect named Howard Van Doren Shaw acted the part of the tintype artist, J. Milton Brown.

I admired Mr. Shaw's characterization very much, and it diverts me to imagine how astonished we both would have been to realize then that he was eventually to become my father-in-law.

## ～ 28 ～

# Changing to the Tribune

THESE three series of cartoons, the Boy, the Prince Henry and the Bird Center, together with the one about the French Emissaries and still another called Pictorial Sunday Sermonettes, attracted the attention of James Keeley, managing editor of the *Chicago Tribune*. For some months the *Tribune* had been without a cartoonist, Harold Heaton having left to undertake a stage career.

Mr. Keeley sent for me and offered to double my salary if I would come to them.

I liked the *Record-Herald*, I liked Mr. Lawson and I liked my associates there. My relations with them all had been very pleasant, they had been very kind to me during my first struggling years of newspaper work, and I was not disposed to leave them.

I told Mr. Keeley I owed Mr. Lawson a good deal and couldn't accept any offer without giving the *Record* a chance to meet the raise. It jumped my pay from $65 to $110 a week, so I told Mr. Keeley I intended to stay where I was.

In June 1903 he sent for me again and offered me $250 a week.

"The same condition still exists," I said. "I won't leave without giving them a chance."

"Name any figure you like," said Keeley.

"No, I can't," I replied.

There was a great consultation. Everybody went into a huddle. Nobody on the *Record*, not even the managing editor, was getting that much! It would have thrown the whole paper out of kilter. They would have had to raise everyone all along the line.

I said, "I like it here. I'm grateful to you for my start. I'll work for you for a hundred dollars a week less than the *Tribune* offers me."

But even $150 was more than anyone else was getting! There was more deliberation. It raised the devil among the directors. Frank Noyes, Alexander McCormick and the rest wanted to see the raise. But Mr. Lawson couldn't bring himself to it. Giving any sort of raise was never his strong point. And Mr. Lawson owned the bonds. So I went back to Mr. Keeley and took up the *Tribune* contract.

On the first of July, 1903, my first cartoon appeared in the *Tribune*.

Within three weeks after I joined the *Tribune* came the news of the death of Pope Leo XIII. I read this in a noon edition in my studio and hurried over to talk with Mr. Keeley.

I was still going through an attack of stage fright. The first days in a new job one tries too hard, which is like pressing in golf.

We discussed the cartoon and he suggested: "Why not a globe with a band of black?" I went back to the studio, and in as simple a form as possible I drew the world tied with a great band of crepe, the bow draped over the approximate location of Rome. The cartoon was presented to Archbishop Quigley, and I have reason to believe it ended in the Vatican among the souvenirs of Leo XIII.

This was the beginning of a long and very pleasant association with a man who was called the ablest and most colorful managing editor in the country. By sheer ability and a natural intelligence in newspaper work Jim Keeley had risen from the bottom to this commanding position. Stocky, brusque—in his working hours at any rate—with driving mannerisms, he had a genius for playing up a news story for 100 per cent of its worth.

In shirt sleeves, gripping his cigar in his teeth, he was always to be found in the composing room late into the night, with his assistant Edward S. Beck, who became his able successor. Keeley loved music; he had a very sentimental side which came out occasionally in spite of his efforts to smother it. Behind his abrupt way of giving his staccato orders, he had a venturesome soul; he would have liked to be off doing the things his correspondents were doing. He was always sympathetic with my desire to go adventuring and with any departure I made from the routine cartoon. In after years I had many occasions to be grateful for the permissions of absence he granted, and the way he played up my stuff.

Early in May 1914 Jim Keeley left his *Tribune* desk forever, to go, curiously enough, to the *Record-Herald* whence he had lured me. He bought the paper, with the backing of a number of rich men such as Charles R. Crane, Julius Rosenwald and Samuel Insull, and became its publisher. When this paper later merged with Hearst's *Chicago Examiner*, Keeley went into the Pullman Company and remained one of its vice-presidents until his death.

I, too, had gone into the Pullman Company in a small way about ten years before Keeley joined it. I made a very modest investment in Pullman stock. I think I bought fifty shares. It went up a point or two, then sagged back, never again to reach the figure I paid. That is a habit most of my stocks have had.

Some weeks later I received a notice of a stockholders' meeting in the Pullman Building. Not being too well acquainted with higher finance, I assumed that all stockholders who could do so made a point of attending. I showed up at the appointed hour and place, and was directed to a small room adjoining the president's office. Except for a secretary at a desk, I was the first arrival. Presently John S. Runnells, general counsel for the company, came in. I knew him and he greeted me with the utmost friendliness and suavity. Immediately afterward Robert T. Lincoln, president of the company and eldest son of the Great Emancipator, entered and took his seat. Several lesser officials arrived. The meeting was called to order. There were no other stockholders present.

It began to dawn on me that perhaps I had taken the notice too literally. Another disturbing thought assailed me. I was known to be a newspaperman. Did they think I was there as a small stockholder to observe the secret workings of the corporation? Mr. Runnells' affability was somewhat reassuring, but in Mr. Lincoln's rather dour features I could read no particular sign of welcome. The rest never indicated that my presence was a surprise, although they all must have been intensely amused. The formalities of the meeting proceeded—it may have been a routine affair of no importance. In any case, I had no idea what was going on.

At the conclusion Mr. Runnells shook hands cordially, Mr. Lincoln nodded gruffly and I departed in a daze. It was the last stockholders' meeting I ever attended.

One of my most prized possessions is a picture taken at the Keeley farm in Wheaton. I am seated holding a little pig, all bedecked with ribbons. Looking down on this Madonnalike couple are J. K., Senator Beveridge, Dick Little and William J. Calhoun. I think it was some sort of christening, but whether I was supposed to be the father or just the godfather is one of the things that has become confused in my memory.

When I returned from Hong Kong in 1910, I brought with me three little chow puppies. One I had bought from a Chinese steward on the Manila-Hong Kong boat. I paid a dollar Mex. for it and the bamboo cage. Norman Armour and his uncle, Allison Armour, also were on board, and Norman became infatuated with my puppy. When he arrived in Hong Kong he bought two for himself, about the same size and age. He planned to take them back across the Pacific with him but his uncle suddenly decided to go via Siberia and said they couldn't be bothered with puppies.

So Norman gave them to me, and the three little chows were put in charge of the butcher on the ship. One I gave to my brother Ben, and two of them, Tientsin and Tan San, one of which names is evidently feminine, were domiciled on the Keeley farm.

Here they lived happily, and begat and begat to such purpose that I think something like fifty-eight bouncing juniors, boys and girls, appeared and were distributed to friends in and around Chicago, a veritable Chow Dynasty, whose parents had come over on the old *Asia,* counterpart of the *Mayflower!*

## ～ 29 ～

# Lecturing

DURING the intervals when I was not playing hooky—as George Ade so disrespectfully termed my travels—I connected with the Redpath Lecture Bureau. For this it was necessary to keep a notebook, recording the dates and places where I was supposed to lecture.

My method of keeping these notebooks leaves much to be desired by a historian probing the past, but now and then the entries give a skeleton framework of some of my other early activities. Joining things seems to have been one of them.

There is an entry about a meeting at Vogelsang's Restaurant early in 1905. That was when Riley and Landis and Beveridge and George Ade and about a hundred other citizens of Chicago got together to form the Indiana Society and plan its first banquet. There was still some sort of odium attached to the word Hoosier—a sort of synonym for yokel—but the Society boldly adopted it and made it a term of honor.

Another brief notation on May 27, 1905, reads: "Meeting of Club at Wellington Hotel." It is likely that this refers to another historic birthday—the Wayfarers, a small dinner club whose only purpose was to promote good-fellowship among a congenial crowd. Ten of us were present. As sole surviving charter member, I am happy to report that the organization still flourishes.

On the preceding page, May 26, 1905, my notebook says: "Notified of election to Royal Geographic Society of London." I remember clearly the arrival of this document, resplendent with red seals. It came on a morning when I was feeling singularly frustrated in a geographical sense. The evening before I had been out on the far South Side, endeavoring to call on a young lady. For two long hours I had wandered around in the cold and dark, then, hopelessly lost, I had walked most of the way home, unable even to rediscover the whereabouts of the cable cars.

The first lecture I gave was at Fullerton Hall, an invitational affair, for which I had to prepare my speech. After that it seemed not so hard to do it again. The lecture was not a serious one—at least not intentionally so—but in order that it might be dignified by a claim to serious purpose I called it "A Chalk Talk On The Psychology Of The Newspaper Cartoon." The word *psychology* was supposed to establish this claim. The Redpath people thought it was important. And I wanted it to include some constructive ideas on newspaper cartooning. Even the parts where attention usually lagged I retained because I believed they ought to be said.

Usually upon arrival I tried to find someone who could tell me about eight or ten recent events in town. Then at the conclusion of my talk I would draw cartoons with local significance. The audience always enjoyed this.

As I finished each drawing I tore off the large sheet and threw it on the floor. Afterward—especially in college towns—there would be a scramble over the footlights to retrieve them. Sometimes I autographed small pieces of each.

My first paid lecture was at Grinnell College in Iowa. During that winter and the next few I gave the lecture on cartooning usually about once a week anywhere within five hundred miles of Chicago. Although not congenial, lecturing seemed valuable to me. It trained me to appear in public and not to be frightened by a crowd. It also tremendously increased my contact with people and this was an asset not only to me but to the *Tribune* as well.

I never became sufficiently acclimated to the lecture platform to escape certain agonies. It meant doing a cartoon ahead for the paper, something of a strain. Too, there would be a long, tiresome ride in a superheated day coach and an arrival in the early darkness of a winter night on the wind-swept platform of a small-town station. This would be followed by a ride in a rickety bus up to a hotel where the commercial travelers eyed me with gloomy suspicion and wondered what "line" I was carrying.

Sometimes the blackboard or other equipment failed to arrive. This always meant a very unsuitable substitute. It is difficult to draw on an extemporized board and unfamiliar paper.

Supposing the easel was set up and the audience was in the house—except for the late-comers that always blur the point of your opening story with a confusion of shifting feet—then came the worst ordeal of all, getting introduced. I never knew how it would turn out. Sometimes the man who did it talked almost half an hour himself. At one place the mayor introduced me with a wealth of rhetoric and then forgot my name completely.

I delivered my chalk talk so often that I came to know the good parts and the dull parts. When I told about the little dog or the Bird Center episodes, there was a hushed house, not even a cough. When I went on to the salient points about what governs a cartoonist in his work, there was an immediate wavering of attention. Faces drooped, and the younger set began to fidget.

Once, however, when I was in this section of my talk, a part that had never failed as a soporific, I became conscious of a sudden wave of interest that swept the house. People were sitting bolt upright in rapt attention, and I couldn't understand it. I hoped that at last my serious message had come into its own, but, a little later, it developed that a cat had walked out on the stage and was marching and countermarching behind me. There is nothing like an earnest cat to enliven a discourse.

Another time the evening went off beautifully. The audience was suffused with mirth and good nature, and I felt immensely pleased until I reached the hotel and discovered that I had wiped my forehead with a charcoal-covered hand and left most of the charcoal behind.

I never liked to stay in a town longer than necessary. I always took the last train in and the first train out when I could. I tried to escape from the lecture hall by back entries and back streets, because I dreaded seeing people afterward or overhearing unflattering comments.

Getting away the same night, especially from the smaller towns, often necessitated sitting up until two or three in the morning to take a short ride to somewhere else to make connections with a Chicago train. Too commonly it wasn't possible to get away. Somebody had been delegated to entertain me, or some minor-league lion hunter wanted to show me off and I was trapped.

There were other hazards. I missed the last train or got on the wrong one. I remember one occasion that was especially distressing. I started late to catch a train to Whitewater, Wisconsin. In my hurry I got on a train to Watertown. It followed more or less the same route, with a change at Milwaukee. Not until I was almost at the hotel did I realize I was in the wrong town. It was then seven o'clock and Whitewater was fifty miles away. I tried to get an automobile, but there was only one man in town, people said, who would dare to try to do it in less than a couple of hours, and he was nowhere to be found. I called up Whitewater and got the manager, who was taking tickets at the door.

"I'm in Watertown," I apologized.

"I should say you are!" He banged down the receiver, furious.

Later, to make amends, I went to Whitewater for nothing. Ordinarily I received $200 or $250 plus expenses. At one place they paid me with two sheets of five twenty-dollar bills each, still uncut, all signed by the local banker.

Another time I was on my way to York, Nebraska. Around Lincoln we ran into a tremendous blizzard. The big Union Pacific trains ran nineteen hours late, and the local train for York was canceled entirely. Stumped, I telegraphed to York: "No possible way of getting there." The subscribers were offended because I had not driven fifty miles in no time through snowdrifts that had stalled rail service. The letter I received hurt my feelings, too, making it unanimous.

Occasionally one of these mix-ups gave me a cloak of glamour. When my Cousin Rose invited me to speak at a Presbyterian charity benefit in Thorntown, Indiana, my information about train times was wrong because the railroad had changed its timetable the day before and I did not discover it until too late. I hesitated to send an excuse like that; it would undoubtedly have looked as if I were just trying to avoid going.

It was November. After vainly trying to find interurban connections, I talked to an early automobile enthusiast at the Chicago Club about the possibility of getting down by motor. He advised against it. Covering 150 miles on the roads of 1904 to 1909 at about twenty miles an hour was not like driving the same distance today.

My only remaining chance of getting there in time was to adopt Mr. Selfridge's technique and hire a special train. I called the Big Four and they provided an engine and four coaches—four being considered safer than one—for the five-hour run at a cost of $296. I was completely alone save for the train crew. Sometimes I sat in one coach, then I would wander into another. I had telegraphed, of course, so there was quite a thrilled crowd to meet me, and I felt rewarded.

Another time I did drive part of the way, fourteen miles, to reach a town in northern Indiana, and I arrived nearly an hour late. While I was giving my lecture, the driver got drunk and when we started back he got lost. It was a lonely drive, groping in the darkness of a silent country road at midnight, but somehow we finally made a distant railway station. A week later a farmhouse on this same lonely road was burned and the world was electrified by the revelation of the famous Gunness murder farm. I might quite easily have gone in there to inquire the way, in which case I might not have had opportunity to lecture any more.

I never really liked lecturing anyhow. I knew I had the power of drawing people but I never had any confidence in my ability to entertain them once they were out in front of me.

"Well, he ain't much of a talker, but the drawin's were purty pat!"

## ～ 30 ～

# A Fresh One Every Morning

WHEN I started work the only way of reaching the mass of people
was through the press. Movies and radio have changed this. Nevertheless I still feel that in the molding of public opinion for better or
for worse the dominating power and responsibility rest with the
printed columns and cartoons of the country's newspapers.

People used to ask me "Where do you get your ideas—a fresh one
every morning? I should think you would run dry."

The popular impression is that the life of a cartoonist with its demand for a drawing every day, rain or shine, idea or no idea, must be
fairly irksome. I have not found it so. Each artist, I suppose, has his
own way of going about this business. Mine was at least easy to
describe.

Let us assume that it was morning and that I had nothing in mind
for the day's work. My first move was to read the papers thoroughly,
taking note of the news uppermost in the public mind. Nearly every
day presents at least one good front-page story, an election, a notable
speech, a prize fight, a war scare and so on through an endless variety.
By the time I had finished the papers I might have half a dozen suggestions, equally good or poor. One might deal with a broad national
matter; another with local politics; still another might have domestic
interest that would appeal to women and children. This list of suggestions is sometimes submitted to the editor. More often the cartoonist is given discretionary powers.

At other times the papers did not suggest a single idea. Everything
was dull. If nothing was evolved by four o'clock, the situation became
alarming. But there was no use worrying. I knew there would be a
cartoon in tomorrow's paper, and I would get it out, because I was
under contract to do so! Also there was the cheering consolation that
oftentimes the eleventh-hour idea turned out to be the best of all.

When that eleventh hour came, however, I really had to dig. I would put down the date of the next day and look at it hard. Was it the anniversary of any historic event? Was it the birthday of anybody of interest? Then I would try to remember whether anybody had said anything startling recently. Once a university professor was credited with saying—whether he did so or not—that Rockefeller was greater than Shakespeare. Then a doctor came out with the opinion that bathing was unhygienic. Changing fashions offer material; and weather was a last resort—there are enough different kinds in this climate to give us a chance.

Broadly speaking, all cartoons fall into two groups, the serious and the humorous. Each has its place. I always enjoyed drawing a type of cartoon which might be considered a sort of pictorial breakfast food. It had the cardinal asset of making the beginning of a day sunnier. It is safe to say the prairies were not set afire by these cartoons, yet they had the merit of offending no one. Their excuse lay in the belief that a happy man is capable of a more constructive day's work than a glum one.

People prefer to be amused rather than reformed. The American public especially, I found, likes considerable amiability mixed with its lectures. A pictorial sermon once in ten cartoons is more effective than ten pictorial sermons in a row. The diet of daily news is so full of crime, crookedness and divorce that it is sometimes hard to resist the temptation to become a muckraker who allows the dark spots to dominate his vision. A cartoon, it seems to me, does as much good by reminding people of the blessings of life as by pointing out its shortcomings.

However, some subjects should not be treated lightly. Some evils demand more stinging rebukes than can be administered with ridicule or good-natured satire. In such cases a cartoon must be drawn that is meant to hurt. All the same, I have not liked to draw that sort of cartoon, and it was invariably with a feeling of regret that I turned one in for publication. It would seem better to reach out a friendly pictorial hand to the delinquent rather than to assail him with criticism and denunciation.

A most unwholesome type of cartoon is that which strives to arouse the ignorant passions of one element of society against another. There are too many good people in every walk of life to justify assailing the group as a whole. One must try to be truthful and not misrepresent facts to bolster one's point.

This then was the creed which governed my own work. If the one who saw it smiled, its mission was fulfilled; and if, on rare occasions, half a million people smiled in unison, then I felt a great work had been accomplished. I tried to be optimistic and constructive rather than iconoclastic and discouraging. It isn't so important if children don't believe in Santy, but gosh, the world would come to an end if Santy didn't believe in children!

Other principles of journalism further influenced the selection of an idea. There must be consideration for the paper's own point of view as well as for the tastes and prejudices of its many thousands of readers. Quite naturally an intelligent newspaper does not print cartoons that needlessly arouse the resentment of large sections of its circulation, or unnecessarily offend advertisers who of course provide the lifeblood of the newspapers. On the other hand, there is no arbitrary rule. I recall an advertiser who objected to the editorial policy of a certain paper. He demanded that it be discontinued—or else! The publisher, a sincere believer in the policy he advocated, refused to be coerced by any advertiser, however great. In the end, the ultimatum was withdrawn and peace was restored.

In cartooning the President of the United States, most artists seek a manner that does not reflect on the honor of the man or the dignity of the office, but it would be absurd to consider criticism of its occupant as lese majesty.

Similarly it has been an accepted practice, when a woman's activities are to be caricatured critically, that a cartoonist shall blunt his barb by somehow flattering her.

Valuable tricks of the trade were turned up in those early days. We used a lot of stock characters. An anxious-looking man loaded down with bundles stood for a suburbanite; a man in a loud checked suit with a hat down over his eyes was a gambler or confidence man; by adding a horseshoe watch charm, the same man became a race-track sport. Congressmen invariably wore chin whiskers and for years old maids wore spectacles and ringlets.

Then there was the corpulent gent in the frock coat and silk hat, besprinkled with diamonds busily spurting out streams of radiance. Who does not recognize the trust magnate of the last century or, more recently, the capitalist? He used to have side whiskers. Why I never knew for sure but I may hazard a guess. When the first American cartoons were beginning to appear, the late Commodore Vanderbilt was our greatest representative of wealth. The older generation will

STARTING ON OUR WEDDING TRIP

With Barr at the Custom House.     Uncle Charlie gives the figurehead a sponge bath.

The *Lucaya* off Spanish Cove.

The Residency.

TREASURE ISLAND

recall that this particular Mr. Vanderbilt wore side whiskers and expressed considerable disregard for the rights of the public. The capitalists of today look lamentably less and less corpulent.

These purely conventional types were used as symbols, along with other people you've always known but never met, such as Father Time, Cupid, Neptune and the Grim Reaper.

Occasionally real people came to be known by such symbols instead of portraits. In the golden era of Theodore Roosevelt, a pair of glasses and a gleaming phalanx of teeth were unmistakable. When James Hamilton Lewis raised his so-called pink whiskers he changed what may have been an ordinary face—I never saw it unveiled—into a unique one.

An ultra-stout gentleman out fishing, whether shown front, side, or rear, used instantly to suggest to every mind the portly ex-President, Mr. Cleveland. Once when it was incumbent on McKinley to select an American representative to the coronation of King Edward VII, Cleveland's name was mentioned. I drew him far fatter than natural, in a boat fishing, and replying to the President, who beckoned from the shore, "Can't go. Got a bite." A note in Mr. Cleveland's handwriting presently arrived:

> The incident and the ideas it suggests are not only amusingly portrayed, but thoughtfully—except that I have not been invited to attend the coronation either officially or unofficially, and the string of fish is wholly inadequate.

As a general thing, public men have a kindly feeling for cartoonists even though we sometimes handle them roughly. Publicity, good or bad, is the statesman's most valuable asset, and cartoons are as good as first-page advertising.

With a weather eye out for cause and effect, we soon discovered that, to the average mind, a farm suggests honesty, simplicity, democracy. Hence we began to emphasize the farm angle of our favorite candidates whenever there was a ghost of a chance. Conversely, a silk hat was to be avoided.

At the beginning of Carter Harrison's first race for mayor of Chicago, somebody unearthed a picture of the young man in a bicycle suit and cap, bending low over the handle bars. This picture was not one to reassure the people. Obviously the young man lacked dignity and would not do for mayor of a great city. The bicycle cap became an issue and at another time might have defeated the candidate. As it happened, the campaign was coincident with the bicycle craze, and it is presumed that several hundred thousand cyclists rallied round the cap and elected it.

Frequently it happens that the prophetic cartoon falls down with a prodigious flop. However, on the morning after elections there is nearly always a pat cartoon. The method of achieving this dexterous result is simple. Two cartoons are drawn the day before.

In 1902 there was a notable election in Chicago. One of the candidates for alderman was John Coughlin, familiarly known as Bathhouse John; all the reform influences were out to accomplish his defeat. It was a picturesque fight, for the Bathhouse's position in the first ward was well-nigh impregnable and his followers included all the riffraff of the levee district. As the campaign approached its end, the reform elements made a mighty effort and there were some optimistic persons who believed that the legions of the Bathhouse would be routed.

On election morning my cartoon showed an egg, which conformed

fairly well to the architecture of the Bathhouse, and this egg was being pushed from the top of a high building. The cartoon definitely indicated that the Bathhouse was likely to sustain a profound jar in the near future. When the returns were in, he was something over three thousand to the good. It was a mighty victory and necessitated some quick side-stepping on the part of the cartoonist. Next day I showed the Bathhouse exultantly landing in a net held by his friends, the gang down on the sidewalk.

The cartoon differs from any other picture in that the idea alone is the essential requirement, whether it is meant to inform, reform or solely to amuse. This idea should be brought out with directness and simplicity, in such a way that people will know it is a cartoon and not a work of art. It has little to do with beauty or grace; it has much to do with strength and uniqueness. It is a peculiar form of art for a peculiar purpose, and presupposes the ability to say a thing trenchantly, humorously or caustically, in terms of line. However I don't believe drawing has much to do with the success of a cartoon.

Eugene Field, who had only a bowing acquaintance with drawing, could make sketches overflowing with fun and drollery. Mark Twain, who could not draw at all, made crude pen scratches that are extremely funny.

I am always conscious of this dilemma when a beginner comes to me for criticism. Remembering the undoubtedly amateurish samples I brought to Chicago to display to a professional, I hesitate to discourage an enthusiastic aspirant; yet it would not be fair to encourage him to waste time studying when it is evident there is no likelihood of success in the end.

New ideas and distinct individuality in methods of both thought and technique, on a base of sound training, are the steppingstones I try to emphasize.

## ～ 31 ～

# The Cartoon Symposium

EDITORIAL cartoonists on the big American dailies try to draw their cartoons as near the hour of publication as possible. There come times,

however, when it may be necessary to draw considerably ahead of the
hour and even the date of publication.

In 1904, about a year after I went on the *Tribune*, I hankered for
some ocean travel at a time when I definitely did not rate a vacation.
I suppose what I really wanted was a look-in on the Russo-Japanese
War then in progress. I hated having a war going on without my
seeing at least something of the edges of it.

When John Bass and Dick Little packed their bags and left, every
part of me capable of itching was busy! I studied the timetables and
found that by taking an "Empress" at Vancouver on August 15 I
could land in Yokohama on the twenty-ninth; and by taking another
"Empress" on September 3 I could be back in Vancouver on the
fourteenth. Allowing four days each way from Chicago to Vancouver,
I could be back in thirty-eight days.

The call was too great to resist, so I went to Keeley and asked for
about a month's vacation.

"Where are you going, up into Wisconsin?"

"No," I replied, "I'd like to go to Japan."

"Great Scott! You can't do that in a month!"

"Yes, I've figured it out. By catching 'Empress' boats, I can spend
four days over there and be back in a little over the month."

"Well," he demurred, "this is a campaign year. I hate to have the
cartoons stop for so long."

"I'll draw thirty ahead," I said reassuringly.

"What! What about?"

"Oh, some political ones; some about the St. Louis Fair; three about
the weather—we're pretty sure to have at least three kinds of weather.
Then some general ones, and—oh yes, the birth of a son to the Czar."

"Good Lord! But he has only girls!"

"I'm taking a chance it will be a boy this time. I can go and get
back without anybody knowing I've been out of town."

Keeley agreed.

Then came the problem of figuring out what would happen during
that month. In the three weeks preceding my departure, in addition
to my daily cartoon, I drew the extra ones that I hoped would fit any
emergency which might arise during my absence.

The World's Fair at St. Louis was good for three or four, relative to
the activities of the various states. The Presidential campaign—Roosevelt and Fairbanks against Alton Parker—would offer another dozen

timely subjects. I knew also, from my observation of former campaigns, that Congressman Grosvenor of Ohio would issue his quadrennial prediction of the result—a prediction that generally put nearly every state in the Union save Texas into the Republican column. It was also foreordained that the usual crop of campaign lies would blossom forth during my absence, so there was a cartoon to hit off such a condition. September 1 was the opening of the oyster season, and the cartoon of that day expressed the activity at Oyster Bay where Theodore Roosevelt was living. There was a Labor Day cartoon and several to fit assorted Chicago weather. Then I made half a dozen cartoons of mildly didactic nature for the Sunday editions. Half a dozen more illustrated child life in the good old summertime. And two or three war cartoons were prepared to fit probable conditions in the Orient.

The last cartoon I drew was one in which I took a gambler's chance. It represented the Czar smiling broadly as he said, "It's a boy!"

Another reason I was anxious to get away just then was that *Bird Center* was being dramatized by Glen MacDonough. I dreaded the nervous strain of the opening night. It was being widely advertised.

It so happened that the night *Bird Center* made its first appearance on the stage in New York was the night we lost in mid-ocean on the international date line, so I never did live through the opening performance of my first—and only—play.

Martin Egan, with whom I had lived in Manila, was head of the Associated Press in Japan, with access to all sources of news. During my few busy days in Tokyo I sent no dispatches home, but I wrote an illustrated account on the way back. When I got home, few people outside the office knew I had been away. The public evidently considered the cartoons as timely as usual—which may or may not be a welcome commentary.

Czar Nicholas did all he could to help me. It *was* a boy.

A few years later I had in mind a more elaborate vacation. In 1906 Kirk Brice and I planned a trip that would take five months.

I was not entitled to this vacation either, and inasmuch as it was manifestly impossible for me to do *five* months of cartoons ahead, I had to find some sort of substitute scheme that would satisfy the *Tribune*. I asked Tom Browne, the well-known English cartoonist, to come over from London and take my place. But at the last minute he found he couldn't get there until a month after I had to leave.

Then I bethought me of an interesting way to bridge the gap. I would ask thirty eminent cartoonists from all over the country each to do one for a day of the month. This idea, which I called the Cartoon Symposium, met with immediate approval.

I wrote them all, telling them of my projected trip, and of my dilemma, and saying that any subject, in their own style, would be

*W. A. Rogers Expresses Envy*

welcome. They responded generously. Many were famous at the time, others have become so since, and still others have gone into different activities. Clifford Berryman and Homer Davenport were two who contributed. Among them all they covered the country.

With the substitute cartoon business satisfactorily arranged, I could turn to the red tape of preparation for the trip.

If anyone aspires to be a traveler, he must arrive before the picture post card; otherwise he is just a tourist. In 1906 Kirk Brice and I thought we could be travelers in Central Asia. However, it would not be true to say that we had no more serious motive than to get off the beaten track.

No other part of the world has such an appeal to the imagination. Here, Jason searched for the Golden Fleece; here, Mithridates led his armies; here, Tamerlane, Genghis Khan and Alexander exhausted the fields of possible conquest. The Caspian, Khurasan, Samarkand are names that suggest a kaleidoscopic vision of Georgian beauties, Persian gardens, turquoise hills, torrid sands and Mongol hordes. There are frankincense and myrrh in the sound of them; they send one scurrying past more peaceful charms. The region is said to be the birthplace of the human race, and as a birthright it has fallen heir to more sustained turmoil than Europe itself.

Fortunately for victims of the wanderlust, there are interregnums wherein the Christian wayfarer, if properly accredited, may invade the scenes made memorable by ages of warlike khans and bloodthirsty Mongols. The invasion of Central Asia by Kirk Brice and me added nothing to the bloody annals of the district.

The first essential preliminary was to obtain the special permits from Russia, as the district was under military rule at that time, and the ordinary passport would not avail. If you could prove that you were not an Englishman intent on investigation of Russian activities on the northern borders of Persia and Afghanistan, there was no real difficulty in this.

The next preliminary to such a trip is to deafen your ears to the advice and warnings of those who have gone before, else you will never start. But all the drawbacks so persistently offered for our sober contemplation served only to make the outlook more alluring. And as usual we found that the difficulties of travel are proportional to the distance you are away from them. We saw evidence of disease but felt no special fear of contracting any. We were mobbed once in Persia, arrested once in Turkestan, and robbed of some of our luggage in Russia. But altogether the trip was most pleasant and delightful. We ate well and slept well, except for one night in Persia when, for reasons too numerous to mention, we remained in a defensive attitude.

Until we reached Odessa, our track was so beaten it is not necessary to describe it. Once across the border we discovered a very pleasant characteristic of the Russians—a disposition to aid helpless travelers who do not speak the language. This was as useful as it was novel to anyone accustomed to the brusque American way of handling the traveling public.

Odessa was under martial law—"a state of siege," they called it— and looked like an armed camp, but my main recollection is of a boil on my cheek which was conspicuous and painful, and another on my neck. When we dined with important functionaries I couldn't wear a collar, which was very embarrassing.

A Black Sea steamer took us eastward. At Novorossiisk where we had intended to disembark, we found that rioters had seized the railway and no trains were running, so we remained on board as far as Batum. Here we landed during the funeral services of the American vice-consul, who had just been murdered.

From Batum, we took a train to Tiflis, a most curious city. The

Kura River divides it in half, rushing through a great gorge on the
sides of which the city is built. Each of the more numerous nationalities lived in a separate quarter, but there was constant strife between
the Tartars and the Armenians, with the Russian Cossacks always
ready to gallop in with their knouts and rifles.

In Tiflis we engaged our dragoman. We had some trouble in finding one, and were not much impressed with the seventy-year-old
Johannes. When we left him, weeks later, we were convinced he was
one of the most adroit, efficient and companionable people in the
world. He had even shared most of our games and pleasures.

As a starter, to test him out, we made a little side trip down into
Armenia, to Erivan in the shadow of Mount Ararat, and to Etch-
miadzin, seat of the Armenian pope.

When we returned to Tiflis we found that a bomb had been thrown
at the governor the day before. He and the chief of police were driving through the main street when the bomb was tossed, killing a
couple of Cossack guards. The chief jumped out of the carriage and
shot the two nearest innocent bystanders and the incident was closed
with honor to all parties involved.

The Caucasus Mountains cross diagonally from the Caspian to the
Black Sea. The great 12,000-foot barrier of ice-capped peaks marks
the boundary between Europe and Asia. The pass has been a great
gateway since ancient times, and as each century brought its vast
armies of conquest surging through from east to west or west to east,
there were stragglers left behind in the Caucasus. There is probably
no other place in the world where so many nationalities are jammed
together. Ordinarily a mail coach ran through the pass by the Georgian
Military Road, but revolts and rioting had so upset the service that
we had to get our own carriage and four horses.

We left the Hotel de Londres the last of May. From Tiflis to
Vladikavkaz at the northern end of the pass is 135 miles. It was a
wonderfully picturesque drive with old castles and watchtowers and
deep valleys and thousands on thousands of sheep and cattle. In many
respects the people were just as they had been 3,000 years before, and
all the time we were reminded of Biblical characters.

Our carriage was the sum total of traffic on the road. Although we
saw many bands of soldiers in the mountains we were not molested.
By the second night we were driving through the damp and cold of
the dense clouds that were massed about the snowy summits.

We passed Mount Kazbek, where Prometheus was supposed to have been bound. Then came the wildly grand scenery of Dariel Gorge, eight miles long and a mile deep. Valley after valley crisscrossed the gorge, with little villages, each speaking a separate language. The miserable little settlement of Mishket boasted of having been founded by the great-great-great-grandson of Noah. The Crusaders also passed this way, leaving old French names.

On the third evening we descended into Vladikavkaz and took a train for Baku on the Caspian Sea. We found the town barely recovered from riots of a few months before, in which thousands of people were killed. The burned and wrecked business blocks were eloquent reminders, and the nerves of the community were still on edge. A new outbreak was expected momentarily, and the slamming of a door was enough to send the citizens scurrying to the cyclone cellar.

You will, by now, have perceived that the time and place of our trip had been well selected for a couple of romantics seeking relief from the pleasant comforts of conventional summer outings.

To complete our outfit and get our food for the caravan trip, we stayed in Baku several days, and had most delectable squab and stuffed chicken at the little hotel. Just as we had almost run out of cigars, we chanced on a shop which had Corona Coronas, and Henry Clays, and Hoyo de Montereys and other good brands. In our excitement we bought up the whole stock, which cost some 300 rubles—$150.

When we went on board the steamer in Baku the moon was just rising above the eastern rim of the Caspian Sea. I have never seen a richer, yellower moonrise. Perhaps the fact that the Caspian is nearly a hundred feet below sea level imparts to the atmosphere some peculiar necromancy. Or perhaps nature strives harder with its aesthetic effects as a compensation to those who are compelled to live in Baku. For living is hard in Baku. I have never been in a place where the air seemed so full of menace and danger, where there was a threat of tragedy in nearly every face, and where the grim terrors of racial feuds were only half disguised by a barbarous half-drunken gaiety.

We crossed the Caspian to Krasnovodsk, the first town in Russian Turkestan. From here a military railway with good sleeping and eating accommodations crosses the desert to Andizhan, a distance of 1,700 miles.

We took this railway as far as Ashkhabad.

## ∽ 32 ∽

## Central Asian Caravan

To THE average mind the word "Persian" conjures up a delectable picture. Swaying camels resting at a cool oasis, dusky bazaars hung with silken rugs, the bulbul singing in the purple twilight, and soft moonlight flooding the gardens and the poppy fields with splendor.

One by one these ideas crumbled away. They may be found in other parts of Persia, but not where we went.

From Ashkhabad, the Persian frontier lay to the southward just over the blue hills of the Kopet Dagh. Beneath our windows the ancient caravan trail led away invitingly; a four days' "march" would take us to Meshed, capital of the province of Khurasan and the Holy City of Persia, where a Christian is as unwelcome as triplets.

What Mecca is to the orthodox Mohammedan, Meshed is to the Persian. If one of the faithful goes to Mecca, he is henceforth and forever entitled to be called Hadji, a title outranking that of Colonel in Kentucky. If one goes to Meshed, he earns the title of Meshedi. We decided to qualify.

But there were other things necessary besides the decision to go to Meshed. We had to arrange for transport, and also to obtain a special pass permitting us to depart from Russian Turkestan. Furthermore, we needed another pass to enter Persia once the Russians had released us. So the diplomatic machinery was set in motion and we settled down in Ashkhabad to wait.

The guide and interpreter whom we had hired in Tiflis was an Armenian, who for reasons of safety carried a Persian passport. At various times he would alter his nationality to suit the occasion if there was any strategic advantage to be gained thereby. His name, Johannes, made him part German. However variegated his nationality may have been, he was a jewel when it came to arranging details. He was the diplomatic machinery referred to, and to him was assigned the delicate job of obtaining the various permits.

Meanwhile, he said, would we like to see some fine carpets? They were Tekke carpets—he never used the word rug—and excellent specimens.

So we looked—and were persuaded to buy.

That was fatal, for as long as we could be induced to buy rugs in Ashkhabad it could never be arranged for us to start for Persia. The word spread through the bazaars that foreigners were buying. It leaked out through the Akkal Oasis and spread to the desert. Turkomans and Tartars and Persians began arriving at our modest hotel. The air was full of dust from visiting rugs. In one day Johannes' commission on the sale of rugs to us had doubtless exceeded his wages for the whole trip to Meshed.

At last we rebelled, and insisted that unless the expedition to Persia started immediately, Johannes was likely to find himself playing the leading role in a Russian atrocity. So he shrugged his shoulders, mustered up a semblance of energy and fared forth to complete arrangements.

When the day of departure arrived, Johannes became the incarnation of activity, and he could look busier without cause than any human being I ever saw. The hour was set for ten o'clock. At ten Johannes burst in, and at first glance we supposed he had received bad news from home. But no. It was the road, which had been washed away by a flood. We could not go for a day or two.

How far away was the break in the road? we asked.

Oh, out in the mountains, thirty versts.

How did he know?

Oh, a Persian had arrived with the news, but it was necessary to await further details.

He was crestfallen when we indicated that we would proceed as far as possible, and at once.

Out in front of the hotel a peculiar-looking vehicle was drawn up—a sort of victoria built for crossing rock piles. It was dusty and rickety and was preceded by four drooping ponies. Valentine, a Russian driver in a faded pink blouse, sat on the box like patience on a monument. His patience asserted itself as long as the heavy work of loading continued. Johannes did a prodigious amount of ordering around, and I suspect the assembled Ashkhabadians thought Kirk and I were merely part of his suite.

At noon we drove down the wide street, ponies galloping to the crack of Valentine's whip, and clattered out onto the road across the plains to the foot of the Kopet Dagh, eight miles away. Donkey caravans, transport wagons with high wheels and a sort of prairie schooner superstructure, and pilgrims along the roadside, all paused in their progress to watch us pass.

Well, it was a terrible trip. The roads were fearful. The dust was fearful. The heat was unbelievable—110 degrees in the shade, and our carriage was open. Mirages hung in the distance all the time— lakes surrounded by trees—yet it was absolutely barren except where a small village surrounded an oasis. At one town the gutters were running with—could it be blood? Our hair stood on end. But no, there had been a decree to do away with all foreign dyestuffs which were replacing the native vegetable dyes that give the Persian rugs such magnificent colors.

All was dirty, slovenly and backward beyond words. We stopped at night anywhere—the caravansaries were simply native houses which we had to clean out. In the evenings we used to shake dice. Old Johannes joined in with great success, though we watched him carefully.

Early on the first afternoon we entered the foothills of the Kopet Dagh, and for three or four hours wound through a series of stony, forlorn hills. We came upon hundreds of camels feeding by the way, their 500-pound burdens of cotton or oil or rugs heaped by the roadside. Biblical shepherds attended them.

We had hoped to reach the frontier before nightfall, but the break in the road delayed us. A little stone causeway that crossed a gulch had really been swept away—as Johannes had said—and the rocks that had formed it were strewed for a quarter of a mile down the bed of the gulch. A plunge down a perpendicular bank, a wild clatter across the rock-strewed gorge, and a frenzied pull up the opposite bank showed that our equipage was indeed built for such heroic demands. But we made only twenty-seven versts or eighteen miles that day.

Sometimes at night we were awakened by what, in my opinion, is the most characteristic and memorable sound of the East, the sound that marks the progress of a camel caravan.

On the trails, bound for Persia or Afghanistan or India, the camels are roped together in groups of ten. The leader carries a bell of a certain note, the eight middle camels wear little tinkling bells, and the end one has a great copper bell that hangs from its side and with every step gives forth a deep, rich boom as soft and melodious as the gong of a Burmese temple.

For many minutes before the van comes abreast of the posthouse, the bells may be heard. There are no sounds of footsteps, for the camel tread is noiseless. In the uncertain light the swaying figures of the animals pass like so many ghosts, silent except for the sweetest music of bells that one can imagine. This medley of notes produces a curious harmony that ever afterward connotes for you the fascination of the East. Only the tom-tom has a more mysterious potency.

For hours, it seems, the caravan is passing. You are asleep long before the rear guard rocks by and the jangling of bells is replaced by the "silence of the East."

We arose betimes each morning, as the old travelers say, had tea from a samovar, and hard-boiled eggs, and by six o'clock were once more on our way across the gaunt and somber landscape, till we arrived at the walls of Meshed.

There was, according to Johannes, no suitable caravansary, so he took us to the residence of the head of the British bank. This kind gentleman, apparently glad to see a rare outsider, allowed us to make his home our headquarters. It was modern and comfortable, with a lovely garden, inside a high protective wall.

The fame of Meshed is due to the fact that in the ninth century the remains of the pre-eminently holy Imam Reza and about eight other Imams or prophets were here interred.

Also buried here, although quite incidentally, is the Caliph of Bagdad, Harun-al-Raschid, who was to me much more interesting than Mr. Reza.

The holy shrine stands in the center of the city, and there is sanctuary for a quarter of a mile on every side. All criminals are safe within the Bast or dividing line. And no Christians are allowed within it. There had been, in 1906, only a few authenticated cases of successful entry.

Each year thousands on thousands of Shiite Mohammedans come from all parts of Central Asia to worship. As their religion sanctions the custom of temporary marriages during this pilgrimage, it is a religion people seem to like very much.

In Meshed, Main Street is eighty feet wide. Down the center of this Oriental Champs-Élysées runs a canal, or more accurately a dirty ditch, spanned by frail foot bridges and planks. It serves as drinking fountain, laundry and public bath. It is lined by irregular rows of mulberry, plane and willow, mostly rather decrepit and forlorn, and beyond them is the ramshackle arcade of the bazaars.

Within, in a sort of twilight, the teeming life of the Orient goes on amid the rugs and the odors. Among the dense crowds may be seen the white-turbaned mullah and the half-caste dervish; the portly merchant and the travel-stained pilgrim; the supercilious sayid in a green turban and the cowering Sunni who has ventured into a stronghold of the enemy; black-browed Afghans, handsome Uzbegs, wealthy Arabs, wild Bedouins, Indian traders, Caucasian devotees, Turks, Tartars, Mongols, Tajiks. Everybody was shouting and shrieking at the same time.

In our carriage we returned to Ashkhabad by the same route we had come. We then proceeded by train, stopping over at Merv, Bokhara, Samarkand and Tashkent. Merv was at one time called Queen of the World and had 2,000,000 inhabitants. As we happened here to wear our English sun helmets, we were mistaken for Englishmen and arrested, but were released upon proof that we were Americans.

In Tashkent it was necessary to call on the governor and commander in chief for permits for rifles for shooting. It was likewise necessary for this purpose, we were told, to wear long-tailed evening clothes. We had carried them with us especially for such an emergency. Through the broiling streets in the blazing sun we drove, acutely self-conscious although no stir was created. But did the general and his staff, in uniform, greet us with some surprise? Or was it only our imagination? We obtained two little Krupp double-barreled rifles.

Andizhan was the end of the railway. We went on by carriage again to Osh, and from here started the best part of our trip.

We—or rather Johannes—organized a caravan, but not the camel variety. We had horses. There were five attendants for the pack animals.

From Osh to Kashgar in Chinese Turkestan, now Sinkiang, was 250 miles over the Alai Mountains. There would be no houses on the road, only the felt tents of nomads feeding their flocks there in summer.

Our usual method was to send a man ahead to arrange with the headman of a village to have a tent emptied for us and moved to a clean piece of ground. When we arrived the kibitka or yurt was beautifully decorated with carpets, friezes and soft sleeping rugs. A sheep had been freshly killed, and curds and milk brought in and sometimes kumiss, which is fermented camel's or mare's milk.

Then, in exchange, everyone who had anything the matter came to us to be doctored! Being white, we were supposed to know. We prescribed for everything, but drew the line at surgical operations.

My gold tooth caused a tremendous sensation. It served as a further passport into the good graces of the people, who were all kind and friendly.

In the higher mountains we stopped for a couple of days to hunt ibex. We went farther up on yaks—our memorable "yakback trip through the Kipchak country"—and then followed the native mountaineers on foot over places I never dreamed I could cross—up to 14,000 feet. We had several shots at ibex but no luck.

Eleven thousand feet up, we paused for several days in the Alai Valley, to rest among the wild flowers, great masses of color against the dramatic backdrop of the ice-capped Pamirs off to the south.

Sometimes the trails were dangerous. We had to skirt the edge of gorges, with the river below supposed to be ninety feet deep and the footing for our horses exceedingly precarious. Once the trail was broken and we had to descend and ride through the very edge of water, where we could not see what lay under our feet. Often we were lost entirely. Sometimes there were long rides between drinks, a trying ordeal in the heat, though we carried raisins and chocolate to tide us over.

By the end of two weeks of this sort of riding there was not much general conversation left. We used to sing a good deal, and indulge in fanciful conversations.

"How do you like the little sunset I arranged for you this evening?"

"I put a good deal of effort into that particular landscape. Have you any suggestions?"

All our rations began to run out, even my stock of cigars. Kirk eked out his supply with cigarettes, so they lasted longer, and he used to tease me along with "If you're good today, I'll give you a cigar."

Finally we left the grasses and flowers and turned in along great rivers among bare eroded mountains, queer, fantastic and unfriendly. Then we began to meet people, to pass trees, houses, gardens. Away ahead lay the town of Kashgar.

Upon arrival, we went directly to the Russian consul, Colonel Kolokoloff, who kindly arranged for us to take a house which was then vacant, quite an elegant house overlooking the river. It was also arranged for Kirk and me to lunch with the taotai of Kashgar, the native Chinese ruler. We were warned that he would wait on us himself and would follow us out as we backed from his presence.

His was a typical Chinese residence, with several courts and gateways before one reached the main compound. The table was set with a lot of little things, like candied fruit, nothing solid. The taotai poured the tea. We stood up to eat. There was no talking, but a vast amount of smiling and bowing.

Finally the taotai and some other Chinese dignitaries escorted us to the door and bowed extra-ceremoniously. Then they followed us to the next gate. We backed all the way as per instructions. There ensued another formal bowing. From yard to yard we backed, clear to the outer gate, each time repeating the performance. We had difficulty keeping our faces straight.

From Kashgar there were two ways out. We might have gone south over the Karakorum Mountains, 17,500 feet high at the pass, and along the corner of Tibet. An eight weeks' caravan trip would take us into Kashmir; then out through India. Instead we chose to go north by caravan across the Tien Shan Mountains to Russian post roads in Siberia, follow these roads a thousand miles to the Irtish River at Semipalatinsk, and thence several hundred more miles down that river to the Trans-Siberian railroad at Omsk.

After riding through the mountains we reached Naryn on Kirk's thirty-third birthday, which we celebrated with champagne and also with the purchase of a native tarantass, a carriage in which you can stretch out and sleep. You are supposed to change horses at the post stations and thus travel twenty-four hours a day. The vehicle and horses cost us, I remember, 250 rubles or $125. In addition it was necessary to rent another carriage for Johannes and the luggage.

North we went, past Issiq Köl, a lake in which a city is said to be buried whose towers can sometimes be seen. A storm broke, with thunder and lightning—at 12,000 feet we traveled along in the storm clouds themselves. We struck the Russian post road, but even Johannes was unable to get fresh horses at each station, so we gave up riding all night. Anyhow the jolting along without springs hadn't been very soporific.

Vyernyi near Lake Balkash was the first large town. North and still north we drove to Sergiopol and finally to Semipalatinsk whence we went by steamer 500 miles down the river to Omsk, then by courier express to Moscow.

The trip in the tarantass had taken us fourteen days, rather monotonous ones across the steppes, seeing only occasional Kirghiz with their flocks. At Semipalatinsk we naturally wished to sell the carriage, but equally naturally no one wished to buy. I suggested burning it up, but we finally weakened and left it to the crafty Johannes with whom we parted regretfully.

## ~ 33 ~

## Just for Variety

IF I HAVE had any conscious plan of action during my life, it may be based on the theory that each passing year will seem longer if it is marked by some distinctive feature, some new experience. Varying the smooth daily routine of life makes for a feeling of accomplishment, revitalizes a person, and gives him a vantage point from which to evaluate the rut he may have fallen into.

Hence the early summer of 1907 found me again on the ocean, this time with Albert Beveridge.

Beveridge was a fine companion, always interesting, always amusing. While it must be admitted that in his younger days he was too outspoken, too assertive, overdressy, yet the widespread opinion of his conceit and pomposity would have changed, could others have seen him as I did. He knew what people said of him and he laughed about it. He had a swarm of devoted friends, whose friendship he could not have held had they not discovered the sterling depth of his character. Never in all his career in the Senate was there a word reflecting on his integrity.

When I was in college I remember hearing of the young DePauw speaker who was sweeping all the oratorical prizes before him. He was elected to the Senate in 1899. As a visiting Senator to the Philippines, he followed with me an expedition to Antipolo. He was clever enough to realize that the Philippines would in future be a subject of major policy in the United States, and came out to get his impressions first hand. When he returned to the Senate, his voice carried authority.

George Ade, Sam Blythe and I accompanied him on his special train through Indiana in 1910. He never seemed tired, could make many speeches during the day, was always too quick-witted to be caught by the hecklers, and left his audiences cheering wildly. As he grew older his words became simpler, less florid, consequently even more appealing and effective.

In his frequent long letters to me, he always addressed me as "J. J.," which, he explained, stood for "Gentle John."

Since I was also an old friend of Catherine Eddy, I had long been aware of the Senator's admiration for her. This feeling was reciprocated, but her family were unenthusiastic. Beveridge counted on changing their feeling for him. So when the Eddy family went abroad early in the year, he and I arranged to follow. Now, in our stateroom on the *Kaiser Wilhelm der Grosse*, he told me day after day of his hopes.

In Paris Albert and I stopped together at the Hotel Meurice, and in a few days he was happy to announce that the date of the wedding had been set, to take place in Berlin where her brother Spencer Eddy was Ambassador. He wanted me to act as best man, but my leave was too short.

After I knew that the Senator's plans were working out happily, I left for a motor trip through the chateau country. I had some romantic affairs of my own on hand.

On my return to Paris I dined with Booth Tarkington and his wife on the Rue de Tournoy near the Luxembourg Gardens.

The year after I graduated from Purdue, Tark had come there from Phillips Exeter to take a special course. He became a Sigma Chi brother and I used to see a lot of him when I went down from Chicago. With active and oftentimes startling effectiveness he was absorbing the reactions and psychology of youth in all its phases; this was later to enable him to become the literary mouthpiece for "Penrod" and of youth in general. But beside his many pranks he brought into Purdue something of the cosmopolitan East, and he seemed to have been gifted with everything that fortune could bestow. He drew well, had a remarkable singing voice, was a good actor as well as playwright and had a charm of manner that made him irresistible. Not only the nicest young ladies of Lafayette but a procession of visiting young ladies felt his fascination. The only thing that could possibly interfere with a brilliant future was the possibility that he might not exert his undoubted powers; that, being able to do so many things well, he might never concentrate on one. Entirely due to the efforts of his sister, who adored him, he kept at writing until his first stories were accepted, *Monsieur Beaucaire* and *The Gentleman from Indiana*.

The evening in Paris started out normally enough. Also present were Mr. and Mrs. William Hereford. We sang and reminisced until midnight. Then we decided to go to the Panthéon Restaurant for a bite before bed. We were still there when the place closed at two.

Tark suggested that we walk down the Boulevard St. Michel to the

Seine. He had with him his frisky little dog Gamin, and, needing something to hold the dog in check, he hailed a fiacre. He bowed low and addressed the *cocher* as "Monseigneur le Prince." The *cocher* did likewise and asked what he wished. With Chesterfieldian courtesy Tark explained—a strap to tie his dog. The *cocher*, beaming widely, deprecated the fact that he needed all his straps to keep his harness intact, but not to be outdone in civility he dismounted and produced a bit of string from somewhere. Tark gravely offered him a cigarette.

As we walked on, Tark explained vividly the historical significance of the places we passed. By four in the morning the early market carts began coming into the city. Outside the market place dozed an old woman with ferns to sell. Tark gazed at the hollow square of greenery, then removed his hat. The woman wakened and he bought an armful. A little farther on we came to an old man, sound asleep on the curb beside his vegetables. Once more Tark removed his hat and, laying the load of ferns on the sleeper, stood in an attitude of great reverence. This awakened the old man who glanced with astonishment at the funereal effect on his breast. Then he began to laugh.

"Monsieur is most amiable," he said, "but do you not think I will catch cold with these damp leaves on me?"

After depositing the sleepy ladies of the party at home, we decided to walk some more. Tark stopped a gendarme and asked how far to Chartres. The perturbed gendarme gesticulated frantically. "But, monsieur, that is impossible!—but impossible—to walk all that distance in dancing slippers!"

Tark fed some cigarettes to a horse, and when we had walked on a considerable distance, he decided he'd been discourteous, so we had to go all the way back to apologize to the horse. Then we climbed into the fiacre. As we drove past the women flushing the streets in the dawn, he rose up in the carriage and said to each with a great flourish of his hat, "Ah, madame, vous êtes ravissante!"

Tark and I had breakfast at Pré Catalan.

In later life, to my regret, our paths diverged widely, although I always intended, if I was ever in the vicinity, to drop in at his studio, the hull of an old ship grounded near his garden in Kennebunkport.

Twice in 1908 I managed to "play hooky."

During the winter Charles Atkinson and I went to the Grand Canyon. My first view of that immensity was through a snowstorm, with blue-black clouds boiling up out of the gorges. Every time a sight-seer said something complimentary, a new peak blushed rosy-red. According to our weight we were allotted mules of proportionate strength, and we were fortified, as we started down the trail, by the reflection that no one had ever been lost in this daring feat on which we were embarked. These and other reflections I embodied in an article for *Appleton's Magazine*, a reprint of which, published by Fred Harvey, was still on sale at the canyon when, once again in a snowstorm, I took my family down in 1931 for a night at the Phantom Ranch.

By springtime I felt I needed more fresh air.

My very first trip outside of Indiana had been a visit to Chicago with a group of students from Purdue to see Booth and Barrett in *Julius Caesar*. At the old lake-front Exposition Building I had bought for my mother one of those vases of wax flowers cunningly mounted under a glass dome. I thought it the most beautiful thing I had ever seen. All the rest of the time in Chicago I had carried this contraption around with me. When I presented it to my mother, she expressed the greatest delight. Possibly she was as good an actor as Booth or Barrett.

Later I built her a house. Now I was in a position to do something else. I wanted to show her some of the world which I found so intensely interesting. So when the Hamburg-American Line started the first of the West Indian cruises in 1908, I booked passage for a thirty-day trip on the *Oceana*. George Ade and Ort Wells went along, and, as companion for my mother, a female Purdue classmate, unhappily married, and also unhappily grown fat.

It didn't seem to bother any of us, least of all herself, that my mother was suffering from severe neuritis. At the time of departure she was in such a condition that I didn't know whether we could even get her to New York. Then she was seasick. When I saw her lying there so frail and ill, I said, "Why did I do this?" I felt that I had inflicted this terrible ordeal on her just because I was so eager to have her share my pleasure in travel.

At St. Pierre, Martinique, we had to land at a rickety pier high above the water level. Husky sailors leaned down and, one by one, hoisted the passengers up the six-foot gap. Mother's neuritis had settled in her right arm and shoulder, but in the excitement of landing none of us remembered it. One of the sailors reached down, grasped Mother's right hand and, with a mighty yank, landed her on the pier. It must have hurt excruciatingly.

But nothing ever ruffled my mother. Strange to say, she felt much better afterward and enjoyed the cruise enormously. I have often wondered whether she had this in mind when, during the following years, she heard me mention, one after another, the young ladies who occupied my attention.

"Would you like to travel with her?" Mother always asked. This was the acid test.

## ～ 34 ～

## Studio Gossip

MY FIRST studio was in the Fine Arts Building, that unique one among Chicago office buildings, for so many years the center of the city's artistic and cultural life.

In its spacious lobby the patrons of the Studebaker Theatre relaxed between the acts of such productions as George Ade's *Sultan of Sulu* and the Tarkington-Wilson play, *The Man from Home*, with Olive Wyndham and William Hodge.

Roullier's, Ackerman's, Winn's—the shops were famous. On the way up the ten stories in the elevator, one glimpsed kaleidoscopic strata of antique furniture, etchings, lamps, pottery, foreign glassware, handmade jewelry, artistic photographs, fine needlework and old silver. The Alliance Française was here, and the Cordon, a professional women's club within whose portals of carved oak visiting speakers were always being entertained; it was here that the old maids, heavily veiled, and the ingénues, surreptitiously assembled to hear Brieux on Free Love, and all he talked about was stage technique. The French Theatre, the New Theatre, and Maurice Browne's Little Theatre here abode their destined hour. Here also was Mrs. Milward Adams' School of Dramatic Art and the Carruthers School of Music. Down the corridors echoed the mingled jangle of innumerable music lessons, and the penetrating scales of opera stars in the making.

As you rose toward the upper floors, the atmosphere became thicker. Lorado Taft's studio and those of Charles Francis Brown, Oliver Dennett Grover and, later, Ralph Fletcher Seymour were there, and Ralph Clarkson's, a huge one with sloping north windows, where, among his canvases, the Little Room met and exuded a delightful aura of causerie and cleverness, resulting from nothing more inspiring than tea poured by Clara Laughlin or Harriet Monroe. On Friday afternoons local and visiting celebrities such as Henry B. Fuller and Hamlin Garland gravitated there naturally.

Only a few doors down the hall from this was my own studio, a big skylighted one, large enough to accommodate my constantly growing collection of things from everywhere I had ever been.

When the door opened one was confronted with rugs from Bokhara and Ashkhabad, bronze filigree lamps from Japan, the tawny skin of my first lion. There were heads of African game; tribal shields and weapons; assorted guns and historic shell fragments; three of Carl Akeley's groups, inscribed to me in the bronze; the tattered ensign used by us correspondents in going from ship to shore in Manila Bay, to prevent being fired upon by our own ships.

The burlap walls were covered with flags from Spanish ships, pictures, photographs and other mementoes, such as my pass for the Khyber Pass, and the hemp contract. I never allowed that faded burlap to be cleaned lest the old familiar arrangement be disturbed, and the old familiar dinginess be unduly brightened. Here in my shirt sleeves I worked for twenty-three years.

Often there were knocks on my door. Whole grades of starry-eyed youngsters from the city schools came to gaze in astonishment at this strange assortment of things beyond their ken. Occasionally "Seeing Chicago" tours stopped in. Sometimes, if I were too busy, I would not open the door. Once, after a prolonged knocking had ceased, I found William Jennings Bryan's card tucked underneath.

However, I seem to have evolved a system whereby, after I settled on an idea, I could draw steadily on my cartoon, and at the same time entertain visitors who conducted a one-way conversation without in the least interrupting my work.

Charles G. Dawes, not so well known then, was one of my most frequent callers. He liked to sit and talk. He has always been an able raconteur with the keenest kind of wit.

A pleasant young insurance man used to come to tempt me with his no doubt excellent wares. His name was Franklin P. Adams.

Younger artists, aspiring to draw cartoons, began to bring their early work to show me. Among them, as I remember, were Frank King, Frank Willard, Milton Caniff, Harold Gray and Fontaine Fox. I should be happy to feel that any suggestions of mine may have helped them up even one rung of the ladder to fame.

A Mrs. McMartin dropped in often—Laura May she was to her friends. She was a kindly, generous person from Wisconsin and was lonely in Chicago. She lived at the Great Northern where her husband was the hotel doctor. In after years, by one of those tricks of fate, she became the famous international hostess, Mrs. James W.

Corrigan. A very satisfactory story is told about her. When her second husband died, he left to his wife the controlling interest in a large steel company, supposed to be worth upward of $50,000,000. Along in early '29 a group of sagacious capitalists decided to buy her out. It would be simple, they thought, to drive an advantageous bargain with a lady socially occupied in Europe. But it seemed that the lady who was to be so skillfully trimmed turned out an astute businesswoman. Came October 1929 and the great crash—she had all the assets and they had all the liabilities.

She lived in France during World War II and was indefatigable in her relief work, selling her own jewels to augment her available funds. Another story tells how, quietly dressed in uniform for one of her errands of mercy, she was descending in a Paris hotel elevator when Frau Göring entered the elevator, bedecked in all the emeralds that had formerly been Laura May's.

Another person who used to come up and talk to me while I drew was Judge Landis. His sense of humor was superb and an hour with him was certain to be rewarding. Sometimes, too, I would sit in his courtroom to watch him unerringly put his finger on the essential point in a case. He had an effective way of deflating pompous attorneys, and of keeping them down to brass tacks. One of a remarkable family of Indiana brothers, Kenesaw Mountain Landis had been private secretary to Walter O. Gresham, Secretary of State in Cleveland's second Cabinet, before he was appointed a Federal judge in Chicago.

It was he who summoned John D. Rockefeller to come and testify in his court; who found the Standard Oil Company guilty of illegal

"OH, JOHN — THIS TWENTY NINE MILLION THEY ARE TALKING ABOUT — IS THAT THE AMOUNT OF THE FINE OR THE FEE?"

"THAT'S JUST THE FINE, MR. ROCKEFELLER"

"CALL THE NEXT CASE!"

practices which had been enormously profitable, and who fined the company $29,000,000. Probably no more startling decision or one more widely discussed has come from any court. It was promptly overruled by the higher courts, but there were countless thousands who believed in its justice and were convinced that the disclosures fully warranted it. In the more exclusive clubs, to which many of his friends belonged, his name was anathema. On the streets, where his striking figure was always recognized, he was cheered.

When the baseball organization of the United States, reeling under the scandals which permeated the professional sport, felt that they must do something to regain public favor, they asked the judge to become czar of that industry. They needed a man of integrity and courage, in whom the whole country would implicitly believe. It was significant that the baseball magnates should have felt that Landis was the only man to fill the requirements. He discussed the offer with me and asked my opinion. I advised him to remain on the bench where a man of his character was needed even more. I came to believe that he was right and I wrong. He cleaned up baseball, our largest national sport; he was spared financial worry in his later years, and his lean face, mass of white hair and humorous eyes became widely known throughout the country.

Once at a knock I opened my studio door to a tall lady, soberly dressed with an unfashionable hat, who stepped inside and without any preamble announced that she had written a poem about the aftermath of the World's Columbian Exposition, and could I use it in a cartoon? I thanked her and said I would read it. She smiled and departed. I didn't like to use contributed poems in my cartoons. Floods of verses would ensue and feelings be hurt. The chances were infinitesimal that this one would be usable; I glanced at it idly, and to my surprise, liked it. I had no idea who the lady was; the poem was not signed. I used it in a rather elaborate architectural cartoon, about which I heard much favorable comment. But I heard nothing from the poet. For more than a year her identity remained a mystery. Then one night I recognized her in a box at the opera. She was Mrs. Emmons Blaine, sister of Cyrus, Harold and Stanley McCormick.

Suggestions for cartoons were often submitted, but the overwhelming majority of these were for one reason or another not usable. They might be too involved, or too violent, contrary to the policy of the paper, or not sufficiently timely. When once in a while I saw fit to use one, I made a practice of adding a plus sign after my signature with the initials of the sender.

In my studio were held the meetings of an unpretentious organization called the McCutcheon Social and Pleasure Club. John Alden Carpenter was a member, and his wife Rue; Ethel Hooper, Harry Harvey, Laurance Ray and Hazel Martyn Trudeau. Since I had known Hazel, Mr. Trudeau had come and gone. Later she became the wife of Sir John Lavery, the portrait painter. Sir John was born in Ireland. When the Irish Free State was launched, he designed the one-pound note for the new currency, using, as part of the symbolism of the design, a woman's head. It was a portrait of Hazel.

Hazel used to tell a story concerning the time she attended a large and impressive reception. Came the moment to give her name to the announcer. "Lady Lavery," she said softly. He leaned forward and whispered behind his hand, "Two doors to the left, madam."

Both Hazel and Rose Chatfield-Taylor were beautiful and both were talented. For a time Rose had a small studio in the Fine Arts Building where she did notable bookbinding. It was called the Rose Bindery. On my bookshelves is a volume of my first collected cartoons which she rebound for me. And on my studio walls hung several of Hazel's sketches, including one of Rue, Ethel and herself, drawn at one of the meetings of the Social and Pleasure Club.

For these occasions I had a piano moved in from a neighboring music school. To hear John Carpenter accompany Harry Harvey in "Gypsy John," or Laurance Ray in "Rolling Down to Rio," was worth five dollars a ticket any day. When they were all in full voice, they added quite an impressive blast to the cacophony in the Fine Arts Building.

About this time several of us took lessons from Maurice and Florence Walton in the Argentine tango—at twenty-five dollars per!—but my dancing never underwent any discernible improvement.

The Auditorium Hotel next door obligingly served meals, *à deux* or more, in my studio. Once I gave a party for the current debutantes. I spent days in preparation of a little silhouette fantasy called "A Day in the Life of a Debutante," copied after something I had seen at Le Chat Noir in Paris. I manipulated the figures by hand. Also I wrote the words of a song and asked John Carpenter to write the music. It was called "A Cocoon Song." I inscribed it "To a Debutante of 1908" and I sent it to five different buds, Lucy Blair, Marion and Barbara Deering, Harriot Houghteling and Peggy Ayer, better known nowadays as Margaret Ayer Barnes, the novelist. I am afraid I let each girl assume what she would!

During winters at a later period grand opera was the most fashion-

able of social activities, and some people liked to get to it on time—
Edith Rockefeller McCormick, for instance. When you dined with
her, the most delectable food was served on solid gold service, but you
had to hold onto the plate with one hand and eat fast with the other
because a footman was always waiting behind your chair to take it
away. As you set match to your after-dinner cigar, while the coffee
was still too hot to drink, a footman invariably announced, "The
ladies are waiting."

Often I had a hard time making these early dinners. Either an idea
wouldn't come or it proved unexpectedly complicated to draw. My
deadline was then seven o'clock, and I had to send the cartoon over
to the *Tribune* by messenger boy. With one eye on the clock I would
pore over that drawing board in a fever of haste. On such occasions
I used to telephone home to have my evening clothes sent down to
me by cab. Once they sent my brother-in-law's clothes. He was six
feet three. I didn't notice until I got into them and the tails nearly
reached my heels. Another time they sent me everything from pumps
to silk hat—except the vest. Well, you simply can't extemporize a
white vest, and full dress without one is just one of the impossible
things, especially to a rather shy young man. So again I was late to
dinner.

Sometimes I had other kinds of trouble. One night I had been invited to dine with Kate and Walter Brewster in Lake Forest. I looked
forward eagerly to the occasion. In my studio at four o'clock the
cartoon was almost completed. There would be ample time to go to
my apartment, dress and catch the North Western train that would
carry me the thirty-odd miles to the party.

Just then the afternoon papers were dropped at the door. A big
story involving Governor Haskell of Oklahoma was spread over the
front page. Obviously that was the cartoon topic for the next morning's paper. Discarding the nearly finished one, I was soon immersed
in the new. Everything else was crowded out of my consciousness.
Three hours later, at five minutes before seven, I took it to the Western Union desk at the Auditorium and hurried a messenger off with
it. A load was off my mind. The cartoon had been drawn under pressure of quick and hard work. Tired, relieved, content, I started for
home without a care in the world. I dined comfortably and presently
was smoking my after-dinner cigar. That certainly was a big story
down in Oklahoma; thank goodness I had caught it in time! I was
the center of a lot of relaxed well-being.

Four days passed. Again I was finishing a cartoon in my studio. Just what happened I don't know. I only recall that my eyes and pen were suddenly arrested at a spot on the paper. Old Mr. Subconscious Cerebration was doing something, at first dimly, then in an explosion of realization. Great Scott, the Brewster dinner! And I had not telephoned or written. It was a crushing moment. What excuse could I give? I was not dead, nor in the hospital, nor out of town. I had no excuse except the hardest one to give a hostess—that it had slipped my mind!

I must confess, tell all, throw myself on Kate's mercy. So forthwith I made my apology in cartoon form: myself crawling on my knees all the way from my studio to her door. In addition I sent a dozen American Beauties. Then I waited for a friendly note of forgiveness. None came. Not a syllable. A blanket of self-commiseration settled over me as week after week passed. Finally I received a lovely letter. She had just returned from Europe, whither she had departed the morning after the dinner. I was forgiven. The clouds cleared.

It wasn't always for opera that I dressed in the studio. There was the Roy McWilliams' futurist party. The famous Armory show had just struck Chicago like a thunderclap. The guests were allowed plenty of latitude, and, as George Ade so pungently expressed it, some took the whole 360 degrees. Notably me. I elected to go as a Matisse nude. Grace Gazette, with a background of Paris liberalism, volunteered to help me in preparing my costume, a suit of long pink underwear, made lumpy in spots, and touched up by Grace's paintbrush to accentuate the anatomy in true Matissian style. Heavily overcoated, I proceeded to the party, and when I made my entry there was a gasp, then pandemonium. So much so that the *Record-Herald* printed a scathing editorial denouncing the profligate tendencies of the times.

# 35

# On Safari

Here I find myself up against a dilemma. I have arrived in my chronicle at the point where I go hunting in Africa. Now the one real book I ever wrote, based of course on articles written first for the *Tribune,* was about that trip—quite a fat book. How can I wind myself up to write again about those delightful nine months when I seem to have said everything so much better than I possibly could again?

The chance to realize one of the more modest of my boyhood ambitions—to hunt big game as in the old woodcuts of daring hunters charging lions or elephants—came, as did most of my adventures, unexpectedly.

In the spring of 1909, Carl Akeley, already famous for hunting exploits, came to Chicago to speak at a meeting of the Wayfarers and show some of his pictures. I must have listened with such popeyed interest that he was flattered, for when I talked with him after the meeting, he asked me to join his forthcoming expedition. It was to consist of himself, his wife Delia, Fred Stephenson, a hunter of many years' experience, and me.

Akeley had recently been called to the White House to discuss President Roosevelt's plans for an African hunting trip after his retirement in March, and had arranged to meet him in Africa. Consequently the *Tribune* was only too glad to let me go.

During the five months that elapsed before I set forth, I went about my daily work with a mind half dazed by the delicious consciousness that I was soon to become a lion hunter. One of the objects of the expedition was Akeley's purpose to record a rhino charge in motion pictures. Stephenson and I were to provoke the charge and allow the angered rhinos to approach within a few yards of the cameras before springing into action. This lent a piquancy to my reflections. I tried some shooting on the target range at Fort Sheridan till my shoulder got black and blue, and then I took boxing lessons to improve my wind.

Stephenson and I arrived in London in August and finished outfitting in those shops that are known to sportsmen from one end of the world to the other. I bought three rifles, a .256 Mannlicher, splendid for long-range shooting; a 9 mm. Mannlicher, large enough for nearly all purposes but not reassuring at close quarters; and a .475 cordite Jeffreys, which has a tremendous impact. The presumption was that I would shoot a lion at long range with the .256; then in the middle distance with the 9 mm., and finally, if there was time, with the .475 cordite. Several thousand rounds of ammunition were acquired. This did not mean that several thousand lions were to be killed. Allowing for a fair percentage of misses, we calculated, with luck, to get two or three.

**Part of the Equipment.**

I had now assembled such an imposing arsenal that I was nervous whenever I thought about it. With such a battery it was a foregone conclusion that something, or somebody, was likely to get hurt.

When Fred Stephenson and I had collected all the supplies we could get in London, I read in the papers the announcement of the world's first aviation meet, to be held in Reims the last week in August. All the famous fliers in the world were expected—the few there then were!

I knew at once I *had* to see it. Fred also wanted to, and a couple of other people. So we all went over to Paris, to the Hotel Castiglione. Next morning, in order to reach Reims by nine o'clock, we had to get up at five. It was the third day of the meet. All morning we inspected planes—like a crowd in a paddock before a horse race.

The flying began in the afternoon. The course was two miles around, with tall pylons at each end. Blériot was there with his little monoplane; the Farmans and Glen Curtiss. The Wrights were not present in person, but other fliers flew their planes, which were catapulted down a runway. All the planes were supposed to fly around the course, if possible. Some didn't even get off the ground. Most flew at an altitude of fifty or sixty feet. There were two or three smashups during the afternoon, and one or two men hurt.

Hubert Latham, flying an Antoinette, was very daring. He actually got up to 400 feet and made us all gasp. Sometime later he tried to cross the Channel but fell in. After several years of flying, he was finally killed in Africa by a Cape buffalo.

Paulhan, flying a biplane, kept going around and around for two hours and forty minutes, thereby establishing a world's record. It was a tremendous achievement. When he ran out of gasoline and landed his plane, he was carried in triumph on the shoulders of the crowd and cordially greeted by President Fallières.

There was no train back to Paris until early morning, so we tried to get rooms in Reims, an utter impossibility. The hotels, the boardinghouses, even the private homes were completely full. We killed time in a restaurant until it closed, then in a music hall until we were put out. We were unable to get back to Paris until five-thirty—a full twenty-four-hour day.

From Paris Stephenson and I went to Italy and sailed from Naples with the Akeleys on the *Adolph Woermann* bound for Mombasa. On the hottest day of the trip, in one of the ports of call when the mercury was spluttering around the top of the thermometer, we heard that Peary had discovered the North Pole. It cooled us off for a while.

The new governor of British East Africa, Sir Percy Girouard, was a fellow passenger. We made the long ride from Mombasa to Nairobi in his special train, stopping en route at Tsavo in memory of the two famous man-eaters. Twenty-eight natives working on the railroad were eaten by them. Their terrible depredations had taken place nine years earlier, as I was coming up the coast from the Boer War.

Just before dawn we wrapped up warmly and went out to sit on the observation seat over the cowcatcher of the engine. On each side of the Uganda railroad was a strip of land protected from the sportsmen and consequently teeming with big game. There were many lion stories as we rode along. One, in particular, I remember.

It was told by a gentleman high in government service, a man of unimpeachable veracity. He said the story is absolutely true, although he refused to swear to it.

Once upon a time there was a caravan of slaves moving through the jungles of Africa. The slave drivers were cruel and they chained the poor savages together in bunches of ten. Each slave wore an iron collar around his neck and the chain passed through this ring and on to the next man. For weeks they marched along, their chains clanking and their shoulders aching sorely. Life was far from pleasant and they watched eagerly for a chance to escape. Finally, one dark night, when the sentinels were asleep, a group of ten succeeded in creeping away into the darkness. They were unarmed and chained from neck to neck, one to another. For several days they made their way steadily toward the coast. They ate fruit and nuts and herbs. All seemed well.

*They Made Their Way Steadily Toward the Coast*

But alas! One night a deep rumbling roar was heard in the jungle through which they were picking their unanimous way! A shudder ran through the slaves. "*Simba!*" they whispered in terror. Here they were, ten days from the coast, and quite defenseless.

Presently the lion appeared, his cruel hungry eyes gleaming through the night. Slowly, slowly he crept toward them. They were frozen with terror, realizing only too well that the lion's intentions were open to grave suspicion. Being chained together, they could not climb more than one tree, and perhaps no tree was big enough to hold more than nine of them. In any case, the horrid tale goes on to relate how the lion gave a frightful roar and leaped on the tenth man.

*The Lion's Intentions Were Open to Grave Suspicions*

The dilemma of the slaves is obvious. They knew better than to disturb a lion while he is eating. They sat still and waited while he greedily devoured their late comrade. Then, surfeited with food, the great beast moved off into the jungle.

Immediately the nine remaining slaves took to their heels, dragging the empty iron ring. They ran until they were exhausted and, after a nap, hurried on again, hopeful once more.

**While the Man-Eater Finished His Supper**

About suppertime, they heard the distant roar of a lion! Nearer it came, and presently the lion's gleaming eyes appeared among the jungle grass. Once again they were frozen with horror as the hungry beast devoured the last man in the row—number nine. As soon as the full-fed lion disappeared, they scrambled up and hiked busily toward the coast, nine days away.

They began to dread the supper hour. The next night the lion caught up with them and devoured number eight, leaving a third empty ring.

For six nights after this the lion caught up with them and diminished their number by six. Finally there was only one man left, and the coast was a full-day's march away. Could he make it? It looked like a desperate chance, but he still had hopes. With pleasure he noticed that the lion was becoming fat and probably could not travel

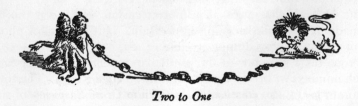

**Two to One**

fast. But with displeasure he also noticed that he had forty feet of chain and nine heavy iron rings to lug along, and the extra weight naturally greatly handicapped him. It was a thrilling race—one day to go, and life or death the prize. Who can imagine the feelings of that poor slave? But with a stout heart he struggled on. The afternoon sun slowly sank toward the western horizon, and——

At this point of the story the locomotive screeched loudly, the wheels scraped on the track, and my official friend leaped off the cow-catcher.

"Here!" I shouted. "What's the finish of that story?"

"I'll tell you next time I see you," he sang out.

The members of the Boyce Balloonograph Expedition also had been on board the *Adolph Woermann*. They were going into the big-game country to photograph wild animals from above. When they had their camp set up outside Nairobi and their 12,000-cubic-foot balloon partially inflated—not fully because somebody thought the hot equatorial sun would expand the gas and burst it—they invited Fred Stephenson to make an ascent. Hundreds of natives sat around spellbound. But the balloon would not rise with Fred, who was six feet five and weighed 230 pounds, until he had thrown out his heavy hunting boots. Then it started at once for some trees a hundred yards away, and was hastily reeled in again.

My turn came next. With only my 140 pounds to lift, the balloon shot up to a thousand feet with no sensation of motion, except that the ground dropped dizzily away. I stood up in the three-by-three basket, clutching the ropes and dramatizing the situation. Supposing the wire snapped? Would I drift a hundred miles, perhaps, into some remote wild region, where the natives would hail me as a god? Or the lions accept me as manna? How would I act under this confusion of identity? I never decided, for I was jerked back to reality with startling abruptness. Everything had been fine so long as we were going up—there was no resistance—but when they started to haul me down, the balloon rushed in wide circles like a kite and the partly filled bag flapped and thundered. That wire looked very frail!

Later Delia Akeley made a 200-foot ascension, which was the last one made by the Balloonograph Expedition. This method of photographing animals proved impracticable.

In 1909 there were few of the gentleman ranchers who later came in such numbers to British East Africa, now called Kenya. The town of Nairobi lay on the edge of the Athi Plains, a broad sweep of sun-bleached grass veldt many miles in extent. Countless numbers of animals fed contentedly within walking distance from the station. Sometimes, as happened the night before we arrived, a lion charged a herd of zebra and stampeded them through the town, trampling fences and gardens.

To supply our expedition of four white people, we had over a hundred natives. There was one headman whose duty it was to run the safari; there were four gunbearers and four second gunbearers; four askaris, armed and in uniform, one of whom was always on guard day and night. Each white person had also his tent boy or personal servant, who took care of his tent, bedding, bath and clothes. Jumma was my tent boy, a Wakamba with filed teeth. Jumma had the happy faculty of never looking rumpled, a trick which I tried hard to learn, but all in vain. Instead, however, I learned from him a useful expression. As nearly as I could make out, his word of approval was "umslopagus." Like smacking lips, the sound of it conveyed satisfaction. When qualified by "eighty-eight," the highest number he was able to count, it signified his highest praise. In subsequent years, when I have opined that certain ladies were umslopagus thirty-seven, or umslopagus minus three, my family has unerringly deduced my drift.

**Our Safari on the March**

There were one cook and four saises or grooms, one for each horse or mule, of which we had four. Then came the many porters. Our eighty were made up of many tribes—Swahili, Wakamba, Kikuyu, Masai, Lumbwa, Kavirondo and others. There were also about twenty "totos" or boys, who started as stowaways, and came out to help when it was too late to send them home. They got nothing but food and lodging, and the experience which would enable them later to become porters.

For weeks or months on safari you live a nomadic tent life amid surroundings so different from what you are accustomed to that you are both mentally and physically rejuvenated. You are among a strange and savage people in strange and savage lands, threatened by strange and savage animals. The life is new; the scenery is new. There are adventure and novelty in every day of such a life, and it is this phase that has the most insistent appeal. Even if one never used his rifle, one would still enjoy life on safari.

Like everyone else who goes to Africa with a gun and a return ticket, I had two absorbing ambitions. I wanted to kill a lion and to

*"A Very Interesting Experience," Said I Coolly,*
*a Couple of Days Later*

live to tell about it. Finally I encountered my first lion. It was not until I had come within forty yards that I could get a clear view of him. He was glaring at me with tail waving angrily, and his mouth was opened in a snarl. I could see that he didn't like me. Luckily I got him before he got me. We had many other lion hunts and tried several different methods of hunting them. We sojourned in the rhino country, where we saw at least a hundred every day. Then we went on to the elephant country. It was of unfailing interest to see how the Akeleys prepared all the animal specimens we obtained for the museum.

A good portion of my African book is devoted to our encounter with the safari of Colonel Roosevelt. This was then news of the first water. All the time I was in Africa I carried an unnecessarily large quantity of Indian rupees, in order to send a cable to the *Tribune* in case anything serious happened to the colonel. I didn't want to arrive at a telegraph station with a world scoop and then be balked by a demand for a cash payment. Years later when I casually mentioned this to Roosevelt's younger sister, Mrs. Douglas Robinson, she was horrified. "Oh, how ghoulish!"

Yes, I suppose so, but that's how newspaper minds work.

When we returned to Nairobi four and a half months later, Fred and I hired a carriage, a low-necked affair drawn by two little mules, and took a drive out of town. Within five minutes we passed sixty impalas, a herd of zebra, and some Coke's hartebeests. They watched us with humorous interest. As long as the carriage kept moving they showed no apprehension. An eland grazed on a hillside and a wart hog trotted away. Suddenly three lions walked slowly out of the nullah and climbed the slope on the other side, not 350 yards away. One was a female, the others were immense males. They stopped to look back, then resumed their stately retreat. Then began a most strange lion hunt. I had heard of the practice of "riding" lions, that is, bringing them to bay on horseback, but to my knowledge no one has ever "galloped" a lion in a carriage drawn by two mules, much less "galloped" three lions at one time. It was a memorable chase. The mules were lashed and the carriage rocked like a Channel steamer. We gained on them, we reduced the distance to 250 yards, we both got

**At Two Hundred and Fifty Yards**

out and knelt to fire. But we both missed and the lions disappeared over the brow of the ravine.

In many respects the technique of hunting has utterly changed since I was there. The hunter now embarks in a well-equipped truck, and in defiance of all obstacles quickly places himself wherever he wants to be in regard to the game. Danger is mitigated to a very pleasant minimum.

There was a good deal of publicity about my return from Africa. Clare Briggs did a cartoon which pleased me very much. It showed a dog, one of my special brand of flop-eared mongrels, standing on the end of a pier looking seaward toward the smoke of a distant steamer. It was captioned, "He's coming back." The *Tribune* took up the refrain "He's coming back" with a series of advertisements. They were inserted into the paper almost anywhere, and were followed in a week or so by another—"Who's coming back?"—so timed that it was topped off with the news of my arrival.

*Retiring in Favor of Rhino*

## ～ 36 ～

## Early Flying

WHEN for the first time I had seen an airplane leave the ground in Reims in 1909, I knew I would never be content until I had flown.

Anything to do with planes fascinated me and I hung around airmen whenever I had a chance. But passengers were not in demand. My own efforts to get off the ground were consistently balked.

In September of 1910 Walter Brookins, up from Dayton in a Wright plane, won a *Record-Herald* prize of $10,000 for flying from Washington Park to Springfield. It is recorded that "as the train had to stop at many stations, he had no difficulty in keeping abreast and at times ahead of it." Before the race Brookins gave an exhibition flight on the lake front. An Associated Press man went with him, so I had no chance.

My disappointment must have been sticking out all over me because the Wrights' manager, Mr. Frank Russell, said he would arrange for me to fly with Brookins in his demonstration in Springfield two days later.

Simultaneously I received a wire saying my Aunt Kate had died and the funeral would be, of all times, two days later! I don't know that it is going to redound to my credit, but I was certainly torn by conflicting emotions. Here was everything all fixed for me to make my first flight, a thing I wanted at that time more than anything else in the world. However, I decided to do my duty, and telegraphed that I could not come to Springfield and why. I have always hoped they believed me!

I wrote to Russell expressing the eager wish that another arrangement might be made. To my delight he told me to come down to Dayton any time. At once I set a date on which I had an evening engagement to speak in Indianapolis. I figured the flight might add valuable matter to my talk. I looked forward to it with eagerness and some apprehension, and I rather hesitated to tell my mother of my plans. What was my chagrin to find myself so delayed en route to the station that I missed my train! I took another one about 11:00 P.M. and woke to find that the engine had broken down! We crawled into Dayton toward noon, three hours late.

"Never mind," said Russell. "We can go out right after lunch."

Simms Station was several miles out of town. When I told Russell of my evening engagement, he said it would be impossible to reach the field, wait for proper flying conditions and get back by traintime. Gloomily I proceeded to Indianapolis.

On a third attempt I got as far as the field. But a heavy wind was blowing; in fact the door of the hangar was nearly blown off, and the plane was not even brought out.

It began to look as though Destiny were doing its best to keep me on the ground.

However, I was not at all discouraged and soon tried again. This time Harold McCormick accompanied me. Orville Wright came out to the field with us, and Phil Parmalee, rather more than a student, and C. P. Rodgers, who was later killed on the Pacific Coast when, it was presumed, a sea gull had in some way crippled his plane.

The plane was brought out and my turn came first. I remember rattling through the weeds at a terrific speed—no concrete runways then!—and circling over the adjoining fields at about 700 feet. I sat on the lower wing of the biplane, with my feet on a small bar below, and clung to the struts. I think the pressure of my grip must show to this day! The pilot sat beside me with two control levers in his hands. The engine was suspended above us and two big propellers, connected by chains, were behind us, between the two wings. It was extremely primitive, crude and awkward, but it did go up, and after ten or fifteen minutes came safely down.

Then Harold went up and came down, and as they turned the plane to run it into the hangar the crankshaft broke squarely in two—granulated!

On my return I drew a cartoon expressing the emotions of a man making his first flight.

The following year I made my second flight. It also had interesting angles. It was on the occasion of the first Aviation Meet in Chicago, August 15, 1911. Grandstands had been erected in Grant Park, east of the Art Institute.

On the first day I lunched with Charlie Dawes, Harold McCormick and Orville Wright, and before I had phrased my hopeful question, Wright interrupted me: "Yes," he said, "you may go in the biplane race." It was scheduled for that very afternoon.

The race was to be around four pylons, over a course scarcely a mile long. There were several entries. I learned with some uneasiness that the pilot of the Wright plane was named Coffin—Frank Coffin. After lunch I was asked to go to the Wright hangar to have my heart examined. It was pounding so hard with excitement that I feared it might not pass the test, but all was well and I walked back to my seat. On my way I passed, still lying on the field, the wreck of the plane in which William Badger had just been killed.

I tried to talk casually to my friends in the box and, when the time arrived, to appear unconcerned as I saw Coffin's plane trundled out before the crowd. Then I had the fun of suddenly arising and handing my hat to one of the ladies in the party.

"Will you hold this for me, please? I am going to fly in this race." The resulting sensation was entirely satisfactory, and I strode down the ramp and out onto the field and took my place in the plane. It was the same open type without fuselage in which I had flown before. The signal was given; we started. Soon we were up and began rounding the pylons, one after another, at what appeared to me a horrifying angle. On the ground, Dawes was standing with Orville Wright and he has often told me how scandalized Wright was at the way Coffin was banking those turns. At no time were we over fifty feet from the ground.

On one of the laps I caught sight of an ambulance racing across the field below us. Turning gingerly in my seat, I followed its direction and saw, projecting out of the lake, part of the plane in which St. Croix Johnstone had just been killed. He had been circling over the water as a side show. Those two men, Badger and Johnstone, were the only ones killed in the meet, one just before and one during my flight.

One of the spectacular features of the meet was Rodgers' big circles over the lake at 400 or 500 feet. He flew them continuously for nearly three hours. Lincoln Beachey did some remarkable stunting. From about a thousand feet he would dive down and then skim just over the cars in Michigan Avenue; or costumed in old-fashioned woman's garb, he would go hedgehopping down the field from end to end. Beachey was one of the first American stunt fliers. In the light of later development his amateurish performances in that pitiful little plane were far more dangerous than the later breath-taking feats of Al Williams or Atcherly.

The next summer Harold McCormick, who, like me, had got the flying fever, acquired the first privately owned plane in our part of the country. He built a hangar on the beach below his Lake Forest house, engaged a good pilot, and in due course the seaplane arrived. I knew nothing about all this until one day while I was working in my studio the telephone rang. It was Harold.

"Hello, John. How would you like to ride home with me in my new plane this afternoon?"

"Great Scott! How long have you had a plane?"

"I just got it. It's a Curtiss. I flew in it for the first time this morning."

"Of course I'll go back with you. When shall I show up?"

"Come to Grant Park about five."

I am afraid I hustled that cartoon through without too much care, packed a small bag and was at the lake front well before the appointed time. It was a hot day. The beaches were jammed. There was prodigious neck-craning as we swooped over the water. At eighty or ninety miles an hour the thirty miles to Lake Forest were covered all too soon.

These were my first three flights—one each year for three years. Planes were still a stirring novelty. Flying for ordinary mortals was a matter of tremendous interest and news value.

It may be wondered why, with all this enthusiasm, I never tried to learn to fly myself. For a fellow who couldn't back a car out of a garage—let alone tune in correctly on a radio football game, even when Purdue was playing—there was never any temptation.

## ~ 37 ~

# Theodore Roosevelt as Cartoon Material

LOOKING back over the perspective of years, I recall only two national political campaigns which have really stirred me from top to bottom. The first was that remote Cleveland campaign when I was fourteen; the second was the Progressive campaign of 1912.

When Theodore Roosevelt succeeded to office after the assassination of McKinley in 1901, a shudder ran through the financial world. Conditions for the prosperity of capital had never been more propitious, and the McKinley boast of a full dinner pail was being amply fulfilled for some if not for all. If my political observations have proved anything, they seem to indicate that our nation cannot stand prosperity—or too much of it at once. Every great wave of it generates abuses of some kind or other. The "hath-er" is not satisfied with what he "hath." He must devise schemes for getting more. Most depressions, if not caused by war or market manipulation, seem the result of battles among industrial giants. McKinley's beneficent complacency in the face of the tremendous growth of business combinations aroused a growing indignation. In answer to this rising clamor of protest, my second Presidential champion rose to prominence.

Big business was very suspicious of the fire-eating Teddy, but while he was filling out McKinley's term, the trust-busting crusade was held in leash. The thunderous excoriations of intrenched privilege were reserved for his own term which began in 1905. That was when, speaking at a Gridiron dinner, he snapped out the words, "malefactors of great wealth," and shook a warning finger at the captains of industry— the elder Morgan, Harriman, Aldrich, Elkins, Penrose, Crane, Stillman, Hill and a score of other sacrosanct guests at the tables, men who were not accustomed to having fingers shaken at them. Perhaps it was bad taste, but it came nearer to being heresy in those days.

I have explained how the duty of a newspaper cartoonist requires him to make a hasty review of the world's doings as chronicled each day in the press, decide which topic is uppermost in importance or interest, and then construct a cartoon about that subject. Thus, in a measure, the cartoons of a period constitute a fairly complete record of the chief events of that period and by scanning them consecutively one is enabled to grasp the general trend of the big news.

Assuming this to be true, whoever delves through the files of the first decade of the twentieth century will come to an inevitable conclusion. The most important news of that time was Mr. Theodore Roosevelt, President, politician, statesman, sociologist, reformer, defender of the faithful, exposer of shams, protagonist, antagonist, hunter, diplomat, apostle of peace, wielder of the Big Stick, and founder—but not a charter member—of the Ananias Club. A historian might be puzzled to decide whether Mr. Roosevelt was an imperialist or a socialist, a Democrat or a Republican.

If he had devoted a lifetime of earnest thought to the best method of capturing the public fancy, he could not have selected one better suited to his purpose than his Rough Riders of the Spanish-American War, that regiment made up of cowboys, collegians, gun fighters, cotillion leaders, millionaires and plainsmen. With the Rough Riders Teddy became a veritable Golconda of inspiration to the cartoonist.

He had a genius for doing provocative, picturesque things that started discussion, stirred interest, aroused the bitterest antagonism and the most devoted loyalty. He kept life in America in a pleasant turmoil.

His variety of mental and physical activities, aided by features that lent themselves gladly to caricature, made him a tempting target for cartoon exploitation. His teeth and eyeglasses became famous almost before he did. When he smiled it suggested a man in ambush behind a stone wall.

THE HISTORIC SPLIT

The friendliness of his nickname Teddy also helped win for him a peculiarly intimate place in the minds and hearts of the nation. It became a habit to think about him, either kindly or otherwise, but certainly to think about him.

In addition he had the invaluable asset of good horse sense which he clothed in graphic language. "Nature fakers," "muckrakers," "the strenuous life," "the crop of children is the best crop of a nation," and many other expressions owe their vogue to his instinct as a promoter and advertiser.

My own experience as a chronicler of T.R. covered all of his official life after 1900 when he had just been nominated for Vice-President. In 1901, as I have said, he acted more as executor of McKinley policies than as a proponent of new ones of his own. But soon thereafter his volcanic energy and initiative began to assert itself once more. Even in his messages to Congress he contrived to introduce little touches of human interest as well as a range of subjects that furnished material sufficient for cartoonists to work on for years. Take, for example, the synopsis of one of his annual messages, that of 1906, which, if supported by a Congress as energetic as he, might have disposed of all the national evils at once.

"Make race war impossible by abolishing lynching," he said. "Abolish lynching by inflicting a summary death penalty on those guilty of assaulting women. Pass a law demanding publicity in corporations; pass another law protecting all corporations from contributing to campaign funds, and a law demanding supervision of trusts." He said also that injunctions should be upheld; that we should save coal lands; that swollen fortunes should be remedied by a graduated inheritance tax; that strikes should be made impossible by a board of arbitration; that public ownership is not desirable, that ship subsidies are desirable; that we need currency reform, a reduction of the Philippine tariff, and scientific agricultural methods. He advised us to respect Japan, annex Cuba if it didn't behave, keep up an efficient Navy and perfect our coast defenses.

Many Presidents have allowed their mental processes to operate in a limited orbit, touching only the weightier problems of statecraft and diplomacy. Not so T.R. He leaped blithely from a discussion of the Open Door in China to one concerning the habits of the bobcat. "How to make farm life attractive to boys" came in for the same eager consideration as the construction of the Panama Canal.

The summer White House at Oyster Bay burst into a sudden, garrulous prominence that made its humble name a misnomer. Here Teddy went for rest and quiet, but if he got it, it was not recorded by the humorists of the pencil who were kept busy by the amazing variety of his visitors. For instance, on Monday the President entertained the champion tennis player; on Tuesday some old Rough-Rider pals; on Wednesday some fellow LL.D.'s; on Thursday a couple of big-game hunters; on Friday a few politicians; on Saturday some brother historians or eminent scientists. Between times he would seek relaxation by chopping down a few trees, swimming across Long

Island Sound or taking ten-mile marathons. No President ever worked so hard turning out material for cartoonists.

When the monotony of life in Oyster Bay or Washington became irksome, he went bear hunting in Mississippi, which activity produced the crowning triumph of his personal popularity, the Teddy bear. Admiring countrymen sent him bear cubs from the West, or hunting dogs from the plains, alligators from the South and turkeys from New England. The state dining room of the White House partook of the character of a zoo, and the four little boys of the family shared the fun.

After his bombshell about race suicide—"an unmarried man is a criminal"—parents with record-breaking families brought them to receive the Presidential congratulations. The cartoons hailed him as the Advance Agent of Posterity. In appreciation he presented a hundred-dollar check to a child who was named after him. Next day hundreds of parents named their babies and sent special-delivery letters to the eminent patronymic.

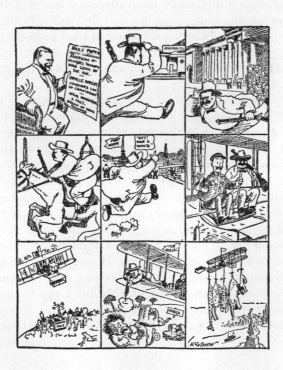

His trip in a submarine, his luncheon with Booker Washington, his Brownsville fight, his boxing and jujitsu lessons, all these sprightly doings kept him in personal touch with more sections of the country and more classes of people than any President before the advent of radio, and he gave us a bewildering lot to think about, talk about, get mad about and cheer about.

As a cartoonist, I was one of those most benefited by these Theodorian characteristics. It was a dull day when I could not turn to the White House for an idea. He was as dependable as the weather. I drew him so often, mostly with sympathetic friendliness, that I received, in the form of letters and invitations, many evidences of his friendliness in return. I don't think I was thus flattered into my attitude of admiration, because other Very Important Persons have been equally nice to me without converting me into a devoted follower.

When T.R. finished his term there was a wide clamor for him to run again; he refused and reminded the people that he considered that he had had two terms, and pledged himself not to seek a third. Taft was his man, and the nation dutifully accepted his substitute, feeling that Teddy's policies would be carried out.

They were. A few weeks after Teddy had gone to Africa to hunt lions, the Roosevelt policies were carried out and dumped over the back fence.

In one of Peter Dunne's Dooley articles which I illustrated, Mr. Hennessey had inquired, before the election, "Has Mr. Taft any chance?" "Did he ever take one?" answered Mr. Dooley. The men who shine in history are not those who sit tight and let well enough alone. I find a tendency, in my cartoons, to represent Taft with an aura of amiability radiating from every square yard of his massive frame, and surrounded by men who knew what they wanted, the very men most active in opposing T.R.

For several years the nation had been amused, shocked, jolted, instructed, "enthused" and entertained by emanations from the White House. Taft restored thereto a measure of peace and quiet.

I saw much of T.R. during the days in Africa when our safari joined his while he and his son Kermit killed three elephants for Akeley's group in the American Museum of Natural History. In the colonel's tent one day, I spoke of the possibility of his running again.

"No," he said. "No, the kaleidoscope never repeats. A lot of people seem to worry about what to do with ex-Presidents. Well, they needn't worry about this one. I can keep myself busy."

I feel sure this was his frame of mind at the end of 1909. Nevertheless in 1912 at the Republican Convention, when Senator Lodge referred to the best-hated and best-loved man in America, although no name had been spoken, explosions of cheers for Teddy battered against the silent block of Taft delegates, uncomfortably conscious of the fictitious nature of their strength. It's an old story now, how Taft's backers jammed the nomination through in opposition to the obvious public will.

The bolt of the Roosevelt delegates was inevitable, and at the Progressive Republican Convention T.R. was supported by the same independent voters, the people seldom stirred to action in party politics, the youth, the idealists, all now burning with the same zeal that had characterized the campaign for Cleveland in 1884.

Albert Beveridge, virile, stormy and elemental, delivered the keynote address, and the keynote was "Pass prosperity around."

It is one of my proudest experiences to have gone through that Bull Moose campaign as a rapt participant. The *Tribune* threw its whole weight behind T.R. My cartoons were 100 per cent for him. I even made my first and last political speech in his behalf.

"I wish to go on record," I began, "as favoring the Bull Moose cause, in case those of you who see the *Tribune* every morning may still be in any doubt as to where I stand! I have no illusions as to my qualifications as a spellbinder. I don't expect you all to rush home after hearing my speech, to vote for T.R., however much I might hope for such a gratifying result. My chief concern just now is that you don't rush home while hearing it!"

With the Republican party hopelessly split, Woodrow Wilson edged into victory with a minority of the votes cast.

# 38

## The Pirate Cruise

THE Pirate Cruise did not turn out quite as planned; still I like to look back on it. It all came about because of my early ambition to be a pirate.

When I was a boy I knew that by following the trades and sailing with America two points off the starboard bow and the broad Atlantic just abaft the weather beam, I should in due course arrive in that alluringly vague vicinity known as the Spanish Main. Duties about the farm and the necessity of going to school prevented the carrying out of any plan just then, but as I lookcd wistfully down the dusty road to where a fringe of maple trees marked the limit of my travels, a spirit of unrest stirred within me which I am afraid I have never outgrown.

Every year there comes, like a recurring fever, an irresistible longing to look at timetables and steamer sailings in the hope that somewhere in this busy world I may find a spot where romance and legend have escaped the cruel inroads of the commonplace.

So when, in 1912, the annual fever struck me, I determined to fare forth and lay a tardy wreath on the shrine of Captain Kidd and his long-dishonored crew.

I wanted to sit on the lonely beach where L'Olonnais sat; I wanted to lie under the palm trees where the swaggering Portuguez cooled his swarthy brow; I wanted to anchor in the leeward coves where Morgan's vessels swung. Perhaps somewhere I might stumble over the edge of an ironbound chest, in which case the expenses of the trip might be defrayed, not to mention the duty on such buckets of pearls and plate as might be uncovered by my questing pick and shovel. And if, perchance, the islands yielded no such material reward, I felt that the trip would be rich in such other compensations as health and recreation, which are equally beneficial and secured without the irksome exertion of digging for them in the hot sun.

In planning to write up the trip for the paper, I considered whether a series of articles glorifying the deeds of the pirates might possibly have an evil effect on the young, but this unhappy result seemed unlikely when one reflected that the pirates are all dead—or most of them anyhow—which proves that a life of piracy is both disastrous to the health and destructive to the hope of living happily ever after.

These matters being settled in my mind, I at once wrote Kirk Brice, setting forth my plan for the cruise. He wrote back enthusiastically, adding "I happened to mention the Pirate Cruise to Elsie Clews Parsons. She says she's coming too."

I didn't know Elsie, but, to balance up, I invited Katherine Dexter McCormick. The idea was for each to pay a quarter of the expenses.

Now in exploring pirate haunts, one should provide oneself with "a long, low rakish craft." I found the perfect boat requisite to the sentimental spirit of such a voyage, Clement Griscom's *Whim*. She was already in Miami, a charming, suitable schooner with all the comforts. Fearing to lose her by delay, I chartered her at once.

That same afternoon I received a telegram: "Have just chartered motorboat Heather in your name. [Signed] Elsie Parsons."

I was sunk. I couldn't get a release from the *Whim* charter, although they said they would try to relet her. Besides, I most definitely did not want a motorboat. But from a rather exaggerated—as I look back on it—sense of chivalry, I didn't say anything. I cheered myself with the reflection that *Heather* rhymed with "always fair weather."

I reached the scene of embarkation first. Kirk and Katherine arrived next day, and presently Elsie turned up. Maybe she thought that two unmarried couples—at least not married to each other—needed a chaperon. Anyway she showed up with an attractive young Englishman, third secretary of the British embassy. She had met him one day at tea, she said, and just invited him along. His name was Archibald Clark Kerr.

We set sail, metaphorically speaking, on the afternoon of February 6. The trouble started right here.

The *Heather* was built like a destroyer, 105 feet long; her two 300-horse-power engines consumed forty-two gallons of gasoline an hour. She was long and low but rather more rockish than rakish, as we were soon to discover. She carried a complement of nine men. There were no sails, nothing but the engines. And to satisfy the enormous appetites of these engines in a cruise through parts devoid of filling stations, a great deal of gasoline had to be taken on board. The tanks, containing 1,550 gallons, at eleven cents, were filled; nine large fifty-gallon drums were lashed to the rails, and twenty-five ten-gallon tins of case oil were stacked on deck. The presence of all this gasoline crowding the living space clashed a good deal with romantic ideals. Also, it raised our center of gravity to somewhere up in the huge funnel. I thought with misery of the smart little *Whim* and her white sails.

The plan was to lie near the Florida Light until dawn, then cross the Gulf Stream. A norther had been blowing fiercely for a couple of days. At five in the morning we got under way and the first half hour was not so bad. Then we felt an ominous shudder. The *Heather's* propellers raced and she buried her nose in the sea as if she had decided to be a submarine. At last she swung dizzily back and then began to slide down a long hill, at the bottom of which a mountain of sea dropped on her bow with a crash.

This was only the beginning. For the next hour the *Heather* staggered, reeled, bucked, plunged and trembled, burying her nose and shaking her tail fearsomely. When a heavy norther traveling south meets the Gulf Stream traveling north, the consequences are open to criticism.

Below, confined unhappily beneath tightly fastened hatches, we had the selfsame sense of security that is felt by a rat in a trap. Kerr got his pistol ready—said he preferred that way to drowning. Kirk, who had been vainly trying to stay in his bunk, was heard to remark to himself that he had had enough of pirate islands; Manhattan was the only island he was interested in. At last, after more than an hour of agony, the sea abruptly subsided.

Hurray! we thought. We're across!

But a look through the porthole disclosed the Florida Light, and it dawned on us sickeningly that we were back where we had started from. The captain said it was the first time in thirty-two years that he had turned back.

With daylight came a slight mutiny of the passengers. Kirk and Katherine announced that they were through with pirate cruises and would cross to Nassau on the regular boat, the old *Miami*. Elsie, her Englishman and I decided to stick with the *Heather*, whatever it rhymed with, and at midnight we made an uneventful crossing and were well on the way to Nassau when Elsie had an idea.

About five o'clock in the afternoon, the sea having calmed, Elsie thought it would be fun to visit Andros Island, then a vast and mysterious expanse populated only by flamingos, myths and a few Negroes who were said to have lapsed back into African barbarism. This was just what our souls craved after the past twenty-four hours.

Inasmuch as the *Heather* drew too much, we decided to let her continue to Nassau without us while we took to the little sixteen-foot launch, *Sundog*. We carried with us food, water, blankets and guns, and one sailor to man the engine. We felt we could safely make the short run to the island before dark. We could see its palms edging the horizon about ten miles away. It took us longer than we expected. For over an hour the *Sundog* chugged bravely on without making any appreciable approach to the fringe of palms. The sun began to sink. In another half hour the sea was in darkness.

Suddenly, to our horror, we found our craft most clearly where she was not supposed to be—in the midst of the tumbling, sinister white waters of a reef. In the dark the great black uplifts of the waves before they broke loomed like huge glistening rocks. There was a grinding of the keel and we lurched over into the lagoon. Here more trouble awaited us in the shape of numberless treacherous coral peaks that lurk near the surface, invisible at night. We struck one but slid off without apparent harm because we were going so slowly.

We waded the last hundred yards, with only a flashlight to show the way, and lugged our things ashore, floundering over the jagged coral and into pools left by the receding tide.

Driftwood furnished a cheering fire, and with all the sensations of shipwrecked mariners we stretched out on that lonely beach to sleep.

By dawn we were cooking breakfast. Then we walked for a mile or two along the desolate shore, but there were only sand, mangroves and the reef, not even a wild bird. We decided to start for Nassau, about forty miles away. As the *Sundog* could do only five miles an hour, it would take us all day, half of the time out of sight of land. We loaded our meager cargo, offered a prayer that the gasoline would hold out, and, at eleven o'clock, embarked and steered carefully across the lagoon, the waters of which by daylight were so clear that fish glided along below like birds in the air. Cautiously we crossed the reef at a point where the foam was slight.

Between Andros and Nassau is the Tongue of Ocean, which is approached, by those who know, with respect and often fear. We didn't know.

The first hour of the voyage was tranquil. Land dropped from sight and we found ourselves puffing along in our tiny boat as much at sea as though we were in mid-Atlantic, and in much more danger, for the Tongue of Ocean is a funnel through which the northwesters sweep down and scatter luckless little boats to the four winds.

At the end of the second hour a breeze sprang up and the water became choppy. Within fifteen minutes the wind had risen ominously and big black clouds were bearing down upon us. Incredibly swiftly the seas became so heavy we feared the launch would capsize. She took the big ones on the bow where they stopped her momentarily, broke and sent volumes of water into the little cockpit. We raised the canvas hood to ward off some of the deluge. It was impossible to keep the boat on a compass course, for the seas beat her off so savagely that we seemed to be making no headway at all. From crest to crest we struggled, the wind and waves growing steadily more formidable. The flywheel of the engine threw out a fountain of spray. One man worked the hand pump, another bailed. We had no life preservers.

The canvas hood was ripping to pieces. Everybody was bailing now. Kerr, knee-deep in water, got out his revolver again. Elsie's notion of adventuring to Andros was being fulfilled in a big way.

Finally it became clear that even if the launch held out, the gasoline would not. By this time Andros had been long out of sight. If we turned back, might we not pass it to the north, the way we were being blown?

Between crests we turned hastily and headed back. Going with the waves was like the wild rush down a roller coaster, a pause at the top and another dizzy plunge. One man kept a lookout behind and signaled when a wave heavier than usual was coming. The *Sundog* was then eased over it and afterward resumed her course for a few minutes in what we hoped was the general direction of Andros. In this way we zigzagged for over two hours, bailing steadily, till at last we sighted land and nerved ourselves for the reef again. Elsie and Kerr took off their shoes in preparation for disaster. I didn't. I knew that if the boat capsized, I could not swim the mile to shore with or without shoes.

The reef was roaring like Niagara, and an endless line of foam marked it. Far away on shore we sighted a few houses beneath the palms. Along the beach we could make out figures frantically rushing back and forth and making signals at us. We presumed they were trying to tell us not to cross. But we had to, and we did. A lucky lift of the sea must have cleared us momentarily, for the great purple rocks were so near the surface it seemed inevitable we should strike them and be overturned.

A quarter of an hour later, drenched to the skin, chilled and disheveled, we landed on the beach of Mastic Point amid a throng of excited natives.

"It was an act of God," they said. "No boat can cross that reef!"

We were pleasantly surprised to find ourselves greeted with friendliness. If these people were wreckers, they seemed to be agreeable ones. Soon, the sponge trader appeared; his whitewashed cottage was the nucleus of the little community, and in his warehouse the various kinds of sponges were sorted and prepared for shipment. His name was Pemmy Smith; a benevolent autocrat, he administered a paternal form of government which seemed to work beautifully. Everybody was happy, good-natured and as prosperous as the simple necessities of island life demanded. After welcoming us and expressing amazement that we had crossed the reef safely, he escorted us to his house, where his wife, a tall, soft-eyed Nassau girl, gave us dry clothes and spread our waterlogged belongings in the sun.

That evening on the shadowy porch the talk turned to the subject of our quest. Morgan's Bluff was not far away. Sir Henry was supposed to have used this spot as a rendezvous and haven of refuge. Very little imagination was required to see his swift sloop bearing in toward the safety of the quiet lagoon. Pirates, wreckers, blockade-runners—it was worth floundering over the reef just to hear the atmospheric words roll out in such a setting.

Next morning the northwester still raged. It had been arranged with Captain Haines of the *Heather* that if we did not return in two days, he was to search for us along the coast of Andros. But it seemed unlikely that on such a day he would venture outside of Nassau harbor. His only justification would be his belief that we were in distress.

There was no cable or radio in those days. Once every week or so a little schooner, manned by blacks, made the run with mail and a miscellaneous cargo. By midafternoon we gave up hope of the *Heather's* arrival and arranged to go on the schooner which was due to sail. The *Sundog* was loaded aboard and we climbed after her onto the cluttered deck. Cargo was piled on wherever it could be secured— firewood, sponges, garden truck. Several pigs ambled about and a goat was tied in the stern. Cordage was coiled in inconvenient places, and the quite discouraging-looking little cabin below was crowded with natives.

Thus we sailed from Mastic Point, beating down the lagoon for Nicholls' Town and the channel through the reef. Soon afterward the *Heather* hove in sight and the launch, her sailor and Kerr were taken aboard.

Elsie, still game and venturesome, and I decided to try a night on the schooner. We stretched out in as open a spot as we could find, between the charcoal brazier and a heap of conch shells, and went soundly to sleep with the helmsman's song as lullaby and the creaking shrouds and swaying masts outlined against a brilliant tropic sky.

At daybreak, after a twelve-hour voyage, we tied up at the wharf in Nassau, very bedraggled and very hungry. The *Heather* was not yet in. Kirk and Katherine had definitely abandoned the expedition and removed their effects to the Colonial Hotel. We were face to face with the necessity of joining them at this fashionable hostelry, looking like beachcombers.

In the meantime other things had been happening. The two storms which the *Heather* had already encountered had shattered the confidence of the crew. The engineer and the steward quit and had to be replaced.

More gasoline had to be bought at a shilling a gallon, and nineteen large steel drums were lashed to the rails. This made 1,390 gallons on deck besides that below in the tanks. It would be weeks before we could get more.

In addition to gasoline we had instructed the cook to stock up with such things as meat, ice and fresh vegetables. With fatalistic accuracy he had fallen into the hands of a yacht supplier who bore the same name as a famous pirate, and it is presumed that a smoldering ember of inherited iniquity was stirred into action. He and the cook had stowed away enough supplies to equip a man-o'-war. When the bill was presented to us the night before we planned to sail, we were staggered. There were items on it that would have jarred a fixed star. Among the things we had not ordered was enough beer to float the boat. None of us drank beer, and even if we had, there was no good reason for getting so much that merely the drinking of it would have left no time for anything else. We refused to accept this item together with others equally preposterous, and the cook was detailed to help the piratical agent carry the stuff ashore.

Then in the midst of our dinner the cook announced that he too was going ashore, and he put on his coat and deserted.

The outlook was gloomy. There was none of that joyous sparkle to life associated with a pleasure cruise. Elsie and Kerr seemed to feel that as the whole plan was my idea, I should be given free rein to fix things up alone. As I dismally pushed off for shore, I envied old Blackbeard and wished I had more of the dictatorial endowments of a man of his stripe.

However, with the help of the pilot, a cook was found, and in the morning we sailed out of Nassau harbor with renewed anticipation.

At Wemyss' Bight on Eleuthera, the natives were terrified by our searchlight, the like of which they had never seen before, and when we took our phonograph ashore, the excitement was wonderful to behold. There was one white man in the village, an English preacher, who had always dreamed of hearing Caruso. We were happily able to fulfill his dream. When we questioned the people about pirates, they would cheerfully agree that in the old days this man or that had touched here, but we suspected they were telling us what they shrewdly guessed we wanted to hear. If we had inquired about troglodytes, I think we would have received just as satisfactory information.

Next on our chart we picked out Cat Island. We anchored in a little cove and a fisherman sculled us through the reef. School adjourned at our approach and the entire population came out to inspect us. Incidentally, there were many more goats than cats on Cat Island.

The name Rum Cay fairly reeked with piratical suggestion. We could not help visualizing a rollicking company of Brethren of the Coast, all bronzed and bearded and tattooed, with striped sashes and turbans, and cutlasses ready to hand. In addition we had been warned that the 400 inhabitants were ill-disposed and untrustworthy, so I was especially desirous of making an impressive landing on Rum Cay. I wanted them to gaze on me with awe and whisper among themselves, "Here is a man who will brook no treachery!"

But alas! With my arms full of sweaters and cameras, I seized the sea ladder. A wave carried the launch out from under me and left me dangling in the water. When they hauled me out onto the rickety pier I fear the natives were not struck dumb by my commanding presence. A broad grin spread over the faces of the Rum Cay reception committee.

In his journal Columbus describes his first landfall as being beautiful as Vallombrosa in June, but it seems improbable, even after seventy days at sea, that he could have been speaking of Watling's Island. It was bleak and unlovely and hadn't a smile in the whole landscape.

From there we sailed south, full of eagerness as we raised the turtle-like bulk of the most famous of all buccaneer strongholds—Tortuga. Not much remained to mark the place where once Levasseur, Pierre le Grand and a host of other chieftains who terrorized the Spanish Main were wont to rest and frolic after their bloody sorties. We saw only a peaceful valley and a sleepy sprawling little town, whose colorful history was far more familiar to the visitors than to the residents. If there was buried treasure, it was surely safe, as the idea of doing any voluntary labor seemed far from their minds.

That same afternoon we cruised eastward along the mountainous shore of northern Haiti. Perhaps no district in the world has seen more bloodshed and massacre than Haiti. We got our first impression of the black republic at Port de Paix, a shipping port for logwood and coffee. The little town was in the throes of mid-Lenten ceremonies, a sort of mi-carème, which among those Negroes became little less than orgiastic. As we walked through the dirty cobbled streets full of dogs, pigs, sheep and donkeys, mobs of masked figures circled around us with beating drums and loud clamors for money. If their attitude had been one of good-natured revelry, all would have been accepted in a complaisant spirit, but civilization had touched them only enough to make them insolent. In the evening, we were led by the sound to a dance hall, and took our places at the side of the wretched close low-ceilinged room. The dancing was offensively suggestive, many of the costumes were obscene, but all were interesting from an ethnological point of view.

Here for the first time I heard the music which afterward invaded America and spread throughout the world under the name of jazz. It was a wild, haunting blare of brass and drum, the general effect one of barbarous indecency.

The evident hostility of the people made us uncomfortable, so we soon returned to the *Heather*, Kerr to his *Oxford Book of Verse*, Elsie to her memoranda on the folk tales of Andros and other Bahama islands, later published by the American Folklore Society.

When Columbus was asked to describe Haiti, he crumpled a piece of paper in his hand and laid it before Isabella. "That is Haiti," he said.

We were conscious of this description as we scrambled up the steep, tangled path to the Citadel, sometimes dragging ourselves up by roots and vines. When we gazed over the sheer drop at the top, we remembered the story of how the black slave who became emperor illustrated for his foreign visitors the discipline of his troops. He gave the order to march, and as no other order followed, the whole troop of 300 marched over the edge to death.

Our enjoyment of scenery and historic association was constantly shattered by anxiety about gasoline. For three days I combed the little shops of Cap Haitien and got in touch by telegraph with officials in Port-au-Prince, till I finally collected enough to get the boat around to Gonaïves, running at the most economical speed.

We ourselves wanted to make the trip overland, lured by tales of the mysterious interior. Voodoo worship was supposed to flourish, just as it had come from the west coast of Africa: charms which could bring death; human sacrifice on the altar of the Great Green Serpent.

Just before our arrival an American named MacDonald had obtained, by intrigue and bribery, an unpopular concession for a railroad across the island. Mademoiselle Celestina, the president's daughter, who had helped him, was being burned in effigy by disrespectful crowds and the term "MacDonald" was applied to all Americans in reproach and bitterness.

After securing special permits and a guide, and carrying almost no baggage aside from some tinned food, we started across on horseback. I lent Elsie a pair of khaki trousers, and she strapped a huge six-shooter about her waist. With her long hair difficult to conceal under a slouch hat, and her conspicuously feminine features, she presented a much odder appearance in those days than she would now when all the girls wear slacks. I think it was largely due to this that we got through without trouble. The unfriendly glare of the semisavages at the approach of three white men changed to curiosity when they realized that one was a woman. Their own women were extremely modest in long voluminous skirts. Consequently Elsie was something of a sensation as we passed through the mountain villages.

We encountered a wedding and several cockfights, and spent the nights in the huts of French priests. The proprieties were observed by introducing Elsie as Kerr's sister. Once we came suddenly upon a ritual dance, the significance of which we could not detect; the dancers did not stop, but glowered at us so malevolently that we went hastily on our way.

Deep in the bush, voices muttered, "MacDonald! MacDonald!" Almost continuously, during our ride, we could hear, sometimes near, sometimes far back in the hills, the hypnotic and always rather ominous beat of the tomtom.

After three or four days, we reached Gonaïves, dirty but healthy. The *Heather* was waiting and took us down the coast to Port-au-Prince, where we made a ceremonial call on President LeConte in the Palace. The large Columbus anchor stood in the hall. About a month later LeConte was assassinated and the Palace burned, but the anchor was saved.

As usual the question of gasoline dominated all our activities. By dint of seeing nearly everybody in town, and paying sixty cents a gallon, I managed to scrape together 1,080 gallons, just enough to get the *Heather* across to the nearest port in Cuba, Nipe Bay. Here there was none, nor was there any at Santiago, a telegram revealed. The nearest source of supply was Havana, far at the other end of the island.

So we said good-by to Captain Haines, promising to send him 2,200 more gallons, and when that job was done I started immediately for home, having had all the pirate cruising I wanted just then.

There remained, for me, as a last piece of business connected with the trip, the little detail of paying for the charter of the *Whim*, which had not been relet.

The following autumn Dr. Carlos Montezuma, an Apache Indian, asked if I would care to join the tribe on their annual deer hunt. When he was a child, his family had been killed or driven away by enemies. The little boy had been found and cared for by a photographer. Subsequently he was adopted and educated by an Army surgeon, but he had retained his interest in his native tribe.

We were to motor back from Phoenix into the Indian Reservation, then proceed on foot with the Apaches for two weeks, sleeping as they did on the ground, eating Indian fare, and seeing amazing exhibitions of Indian tracking. It would be an unusual experience because one must be invited by and go with a genuine Apache. There were to be thirty-eight Indians and four or five whites.

I knew him sufficiently well to ask if I could bring Kirk Brice, and Montezuma agreed. Presently Kirk wrote me in a great state of excitement. He said he had mentioned the trip casually in Elsie's hearing and she said she was coming, too!

I told him for God's sake to head her off!

Kirk telephoned me on his arrival in Chicago. He said he had recognized Elsie's duffel bag in the lobby of the Blackstone. I hit the ceiling.

"Come on down and tell her yourself!" he said.

I went down and there she was.

"What train are you starting on?" she inquired enthusiastically.

"Now, here, Elsie——" and I started in.

Then it transpired that they had been playing a joke on me. The train stopped at a lonely little station and Elsie and her duffel bag disembarked on some tour of her own.

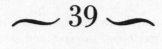

## ~ 39 ~

## Mexico

WHATEVER the shortcomings of the Pirate Cruise, it gave new life to another of those boyhood ambitions of mine that seemed to be perennial. I had wanted not only to visit tropical islands—I had wanted to *own* one!

Often from the airy heights of the haymow I used to gaze over the cornfields, and after looking intently for a while I could see green seas tossing on my own private coral strand. In the early stages of this ambition the island was not particularly peopled by anybody but me and a few trusty retainers. As my reading progressed I discovered that island life need not be wholly spoiled by the presence of beautiful ladies. But until I was grown-up, the only islands I knew were those of my dreams and books. As far as I can remember I had never laid eyes on a real one unless at low water a mudbank appeared above the Wabash.

In the Philippines I saw thousands of them, real ones with cocoanut palms and more or less languorous native girls; but I had other affairs on my mind. Years passed; straphanging and deadlines failed to dim the old dream.

Nineteen hundred and fourteen was plodding along. My contract with the *Tribune* was to expire the first of May. In a new one the starting date was set six months ahead.

"Now," said I, "I'll do something about getting an island!"

Some preliminary correspondence with people in Sydney disclosed that one Melville Island in the Arafura Sea near Port Darwin was available at a price within my range, probably because of its inaccessibility. It contained 10,000,000 acres and 10,000 head of wild cattle.

I determined to visit this island.

Viewed in retrospect, there were quite a lot of things wrong with this idea. For one thing it would take at least three months just to get there and back. Paying such a large slice of a not very large capital for an island I might never set foot on a second time seemed of dubious wisdom. I think I've always been a practical realist in working for my money, but I suspect I'm something of a starry-eyed idealist when it comes to spending it. I'm afraid I thought it would be worth the money.

This point of view may be incomprehensible to those who see life wholly in terms of percentages, invoices and overheads, and I mean this in no way derogatory to businessmen. There are many times when a bank balance is more beautiful than a palm tree waving in the trade winds.

In any case Melville was as good an objective as any. A steamer left San Francisco on July 25. In the meantime there was a Manila Bay dinner in Washington on the anniversary of the battle sixteen years before. As Ed Harden and I were the two civilian members of the society, and the dinner was to be held at the home of Admiral Dewey, I was eager to attend. Accordingly I made plans for a quick trip east before preparing to start for the island at the other end of the world.

That dinner proved one of the little events in my life out of which arose unexpected consequences.

I sat between the admiral and Captain Pitt Scott who had been on his personal staff when he was commodore. Other old friends were there, a little older, a little stouter, a little less romantic-looking than when they were pacing the quarter-decks in a strange half-known place called the Philippines. In the glow of candles and the warming presence of friends the admiral thawed with courtesy.

In addition to reminiscences, there was, as I had anticipated, much talk of the recent Vera Cruz incident. Seventeen of our battleships were flung in a massive crescent before the city, which our soldiers were holding against the Mexicans. Carranza and Villa were heading rival armies in northern Mexico, and Huerta was drinking his brandy while he scoffed at Wilson's attempt to get an apology for not saluting the American flag. The Navy was preparing a formidable demonstration. Pitt Scott had been put in command of the *Marietta* which was outfitting in the Brooklyn Navy Yard. She was a small gunboat which might be sent in close, possibly up some river to do bombarding.

"Gosh!" I said. "You're likely to see more action than any of the other ships!" There must have been a wistful note in my voice.

"Why don't you come along?"

"I'd have to get permission of the Navy Department."

"Well, here's Admiral Fiske right now."

The admiral was kind enough to endorse the idea, and the following day I called on Secretary Daniels, incidentally meeting Assistant Secretary Franklin D. Roosevelt. I was given permission to go on the *Marietta*, so I proceeded at once to New York and sent my baggage aboard. Then a monkey wrench was dropped into my plans.

As Pitt Scott and I were standing together, an orderly approached and handed the captain a long official envelope. He opened it and I knew instantly that something was wrong. He read it twice, then handed it to me.

It was an order for the *Marietta* to proceed to Guantanamo to relieve another ship on patrol duty at Santo Domingo. She was to go nowhere near Mexico.

Well, it was one of those things! I didn't want to go to Santo Domingo! After a few shoulder shruggings, meaning what-the-hell, I took my bags, said good-by to Scott and headed for Harden's office on Wall Street where I immediately called John Callan O'Laughlin in the *Tribune* office in Washington. O'Laughlin was short and dark and vital with enthusiasm and *joie de vivre*. His eyes sparkled with good-fellowship. It is easy to understand why he has always had so many friends. A short time before Theodore Roosevelt retired, there was a vacancy—first assistant secretary of state. He gave the position to O'Laughlin. For many years he edited the *Army and Navy Journal*.

I explained my situation to him and he said, "Wait a minute." Soon he called me back. He had got in touch with Secretary Daniels and had me transferred from the *Marietta* to the flagship *Wyoming*, our most imposing battleship! She also was lying in the Brooklyn Navy Yard. I hurried back and Pitt Scott took me over to her. The executive officer, Commander David Todd, turned out to be a Manila friend. He took us to Captain Glennon.

"I am to have the honor, sir," I said, "of accompanying you to Vera Cruz."

"Vera Cruz!" he exclaimed. "We have no orders to go to Mexico!"

"Why, it's less than an hour since I was told I was to go there on the *Wyoming*."

"I'm sorry," said the captain shortly. "There must be some mistake. If anybody knows the ship's orders, I should."

It looked like an impasse. I had almost reached the shoulder-shrugging stage for the second time when—also, for the second time, like something out of a storybook—an orderly approached and handed the captain a long official envelope.

He read it over slowly. "Well, you're right," he said huskily. "Here are my orders to go to Vera Cruz." Then with cordiality he told me to send my things aboard.

It was something to remember—to have been able to give the commander of a battleship his first news of his orders from the Navy Department. My telephoned instructions had simply outstripped the slower Navy order which had to go through several hands.

Next morning I joined the ship for one of the pleasantest seven weeks of my life. At Vera Cruz we found thirty-five other ships, including seven superdreadnaughts. Admiral Badger, who was in command, transferred his headquarters to the *Wyoming*. I was supposed to go ashore, but to my delight by a general vote of the wardroom I was invited to stay on board where I could continue to enjoy, among other things, those glorious nights of delicious coolness, with the admiral's orchestra and the ship's band, and a thousand sailors perched on the turrets and scattered about the decks to see the moving pictures. The wonderful spirit on the *Wyoming* won for it the name of the Happy Ship.

All the war correspondents in the world were on hand. There was not much to see or do, but the air was full of rumor and possibilities. I went ashore every day. Richard Harding Davis and I made a trip with the cavalry to El Tejar, ten miles inland; Frederick Palmer and I went with Admiral Winslow on a destroyer to Puerto México, but couldn't get in because of Mexican gunboats. One night I slept out with the marines on sentry duty. Another night I gave a dinner on board for General Funston, in command of the land forces; I had not seen him since Manila.

It happened that still another Manila friend, Henry Mustin, was commandant of the *Mississippi*, the aviation headquarters of the fleet, and he was disposed to help me in my persistent desire to fly. Dick Davis had been up a few days before and reported that the Mexicans had fired on his plane. This made a fine news story. I was assigned to the care of a naval flier named Geoffrey Chevalier, who took me over the town and the harbor, over the greatest concentration of American naval power up to that time. It was a beautiful flight but without incident.

On the first of July, by order of Secretary Daniels, the Navy went dry. Admiral Badger and Captain Glennon immured themselves in their quarters, stopped up their ears and ignored the revelry that resounded throughout the ship. It was a wake, and a noisy one, and it lasted until midnight, at which moment any leftover liquor was thrown overboard.

By this time most of the correspondents had departed.

As public interest shifted from Vera Cruz to Carranza and Villa, the *Tribune* cabled me to join them. Palmer also decided to change his base of operations and went with me to Saltillo where I made a sketch of Carranza. Since communications between the two warring districts had been stopped by then, we went back together by a long roundabout way to Chihuahua where we found Villa. A meeting was arranged by a Hearst correspondent named Roberts who acted as interpreter.

I had some misgivings about drawing this picturesque character whose exploits were filling the columns of all the papers in America. He had been represented as a person of such impetuosity and at times violence that I worried about the form his displeasure might take in case the portrait did not please him. He buckled on his holster and

cartridge belt, seated himself at a table and laid his six-shooter in front of him. This was not calculated to quiet my nerves. He wore a light-gray uniform and shiny riding boots; it was evident he had bestowed some pains on his appearance. He had a fine forehead and a well-shaped nose. The one unpleasant feature was the pendulous lower lip which, as he sat listening, with his suspicious eyes darting from one person to another, had a most disturbing effect. In view of the revolver, I wondered whether I should draw this as it was, and yet I realized that it was absolutely essential to a true likeness. So I drew what I saw.

When I had finished I asked, with some trepidation, if he would sign it. He looked at my sketch without indicating any emotion whatsoever, and in a sprawling hand, thereby refuting the story that he could not write, he signed "Francisco Villa."

Meanwhile time was passing. If I did not catch the boat on the twenty-fifth of July and get to my South Sea island in a hurry, I knew I could not get home in time for my new contract. It was because I was having such a good time with Palmer that the sailing date came nearer and nearer without my starting for San Francisco. He had nice gray eyes, prominent jaws, an easy joshing manner and striking ability. He was the only man I ever knew who ordered mashed potatoes all the time. Usually you get them without premeditation. He had just written his prophetic novel *The Last Shot*, the purpose of which was to show that war would become so frightful people would get sick of it.

Little by little I slipped into the easier way, and when the last minute came, as in the old time in Bombay, I trusted to luck. Thanks to the toss of a coin in El Paso I was not westbound in the middle of the Pacific when the First World War began.

# With the Kaiser's Army

ALL interest had been squeezed out of the Vera Cruz situation, especially after the Navy went dry. While there had not been a visible cloud on the European horizon, yet all the ingredients were in the pot. Had I dreamed that war in Europe was at last so imminent after the many false alarms, I would never have been loitering in Mexico covering our little fracas with Huerta, and fighting mosquitoes.

Then things began to happen. On the evening of July 27, Palmer received a telegram from Trumbull White, editor of *Everybody's*: "Conditions very grave. Leave at once for New York and Europe."

A couple of hours later we were both on a northbound train, leaving Mr. Carranza to his own devices. We separated in St. Louis. Palmer caught the *Lusitania* on the fourth of August. I stopped in Chicago to arrange with the *Tribune* for money and credentials and booked passage on the *St. Paul* on the seventh.

It was a week of terrific climaxes—the flaming bulletins, the staggering succession of crises in Europe as one nation after another declared war. During my few days in Chicago I drew five cartoons: "The Christian Nations," "On Guard," "The Sport of Kings," "The Crime of the Ages" and "The Colors." All five won favor. All were conceived in the profound emotion of the hour and had the advantage of a background of events which were stirring humanity to the depths.

In the confusion of news reports were many which told of Americans stranded abroad with letters of credit but without cash. So in addition to a letter of credit the *Tribune* supplied me with $5,218 in gold coin, American, British and French. The gold was in two stout canvas bags and weighed over nineteen pounds. On the train I carried it in my suitcase. On the ship I transferred my burden to my trunk where I used to verify its presence several times a day. Arthur Ruhl, Will Irwin and Irvin Cobb were on board, all weighted down with coin.

There were no porters at the dock at Liverpool. Passengers had to rustle their own luggage, assisted by cabbies. By the fifteenth I was in London, and on the seventeenth in Brussels. Palmer had arrived two days before me.

We all knew that there would be an iron determination on the part of the military commanders to bar correspondents. We were told no man could go with the French Army unless he spoke French and filed his dispatches in that language. Lord Kitchener was notoriously hostile to newspapermen as well as supremely indifferent to how they felt about it.

Certainly none of us had the slightest hope of seeing anything of the German side because of the widespread belief that in no circumstances would correspondents, German or alien, be tolerated in the German lines. News was not leaking out; no correspondents seemed to be leaking in.

The outlook was not promising. And I think we all felt that the military authorities were more than half right in their wish to exclude writers who might unintentionally betray an important operation with disastrous results. It almost seemed as if the day of the war correspondent might be over. Yet nearly all the men who had been in on the war game during the last twenty years were dropping down on London like birds coming home to roost.

I had all sorts of credentials to impress the French Army. My plan was to stay a few days in Belgium, then to return to London, thence to France. After taking out $700 in gold, I left the remainder with Sam Blythe at the Hotel Savoy to hold until I returned in a few days. When weeks passed and I failed to return, Blythe transferred my gold to Mr. Selfridge, in whose vault it reposed for several months. I brought home $4,300 of the original gold.

Once again the element of luck intervened.

Instead of staying a few days, I stayed eight weeks. Instead of joining the French Army and needing my letters of introduction, I joined the German, against all advices to the contrary—and my letter of credit was good in Germany. It was indeed a piece of journalistic good luck to be one of the first four correspondents to see behind that shroud of mystery.

Irvin Cobb and I put up at a big Brussels hotel and lost no time in calling on my old friend Brand Whitlock, the American minister to Belgium. The Germans were still in the east, having been delayed by the forts at Liége. The tension in Brussels was crushing. New York and London papers were painting the Kaiser as a mad dog, the German soldiers as barbarous Huns. In imagination one saw them slashing a murderous road through helpless Belgium. Behind this immediate picture, in my mind, lay the background of Manila episodes, where also the Germans had been given the role of brutal aggressors. I did not realize it at the time, but in Hong Kong in 1898 the devious propaganda war between Britain and Germany had begun, with the United States as prize.

I can also remember, in Brussels, how hopeless it seemed that I could *see* anything of this war. We tried in every way to get permission to go out toward the German advance. In despair we decided to try a subterfuge. We applied to the American consul, who gave us each a formidable-looking document dripping with large red seals. There was nothing in this to enable us to pass lines. All it said was that we were American citizens. Yet on it four of us started out in a taxicab, Irvin Cobb, Will Irwin, Arno Dosch and I. We all climbed in, intending to go as far as we could and return to Brussels well in advance of the invading legions.

We were stopped at each barricade. The soldiers looked at our documents, shrugged their shoulders and let us through. One by one we passed the various guards and outposts of the Belgian lines. We passed breastworks and trenches and streetcars that had been thrown across the street. It amazed and amused us to find how potent our worthless passes seemed to be. Before long we were out of the city and headed toward Louvain. That was a dramatic road. We passed through large detachments of Belgian soldiers, tired and worn, and machine guns drawn by dogs. Then we began meeting refugees, first in little groups, later in solid streams. Some had carts or wagons loaded with household goods. Men, women, children, dogs—a sorry procession, silent, resigned, helpless victims of war.

Nobody stopped us. Nobody tried to stop us. Then it dawned on us that nobody wanted to stop us. When a city is about to fall, all precautions are relaxed. A car dashed by, loaded with newsreel photographers. They waved us to turn back. "The Germans are coming!"

The taxi driver didn't look happy, but he took us in a reflective sort of way to within a couple of miles of Louvain. From a slope we looked down on the town. The sound of firing came from somewhere beyond. Then the driver got off his perch and made a long survey of the machinery under the hood, coming to the conclusion that the car had arrived at a state in which it would travel only in the direction of Brussels.

"I go no farther!" he said. "If I am cut off, they take my cab!"

All persuasion being useless, I left my light raincoat in the car, we obtained his promise to wait for us and started toward the town on foot.

People were grouped in every doorway. Some priests waited in a walled garden. The occasional shots sounded nearer. In the streets there was an absence of hurry and noise, but the silence here was not the silence of unconcern. The king had left two hours before.

"I understand any correspondent caught in the German Army will be shot," remarked Irwin.

Suddenly a group of Belgian soldiers ran out of one side street and into another. A second group darted across. We had gone only a few more steps forward when two figures rounded a corner. It was almost a minute before we realized what we were seeing. One was a uhlan on a horse, his rifle lying across his saddle. The other was a German soldier on a motorcycle. We flattened ourselves against the wall. The Germans rode slowly by, their steel-blue eyes scanning the street ahead. I shall never forget them.

War in the streets seemed imminent. Not wishing to be caught in the cross fire, we hurried back toward the taxicab, but when we reached the Brussels road, we found we had been cut off. A column of troops had swung into it and was marching toward Brussels in clouds of white dust. Our taxi man was doubtless going in the same direction, but in a little cloud of dust all of his own making—with my raincoat in lieu of fare!

I had been worrying about not getting to the front in this war. Now the front had come to us. We were engulfed in the mightiest front in Europe—straw-hatted, without so much as a toothbrush, speaking only English, and I with a letter to the President of France in my pocket. We felt reasonably sure we could not be mistaken for Belgians. Cobb couldn't look like anything but an American if he tried. Indiana stuck out all over me—as it always does. But we decided to report ourselves at the first possible moment, to tell them that we were not there for any malicious purpose, that we were simply there because we had come in a taxi and could not get back.

Meanwhile we watched the river of gray flow down the Rue de la Station on its way to Brussels and France and history. Two solid streams of soldiers, thousands and tens of thousands of infantry, tens of thousands of cavalry with poised lances, hundreds of artillery pieces, and thousands of soldiers on bicycles rolled into the Grand Place like a flood that had no end. The roar of motors, the clatter of hoofs and the measured fall of thousands of heavy boots on the pavements were both stupefying and hypnotic.

The columns flowed in, singing in great choruses. The songs swelled in thunderous strains above the plaza beneath the Hôtel de Ville and the Cathedral of St. Pierre.

We waited until we saw an especially jovial-looking German officer and then reported to him, explaining in some trepidation how we happened to be there. Instead of ordering us to be shot immediately, he laughed heartily. Then he called other officers and together they laughed over the circumstance of the American correspondents caught between the lines, who had come out in a taxi to see the war.

They would not give us permission to return to Brussels. It would have been too dangerous for us, with sniping and reprisals, as well as imprudent for the army to allow us to go after having seen so much. We were not made prisoners, we were at liberty to go about the city, but we must not leave until we had permission. This was partly for our own safety. The fact that in many eyes we may have looked English made us marked men. In the few hours that we had been in town, our presence had been reported to the authorities by the secret-service agents fifteen or twenty times. So we found a little hotel facing the station, Hôtel des Mille Colonnes, from which hour after hour we watched the unbroken stream of gray-clad soldiers pouring through the town, on and on without end, forenoon, afternoon, evening and night. In the morning we awakened to the same roar in our ears, the same compact volume of German power still surging and singing onward.

The landlord could give us nothing to eat, but at a little delicatessen store we bought some bread and cheese and a can of pineapple. A number of German soldiers were in the shop at the time, and we noticed with some surprise that they were paying for their purchases. It was a pleasure to find that the invaders were not the maddened barbarians we had been led to believe. During the three days in Louvain I never saw a single exhibition of rudeness or discourtesy from a German soldier or officer to a citizen. In the barbershops I saw officers patiently wait their turn while citizens preceded them into the chairs, a small matter perhaps, nevertheless an indication of the desire of the soldiers to avoid giving offense to the people.

Two days later we were free to leave Louvain.

Our ride back to the capital was in striking contrast to the ride out three days before. Gaunt walls were all that remained of many houses. Rude mounds with extemporized wooden crosses stood by the road here and there. But the fields of grain were undisturbed. The wake of the army showed no instance of wanton destruction. On entering Brussels, we saw where a camp had been made in a park. None of the trees had been damaged, and even the sod that had been removed lay carefully stacked up for replacement. This careful preservation of the park was as thorough as the careful destruction of the Belgian snipers and their homes.

Within three or four days after we left Louvain we heard of the tragic outbreak there that shocked the world. In view of the historic importance of events just preceding and following the partial destruction of the city, I described rather fully in my dispatches the events I saw. The fact that I was one of four American newspapermen in a position to chronicle first impressions gave my observation an interest it might not otherwise have had. Much war news that reached American readers was somewhat one-sided. I endeavored to give both sides.

For days the endless German column marched through Brussels, so long in fact that it seemed to have become a fixed feature of the landscape, like the rows of trees or the monuments. Hundreds of thousands of men and horses passed, so many that the magnitude of the movement benumbed the senses.

Business was resumed and the city overcame its nervousness. It was learned that England and France were rushing their troops up from the border and massing near Waterloo. It seemed probable that a second battle, on a larger scale, might be fought ninety-nine years later on that historic field.

We were impatient to get out there as soon as possible. We each obtained a pass from General von Jarotsky, the German Commandant of Brussels. It stated that Mr. Whosit, American journalist representing the *Such and So*, was permitted to pass through the German lines. To this brief document was affixed the photograph of the bearer. It was probably intended for use only in the environs of the city, but anything with the stamp of the German Government on it bore a magic potency which we used to such excellent effect that it carried us past thousands of Germans all the way to the French frontier until that ill-fated day when we ran into an officer superior in rank to General von Jarotsky.

This time all the taxis and cars in the city had been commandeered by the Germans. Two street hacks were finally subsidized for the short trip. One of the drivers had served in the Belgian artillery and presumably was a man of great courage. We started out at four o'clock in the afternoon with the intention of seeing something of this great battle of Waterloo and getting back in time for dinner.

There were seven of us in the two hacks, plus the two drivers in their rumpled silk hats. Many people in Sunday clothes watched our exodus with amusement. When we reached Waterloo there were no armies, but we could hear the distant rumble of artillery. A good deal of diplomacy was necessary to induce the drivers to proceed. At an inn an excited landlord assured us that a great battle was raging only eight miles farther on.

The battle which began that day was the famous Battle of Mons in which the great force of Germans commenced to push back the English and French. Here the English General French showed brilliant strategy, saving his army from the enveloping tactics of the Germans. For three days we followed this battle without catching up with it.

That first evening, at dusk, our drivers obstinately deposited us in front of L'Aigle Noir in the Grand Place at Nivelles and, scarcely stopping to breathe their weary horses, again set out along the twenty miles to Brussels. Will Irwin, who was suffering from tonsillitis, decided to go back with them. This left Cobb, Dosch, James O'Donnell Bennett, Harry Hansen, Roger Lewis and me. We gathered round a table in the barroom where the landlord provided a banquet of cold meat, eggs, coffee, bread and cheese. We were the center of an excited, curious crowd all talking at once. To our chagrin we learned that the town was practically devoid of all means of transportation. The army had commandeered all cars, horses, vehicles and gasoline. We decided to proceed on foot.

At six o'clock next morning we started out. Except for sandwiches and two boxes of cigars, we were unhampered by impedimenta. A somber hush hung over the country. In spite of the bright sunshine, the orderly fields, the tree-lined roadways, there was that in the atmosphere which betokened sudden calamity. The people who remained stood in little groups, talking in low tones, and regarded us in wonder. Often we caught the word *"Anglais."* We hoped to reach Mons, eighteen miles away, in five hours. We passed through Seneffe and Manage and presently came up with a German column.

"Who are you? What are you doing here?"

We showed our passes and the officer received us with an address of welcome. Would he honor us by having a drink? we asked.

He would, with pleasure.

An hour later other officers invited us to come and try some of the army soup. It was then noon, we had come only nine miles. We began to fear the battle would not last long enough for us to catch up with it, but we needed sustenance. Also, the German officers did not seem to fit my preconceived picture of insolent, domineering creatures who pushed people off sidewalks. Instead I found a degree of courtesy which was as pleasing as it was surprising.

After luncheon, as the column began to move, our friends waved to us from their horses and called *"Auf Wiedersehen."* Thanks to our potent passes, all afternoon we were able to march along beside the baggage train. We were turning down the road into Bascoup

ISLAND SCENES

The *Windrift*.

The Admiral doubling on the banjo.

Barr, Shaw and Jackie.

The Watch Tower.

VIEWS OF THE ISLAND

when an officer in a passing car hailed us. Confidently we explained ourselves.

"I'm sorry," he said politely, "but you cannot go any farther. You must go back."

"We have passes," we assured him.

"It is impossible for you to continue. We do not allow newspapermen with the army. You must go back immediately."

His voice carried conviction. Our hearts sank but we extended our passes.

He looked at them, whistled low and made a gesture of despair. "Very well," he said, "you may continue!"

Our spirits rose like rockets. We forged ahead of the baggage train. But all was not well with us.

Cobb weighed over 200 pounds. He was an excellent walker, but unfortunately he wore rubber-soled shoes. Every step had become an agony. The rest of us, too, were more or less disabled by the day's walk of twenty miles. As we limped into the town of Binche, it became evident that if we wished to go farther, we must find some other means of locomotion.

In the morning we resumed our quest for transportation. Lewis who spoke a little French, Hansen who spoke good German, and I who spoke neither, spent hours tramping from one stable to another in search of a horse. By the middle of the afternoon we closed a deal for a roan mare, aged about twenty, an old cart and a set of harness for 775 francs.

The horse's name was Bulotte, meaning Fat Girl, alias Gray Gables in honor of her prominent hipbones.

On the advice of a young German who called to see how we were getting along, we bought also two bicycles and I spent part of the afternoon learning to ride again. A collection of Bincheans watched me delightedly.

In the morning we left Binche. Lewis and I rode the bicycles; Cobb, Hansen and Bennett followed in the cart. Dosch had left us to make his way forty-five miles back to Brussels to get a magazine article off before his deadline. We started in a direct line for Maubeuge although the army took a different route. It seemed lonely without the familiar rumble of columns under way, but we decided we could make better progress without them.

In the town of Merbre-le-Château we found the first evidence of an atrocity and we stopped to investigate; a man had had his throat cut and several houses had been burned. From one source we heard that the citizen was deliberately murdered; from another that he had been studying the German troops with field glasses; and from still another that English soldiers had been firing from the house at German skirmishers. The last explanation I believe to have been the most probable one, for the Germans made no secret of the army's policy of killing citizens in houses where sniping had been done.

The bridge across the Sambre at this point had been destroyed and we were obliged to go several miles out of our way to Buissière where there was another. Once across the river, we could swing back to Maubeuge. At the bridge our passes were examined by a German outpost and found sufficient. The young man asked if we would like to see how the battle had been fought, which of course we would. So we followed him up a steep path under the bluff, along the edge of which ran the earthworks. The town lay compactly below. Even from this incomparable position, the French failed to stem the Teuton advance. The scene in the trenches was one of great confusion. Caps, haversacks, food, tobacco, broken rifles, bloodstained notebooks told eloquently how precipitate had been the flight of the defenders.

Beyond Buissière a broad road led to Beaumont. We decided to try that direction. If nothing was happening there, we might still get back to Maubeuge in time.

This maneuver led us quite unexpectedly into the general staff headquarters of that part of the German Army operating in France and Belgium, and when they found these American correspondents riding along in advance of a large part of their troops, I am sure it must have occasioned them surprise and wonderment! But I am ahead of my story.

By this time a drizzle had set in and it was pretty late. We had great anxiety about approaching the German outposts after dark. Also, there was danger of a French scouting party swinging in from the south. We were, in fact, between the two armies. For three days now we had kept on and on, always expecting to be stopped but always, by some freak of luck, being allowed to pass still nearer to the front. Ahead, the road ascended steeply to where it merged into the winding street that led into Beaumont. We knew that if we followed it, we should reach the inevitable square. The town was jammed with troops. We decided to report to the officer in command, as we had done with such excellent results before.

The war correspondent, according to popular conception in those days, was generally a dashing sort of person in smart riding clothes. Not so, however, were the correspondents who found themselves on August 26 down on the French frontier with the sound of great battles to right and to left. By no stretch of the imagination could we have been considered dashing. We had unshaved faces, soiled linen, dusty rumpled clothes now wet with drizzle. I prefer not to dwell on what we looked like when we drew up before the town hall in the square in Beaumont.

Soon an officer came out, a stern, handsome man on whose coat was the white cloth cross indicating high nobility. He took us in in one sweeping glance, an all-embracing glance which missed nothing—not even the fact that two of us wore straw hats.

"Who are you and what are you doing here?"

He spoke excellent English and he was polite but with an absence of that warmth we had hoped for.

We explained that we were American correspondents.

"How did you get here?"

We indicated the tired little mare and the bicycles, parked among the high-powered cars.

He smiled grimly. "The German Army," he said, "allows no correspondents with it."

"But we've been with it for several days," we said. "Our passes have always been accepted." We handed them to him and he studied the official stamps carefully. Then he conferred with another officer. They spoke together and Hansen understood.

"They are part of the same outfit," said the first one. "The others had passes like these which are meant for Brussels."

We were then asked to wait, something we soon got accustomed to doing.

Presently a more friendly general came out and informed us that if we had gone forward toward Maubeuge as we had intended, and had been found, we would really have been shot; that two men with the same sort of passes as ours had already been found within the lines and arrested.

"Those two men will be sent as prisoners to Liége," he said, "but you will be sent back to Brussels tomorrow." Then he asked us, "How do you get your reports in?"

We told him we had not sent a word, that there was no means of doing so. Our desire, we said, was to follow the army in order to tell the truth about what we saw. We pointed out that our reports might have the effect of counteracting the stories of alleged German atrocities which were flooding the world, for we had seen no evidence of such things.

The general shook his head.

"You are not prisoners, but you must not try to escape. Return here tomorrow morning when arrangements will be made for sending you back."

It was some time before we could find quarters for ourselves which would also accommodate poor old Bulotte. Finally some obliging soldiers directed us to a schoolhouse where we pushed Bulotte into the playground through a tiny door in a wall.

As yet we had not eaten. In our pockets we had some chocolate, sandwiches and eleven hard-boiled eggs, also the remnants of two boxes of cigars and cigarettes. With these we made our way back to a schoolroom where some soldiers were singing, and ate our supper on a bench.

Of all the vivid impressions of the days in Belgium, this one is most vivid—and how those men could sing!

I wish I could have sketched it on the spot instead of from memory, but sketching is dangerous in an army. The ability to draw focuses suspicion on one's motives. Next to a camera a sketchbook is the surest way to invite trouble.

Early in the morning we set about trying to sell the horse and cart. No one in town would give anything for them. We offered the whole outfit to a soldier for one mark, but he just laughed and there was no deal. In the end we gave them to a young Belgian who accepted them without enthusiasm, hitched up and drove away.

We then reported once more to the town hall. Columns were forming, motor vans pulling out, official cars purring in readiness. In the colorful picture of that quaint plaza of Beaumont, there was only one incongruous note—a group of five very disheveled, hungry-looking Americans waiting by the door. That we were being observed and discussed was painfully evident. For an hour or more we waited. At ten o'clock the staff departed. One of the last things that one of the last departing officers did was to turn us over to a tall young lieutenant named Mittendorfer, who informed us there was no way at present of returning us to Brussels.

As long as the general staff was in Beaumont, we had been reasonably free to move about the town. As soon, however, as they left for the front, the responsibility of his charge must have weighed heavily on Lieutenant Mittendorfer, for he placed us under a guard armed with a rifle and bayonet.

"You are not prisoners," he said, "but you must not leave this spot."

We sat on the spot, which was a stone bench in front of the guardhouse, until the middle of the afternoon. At three o'clock it began to rain and we were asked to step inside.

In another moment we had been marched into the guardhouse.

There we found a French suspect, a Belgian suspect, a Congo Negro chauffeur and a couple of French prisoners of war. The first two were doubtless the ones who had passes like ours, mentioned by the German officer. The room was twelve or fifteen feet square and the floor was half a foot deep in straw. A sentry stood at the door, another at the window. Of course we "were not prisoners" but we could not leave the room under penalty of having a bayonet run through us. Our sensations were far from exhilarating.

The next time we saw Lieutenant Mittendorfer, we hailed him earnestly. He was profuse in his apologies and permitted us to transfer from the guardhouse to a little café next door.

There was no exit in the rear, for a high wall surrounded the tiny courtyard. Always in the doorway sat the guard with the rifle and fixed bayonet. Mattresses covered the barroom floor, on which we slept.

Two long days of imprisonment dragged by. Food was scarce, but of wine there was an abundance. Twenty thousand bottles had been found in the near-by cellars of Prince Caraman Chimay. For dinner we had rye bread and old Bordeaux, probably worth many dollars a bottle.

We heard the officer in charge giving his night orders to the guards on duty. "My children," he said (he was only twenty-six), "you must behave well, like German soldiers. You must not drink too much, for if you get drunk, no matter how much I like you, I will have you sent to prison for seven years."

This was the German penalty for drunkenness while on duty.

Next morning for breakfast we had rye bread and another rare old wine. At noon one of us, under escort, was sent out to forage for food. He came back with a few potatoes, some onions, a can of apricots, a jar of honey and a box of cigars. The landlady made stew and for the first time in three days we had something hot.

Toward evening we were finally told to be ready to leave in two hours. Two minutes were all we needed. At nine o'clock we marched to the railway station with a column of 250 French and English prisoners. We were not allowed to talk to them, but marched at the side between the guards. Our party was crowded into a second-class coach half full of German wounded. We pulled down our curtains as we were warned we might be fired upon. At midnight the train got under way. For where? We had no idea.

One of the lightest of us climbed into the rack for hand baggage and tried to sleep. By morning we had gone twenty-five miles to Charleroi. Then we lay at Gembloux for six hours while 700 more French and English prisoners were added and German troop trains rolled by. For breakfast we had rye bread, honey and Bordeaux; for lunch rye bread and honey. Later some Red Cross people distributed sausages and we got one or two. That night two of us climbed into the baggage rack. On the second morning, at Aix-la-Chapelle, we were put off.

"You may go to the American consul and get permission to leave Aix. After that you must report to the police for instructions."

Relieved, but looking scarcely human after the many nights in our clothes, we hurried to the consul's residence to find that he was out of town. The vice-consul made out papers for us. Then for twenty-four hours we shuttled between the military authorities and the secret police, who were reluctant to let us out of their clutches.

When the American consul came back from Liége, I discovered that he was an old friend, Robert J. Thompson of Chicago. He had long been an admirer of Cobb's work and of Jimmy Bennett's brilliant dramatic criticism for the *Tribune*. He speedily established our identity so that we were released from further surveillance; and he verified our newspaper connections so that the German officials recognized us as accredited correspondents. Thus the circumstance of our arrest at Beaumont, at the time a crushing disappointment, turned out to be a real piece of luck.

Bennett, Lewis and Hansen stopped at the large, gay Kaiserhof. Cobb and I took up quarters in the Hotel Nuellins, a quiet, conservative place in which the great of Germany were wont to stop.

From the time we had encountered the Germans in Louvain, especially during the trip down to Beaumont, we had been constantly impressed by the orderliness of the German behavior, not only to us, but to the native people of Belgium as well.

"Where are all these atrocities?" we asked one another. We had seen none. We had tried over and over to trace an atrocity story to its source. It was always elsewhere. Over and over we discussed this phase of German conduct, so very different from what the London papers had led us to expect.

Here we were, five American newspapermen, who, by a set of curious chances, had seen much of the German Army in its passage through Belgium, who had followed closely in its wake; here we were with a news story that Americans should hear. It seemed only fair to the Germans that we should say what conclusions we had reached, wholly independently and without coercion or bribe, about a situation that was stirring the world. Even though none of us was pro-German in his sympathies, it was the unanimous opinion of all of us that the atrocity stories were being tremendously and intentionally exaggerated. I feel I should add that we were not nearly so anti-German as we had been before seeing so much of them at close quarters.

I don't recall how the suggestion of a round robin came up. It may be that I mentioned the one we had sent from the Philippines in criticism of the Army. In any case it seemed the obvious way to make such a unanimous statement.

So a statement was prepared that expressed what each of us was willing to sign as representing his views. The five of us signed it, Jimmy Bennett and I for the *Chicago Tribune,* Cobb for the *Saturday Evening Post,* Lewis for the Associated Press and Hansen for the *Chicago Daily News.*

This statement, which was made entirely on our own initiative and in a spirit of justice, was sent to Berlin for transmission by wireless to the United States. It was known that it could not be sent by cable, for it could not have passed the London censor, through whose hands it would have to go.

Finally, of course, through the German war office, our statement reached the Kaiser and in due time we received a letter of thanks from the Reichskanzler or prime minister.

We never knew whether it had reached America at all until long afterward. Evidently there was much "interference" in that early wireless message. The AP man in New York had to do a good deal of guessing when he pieced it together.

Meanwhile there was not a great deal of news in Aix, although what there was we were free to send home from Vaals, just across the border in Holland. Lewis and Hansen departed for London; Cobb, Bennett and I stayed on. Hopeful of seeing more of the German Army in action, we wrote a respectful letter to the Kaiser asking permission to go to the front, and this, together with Consul Thompson's recommendation, enabled us to gain facilities which we might never have obtained had we been sent to any other city.

Captain Alfred Mannesmann was sent to take us back through the German lines. Thompson also went along. Except for the car, we newspapermen paid our own expenses for the next ten days. The contrasts were vivid and striking between our recent sojourn at the front and our present trip, accompanied by an officer with a Kaiser's pass.

On the first occasion, as quasi-prisoners, we had slept on straw with suspected spies. Now, Prince Reuss, ex-German minister to Persia, "bestirred himself to find lodgings for us," as Cobb put it. On the first occasion we ate only rye bread provided by our armed guard. Now we dined in the big hall of the Prefecture as guests of His Excellency Field Marshal von Heeringen, commanding the Seventh Army of the German Kaiser.

One of the staff officers greeted me courteously and referred to my Prince Henry cartoons which he said he had seen recently on the walls of the Prince's castle at Kiel. I cannot help wondering where they are now after two world wars!

My useful cartoon caption "The Changing World" seemed peculiarly applicable to ourselves just then, and I hope I am not overly optimistic when I opine that our personal appearance was similarly improved! Poetic justice would have been better served, had we encountered the same general we had come up against in Beaumont.

During those ten days with the German Army we saw the great fortresses of Maubeuge battered and smashed. At Brimont, with the twin towers of Reims Cathedral only a scant three miles away, I stood by the guns that had shelled it less than a week before.

We were told and retold how the French were using the towers as an observation post; how two German officers under a flag of truce had been sent to warn them to cease; and how those officers had never returned. It became one of those interminable war controversies, in which each side sticks to an opposite story.

In Laon, it was arranged for me to fly with Ingold, already a well-known aviator. A Bavarian staff officer lent me his leather coat.

"It has my shoulder straps," he said. "If you fall into the hands of the enemy you will be treated as an officer, not as a spy."

I was conscious of a new thrill of interest.

"Be careful not to bump against the gasoline tank," I was cautioned. It was just above my head in the biplane, which was not a combat plane and was not even armed. In the open cockpit were two handles to which I clung. The propeller was in front but high enough so that the blast passed over me. The wind was erratic and full of pockets. I became a fatalist. No amount of anxiety could affect the outcome of the voyage.

A smoky blur seventy miles to the southwest was Paris. The entire battle front along the Aisne was dotted with microscopic figures. Huge clouds of belching smoke from the French and English batteries, and answering bursts of unfolding white billows from the German side, told how savagely the great duel was raging, and meant that every moment men were being torn to pieces. But I could not hear the deep growl of the guns above the noise of our motor. From our 3,000-foot height we could watch the battle more or less relieved from anxiety of being shot. If an Allied balloon gun had fired on us, we could not have

*The Balloon Gun Shelling a French Airplane*

known it unless we saw the white puffs of smoke; if a hostile plane were hovering over us, we could not have heard it.

Such indeed proved to be the case—a Frenchman *was* high in the clouds above us but we were happily unconscious of the menace of his movements.

A crowd gathered about us as we landed.

"See the Frenchman!" they cried, and we watched with interest as the exploding shells, like white flowers, bloomed in the sky around him. In view of subsequent experience of plane warfare in the First World War, we had been in no very great danger from him, nor he from the shells, but at the time it gave an added zest.

The *Tribune* gave this flight of mine much prominence. Up to that time I am not aware that any civilian had flown in either a German or an Allied plane over the lines.

From that gun emplacement at Brimont, I had gazed out over the broad plain, where only five years before I had attended the first aviation meet ever held. Under the impetus of war necessity already that incredible development was under way which was to scrap all the military strategy that had governed war since the beginning.

## ~ 41 ~

## Lord Roberts

As MEN fresh from the German side of the battle front, we were objects of much curiosity to the London war leaders.

Lord Northcliffe was particularly kind. In front of the roaring fire in his chintz-curtained office in the *Times* building, he asked whom we would like to meet. Cobb aimed at the top, Lord Kitchener. To my knowledge Cobb was the only newspaperman to meet the illustrious Field Marshal. His story of this exclusive experience was a milestone in reporting. I felt that it was much more important for Kitchener to meet Cobb.

I myself was more interested in two men whom I had long admired: W. W. Jacobs, author of my favorite book, *Dialstone Lane*, and Haselden, cartoonist for the London tabloid, the *Mirror*, owned by Northcliffe. Unfortunately neither Jacobs nor Haselden was around.

On a memorable day, October 22, 1914, Northcliffe took Cobb and me to lunch with Lord Roberts at his house in Ascot.

The great hall was a perfect setting for one who had served his country for sixty years, and who was now spending the twilight of his life in peace surrounded by reminders of his thrilling days. Above the fireplace was a tremendous picture of a detachment of courageous Gurkhas fighting their way up a steep mountainside. To right and left of this were the heads of an ovis poli and an ovis ammon, those mountain sheep of Central Asia considered by sportsmen to be the greatest prize in big game. One had come from the Tien Shan Mountains in Chinese Turkestan where I had been eight years before. This established a bond of interest and helped me to get acquainted.

Lady Aileen Roberts preceded her father into the room by a few minutes. Then Lord Roberts entered. I had expected to see a larger man, certainly a much older-looking one. His height was only five feet three. His face was ruddy and his hair so thin that he appeared bald. There were deep lines under his alert eyes, and good-natured wrinkles radiated from the corners of them. There was no military effect to his appearance. His voice was clear and steady and he seemed sixty-five rather than eighty-two.

We were immediately made to feel at home.

"They must have a great army," he said when his daughter told him where we had been. He was eager to know the spirit of the German soldiers, and when we told him that the army, as we had seen it, seemed a unit in enthusiasm and confidence, he nodded as if that were what he had expected. He asked detailed questions about how we had come to be caught in the German advance and how we had been treated.

I was struck by the impersonal attitude both he and Northcliffe exhibited when discussing the enemy. They did not show the same bitterness I have found so often among Americans. When we told him that, in our observation, the Germans had been operating with discipline, and that the stories of atrocities were undoubtedly exaggerated, we were surprised to find that this was his own opinion. In the course of his long experience he had learned war psychology thoroughly.

Presently Lady Roberts came in on the arm of her elder daughter, Lady Edwina Stewart. Lord Roberts went at once to her side, and a few moments later lunch was announced. Lord Roberts' attitude toward his wife, who was suffering from the infirmities of age, was one of great devotion and deference. His demeanor could not have been more attentive, considerate and affectionate if he had been a young man in the courting period.

I suggested that his family must be finding it difficult to keep him from the front. He smiled and said he was sending his grandson instead. Above the mantel in the library was a portrait of his only son, who had been killed at the Battle of Colenso in 1899. It is said that at the time the casualty list was posted, officers who had not dared tell him the news watched with concern when he went over to scan the names. He read the list from top to bottom without any sign of emotion, then turned gravely and resumed his place at the desk he had just left.

Lord Roberts was good enough to consent to be sketched. Lady Roberts sat in an easy chair near by while her husband patiently, if somewhat sleepily, underwent the ordeal. He kindly signed the drawing, the chief value of which, I fear, lies in the fact that it was probably the last picture to be made of him before he died three weeks later.

It will be evident to readers who have got this far in these memoirs that the courtesies which the officers of the German Army paid us, and the kindnesses now offered us by Englishmen in high rank, came at a time when, by the chances of war, Cobb and I were in a position to be of great service to the cause they represented. We recognized this and realized that these marks of thoughtful hospitality were not without ulterior motives. The Germans wanted us to shade our reports in their favor; the British wished to counteract any influence which the Germans might have used to affect our neutrality. Hospitality, skillfully used, is the most insidious of all propaganda.

In contrast, the sincere welcome of old friends was a relief. I saw

Sir John and Hazel Lavery again and, on the night before sailing, I dined with the Selfridges at Landsdowne House.

I reached Chicago just before November 1, when my new contract with the *Tribune* was to go into effect, and I had been nowhere near Melville Island.

~ 42 ~

## Paris with Joe Patterson

IN 1915 Joseph Medill Patterson was coeditor and copublisher of the *Tribune*. He and I left for Paris in August on the new French liner *Provence*. It was the first time I had ever traveled with Joe. He told a friend of ours that he was almost afraid to go with me because he liked me so much, and he felt certain we would not come back friends. This was his way of saying that he considered himself very hard to get along with.

I had known Joe ever since I went on the *Tribune* and had always been interested in his philosophy. He had a keen zest and curiosity about life, a great desire for firsthand experience. He was intellectually honest, and though one might not agree with his opinions, one respected his courage in asserting them. I could not imagine Joe Patterson misrepresenting a fact although the truth might be awkward and have unpleasant consequences.

In his earlier days his novels and plays showed a social consciousness which drove him to give up a promising literary career for more direct public service. He went to the Illinois House of Representatives; he became a Socialist for a time and supported for mayor a municipal-ownership candidate, Edward F. Dunne. After Dunne was elected, Joe was appointed Commissioner of Public Works and, in the occasional absence of the mayor, acted for him. He was among the first to join the Army at the time of the Mexican border trouble and again when the United States entered the First World War. In both cases he enlisted as a private. He would not use pull to get a commission, although ultimately he became a captain.

Our common love of adventure gave us a fellow feeling. We started off together in the hope, this time, of seeing something of the French

side. We had a suite on the French liner and played dominoes a good
deal. One could not have wished a more interesting and companionable shipmate. In those days Joe had never asserted the importance
which his position gave him, and it was not difficult to abandon the
relation of employer and employee. In Paris we stayed together at
the Crillon for several months.

Again I was the bearer of a letter from ex-President Roosevelt,
which again I had no occasion to present. I still treasure this letter
along with others from the colonel—one of which signifies his intention of giving me a commission as captain if he were permitted to
recruit a regiment similar to his Rough Riders of the Spanish American War.

On reaching Paris Joe and I at once applied for permission to go to
the front, and were thus in line for any expedition which the French
Ministry of Information might authorize.

We found the airdromes much the most interesting places. In one
I saw the first sample of a new triplane, shaped like a ship with a
curving bow, and with places for cannon as well as machine guns.
There were three tiers of gun ports. I observed it carefully, and from
memory drew a picture of this amazing aero-battleship. When all
my sketches and reports were submitted later to the French liaison
officer, Prince d'Ahrenberg, he brought back everything duly O.K.'ed
except the picture of the triplane.

"I showed it to the Minister of War," explained the prince, "and he
was so interested in it he wanted to study it further. I felt sure you
would be glad to let him."

This was putting the matter with charming and effective indirec-
tion. They had, of course, good reason for keeping it, but I was interested to note that they did not black out my written description of
the plane. In subsequent years I never heard any further news of this
triplane, so I assume it did not work. It was a far cry from a Flying
Fortress or a B-29.

At Villacoublay, where the headquarters of the Morane Company
were based, we were shown what I think must have been the first of
the devices whereby a machine gun could be fired through the propeller.

We were both eager to fly and Joe got the first chance. One of the
Moranes took him up in a fast little monoplane. When he came
down he was excited and happy.

"Pretty high up, Morane turned around and said something that sounded like 'Voulez-vous loop?' I wasn't quite sure but I nodded anyhow, and pretty soon we were diving, and then with a terrific whirl I found my head hanging downward. After another dizzy whirl I was straight up again."

I congratulated Joe with real sincerity, if also with intense envy, but there was no opportunity for another flight that day. The best I achieved was to fly over Paris with a handsome young Frenchman named Jacques Baudry in a Parosol monoplane, a type I had never seen before. The fuselage was suspended below a broad wing and entirely separated from it. I devoutly hoped the fastenings were secure. No mention was made of looping, so there was no unusual thrill about this brief flight.

During periods of professional inactivity we found Paris pleasantly stimulating. This was before the air raids, and before Big Bertha, the seventy-five-mile gun. Every day I used to bring back to our room a copy of the *London Mirror*, in which lively tabloid Haselden's cartoons were then appearing. I have always felt that I may thus have contributed to the birth of Joe's idea for the *New York Daily News*, four years later.

Finally Joe left for home. The conducted tours to the front had amounted in the aggregate to disappointingly little that was worth while from a news point of view. I have no doubt that he could have used the power of his position more effectively had he cared to, but as far as anybody could tell from his own actions, he was merely another correspondent of the paper.

I hated to see him go. Instead of straining our friendship, these three months of sharing cabin and hotel room, and being together almost constantly, had made us, I think, better friends than ever.

At any rate that was the first of several trips we took together. In 1924 he asked me to go to the Texas border with him. Planes were patrolling it day and night, partly to prevent smuggling, partly as a military gesture. We flew in a large circle over the Mexican side, in spite of the fact that Mexicans considered planes over their territory in the light of invasion and made it unpleasant for any that landed. The novelty of this particular flight for me consisted in flying over mountains. I had never done that before.

Another time we went hunting in New Brunswick. Joe got his moose; I didn't. At home in Chicago, he used to come up to my apartment of an evening, and I don't know how many hours we spent playing dominoes and dice golf.

It is an interesting fact that the four grandchildren of Joseph Medill, founder of the *Chicago Tribune*, turned out so well. With all their wealth, power and influence, they had every facility in the world to spend their lives in self-indulgence or the excesses of extravagance. Yet each of the four led a life of usefulness and achievement. They were all hard workers. They were born to their jobs, of course, but they could hardly have held jobs like theirs without native ability and personal effort.

All three boys gave their services to public affairs. J. Medill Mc-Cormick served in the legislature, then as congressman at large, and ended his life from the lofty eminence of the United States Senate. His brother, Robert R. McCormick—or Bert as he is known to his closer friends—served in the Chicago city council and as president of the sanitary district. Joe Patterson served in the state and the city government. Joe's sister Elinor, better known as Cissy, the fourth grandchild, had a literary career of merit and was herself a newspaper editor.

When Jim Keeley left the *Tribune* to undertake a newspaper venture of his own, I had a feeling that the *Tribune* had suffered a serious loss. Yet inside of a year the circulation had increased by 40,000. The cousins, Joe and Bert, had become joint editors and publishers of the paper. They alternated each month in the direction of the editorial policy. Although this arrangement worked unexpectedly well, it was not ideal.

After the founding of the *New York Daily News* in 1919, its steady growth to the greatest circulation in the United States made it necessary for Joe to transfer his headquarters to New York, and Bert Mc-Cormick, now a colonel, assumed sole direction of the *Tribune* and its allied industries, paper mills, shipping lines and other vast ramifications reaching to every great capital in the world.

Joe was a very considerate employer. I always had a feeling that he was behind me, that he believed in me, was sympathetic with my point of view, although that point of view often departed widely from the conservative. He liked cartoons that differed radically from the conventional, no matter how unusual or bizarre they might be; I think he approved of anything that aroused curiosity, speculation or interest of any sort among the readers. He had confidence that my cartoons sensed what people were thinking about, and represented and analyzed public opinion correctly. He was often kind enough to tell me that he had great respect for my judgment in consequence.

It is true that he said, "John *feels*; he doesn't think!" But he also said—and this pleased me very much—that I was the only person with whom he really liked to travel. I have always regretted that his fortunes took him away from Chicago. I saw little of him after that.

Joe was dominant, forceful, wayward. It was characteristic of him to learn to fly after he was fifty, especially as I do not think he was in any way mechanical-minded. He had his moods, sometimes of deep gloom; yet he had an amazingly likable streak that could almost be called winsome. With his outstanding capacity for directing newspapers, he was one of the great publishers of the country.

I never had the opportunity to know Colonel McCormick as intimately as I knew Joe. He is a different type. With a similar educational background superimposed on a boyhood in England, Bert has been more the expression of his class than Joe was. He has appeared more to enjoy and exercise the reins of power. He doesn't thaw out and sit about with the crowd, not because he is unwilling to, but simply because his nature is different. A familiar figure in the hunting field, an ardent polo enthusiast, he has used these sports to keep in good physical condition, enjoying as he does the possession of a notable physique. He is six feet five inches tall, powerfully built, without excess weight.

Joe's purpose was to get what he could out of life in his various undertakings, largely for the adventure. In the case of his cousins, Bert and Medill, I think they embarked on political life with much the same motives that actuated Theodore Roosevelt, when, as a young man, he ran for the New York State Assembly. They had the ambition to make something of themselves, and at that time political life seemed to offer the best approach. Fortune diverted Bert to the responsibilities of a great metropolitan journal.

Bert's devotion to work and attention to detail has been amazing. Weekly conferences with the heads of all departments, held at luncheon in the directors' room, keep him in the closest touch with everything about the paper. Daily conferences with the editorial writers, cartoonists, managing editor and other keymen of the organization fill his days. When not actively occupied at the office, he is generally attending meetings in other cities and making addresses; or he is tramping for miles through the *Tribune's* timberlands around Shelter Bay; or he is supervising the *Tribune's* experimental farm; or reading until late at night. He has a keen, historically trained mind; his knowledge of both American and European backgrounds is matched only by his editorial writer Clifford Raymond, now retired, whose knowledge also appears boundless. Bert has a great sense of pictorial journalism and the *Tribune* has made a larger demand on the cartoon than most papers.

That the *Tribune* remained in the family after Robert W. Patterson's death in 1910 was due to Bert's successful intervention. Fearing that no satisfactory form of management could be arranged under the two Medill daughters, the directors thought of selling the paper to Victor Lawson.

At first encounter with the then redoubtable publisher, Bert tells how in his nervousness he found himself lighting one cigarette after another. Displeased with this reaction, "I'll stop smoking," he said, and he did.

But this self-discipline is leavened by his sense of humor. "I have observed," he says, "that the man who catches the eight-o'clock train catches the eight-o'clock, but the man who catches the nine:ten is apt to miss the twelve:fifteen."

Steadily, since Bert assumed direction, the paper has continued its march to greater influence and power, and this in spite of the terrific drain of depressions and wars. His justice in the conduct of the paper and his generosity in his dealings with his employees are outstanding. My relations with Bert, while not so close as those with Joe, have always been marked by a consideration and kindness on his part for which I shall never cease to be grateful.

The *Tribune* is controlled by a small group of stockholders dominated by the Medill family interests, and having no outstanding bonds. It is in a position of complete independence and can be influenced by no outside pressure. The *Tribune* has always swum against the tide. That is one of its historic virtues. It has been truly liberal in the old-fashioned sense of the term, not the present sense. It has fought against things in public life when the popular and easy thing would have been to go along. When it might have trailed, an acquiescent follower, it has struck out boldly on its chosen course. There have been many times when the *Tribune's* policies have at first lost, so many, in fact, that politicians are wont to say that its support means certain defeat. But in the long run, in the issues that cover years, I believe the *Tribune's* stand has usually been vindicated.

It has inherited its character honestly from a family of strong characters. The Medill daughters, Mrs. McCormick and Mrs. Patterson, both were positive in their convictions, and both had rapier wit which

they were too often apt to use against each other. The *Tribune* cashier
was said to have standing orders to buy a ticket for the one to leave
town at once, should the other arrive.

Once I received a letter from Mrs. Patterson, in which she bewailed
the fact that my cartoons were so critical of the dominating Republican regulars. "Why is youth so harsh? As you mature, you will grow
kinder."

A day or two after the United States had declared war against Germany in 1917, I was looking into a bookstore window on Michigan
Avenue. Suddenly I heard a voice at my elbow:

"What do you think of this goddam war?"

It was the elderly Mrs. McCormick.

## ～ 43 ～

# Saloniki

"Go to Saloniki stopping Athens for interview with Venizelos."

This cable from the *Tribune* suddenly ended those agreeable days
in Paris. After Joe left, I had moved to a small room up on the
mansard floor of the Crillon, where from a little balcony I could look
across a sea of treetops to the Arc de Triomphe.

Now I started for Italy and the Levant. Bill Shepherd of the U.P.
and Jimmy Hare representing *Collier's* decided to come with me.
Jimmy had photographed all the wars for many years. The three of
us proceeded to Athens by way of Messina and the Corinth Canal.

When the ship came to anchor in the port of the Peiraeus, I had
three hours in which to get my interview with Mr. Venizelos. Athens
was not far away, and I found the American minister, Mr. Trotter,
friendly and helpful. But a correspondent cannot drop into an ancient
capital and find its eminent statesmen sitting about waiting to be
interviewed. Neither diplomacy nor personal dignity works that way.
By the time I walked up the steps of Venizelos' house, two of my
three hours had elapsed.

The prime minister was dignified and polite. He talked frankly
and without reservations. Venizelos, Greece's greatest statesman, was

pro-Ally, but Constantine, the Danish King of Greece, had a pro-German slant. Conditions in Greece at the end of October 1915 were of deep concern to all of Europe. But my mind was on the clock. The interview seemed to last a long time. Finally I rose, thanked him respectfully and departed, making a mighty effort not to show the haste I felt consuming me. I dashed to the cable office. There was no censorship to delay me, but the painstaking care of the operator, counting the words and then recounting them, was a terrific ordeal. Then he had to figure out the amount due, and he did that twice.

At last I was in a taxi; we sped to the Peiraeus, to the pier, into a rowboat. But there was a solid mass of small craft hemming me in. I pointed to my ship—she seemed to be lying miles away. We pushed and prodded the boats aside and reached clear water. I looked at my watch. The time was up. I looked at the ship. The anchor was up. I rose in the stern sheets and waved frantically. Shepherd and Hare were watching for me and rushed to the captain. We reached the ship's side. Rather than risk an argument, I pressed on my boatman an amount liberal enough to leave him almost as breathless as I. I caught the sea ladder and climbed to the deck of the moving ship, gasping and panting. I felt ten years older.

Saloniki was a bewildering confusion of ships and soldiers and monumental uncertainties. On our way to the Olympos Palace Hotel, I stopped to photograph a body of Greek soldiers, and escaped arrest and detention only because the Greek policeman spoke English and had lived in Chicago.

"Where do you live?" he asked.

"Corner of Astor and Schiller," said I.

"Ha!" he said. "I lived on Division."

Only a few streets apart. We became at once old friends.

There was only one room vacant in the hotel. It was forty feet long by twenty feet wide and had formerly been the Austrian Club. The three of us established ourselves in the spacious domain. Just across the street below our windows lay the panorama of the water front. Greek fishing boats lay side by side, moored to the old stone sea wall, their gaily painted prows headed seaward. Far to the right, invisible from that distance, but manifesting its presence, was Mount Olympus.

A couple of days after our arrival Richard Harding Davis turned up. As there were no more rooms available just then, we invited him to share ours. He used to take an ice-water tub every morning, causing the rest of us to shiver in our blankets. It was cold enough in the room as it was.

Eventually Dick found a room for himself, and when I used to go up, he was generally writing, with several sweaters on and his feet wrapped around a red-hot oil stove. He did not seem to be reacting properly to his ice-water ordeals.

When we first reached Saloniki, there were few foreign correspondents. Two months later there were at least twenty, representing the leading news agencies of the pro-Ally or neutral world.

With the evacuation of Gallipoli, the British forces had come to Saloniki. The bay was jammed with warships, battleships, transports and hospital ships. The big hotel was thronged with officers. The ancient Thessalonian city had become an important news center.

Every morning we could be seen at the daily conference held in the office of the commander in chief of the Allied forces, General Sarrail, where the general or a member of his staff revealed as much as was prudent of the news of army movements. Questions were permitted; some were answered; some were not. The custom of seeing and talking to correspondents is a good one, although it was most unusual in that war of official aloofness.

No one was permitted to quote General Sarrail. He did not give out interviews or talk for publication, but in a situation as complicated as that in Saloniki where rumors and alarums spread like wildfire, it was well to have some place where authoritative statements might be obtained.

One day, when rumors of Allied reverses were persistent, the general sent for the newspapermen. He leaned against a window sill and confronted the correspondents who were standing, paper and pencil in hand. It was the tenth of December. He then announced that the British and French troops were retiring. There was no further value in retaining an advanced and dangerous position in Serbia. Prudence required withdrawal to a strategically safer line of defense. Bridges were being burned, tunnels destroyed, all matériel and equipment were being saved. In its first few days the retreat had been remarkably free from casualties. Only about thirty men had been lost.

There was complete silence in the little room in the Mission Saïque Française. No one was taking a chance of misquoting a general who was explaining why his troops, after two weeks' fighting, were giving up their positions and retreating.

As soon as this momentous conference was over, we caught an empty freight train headed for the front—Shepherd, Hare, Bass, Davis and I. In Gradek and Strumitsa we saw the first detachments of the retreating French Army. We were not allowed to proceed farther, but did make a short detour to the near-by border of Bulgaria where, across a wide valley, we found ourselves under fire from a Bulgar battery.

The long, halting night trip back to Saloniki in a freezing-cold freight car, without blankets, was one of utter wretchedness. I don't believe Davis ever really got thawed out.

During the retreat the Bulgarian forces pressed forward relentlessly and the casualty lists increased. At last the Allied forces were in Greek territory. Would the Bulgars follow? Greece indicated she would resent the Bulgars advancing alone and stipulated that German troops must lead the invasion and guarantee that the integrity of Macedonia would not be violated. The Greek Army marched out of Saloniki and massed west of the border. To the north were the Allied lines, with the Central Powers beyond; to the south was the harbor crowded with battleships. It was a four-sided front, the whole situation loaded with TNT.

In the midst of this electric tension came the German air raid of December 30, the first move in German hostilities against Saloniki. On a day of brilliant sunshine three planes flew over and dropped about forty bombs. One struck near the Greek barracks while General Moscopolos was reviewing a cavalry regiment; another killed a shepherd near the aviation camp; three British soldiers on a transport were wounded; and a few bombs landed in the French camp. Enormous crowds watched the raid, which had instant repercussions.

The Allies were preponderant in Saloniki and at once arrested the consular staffs of Germany, Austria, Bulgaria and Turkey, and imprisoned or interned them on a French warship. All those scrambled evenings at the Olympos Palace Hotel café were over—no more would German officials sit cozily alongside British officers slightly in their cups. Greek neutrality was put aside; Venizelos quickly capitalized on the raid and King Constantine had to support him.

It was during these supercharged days that I had an amusing experience. I had written a note to Captain Metaxas, aide to Crown Prince George of Greece, asking if I might have the honor of making a sketch of His Royal Highness, who had just come up from Athens for a few days. I had never seen the Crown Prince, nor was I familiar with his pictured features. After some delay I received a note from Captain Metaxas asking me to come to the headquarters of Prince Andrew, brother of King Constantine, for tea at four o'clock the following afternoon.

I appeared with my sketching pad and materials, which were deposited with my hat in the reception hall. I was led into a salon where I was presently joined by two gentlemen in Greek uniform. The older one introduced himself as Prince Andrew; the younger, from his manner, I guessed to be an officer on Prince Andrew's staff. Tea was served and the conversation was easy and pleasant. I assumed an attitude of deference toward Prince Andrew, a brother of a king, but with the younger officer I quickly reached a state of friendly comradeship in which I invited him to come to America sometime.

"Yes," he replied, "I'd like to. My uncle had a great time everywhere he went over there."

His uncle? For the first time a glimmering of the true state of affairs penetrated. His uncle could be none other than Prince Henry of Prussia—then this must be the Crown Prince! I am afraid my sudden realization must have been evident.

"Well, do you want to sketch this young man today, or would you rather wait till tomorrow?" asked Prince Andrew kindly. As I had already been enjoying myself tremendously for an hour or more and it was getting late, I chose tomorrow at any time convenient to His Highness.

So at eleven the following morning I had another couple of hours with the Prince, and the sketch turned out fairly well. He was a friendly, well-bred, English-appearing young man, with an Oxford education and an extremely magnetic personality.

By this time our huge bedroom had become a gathering place for all kinds of people. While events of war were marking time, we played dominoes. We played and we played. Once on a short trip back from Monastir, we forgot the set and made a new one out of paper.

Hours of earnest endeavor were spent at this ancient and beguiling game. I usually kept score, one vertical mark for each point, one horizontal mark across four vertical marks representing every five points. By the time we had played an hour or so, these scores looked like long files of marching men. Being, like everybody else with a pencil in his hand, a doodler, I made rough sketches of Shepherd and Hare and what not. Shepherd kept one particular score sheet as a souvenir. But when it came to light on the Italian frontier, there was a terrible to-do. It looked like nothing so much as cryptic notes made by Enemy Spy Number One. His bags were turned inside out; he was put through a long and rigid cross-examination; and only when a young woman in some way recognized the scoring system and explained it to the authorities was he allowed to proceed.

The night before Dick Davis left for home and comfort, John Bass gave a dinner for him. Everyone was gay; there were many stories told over the wine. After dinner we all rowed out to his ship with him, and he waved from the sea ladder until we reached shore again. It was the last time I ever saw him. Back in New York, while talking to Martin Egan on the telephone, he dropped dead. I've always thought the shock of those icy morning tubs had something to do with it.

My acquaintance with Dick had begun in Vera Cruz the previous year. I had heard he was conceited, a little brother of the gods. Many stories in support of this impression floated around. That he was a marked man was evident. He dressed the part and was a striking figure wherever he went. His background was impressive, his acquaintanceship wide, and his ability outstanding. Fortunately for me, I was with him a great deal both in Vera Cruz and Saloniki and found in him none of the qualities that I had heard criticized. We lunched or dined together constantly. He was wholly congenial, friendly and unspoiled. I had known his first wife, Cecil Clark, for years and I think the fact that I could reminisce about her, even though they were divorced, was a bond that he greatly enjoyed.

By this time the Germans had taken Monastir and driven the French back along the Strumitsa. The lines were drawn in about

Saloniki. The situation had developed into a deadlock and there was little likelihood of further military activity. With Davis gone, with Bill Shepherd in the hospital for a minor operation, with Jimmy Hare in the throes of trying to get a new passport to replace the one he had lost in the confusion of the evacuation, I was rather glad to get a cable from the *Tribune* to come home.

For the last time we went to the French officials to see if we could get permission to fly over Saloniki. They finally relented and authorized us to go to the airport a few miles outside the city. Each of us was taken up in a Farman. We sat in a balcony effect sticking out in front of the wings. Five thousand feet up I took photographs of the city and harbor, crowded with all its varied shipping. When I landed, my exuding enthusiasm was so evident that the officer offered to take me up again in a Nieuport two-seater combat plane, the fastest small plane in use at the time. All my impressions of flying heretofore were changed at once.

On our way to the little Greek ship next day John and Abba Bass and I stopped to get the developed films of the pictures I had taken. They covered several other things as well as the flight. And as usual there had been a delay. With the boat sailing in half an hour, we were obliged to carry off this great mass of film still dripping wet. Our hearts sank when we reached the ship. It was tiny, not over 600 tons, crowded to suffocation, with cattle and pigs on deck. Very kindly the Greek captain let me drape my films around the pilothouse, where there was a cooling breeze and a minimum of disturbance. The little room was festooned in shiny black. Surprisingly enough, the films were not hurt. In fact they were so good—especially those of the new French lines surrounding Saloniki—that they landed me in Scotland Yard.

Of this however I was happily unaware on the trip through the Greek Islands. I left the Basses in Athens and for the rest of the way to Paris I teamed up with Louis Edgar Browne of the *Chicago Daily News*.

The customs man at Dieppe at once spotted my films, now in a neat package. Skimming through them, he saw French uniforms, guns, trenches. "Ah!" He raised his eyebrows, shrugged his shoulders and shunted me aside until all the other passengers had been passed. Then I was allowed to go on board, with the word that I would "get the photographs later."

At Folkestone I had the distinction of being met by a Scotland

Yard man with my pictures in his possession. He escorted me right in to my London hotel and instructed me to report to Scotland Yard next morning at ten. I was there betimes, dreading any sort of delay, for I was sailing for home the next day on the *Nieue Amsterdam.* Time passed. I waited longer and longer. My anxiety increased. Finally a man came and said peremptorily, "Follow me!"

I followed him into a huge office where I waited some more. Then Sir Basil Thompson appeared, head of that grim organization.

"These films," said Sir Basil, "have been examined by the War Department. All pictures showing buildings, together with troops, have been held. The buildings could be identified and reveal troop locations. The rest of your films are here." And he handed them to me. Then he questioned me in such a way as to reveal a complete knowledge of my previous trip to the German front the year before. It was evident that a dossier relating to me was in his files.

"Wasn't the Countess Gizycka connected with the *Tribune?*"

"Yes."

"Wasn't she a friend of Count von Bernstorff?"

"I believe so."

"What are your sympathies?"

"Pro-Ally, naturally."

"Whom do you know here in London?"

"Mr. Selfridge, Lady Lavery, Lord Northcliffe."

Ultimately I was given permission to sail next day, and I departed from those sinister portals feeling considerably relieved.

# ∼ V ∼

# TREASURE TROVE

*when, in a moment of great sentimental exaltation—*

*you are reminded that you are needed at home.*

## The Main Adventure

At various stages of this narrative I have noted how small circumstances profoundly affected my professional career. There was one which even more profoundly affected my personal life. All of the things I have most to be grateful for may be credited to this rather trivial happening.

One Saturday when George Ade and I were loafing around our little hall bedroom on Peck Court, our meager resources depleted until payday, there came a knock at the door.

A handsome stranger stood there. It seemed that he had bet on the wrong end of the Sullivan-Corbett fight and wanted me to draw ten place cards for the dinner he was to give in payment of his debt. He had seen my name on the *Record* drawings, had secured my address from the office and subsequently made his devious way up the two darkened stairways to our door.

He was a tall gentleman, pleasant and courteous. I was glad to do the drawings for him—they were to be pictures of some of the striking moment in the fight—and I said they would be ready at five.

The drawings were done in a couple of hours, and then the big question arose: what should I charge for them?

"You'll never see him again," suggested George. "Why not soak him?"

At five the gentleman returned and was delighted with the drawings. That served to stiffen my "soak the rich" platform. So when he tactfully asked what he owed me, I braced myself and blurted out the exorbitant ultimatum, "Five dollars."

He never flinched. He met the shock like the thoroughbred he was and paid the price in a spirit of utmost cheerfulness. In fact, we afterward thought we could have asked six or even seven dollars.

But George was wrong about our never seeing him again. I married his niece.

The gentleman's name was Charles T. Atkinson. The acquaintance thus begun led to a close friendship which lasted until his death. I used to dine with him and his wife Martha, in their small apart-

ment on the second floor of a narrow-fronted house on Groveland
Avenue near Twenty-ninth Street. Even the street is no longer there.
In due time I met Martha's sister Frances and her husband, Howard
Shaw, who lived on the floor above. I also met the infant daughter
of the Shaws soon after her arrival. It was Charles Atkinson who
hurried out on that blizzardy night in March of 1894 in search of
Dr. Frank Cary.

Time passed. The Atkinsons and Shaws moved down to a pair of
gray-stone houses on Lake Avenue. Miss Evelyn Shaw, then two or
three years old, welcomed me on the stairs with a wide grin. But many
things were to happen before my thoughts were to linger romantically
on this young lady.

In fact, they lingered elsewhere in various directions long before
they showed a disposition to focus on any one spot. I was busy
drawing cartoons, and my love life made but slight encroachment,
apparently, on my daily cartoon life. Matrimony was not on my
agenda. When something of that sort conflicted with other adventure, the entangling alliance was always routed.

When I embarked on the *McCulloch* I was more or less engaged
to a young lady. But when I returned three years later from this

Inside the yurt a high lama watches us.

Sandstorm on the Gobi.

ACROSS THE GOBI DESERT

eventful Odyssey, the young lady had long since married a handsomer man.

Meanwhile, the Atkinsons and Shaws had acquired places in Lake Forest. As I told of my travels by the wide fireplace in the library at Ragdale, a lanky seven-year-old Desdemona listened spellbound. I was quite conscious of this flattering attention and definitely pleased to be the object of her childish favor. She still has a framed drawing I made for her on a sheet of Ragdale notepaper, of herself mounted loftily on a camel, and an illuminated acrostic: "For Evelyn Shaw on her Eighth Birthday."

By now she was a slim girl with bobbed hair, not yet emerged from the gangling stage, yet showing evidence of the distinction of appearance which has always been hers. However, I kept this particular romance entirely detached from others of a more mature nature that came and went.

*Eight and Ten*

It seemed that I was always going away on long trips, then coming back to tell her about them in front of the fire. There were Samarkand and Kashgar, remote, almost mythical lands. Then Africa, with its exciting words—jungles, elephant guns, safaris, lions, charging rhinos—all calculated, perhaps not unintentionally, to transform a rather mild man in his late thirties into a somewhat heroic figure, especially in the eyes of a young girl who was predisposed to regard him in an admiring light.

It was on this last return, from Africa in 1910, that I made the arresting discovery that Evelyn, a tall girl of sixteen, was charming in her riding clothes as we cantered through the fields west of Lake Forest. It came as a surprise that the "little girl—grown-up man" relationship was in a state of change.

Whenever she admired one of my cartoons, it was at once sent to her, appropriately autographed. These reminders of me may have stood guard as sentinels which kept me from being obliterated by the new interest that four years at Bryn Mawr presented.

Then came the First World War. In 1916, after months in the battle zones, I came home to a country seething with propaganda designed to get us into the war. Against the portentous background of a Preparedness Parade I was conscious of a highlight of interest when I caught sight of Evelyn Shaw standing on the opposite side of the street. I crossed over and we had a pleasant reunion.

For the summer I rented a little frame cottage in Lake Forest near the Aldis Compound, charming and informal gathering place of literary, social and artistic circles. I called the cottage "the Château Chic," and in it I drew "The Rhyme of the Restless Rover," "The Munition Maker's Daughter," and a number of other cartoons that I like to remember.

On a near-by tennis court Evelyn and I began a new phase of our relationship. She had weathered her debutante year and was now working as secretary for Harriet Monroe on *Poetry Magazine* and writing book reviews for Ethel Colson on the *Herald and Examiner*.

My tennis helped my cartoons, and Evelyn Shaw helped my tennis, and I soon became aware that this pleasant companionship seemed to take no heed of dates and years. Whether or not by comparison I was elderly, I was certainly given no reason to think so.

In her mother's open electric we took our first moonlight drive down the curving road to the beach, and I began to wonder very intensely just what she was thinking—whether I was for her only the "old family friend" whom she had always known. It was natural that I should fall in love with her. I remember how pleasantly and easily we advanced through the twilight zone of uncertainty to the point where I became very sure how *I* felt.

Much later I learned that she had once told a group of her college friends that she would probably never marry, because the only man she could imagine wanting to marry—the cartoonist John McCutcheon—was not likely to be a candidate.

Evelyn went west for August to a ranch in Wyoming. My letters to her during that month indicated that the summer for me had been more court than tennis. Soon after she returned home from the ranch, we became engaged.

Just about this time another dream came true, also thanks to Charles Atkinson. When I had returned from Saloniki in March, he asked if I was still interested in islands. I assured him I was. He told me there was one for sale near Nassau in the Bahamas, in the heart of the pirate belt. The late owner, Abraham Van Winkle, had looked the world over for such an island, had settled on this as the best to be found for his purpose, and had put in fourteen years developing it.

Although I had been to Nassau I had not seen the island. It was enough that Atkinson had. Besides, it seemed to have all the necessary requirements as to location, climate and piratical antecedents, including some splendiferous beaches with all the Atlantic Ocean to bathe in and all the sunlight in the world to dry in. The war still raged in Europe; the demand for tropical islands was in the doldrums. Nobody wanted any—except me. It was likely that this one could be acquired for a fraction of what had been spent on it, which might bring the price within the means of a newspaper cartoonist.

I lost no time in getting in touch with the agent in Nassau and made an offer. As soon as possible an answer came back declining it. I made another, somewhat larger, and waited anxiously. Within a very short space of time my heart had become set on that island although I knew very little about it. Presently the agent appeared in person—to gauge my sanity, I have always suspected. Doubtless he mistrusted a fellow who wanted an island he'd never seen. However, he must have been convinced of my financial, if not of my mental, responsibility, for we got together on an amount halfway between the asking price and my last offer, although the trustees were honorable enough to suggest the wisdom of my looking at the island before paying the money. In September 1916 Salt Cay with all its improvements, buildings, goods and chattels, including a small yacht, none of which I had ever seen, passed into my possession.

Thus at last I found myself owning an Island.

George Ade, when asked why I bought it, always said, "To refer to." This was not entirely incorrect, for I found myself referring to it with much pleasure. As I sat by the steam radiator with the sharp winds whipping in from Lake Michigan, there was real enjoyment in the thought that somewhere the trade winds were gently waving the palms of my own private tropical Island.

The news of my Island purchase followed by the announcement of my engagement made a combination that my newspaper friends were not slow to make the most of. The linked headlines struck the romantic sense of the public. Syndicated Sunday features glamorized our prospective wedding trip. The Island theme and the pirate background were played up, with plenty of palm trees, rakish schooners and buried treasure.

*Briggs Makes Me The Mysterious Stranger*

My fellow cartoonists all took note, with sympathy and humor, of my belated entrance into the bonds of matrimony. We were somewhat curious ourselves about what awaited us on the Island. The only photographs we had were old and poor. How handsome or how simple the dwelling might be remained a mystery. The inventory of contents was scarcely more illuminating. We speculated in bewilderment over its odd sequence of items: "eleven bedsprings; three bird cages; nine sadirons; eight bridge tables; two galvanized tubs; plates for one hundred twenty-five; one telescope. . . ."

The wedding was set for January 20, a good day to start things, as Congress came to realize, judging from the date set for future Presidential inaugurations. I found it so difficult to reduce my list that we sent out an absurd number of invitations! Many of these friends, according to the press, had evidently "been brushing up on their Stevenson and Defoe to aid them in the selection of appropriate gifts, which ran the gamut from chronometers and picnic baskets to fancy cages for the housing of tropical birds."

Contrary to custom, it was my friends, many from the Indiana Society, who gave the bachelor dinner. Across one end of the Blackstone ballroom extended a backdrop of azure sea. A coral strand in the foreground was strewed with casks of rum and chests of gold. The waiters were swarthy buccaneers. Judge Landis, General Dawes, Dick Little and Ring Lardner made remarks bearing on the earlier activities of the groom, and there were many variations on the theme "Good-by, girls, I'm through."

We were married in the Fourth Presbyterian Church, the interior of which Howard Shaw had designed and which he took pleasure in decorating for the event with Flemish tapestries borrowed from the Art Institute, wrought-iron candlesticks and bay trees studded with roses. The aisle appeared very long before we came smiling out into the bright January snow.

My brother George had reserved a suite for us at the Ritz in New York and filled it with flowers. A fire glowed in the grate. It was hard to leave such a friendly spot even for the theater and a drive through Central Park in a hansom cab.

I had written to E. N. Todd for instructions about how to have the Island prepared for us. He answered that all I had to do was to notify an agent in Nassau that we would arrive on a certain date. Mr. Todd was Mr. Van Winkle's son-in-law. His own children had grown up on the Island. He wrote, "It is generally conceded that letting George do it is the proper method of procedure in the tropics." He added, "I am not sure, but I think I inadvertently left a bottle of champagne in a closet." At the end of the letter he said, "There is a great treasure upon the Cay and it is not buried, but there are many people who could not find it."

So we set out happily and hopefully.

Partly because I wanted the Island to be the climax of our honeymoon, and also, I confess, just in case it should prove in any way disappointing, I arranged to go elsewhere first.

We were in Jamaica when the United States broke off diplomatic relations with Germany; in Colón we found the officers of several interned German ships quartered at our hotel. One of the usual Costa

Rican revolutions was brewing, and armed sentinels patrolled the governor's palace in San José. In Cuba we expected to connect with a ship for Nassau, but as we sailed in under the walls of Morro Castle, we passed it outward bound. There was no other for a week. However, a fierce uprising was in progress in Cuba also. The fighting was supposed to be near Santa Clara and Camagüey. We met Junius Wood of the *Chicago Daily News* on his way to the front, and while war corresponding is not normally part of a honeymoon, we presently found ourselves provided with passes from the Minister of War and boarding a train for the interior. There was more or less activity in Santa Clara, but the big battle was vaguely scheduled for some time in the future, and, the week being soon up, we started back to Havana. Even that way lay excitement. A vast forest fire was sweeping through the cane fields. For some minutes our train was an inferno of flame. We had to lie face-down on the floor, thus obtaining a measure of relief.

In fact, it was quite a honeymoon. Evelyn was at last getting her experiences firsthand, instead of relayed to her by someone else in front of the fire at Ragdale.

We approached Nassau, eager and apprehensive.

Charles Atkinson and his wife, inveterate Nassau lovers, had preceded us to see that all was in readiness. Our ship anchored in the roadstead beyond the bar. Nassau lay smiling on her hillside above the gay harbor. So far, so good. A tender came out. Charles greeted us affectionately, but to every question concerning the Island he countered with another about our trip. It seemed to us he was evading direct answers. Our imaginations were full of misgivings which increased when we joined Martha for breakfast. She showed equal skill in parrying questions. Subdued and disheartened, we asked no more. Perhaps it would have been better never to have come—always to think of it in the bright colors of imagination.

There was the *Alice*, however, lying at the steps of Rawson Square, a fifty-foot yawl with towering spars. She was manned by the captain, a coffee-colored Carib, one of the few remaining in the West Indies, and a couple of dusky sailor boys in spotless white. This was something at least. We embarked, and the Atkinsons waved us off with sphinxlike faces.

We steered down the harbor among the shipping, past flat little Fort Montagu on its flat little point. With expectations keyed to the utmost intensity we turned through the Narrows where, out to sea a couple of miles, lay a long, low reeflike affair—our Island! From charts we knew it to be about three miles long. It did not look too inviting, in fact rather bleak. There was a brisk sea running, making a landing on the south side difficult, so the captain chose the other side.

As we rounded the eastern point, the true Island met our eyes. Long white beaches, thousands of cocoanut palms, red roofs topping a thirty-foot bluff. From then on it was a succession of "Oh's" and "Ah's."

We have since learned to anticipate the sudden shock the visitor receives when he rounds that point, or, more often, climbs the Custom House steps from the south and gets his first glimpse of the color and luxuriance beyond.

We dropped anchor in a white hole inside the reef and went ashore in the dinghy, to a landing place on the rocks where our staff and their families awaited us, shy but smiling. There were about a dozen or so, of all ages, the entire population of the island.

After climbing from the beach up the steep hillside, we followed an aisle of clipped casuarinas to the house, a low, rambling bungalow, with broad porches and cool airy rooms, the most suitable dwelling imaginable. There were cocoanut mats, wicker chairs, a faded rosewood sofa and a wide desk, a roll of charts, a telescope and a case of seafaring books. Shutter doors, faded coppery green, were heavy to resist the battering of storms. The windows were salty from spray. Gloucester hammocks hung in sheltered corners. Two bedrooms adjoined the living room, with cedar closets, and beyond—an honest-to-gosh bathroom. The long veranda connecting the main house with the service quarters was bordered with potted palms. A stone kitchen was immaculately whitewashed; a glowing wood stove was set back in the chimney breast.

From the part of the porch where the dining table stood, an arbor covered with bougainvillia led down some steps to a stone path bordered with spider lilies and hibiscus, which soon branched three ways. We followed these paths as if in a trance. One led to the east, down a steep incline, past a sandy cove, to two guest cottages half hidden beneath their own jungle, then on and on to a little crescent beach tucked between ridges of sharp weather-beaten rock. A hexagonal bathhouse, a sort of little pavilion, stood there, with steps to the roof, whence the rising of the moon could be seen to spectacular advantage.

The middle path led us below the overhanging cocoanuts until we emerged onto a stone pier extending out into a lagoon, a couple of

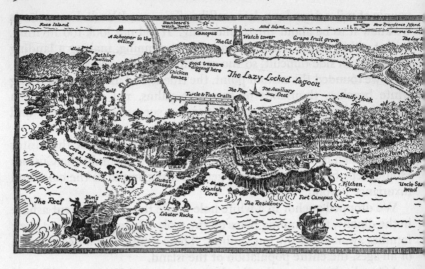

hundred yards across and a quarter of a mile long. Beside the pier
were two stone-walled storage pools or crawls well-stocked with bright-
colored fish. On the opposite side of the lagoon, a cut had been blasted
through the coral limestone to the sea, and twice a day the tide flowed
in, transforming what had once been a malodorous salt marsh into this
clear lake. Beside the cut a high frame tower had been rendered
somewhat perilous by lightning. At anchor in this peaceful haven lay
an entire auxiliary fleet—a fishing smack, a dinghy, a skiff and a canoe.

The third path led around the west end of the lagoon, past the
cottages of the caretaker and his assistant, to the Custom House. This
name was given by Mr. Van Winkle to a thatched shelter surmounting
a flight of stone steps, at the bottom of which a heavy drawbridge did
duty as pier. It could be lowered to receive the occupants of a boat,
then raised to stand high and clear of the devastating rages that might
otherwise wash it away.

We wandered about in a haze of wonderment. Everything was so
far beyond my most optimistic flights of fancy!

At once we realized the reason the Atkinsons had been so mysteriously evasive. They did not want to take the slightest edge off our
first impressions. Their reserve had only heightened our thrill of discovery.

We couldn't explore the whole Island the first day. Marveling and
ecstatic, we sank into the hammocks and lay there until the tinkle of

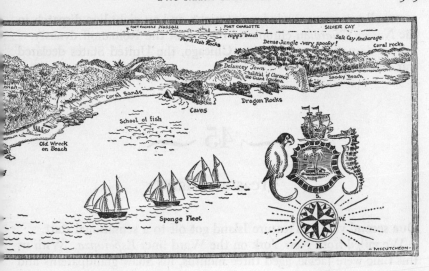

the supper bell broke in on our raptures. Above my chair at the table on the porch hung a painted wooden sign with the old familiar stanza:

> I am monarch of all I survey,
> My right there is none to dispute;
> From the center all round to the sea
> I am lord of the fowl and the brute.

I am conscious that I am not the swashbuckling type, but the legend has swung over my head for over thirty years. And certainly on that first day of realization of a long-cherished dream, it suited my frame of mind to perfection.

As we ate our simple meal by candlelight, suddenly there came singing. Josephine the cook, Beatrice the maid, Loretta the laundress, Barnabas and Sammy with his guitar—they had all come out into the shadows of the long veranda. The wind rustled the palms, the surf murmured gently on the beaches, accompanying the plaintive local melodies.

No South Sea idyll, no Louis Becke story, could improve on this.

The days passed swiftly, with our swimming, sunning, sailing and sleeping. And soon our long honeymoon came to an end. The international cloud was growing more ominous, more insistent on our attention. Rigid government regulations made us draw dark curtains across all our seaward windows at night, and an eight-line dispatch in the *Nassau Guardian* chronicled the fall of the Romanoff dynasty.

Two days after our return to Chicago, the United States declared war on Germany.

## ~ 45 ~

## Treasure Island

OUR second visit to Treasure Island got off to a sensational start.

We sailed from New York on the Ward liner *Esperanza*. With us this time were Jackie, aged three months, his Shaw grandparents and the Atkinsons. Our four cabins were in a row on the lower deck.

It was Valentine's Day 1918. War measures were being observed by ships at sea; the papers reported many vessels sunk without a trace, even outside the war zones. Rumors of German raiders were incessant, insistent. New York harbor was heavily mined and our own destroyers were actively patrolling the sea lanes along our coast. On our way out of the harbor early in the evening a destroyer camouflaged in large blue and yellow diamonds raced past us and disappeared seaward.

At midnight off Barnegat we were running through a dense fog. The *Esperanza* with all ports darkened was steaming slowly. I lay in my berth listening to the periodic hoot of the foghorn. Suddenly there came a blast of an alien whistle, short and sharp with a note of danger, followed by a frantic and prolonged shriek from our own. On the instant our ship shook with a frightful impact, there was a ripping crash, the screech of rending steel, then utter and sinister silence.

I leaped down from the upper berth. "Get up. Get dressed. We've been hit!"

"What is it? What has happened?" Evelyn was hardly awake.

"We've been hit," I repeated. "From the sound I think we must go down very soon."

"How soon?"

"Oh, a few minutes, maybe five."

Sounds of hurrying filled the gangways, but there was no panic or rushing water. I threw on some clothes and a life preserver. Evelyn began preparing herself and the baby for a lifeboat—or the sea, not a pleasing prospect in midwinter. Just then Howard Shaw, who had gone below in his pajamas, returned with word that we would not sink immediately. This gave Evelyn more time. She was relieved that it was "only a collision," not a torpedo. But what had struck us? Nobody had seen anything. Nobody was standing by. Whoever it was had faded back into the fog. The officers were noncommittal. Had an S O S been sent out? We could not learn.

Once more Howard went below and I went with him. We found that the *Esperanza* had been struck amidships on her starboard side—our side. A glancing blow had gouged out a gash in her hull fifty-five feet long and six feet wide, about three feet above the water line. The bolts had been ripped, the steel plates rolled back like tinfoil. The cabins just under ours had been opened to the sky, and a camouflaged anchor had been deposited at the feet of the chief engineer who was shaving. Near it lay broken lengths of anchor chain freshly painted in bright blue and yellow diamonds!

Providentially the sea was smooth. Even the slightest roll would have foundered us. The ship turned and limped back to New York. Two Navy tugs were sent out to bring in the destroyer. Thirty feet of her bow had been telescoped, but her bulwarks kept her afloat until help arrived. No publicity was given the incident.

This was far and away my most terrifying experience. Through it all the baby never woke. For years after that I could not hear a foghorn without a shiver of dread.

But such was the lure of the Island that we transshipped at once, and three days later found ourselves falling into an idyllic routine of existence, apparently established through the years by Mr. Van Winkle, and carried on by our staff, several of whom had been with him on the Cay.

"How was this done in Van Winkle time?" we would ask. "Well then, go right ahead."

For us, Van Winkle time covered all previous recorded history. It is strange to think that now we ourselves have carried on for over twice as long as he did.

As far as we were concerned, there was little to do except enjoy ourselves. The housekeeping seemed to do itself. The cook made out a daily list of articles desired for the kitchen and handed it to the captain, who, being unable to read, handed it over in turn to Cyril Solomon in Nassau.

Mr. Solomon was perhaps as vital a part of the Island regime as were the sea and the sun. I was frequently disposed to wonder whether the Island could function at all without him! Certainly our vacations would have been less restful. Officially he occupied the position of "agent" for the Cay. He was our liaison officer ashore. He saw to it that the cook's order was filled and aboard next morning for delivery on the Cay; also the mail, the *Nassau Guardian* and any errand we had written over about. There seemed to be nothing we could send for that he or his able assistant Oswald Sweeting was unable to produce. When our boat brought over parties, he stood by with another list, this time of guests, and checked them all safely aboard before she sailed. He handled our finances, hiring and paying the staff, and occasionally acting as peacemaker in an emergency. He supervised the opening and closing of the house and all we had to do was to walk in and walk out.

All this, however, was merely a side issue with Mr. Solomon. He and his brother Eric had a cool, commodious tobacco shop in Bay Street, happily called the Pipe of Peace. In addition to a wide variety of smoking equipment, their counters displayed tortoise shell and pink pearls and other articles which appealed to tourists from the winter cruise ships. Centrally located, the Pipe of Peace was a friendly rendezvous. Nobody passed up or down Bay Street without stopping in.

Thanks to the felicitous arrangements set up in Van Winkle time, we were able to establish at once an organization known as the "Nobody Home Society." Anyone guilty of a single good northern *idea* was promptly penalized.

Uncle Charlie was wont to come to the breakfast table with a harried look, saying he was so busy he didn't see how he could squeeze in a swim or a sail that day. Come to find out, he had to blanco one pair of sneakers!

In 1946, with many expressions of regret on both sides at the severance of such a long and pleasant association, Mr. Solomon turned the care of the Cay over to his sympathetic and competent nephew Gurth Duncombe. A couple of years afterward we sorrowfully attended Mr. Solomon's funeral.

Over the years, too, the Island personnel had shifted. The positions of honor and responsibility in the kitchen have descended from mothers to daughters. When Captain Alfred Sweeting died, after transferring his affections from the old *Alice* to the *Lucaya* and finally to the *Windrift,* his nephew Wilfred took over. Sammy, our first caretaker, also inherited from Van Winkle time, was followed by Levi, still later by Josephas.

Sammy was with us for twelve years. He was a man very much out of the ordinary. He was smart and likable and could tell native stories and sing an endless number of beguiling local songs to his guitar. He and his assistant and their families lived on the Island the year round. Their job was to guard it and its belongings, to keep it neat, to plant new cocoanuts, sweep the paths, rake the groves, keep the bathing beaches free of seaweed, tend the rain-water tanks (our only fresh water supply), keep the kitchen in fuel for the wood-burning stove, collect driftwood for picnics, raise and lower the drawbridge, and to understudy in anything else that might be required.

When the boat arrived each morning, they met it and soon we heard the wheelbarrows clattering houseward on squeaky wheels, ice dripping, fish flopping, and like as not a huge bunch of bananas balanced on top.

Sammy's ordinary costume was characterized by a conspicuous lack of fastidiousness, but when called on to act as butler at a chowder party, he appeared in crisp white and passed the cocktails with a distinguished air. There was always a twinkle in his one good eye. The other was rather droopy.

His wife Josephine was our first cook. She also was a superior character of outstanding dignity and intelligence. Upon her death one summer, Sammy married her younger sister Priscilla. When we came down we discovered Priscilla established in Sammy's cottage with a ready-made family, aged two and four.

In the Bahamas it was not uncommon to be "bo'n outside," meaning out of wedlock. There was apparently no odium attached to this little oversight of the legal preliminaries, and the children become respected members of the community. Sammy told me with no feeling of embarrassment that he himself was "bo'n outside." His father used to visit us occasionally, a very dignified and self-respecting old gentleman who played his part in this world with much the same manner as the actor who played God in *Green Pastures.*

Sammy always kept what he called a "jibdog." In common parlance, a jibdog is the female of the species in contrast to bulldog or male. You see, Sammy explained, leaning loosely against a palm tree, lots of ghosts come out on moonlight nights, and if they meet a bulldog, every hair on the dog's back rises in horror and can be counted, whereupon he becomes powerless. But the jibdog's hair doesn't rise; she can keep the ghost at bay until you can "take measures."

The "measures," I gathered, referred to some sort of obeah. Whether the more intelligent of our staff believed in obeah and voodoo charms or not, they were clever enough to use the signs to terrorize a big, lazy second-man into leaving. He found the well-known marks on the paths about his cottage and dared not step over.

Once we took Shenzi to the Island. Shenzi was the direct descendant of the chows I had brought home from Hong Kong in a bamboo cage in 1910. He had been given to us an an engagement present. Being just a year older than our first-born, Jackie, he became in the course of his thirteen years just as much one of the family. We speculated on how Shenzi would pass the time on the Island. Although his grandparents had crossed the Pacific, Shenzi had never seen salt water. After a first drink, he eyed it with solemn disdain. He was not amused by the lizards and soldier crabs.

As for Sammy's jibdog, he favored her with haughty indifference. She was always in the offing, but Shenzi gazed over her head with Oriental aloofness and appeared to us to spend his entire visit in resigned boredom.

The following winter, however, Sammy proudly exhibited a group of most strange animals. Their hair was short, their architecture lean and houndlike, but their slim rattails curled up over their backs absurdly, they had Shenzi's perky ears and coloring, and unmistakable chow black tongues!

A good deal of the fun of owning a coral island comes from the exercise of imagination. It is easy to develop the "I am monarch of all I survey" idea, and to pretend king and queen, even in bathing suits, holding daily audiences down on the beach, conferring decorations, and issuing mandates and pronunciamentos every few minutes when not otherwise and more pleasantly occupied. The formation of a Cabinet came as a matter of course. In appointing these officials I suspect I have followed somewhat the system of the Kentucky governors in selecting their colonels, of whom I am one.

Charles Atkinson, whom we justifiably consider the patron saint of the Island, was at once made Admiral of the High Seas Fleet, consisting at that time of the yawl *Alice,* a smaller fishing sloop, two rowboats, a canoe and *Winnie-the-Pooh,* a strange craft, four-square, which drifted onto the beach. His duties in this ministry involved anything that concerned water. Thus he collected blossoms to fill

the finger bowls for chowder parties. Also, when the female figurehead
we bought in Barbados arrived, sadly in need of attention, it devolved
on the Admiral to give her a bath. He doubled in the job of poet
laureate and spent much of his time playing the banjo.

The position of Chancellor of the Exchequer was naturally assigned
to a Wall Street man, Ed Harden. He has had very little to do up to
the present, but if we ever require an Exchequer, he will no doubt
spring into action. He rated the job because of his financial acumen
as exampled by the time he sent us our living-room table. Its beautiful round top, five feet in diameter, is made of a single piece of Philippine mahogany. The carved apron and ornate legs are impressive. It
was built for General Bell in Manila. Ed came across it at a sale and
knew I would have a sentimental appreciation for it. A letter preceded
its arrival:

Dear John Tengo [he always called me that]:
Recently I sent down to you a table which I thought you might
find of interest. However, I have just received the bill for crating
and shipping it, and now I suggest that you chop the table up for
kindling and keep the crate in the parlor.

If there were not enough suitable positions in the Cabinet, new
ones were created to fit the occasion. George Ade was tendered a port-
folio in recognition of services rendered in the establishment of a five-
hole golf course. That is, there were five places from which one might
drive toward a single hole. A slight hook landed the ball in the lagoon,
while a slice made a splash in the Atlantic Ocean. As long as George
stayed—and the balls held out—the golfing was on. But when he and
his enthusiasm departed, there was a decided slump in favor of the
Gloucester hammocks. The course has since been swallowed by the
omnivorous bush.

All three of our sons made their first visit to the Island when they
were brand-new, then not again until they were four years old, owing
to commissary complications. Today our grandchildren come at any
age, accompanied by a suitcase full of all the necessary canned goods.
In 1918 our friends were scandalized at the idea of taking a baby to
an island "'way out in the middle of the ocean."

But Jackie thrived, acquired a fine tan and appeared to enjoy the
scenery as much as we. When Evelyn and I dined ashore, we took
him with us so as not to upset his schedule. On such occasions we

usually parked him on a pillow in a bureau drawer. Left half open, this makes an excellent crib. There is always one handy; a baby can't roll out and he is free from drafts. An empty suitcase will do as well. Of course this particular baby was brought up to be as obliging as possible in such matters. He quite understood that life on an island would have been impossible on any other terms. He could be trusted to sleep anywhere at any time. The ears tuned for his cry were never pressed into service.

On one particular occasion we decided to return to the Island after some festivity ashore. It was calm moonlight and we asked several friends, newcomers to Nassau, to sail out with us just for the ride over and back. Evelyn gave the baby his belated "ten o'clock" supper, then pinned him securely to the bunk mattress in the cabin. He went to sleep instantly as usual.

When our friends arrived, we spread ourselves on cushions on the cabin deck. Between the lighted yachts of the harbor, down along Potters Cay and into the wider bay beyond Fort Montagu, we slipped along smoothly while the crew sang.

But as we passed through the Narrows, the moon clouded over, the breeze became fresh. Beyond the lee of Hog Island, a choppy sea was running. The boat began to pitch into the waves and we clambered down into the cockpit to escape the spray. The singing stopped, the night became darker and darker. The captain changed his course and we could see the distant flash of Sammy's lantern as he left his post of waiting at the Custom House; from time to time we caught glimpses of it bobbing about as he made his way down the mile-long sandy path to the Emergency Steps where the water would be quieter.

Presently the captain hove to. One of the sailors brought the dinghy alongside where it rose and fell perilously.

"You're not going to get down into that?" someone exclaimed.

"There's no other way of getting ashore," I said.

It was indeed a piratical setting—the black heaving water, the mysterious uplift of the Island, the glow of the lantern casting shadows on the rocky steps.

As the captain steadied my wife, while she "picked chance" to step down into the dinghy, I descended into the cabin, and emerged, grasping the knotted corners of a large triangular bundle which I held gingerly over the side until it was seized from below by Evelyn.

"What's that?" asked a curious guest, struck by my evident caution.

"Oh, that's the baby," I said casually.

"The baby!" . . . "Has there been a baby on board all this time?" . . .
"Don't tell me you take the baby back and forth like this!"
Everyone talked at once.

"He always travels with his meal ticket," I explained as I followed
him into the dinghy and we shoved off into the dark. Instead of a lazy
tropical romance, the night had become for them quite an adventure,
but for us it was just another diverting phase of Island life. Sammy
carried home the peacefully sleeping baby.

## ～ 46 ～

# Between Wind and Weather

ISLAND life never became monotonous even though there was nothing
we need do. This is probably true of any life that is largely dependent
on the weather.

We soon became as weather-conscious as an old sea dog and tapped
the barometer professionally on the way to breakfast.

On a dead-calm morning the wood smoke from the kitchen lay over
the hilltop in an aromatic haze. It seemed a perfect day for sand-
dollaring on the bar. But a perturbing cloud bank lay low in the
northwest.

"De root o' de vind be's up dere," we were told; " 'tis just fullin'
in."

Soon we could feel the shift of weather, and watch and almost time
the approach of a "white squall" across the water, veiling it like a
curtain. The squall closed in from the west and north at once; large
drops danced on the paths; then horizontal sheets of rain slanted in
under the low porch roofs and there was a scurry to bring in the
cushions and close the doors. The gutters overflowed in a continuous
fringe of mobile icicles. The children from the kitchen, Fanny and
Vernita, danced in and out of the rain with little squeals of delight.

"It fallin' off now." The north sky brightened again, the canvas
chairs were full of puddles and we could smell the sweet, still damp-
ness. Already the soldier crabs were dragging their shell houses out
from under the casuarina roots, and the sand crabs were pushing their

stilted eyes up through the ground, leaving little holes and hillocks, all hurrying to get a drink. Water flowed along the grooves of the crinum lily leaves till they bent over and spilled it out in tiny individual waterfalls.

Often we were just on the edge of the squall. Deep mysterious overtones of the usual brilliant colors were reflected on the sea from a steely sky, but we got only a teacupful of drops.

The force and direction of the wind regulated everything on the Cay from what we wore and did to where we ate. Our plans were always conditioned by them.

The Bahama winds have a curious way of boxing the compass. Winter rarely followed us down into that part of the world, but occasionally when we had boasted, the pride of the north lashed back and sent a chill nor'wester for two or three days. We would get out our ear muffs and cry, "Hey! You can't do this to us!" We had to swim on the south side and keep the north doors resolutely closed against the sparkling color.

Then, after some hesitation, the wind would lighten and shift north, northeast, east, with a few days of brisk sailing weather before the soft southeast trade brought a steady barometer and a series of perfect days. Then it would resume its leisurely course around the circle. It is all part of the game in those latitudes.

The natives call the heavy seas that follow a strong half gale a "rage." Following these rages our beaches undergo certain changes. Sand is carried out to sea. Where before there has been smooth sand, there is now a perpendicular drop of two or three feet—splendid precipices for juvenile jumpers—or there are only rough rocks to clamber over. In a day or two the sand returns and the beaches are smoother and more inviting than ever.

The comings and goings of the *Alice* were dependent on the weather. When it was calm outside the Cut, the captain anchored there and one might dive from the boat's deck down to where the shadow of her hull was outlined on the sand twenty or thirty feet below. She seemed to be floating in air. Or one might accept the challenge of the ebbing tide to fight one's way through the fifty feet of the narrow Cut, usually a losing fight. The depth of the Cut was not over one's head but it was a favorite haunt of prickly black sea urchins, and woe to whoever sets foot on one!

On these smooth days even the youngest might take the canoe outside and make excursions along the coast. Contrariwise, when great swells surged around the eastern point, it took skillful sculling to negotiate the Cut. If you could time it successfully to shoot through into the quiet haven of the lagoon on the crest of a wave, it was a breath-taking thrill. But if you lost the crest, a following sea would tower behind you and break into the stern with dire results to white trousers and silk dresses. Going out, too, you must "pick chance" between the larger seas and scull for dear life, for if you met an incoming comber midway, the bow would rise high in the air and only an expert could prevent disaster.

Sometimes the captain would come around to the north side. Then the *Alice* made a pleasing picture, appearing suddenly around the point, the white of her hull and of her sails against the turquoise streaks in the water. She nosed over the reef with tremendous headway; the captain checked her over the "white hole" below the Fort and Henry Lee let go the "hanchor."

Most often she lay off the Custom House. When we first came, we found two weather-beaten signs hanging there, one over each doorway. One was an old song:

> A strong nor'wester's blowing, Bill!
> Hark! Don't ye hear it roar now?
> Lord help 'em, how I pities them
> Unhappy folks on shore now!

The other was by Whittier:

> I know not where His islands lift
> Their fronded palms in air;
> I only know I cannot drift
> Beyond His love and care.

Between these, on the whitewashed walls, in a burst of industry I painted some black and white murals of pirates.

We lived pretty much in the open. A typical day ran gently, something like this. . . .

Seven bells. Sammy sounded the strokes on the old bronze ship's bell that hung in the grove at the foot of the hill. It was cracked and untuneful but somehow we never minded. It hung there until Jackie replaced it with another old bell from an Indiana farm.

Doves cooed in the path. In the distance Sammy's rooster crowed. Immediately there followed sounds of domestic activity. Sammy's bare feet padded along the porch as he watered the potted palms in their green tubs. Gladys' broom swished leisurely over the palmetto mat in the living room. Then through the slats of the door we could see her flowered bandanna and hear the appetizing clatter of breakfast dishes and the soft voice, "Hot watah, suh."

Within easy reach of the Residency on the hilltop are several beaches. For the morning dip we preferred the South Beach, a little crescent that affords easy privacy, making even a modern bathing suit superfluous. But just in case, we had a sign to swing out: STOP! LISTEN! BUT DON'T LOOK! No swim ever felt so good as that morning dip in the velvety-clear water.

Then came almost the highest spot of the day when we arrived together at the late, unhurried breakfast. Somehow the display on the table, capped by a supreme sense of irresponsibility, with the whole beautiful day ahead to spend as we pleased, seemed to whet not only the appetite but the wits as well. Often we were still at the table when the boat arrived with the mail and supplies.

While we ate, black and yellow banana birds and moss-gray parakeets hopped hopefully about the floor or flew into the open cages which we kept supplied with guava jelly. Occasionally one of them mustered up enough courage to reach the source of supply itself and perched nervously on the edge of the jelly bowl, took a few pecks, then darted swiftly away to tell the folks what a narrow escape he had just had.

"Well," Uncle Charlie would say finally, "I think I'll see what's doing." And he would go out to the Fort with the binoculars. Below the wide parapet the sweep of the north beach lay smoothed by the tide. What of the weather? If there are small fishing boats in sight, it promised fair. What else was to be seen? Was there perhaps a schooner from Exuma or Ragged Island, loaded with produce and "creatures" for sale? Was the *Alice* in sight yet? Not even the tip of her spar as she rounded the end of Hog Island? Or was she nearer, hidden for the moment by our own tall palms? Was she headed for the Cut or the Custom House? What could be heard? The chug of the interisland mail boat, or some yacht? The hum of the Eleuthera plane should come at nine; at ten-thirty, if the wind were right, the drone of the big clipper from Miami. When the boys were due for college vacations, we used to watch it take shape suddenly in the west, out of the haze, then sink from view as it landed among the masts in the harbor. Was there, perhaps, a cruise ship in—or two or three? Five miles beyond our western end they would lie, outside the harbor bar. Once the *Normandie* and the *Bremen* were so silhouetted against the horizon that they merged together with their funnels equidistant, startling us with the effect of a huge five-funneled leviathan. On these days we took care *not* to go ashore.

So, Uncle Charlie would return with a full budget of news. By this time the boys and I would have done a good job—half a grapefruit, an orange Nassau-style, peeled and impaled on a stick, a couple of tiger-striped bananas of perfect consistency and sweetness, a dish of hot cereal with tinned cream and brown sugar, a couple of eggs and three slices of thick bacon, and finally corn muffins and syrup.

After this it was permitted us to rest a bit, with maybe a game of chess. Long tanned legs were draped over chairs. Then the serious work of the day began. In the early days when we took the boys out of school, there were lessons to be supervised. Whenever Bruce Rogers was with us, we set out with our water colors. Bruce was neat and meticulous; I was bolder, but of late years rather wobbly.

By twelve o'clock everyone was sunning or in the sea. If ground swells were breaking, the boys rode them in. Up to within a few feet of the beach they slid, hidden in the foam beneath the curl. Or if it

was quiet, they wore goggles and prowled along the edge of the reef. I would not have been surprised to see them sprouting gills!

It might be nearly two before we sat down to lunch—stuffed black crabs, maybe, and "hopping John," the native dish of pigeon peas and rice, and buttery beet cubes, with generous slices of bread and guava jelly, topped off with Heavenly Hash.

After that we sailed—or else we didn't. Everybody might be too busy. Bruce Rogers always wanted to mount the morning's output of art for an exhibition; the boys wanted to adjust the rickety old telescope. Some of the rest of us collapsed in Gloucester hammocks.

*Some Serious Reading*

Then we exclaimed over the artists, and peered through the telescope, and warmed up with some ping-pong. Later we swam again in the slanting light, but the chances were the boys had disappeared. They might have gone out in the glass-bottomed boat but found no sand dollars to repay them, only a few starfish. Or else, as sunset approached, we took the glasses to the Fort and there, far down, some little black specks could be seen rounding the Delanceytown point, homeward-bound.

Lowering the flag was one of Uncle Charlie's favorite ceremonies. Every evening he was to be found on the bench beneath the Fort wall, in his plaid smoking jacket, his cigarette poised at the end of a Nassau tortoise-shell holder, visiting with Sammy, waiting for the sun to sink out of sight. Below, if it were calm among the rocks, bluefish and houndfish and red snapper swam in and out. A big kingfisher might swoop around the cliff into Spanish Cove. At other times the surf broke in a mile-long plunging curve from the Fort to the tip of Delanceytown. Sometimes the mossy reefs lay exposed, and each quiet tide pool reflected the gold and green and flame color of the sky.

This would bring us to supper on the porch, or better yet, of a windless evening when the quarter moon hung over Balighitghit, we liked to have supper there. This was where we had set the carved stone temple statue that Uncle Charlie had brought back from Bali. We are under the impression that *ghitghit* means temple. Table and chairs were brought, a yellow cloth, a couple of hurricane candles, a few Chinese lanterns in the branches; and whelk soup off our own reef, macaroni au gratin, juicy and tender, cold tongue and scrumptious lemon soufflé. Sammy sang unobtrusively in the shadows, while the fat little temple god smiled up from his coral pedestal at the tall golden heads of the sisal plants.

Long after Gladys had cleared the table and Ronald had carried it away, we would sit in the canvas chairs and there would be much joy and hilarity and warmth and ease. Then Uncle Charlie would get his banjo and sing: "His Heart was True to Poll," "My Love Works in a Greenhouse," "The Laird of Cockpen" and, best of all, the songs he wrote about the Island.

When he fell silent, there was no sound save the several voices of the sea.

## ∼ 47 ∼

## After the Armistice

DURING the first part of the war in Europe the possibility of America's becoming involved never entered my head. I had been sympathetic with Wilson's early performance as President. I took pleasure in drawing several complimentary cartoons about the conscientious effectiveness of his work in redeeming his platform pledges. My admiration for him cooled as it became evident he was treading the path to war, a course to which my cartoons had been consistently opposed.

The Eastern states were intensely pro-Ally; the Middle West was much more restrained, and the Far West controlled its emotions very thoroughly. I drew a cartoon expressing this idea, and from the letters I received, it was evidently considered by many a fair statement of the sentiment of the country. The people of America did not want to be drawn in. Nearly two years of insistent pressure, of skillful propaganda and Eastern editorial clamor, at last got under the skins of our citizens who, it has been my observation, are very allergic to sob stories and atrocity propaganda. However, the first month after Wilson declared a state of war to exist brought fewer than 4,100 recruits. Where, one asked, was this widely heralded eagerness to leap to arms?

This, in short, served to describe the attitude of mind of an average Middle Westerner. I don't think I made any cartoons prior to our entry into the war which helped to inflame public sentiment.

My earlier trips to the war zones and the birth of my first son combined to hold me at home during 1917 and 1918. At the first inkling of an armistice, I became restless and eager to get over again before the finish. However, I was still in Chicago on that memorable day when the whole city went stark-staring mad; when the papers were literally afraid to print bulletins denying the report for fear of having their windows smashed, or worse damage, by the hysterical crowds.

Early on the morning of November 11, my wife and I were on a train to Washington. As we passed through Pittsburgh, the long sustained chorus of engine and mill whistles advised us of the real Armistice. That night we were part of the milling mass on Pennsylvania Avenue when searchlights and planes crisscrossed the skies and President and Mrs. Wilson waved from an open automobile to the delirious crowds. It was a highly satisfactory and deafening celebration, but not nearly so explosive as the fake one.

Although Arthur Henning of the *Tribune,* Secretary of the Navy Daniels and General Peyton March, whom I had not seen since Tilad Pass, did what they could to expedite matters, it seemed unlikely I could be wedged into a steamer until the following week.

We went on to New York. On the train I was dictating to Evelyn earlier parts of this "Opus"—that was the name we gave to this plethora of prose—when Edward N. Hurley happened to pass through our car. He was head of the Shipping Board, and czar when it came to sailings.

"Going over?" he said. "Well, you must come on the *Olympic* tomorrow with Herbert Hoover and me."

I was elated at this chance of getting away so soon. Next day I found myself in a palatial cabin called "Louis XVI," with three beds and a bath, but my first night in my sumptuous quarters was something of a nightmare. I had been given a three-in-one typhoid shot. Soon after I turned in, everything began to happen to my vitals. I wondered if I was on my way out, and in a panic of alarm I telephoned the doctor who explained the probable cause of my misery.

In London I called as usual on the Laverys, and Hazel secured an invitation for me to the weekly luncheon given by ex-Prime Minister and Mrs. Asquith. I was the only American there, and was given a seat on Mr. Asquith's right. It was too late for propaganda, but I presume at the time he was feeling grateful to America. Many notables were present, among them, to my great surprise and delight, Archie Clark Kerr! It had been six years since we had ridden across

Haiti together; since he had stood in that leaky launch off Andros Island, ready to shoot himself rather than drown. I saw him again in 1947, when as Lord Inverchapel, British ambassador to the United States, he knocked at my door in Chicago to reminisce about the Pirate Cruise.

I found France rubbing its eyes to make certain that the long agony was over. There were scenes of great confusion in the railway stations. Swirling throngs of troops and civilians battled for places on the trains. Even if you reserved a seat, the chances were that at least two others would be firmly established in it before you reached it. Taxicab drivers were independent to the point of insolence; they wanted a short haul and a big tip. Once when I returned to Paris after a trip of several days, I had to try twelve hotels before getting a room. Even the second-rate places were asking sixty francs a day and the franc was still twenty cents.

Prices throughout France were soaring. The American soldiers were saying the French were robbing them, and the French were saying that American prodigality in spending caused the prices to rise. Perhaps both were right. I know that American troops in the Philippines spent right and left and completely disrupted local price standards. Out there things were finally stabilized by a double standard, twice as much for Americans as for natives.

One reason for the room shortage was that a number of hotels had been taken over entirely by the nations represented at the Peace Conference. Paris was a seething swarm of delegates, journalists, soldiers of nearly all nationalities, women war workers, visiting committees and investigating junketeers, joy riders camouflaged as Red Cross and Y.M.C.A. workers, and a hundred other classes, all jostling about in the overcrowded city. A little of Paris this time went a long way, and I was glad to get out of it.

General Dawes lived at the Ritz. He was there the night the German bomb mussed up the courtyard. He had his own table in the dining room, and every day at luncheon he collected around it whomever he might have come across during the morning. It was always a variegated group, male and female, high and low. Those were the days before the underslung pipe, when he smoked long Invincible Perfectos and gave them out lavishly to his friends. French generals, royalty and other assorted noblemen, American politicians and friends from home all would go miles for the luxury of one of those cigars. At night, to mitigate the harassments of the busy days, he would seek

*The Three Musketeers—Dawes, Pershing, Harbord*

nepenthe over at the Folies Bergère where a rollicking slapstick revue was playing, *ZigZag*. I suppose he saw it a dozen or more times. It was a great palliative, guaranteed to take your mind off whatever it was on.

Thanks to his unfailing kindness, I had many opportunities I might not otherwise have had. I went on General Harbord's private train for a tour of the S.O.S. districts (Service of Supplies), where I saw miles and miles of warehouses, bewildering mazes of tracks crowded with American cars, acres of shells, which had come too late, mountains of food; and on every hand the brisk, unornamental but exceedingly capable Yankee doughboy doing his muddy job in a way that filled my soul with pride. By motor I went through the eastern sectors; with Billy Poland I retraced my steps of four years before, through Brussels and Louvain and Maubeuge.

I sketched most of the American members of the Peace Conference. I cared more about getting a good one of General Pershing. His busiest days were over and he was able and willing to pose. In the early days of my war correspondence, I discovered that the ability to make a portrait sketch offered an easy and valuable way to make contacts. I developed what in retrospect seems to me a remarkable facility for catching likenesses in simple line drawings. Pershing had a face rich in individuality and strength lines. It should have been easy, but in my eagerness I must have tried too hard. Three separate times I tried, and I began to feel as helpless as if I'd never drawn a line in my life. The last time I was licked before I started. Since then I have drawn from photographs of him for cartoon purposes likenesses as good as I had hoped to get in Paris.

I happened to be in Strasbourg on the memorable day when Alsace was reunited to France after a separation of many years. French flags flew where they had not been for decades, while other houses displayed no colors, mutely eloquent of the German sympathies of those who lived in them. Representative troops from all branches of the French Army were there, including Senegalese, Moroccan and Annamese. Bands blared martial music. A grandstand had been erected in which were assembled an overwhelming array of notables: Poincaré, Foch, Clemenceau, Joffre, Pétain, Deschanel, Gouraud; 300 members of the French Chamber of Deputies and the French Senate; as well as Haig, Pershing and a swarm of foreign ambassadors. I made many hasty studies to be completed later. Gay, pretty girls in Alsatian costume flocked to the grandstand and were helped up by willing gentlemen into kissing range of the first row of dignitaries. Clemenceau kissed many; they all did, even the somber Poincaré, so lacking in *oomph*.

With the flier Nungesser, I walked across the bridge. I must have been in quite a fog of excitement, for I lost my London hat in Strasbourg, and my walking stick on the banks of the Rhine.

Meanwhile I had shifted my headquarters in Paris from the Ritz to the Continental where I shared a room with Percy Hammond. I had known Percy for a long time as the brilliant dramatic critic of the *Tribune*, but our trails at home seldom converged. He was active mostly by night, I by day. He attracted people with his scintillating mind and *bonne camaraderie*, and our room was a mecca of congenial spirits at all hours; many a post-midnight visitor pounded on the door; often Percy would be roused from slumber and led off to some convivial get-together.

When we occasionally ate in the big restaurant of the Continental, we would see a group of four always together—Feisal, King of Iraq, and Lawrence of Arabia, with two others, doubtless retainers of the handsome king.

Percy and I took a twelve-day trip around our semicircle of outposts in Germany, and up to Bonn and Cologne. Rigid rules were being made to prevent fraternization. In a quaint old castle at Molesburg, where an elderly count, his wife and four daughters lived among the tapestries and paintings dating back to the thirteenth century, thirty-eight of our soldiers were quartered. The commanding officer, a young

lieutenant, lived in a room grand enough to shelter a king; the young
countesses were trying to be friendly with cakes and little Christmas
trees, and the young lieutenant was trying to remember not to fra-
ternize.

In Coblenz General William Mitchell was superintending the surrender of German planes. Crowded into the airport were many types
radically different from any I had ever seen. The general took me
up in his Lorraine-Dietrich Spad which he piloted himself. Up and
down the Rhine we went at 200 kilometers an hour, not much in
view of present-day speeds, but a star experience then.

On New Year's Day 1919 Percy and I had dinner with General
Mitchell's mess in a little town outside of Coblenz. The centerpiece
was a cheerful Christmas tree which played *"Stille Nacht"* as it revolved on its base, and across it I talked with the Roosevelt boys, Ted
and Kermit, about their father. I had not seen him when I came
through New York, but I had the impression that he was in good condition after his recent illness. Nothing was said to indicate that either
of the boys felt any concern about him. We spoke of his chances in
the 1920 election.

"Your father's opposition to Wilson," I said, "has made him the
logical opponent of any Democratic nominee on a Wilson platform."

We could not suspect that on this very day he was being stricken
with the relapse that carried him off six days later. Percy and I had
no more than reached Paris on the sixth of January when we were
thunderstruck by news of Colonel Roosevelt's sudden death.

Sometimes I have tried to list the ten greatest events I have ever
witnessed. The opening of the "Court of Honor" at the World's

Columbian Exposition; Bryan's Cross of Gold speech; the Battle of Manila; the march of the German Army through Louvain—such things I would include. Certainly another was the arrival of President and Mrs. Wilson in Paris on December 14, 1918. At that time, in the eyes of Europe, he was little less than a Messiah. From before dawn the people of Paris had been converging on the Champs-Élysées to see him pass. Traffic was excluded. Many people carried stepladders. Every window, every roof, every tree, was packed with eager eyes. From where I looked down from General Dawes's offices in the Élysée Palace, it seemed that not another human being could be wedged into the picture. It was something elemental, like a tidal wave caught in a still. Into this breathless expectancy came two open carriages. President Wilson and President Poincaré were in the first, the ladies in the second. There may have been other things in the procession, Guards of Honor, French cavalry; there probably were. But I did not see them.

As the carriages passed, there was not a cheer, not a rustle; it was as if the millions that lined the way were observing some solemn ceremonial in a vast cathedral. That was Wilson's great moment—before the Peace Conference, before they began to remove his statues, before they changed the street names back to something else.

With the peace treaty came the issue of the League of Nations. I think most people at first favored such a body which could act collectively against further war tendencies. I know I did. During the three months I was in Europe after the Armistice, the *Tribune* asked each of its correspondents to write occasional personal letters not for publication, giving their private opinion of things. I remember writing such a letter, expressing the hope that the League might be saved from defeat. Then came the Versailles Treaty and the Covenant of the League, revealing so unmistakably the injustice of the treaty and the underwriting of that treaty by the League. It seemed to me that the League, far from being an impartial body of cold justice, was to be a manipulated device designed to secure to Britain and France the immense advantages they had gained by the treaty. As this became more evident, my sentiments recoiled and I became intensely skeptical of its honest purposes and possible benefits. Only a few years of its operation bore out these misgivings. My cartoon indicated that "according to the autopsy, she was constitutionally and economically unsound, but meant well."

When Wilson left Paris, the *Tribune* began to shift its correspondents. Tiffany Blake was ordered home, and Arthur Evans. I had been half expecting the cable from Joe Patterson which read, "Urge McCutcheon return at once." "He's been off the front page long enough," he explained, and I knew that my cherished plans for a reunion on the Island must be scrapped. It was a keen disappointment; I had already arranged to have the house opened and the boat put in commission. Nevertheless, I realized that my enjoyment of the lazy days down there might be seriously diminished if I were buying them at the expense of my relations with the paper.

There was one gleam of humor in the situation. That was Joe's use of the word *urge*. As if I needed urging! Never before had I felt this tugging at me to return home! A far greater calamity would have been a cable saying, "Have McCutcheon remain abroad until peace is concluded." There's no use talking, things were different. I was finding that a family crowded out a great many other interests.

For my return to America I was assigned to the armored cruiser *Pueblo*, which was taking 1,500 discharged soldiers. Before sailing, however, there were two things I wanted to do. One was easy. I bought Evelyn a jade necklace in the Rue de la Paix. I wished also to get her a Paris gown. This was more complicated. Now General Pershing had a staff officer who had an obliging wife who volunteered to steer me through the mysteries of the Paris *couturières*. I had no measurements but I could say she was about so high and about this far around. At Callot's I bought her an evening gown of green satin, the color Evelyn liked best. There was a frantic rush to get the dress finished; it had not arrived at the hotel an hour before traintime. I aged several years in that hour. Finally I took a taxi with my bags, made a stop to pick up the big dress box, and reached the train for Brest just as the bell rang.

I found myself the only civilian on the *Pueblo*, whose captain, Brooks Upham, turned out to be an old friend from the *U.S.S. Olympia*. I had his quarters, since he himself slept on the bridge during the entire voyage which was delayed four days by tempestuous buffetings of weather.

Evelyn and my brother George were waiting inside the picket lines on the dock. Both the necklace and the dress fitted perfectly. After a few days at Atlantic City—a poor substitute for the Island—I settled down to my drawing board.

However, in order that the year for me might not be without its distinguishing variation, in June I planned to attend the thirtieth reunion of the Class of '89 at Purdue. Now a reunion dates you. Any undergraduate with a pencil and a cuff can figure how much of a fossil you are. Therefore, since travel by air for civilians was still sufficiently unusual to be of real news value, I determined to return in very up-to-date style. My plan was to circle high over the Class Day celebrations on Stuart Field, tailspin down for a few thousand feet, then spiral out for a neat three-point landing before the grandstand, to the admiring amazement of my bride and the assembled multitudes, where I would step jauntily out of the cockpit, yawn slightly and adjust my straw hat with a maximum of nonchalance. That was the plan.

Everything went according to schedule until we came out of the tailspin and the Army pilot took a good look at the field—and didn't like it. So we flew away and came down in a nice comfortable alfalfa field, without a soul in sight.

As a dramatic achievement it was something less than zero—proper penalty for a fellow trying to show off!

## 48

# Delanceytown

WHEN I was in Brussels after the Armistice, a number of prominent women were making an effort to revive the lace industry. The American minister, Brand Whitlock, and I were one day taken through an exhibit by the Countess de Beughem. My eye was caught by some handsome tablecloths worked with the coats of arms of the different Allies. Wishing to help a little, I sketched from memory as well as I could the Island crest. I had given the original suggestion for this to Gustave Bauman who had done it for me in woodcut form. I explained to the countess about the Island and our enjoyment in collecting things for it. Some weeks, she told me, would be needed to do the work. She was coming to America in May and would bring the order with her.

Carefully I refrained from mentioning this transaction to my wife. I hoped to surprise her at Christmas. May came and no lace. Month after month passed. Still no lace. In December I assumed that something had interfered with filling the order and bought another present.

A few days before we set out on our annual hegira to the Island, I received a letter from the countess. She wrote that at last, after all these months, I had been discovered! It seems that she had brought the lace over in May but had lost my name and address! Remembering only the fact that it was for someone who lived on an island, she took the matter up with the embassies in Washington of all those nations having islands in likely spots. It had become a joke with the various undersecretaries—this search for a mysterious gentleman who inhabited an island. From May to December this problem rocked the diplomatic centers in a mild fashion. The countess returned to Belgium. One day she mentioned the matter to Brand Whitlock.

"Why, that was John McCutcheon." He laughed. "He has an island in the Bahamas."

Appropriately the package arrived, together with a boatload of guests, in celebration of our third wedding anniversary. The lace was put into service at once, and to this day has retained its exquisite loveliness.

We were also celebrating, that winter, the new fortifications. When I had had to give up my visit to the Island on my return from Europe, and our disappointed cable reached Nassau, Evelyn's family had moved over to the Cay, and soon news leaked up to us of how they were passing time. Near the end of the old sea wall around the Colonial gardens, a couple of ancient barnacle-encrusted cannon lay half imbedded in the sandy bottom. They had probably been thrown into the harbor when the battery which used to stand on the site was dismantled to make way for the big yellow hotel. They may have been

About to climb in.

Over the jungle.

FLIGHT OVER THE ANDES

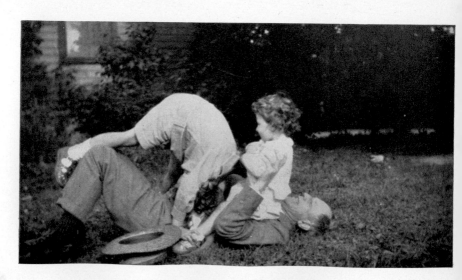

ASSORTED McCUTCHEONS

pointing out over the bar back in the 1700's when the eleven pirates were hanged on the strand a few yards away. On his frequent strolls from the sponge market up along the water front, Howard Shaw had observed them at low tide; with his architectural eye he envisaged them mounted bravely on Treasure Island, and forthwith proceeded to reclaim them. It was easy to get the governor's permission; it was not nearly so easy to get them to the Island. They were eight feet long and weighed two tons.

Native limestone from the New Providence quarries was imported by barge, with eleven masons. According to detailed drawings, they began to construct a fort on the north cliff, at the end of the casuarina alley. Howard used to come quietly up the path from the beach behind them, and find them all leaning on their tools in excited altercation as to whether it was better to serve God or Mammon. After twice the length of time he figured on, and three times the cost, the Fort was ready; one of the guns was mounted on its block, and there we found it when we arrived, its rusty muzzle menacing the tranquil southern sea.

We named it Fort Canopus because of the view it afforded of that most distant and largest star, selected by B.L.T. in his poem, "Canopus," as a haven of rest for distracted thoughts:

> A star that has no parallax to speak of
> Conduces to repose.

The poem appears in our *Island Song Book* and carries this footnote:

> The star so favorably mentioned in this poem is just south of Treasure Island. In fact, our residence has been called the Half-Way House to Canopus. Canopus is visible from all parts of the Island. It is seen to advantage from the parapet of Fort Canopus, but the best view is from the Watch Tower, which is a quarter of a mile nearer the star.

From the Fort of an evening we could look down forty or fifty feet to where the wet sand glimmered as the tide went out, and the water glowed coppery like the young leaves of the sea grapes. We could look away off through the Narrows to where the straggling lights of Nassau sparkled companionably, yet peacefully remote and undisturbing. Or we could look along the dark ridge of the Island to the caves and to Delanceytown and our own west end.

From tip to tip the Island measures about three and a half miles, but it is very narrow. Roughly it is shaped like a spoon, the lagoon filling most of the bowl. The north side levels off to the beach where the slow swells of the Atlantic roll in and deposit their booty: shells and sea fans and bits of sponge and coral; spars and timbers, copper-spiked, and other wreckage; once a long gray battleship oar marked *U.S.S. Maine*, doubtless successor to the *Maine* of tragic memory; and sometimes whole boats, battered but useful.

Above the beach a path leads down this way between green walls of bush, wild sapodilla and tamarind, gum elemi and mastic, buttonwood and blacktorch. Seventy-five varieties of tree and flower and blossoming bush are here. The gnarled forms of the joe-trees accent the heights, the pale gray-green of beach lavender seeks the water line, indifferent to the salty spray.

About a mile down are the two caves, one with a broad mouth commanding the shore; the other a true pirate hideaway with a concealed entrance to which one must climb down from above. Near by were our favorite picnic spots. Gathering driftwood was easy and fun. An armful apiece kept the fire flaring, the shadows dancing and the smoke wraiths vanishing over the water. We used to lie on the sand and sing and stargaze until the children were half asleep. Sometimes the youngest courageously betook himself the long sandy mile home to bed, armed with a trusty flashlight. Walking back along the path, a dark sea on either hand merging imperceptibly into a dark sky, one was very conscious of the *island* feeling.

West from the caves, a wind-swept rocky path leads along the backbone of the Island to Delanceytown. Delanceytown is our suburb, a single tiny red-roofed cottage of two rooms, occupied in Van Winkle time by Mrs. Delancey, the laundress. Wild vegetation has obscured the approaches—hibiscus, oleander and sea grape—while the shuttered doors and windows give it somewhat the effect of a gay little haunted house.

Beyond Delanceytown stretches the jungle, more or less impenetrable without a machete. Sometime—always well in the future—we were going to pretend we were shipwrecked on these shores to see if we could subsist on what we found; but Crusoe had a much more elaborate island than mine on which to exercise his ingenuity. When the

The Crown Prince, the Duke of Delanceytown and Suite —

boys reached a point when they felt sufficiently venturesome, we modified the program somewhat by providing blankets and the wherewithal for breakfast.

The only inhabitant of this part of the Island that we ever knew of was Clarence the giant iguana. Although we often came across his large footprints and the trail of his heavy tail in the sand, it was ten long years before we saw him. Emerging suddenly from the bush above, we looked down on him sunning on a rock, a species of enormous lizard some five feet over-all, the last remaining one of fifty imported from Galápagos in Van Winkle time. They are said to be good to eat. Doubtless they succumbed to the appetites of hungry fishermen, landing surreptitiously. We had scarcely clapped eyes on Clarence when he slithered out of sight.

Beyond the Delanceytown jungle extends the long rough tail of the still greater lizard which by a not-too-great stretch of imagination the Island resembles. The water on the left-hand side may be as smooth as glass, while on the right, separated by only a few yards, the long surf of open ocean smashes against the rocks. The ultimate tip peters off into a series of undulating humps, diminishing in height until they finally become a submerged reef. A few hundred feet beyond, through the clear water, lies the hulk of a sunken ship.

On my first visit to my Island kingdom I could not rest until I had surveyed the whole of it. I summoned Sammy and set off to investigate the remoter reaches. He led me out onto this ridge of eroded aeolian limestone. The Hindu fakirs who dance on the edge of a

sword, or the Fijian fire walkers have nothing on Sammy who, in his
bare feet, stepped nimbly and unconsciously over the jagged needles
which I could feel uncomfortably through my heavy rubber soles.

This trip, made on my second day, has been repeated only two or
three times. I have never set foot on the last three humps which I
named after my three sons. They are almost always awash.

When a rage is on, great walls of water shoot up against this barrier
nearly a hundred feet into the air like a barrage of exploding shells.
We cruise then along the lee side to watch the thunderous seas burst
and crash over and pour down in a series of white waterfalls.

This same lee is called Salt Cay Anchorage on the charts and is
deep enough for large ships to lie at ease in bad weather. Under the
prohibition amendment the sixteenth of January, 1920, was the last
day on which American distillers could legally ship liquor from the
country. Many vessels, loaded below their Plimsoll marks, came to
anchor in our lee. One of them brought 45,000 cases and 5,000 barrels
of whisky. Lighters came out from town to unload them. When the
wind blew from that quarter, there was a decided kick in the atmosphere.

Of course Nassau had made no preparation for these mountainous
cargoes of liquor. They had to be stored any place—in blind alleys,
empty lots, even church cellars. Interminable processions of donkey
carts, pushcarts, human *cargadores* plied to and from the wharves.

Nassau did not realize that another era of prosperity was dawning
on the poverty-stricken colony. The third of the golden B's was about
to gild its coffers—buccaneering, blockade-running and now bootleg-
ging! Through import duties it deepened the harbor, built the docks,
improved the roads and street lighting, purified the water, provided
an elaborate sewage-disposal plant, and brought an invasion of swarthy
hard-boiled hombres whose movements were mysterious and whose
ways were not those of the simple sponging colony.

Often as many as sixteen rumrunners lay in our lee at one time, a
spirited armada. Blackbeard never dreamed of such gigantic operations as these. But many lesser folk were tempted. On a trip to town
I encountered a former Island helper.

"Well, Barnabas," I said, "what have you been doing lately?"

"Oh, bootleggin', suh."

"Any luck?"

"Nossuh, Boss, out o' luck. I los' my liquor, an' I los' my boat, an' I
los' my clo'es, an' I had to swim eleven mile!"

# ～ 49 ～

## Buried Treasure

ONE of the greatest charms of the Island for me was that it lay in the heart of the old pirate belt. Along with Tortuga near Haiti and Port Royal in Jamaica, New Providence was one of the three great rendez-vous of those gloriously inglorious Brethren of the Coast. My Island, providing a safe anchorage outside the range of the guns of the forts guarding either end of Nassau harbor, became their headquarters when negotiating with the governor or doing business ashore. It is, in fact, mentioned by name in the *Memoirs of Peter Henry Bruce, Esq.* (Book XII. 1743):

> On the return of the privateers, the captains were determined not to enter this harbour [Nassau] again and came to anchor at a place called Salt Keys.

The name Salt Cay, by which it is known on the Admiralty charts, was derived from the salt marsh which provided ample stores of this vital substance until, in Van Winkle time, the Cut was blasted and the lagoon dredged clean.

Certainly it is within the bounds of possibility that the pirates may have buried some treasure here. We could not help keeping a weather eye out.

One morning Sammy appeared at breakfast showing considerable agitation. "Boss, my wife Josephine, she done had a dream las' night 'bout dat treasure."

"What about it?" I demanded.

"She dream she mus' go dig under jus' one certain coc'nut tree. Under de moldy fronds she'll meet rottin' boards. She mus' dig till she meet de treasure, an' pay no mind to groans an' moans an' clankin' chains!"

"Did she go?" we inquired breathlessly.

"Nossah, Boss, she ain't go! Boss, she done pull de kivvers over her haid an' shiver de res' of de night!"

Hardly waiting to finish breakfast, we organized an expedition. We

*Treasure digging*

found the right tree, and under the dead branches we most certainly found some rotting boards, but beyond that we had no luck. We urged Josephine, next time, to obey orders and get up and go *at once*. There was no next time.

Howard Shaw, always restless and constructive, approached this matter of treasure hunting in another way. Putting himself as it were in the boots of the pirates, he went about triangulating the higher fixed points of the Island and its nearer neighbors, landmarks that might not have changed appreciably with time, and where these lines converged, he marked an X. We had a season of enthusiastic digging, but it is evident we made some slight error, for no ironbound chest rewarded our efforts.

In order that we should instantly recognize one if we chanced upon it, Howard sent us, soon afterward, a fine specimen he found, dusty and forgotten, in a London basement. We parked it in the living room where it never fails to arouse admiration and curiosity, thereby putting our veracity to a severe test. It is bound and rebound with iron bands; there are faded paintings in the interstices, and when we raise the heavy lid to display the intricate mechanism of the eight-bolted lock, our supply of ping-pong balls and rackets meets the eye.

An old law is supposedly in force in these parts whereby the Crown demands "ninety percent of all treasure trove." This law accomplishes two things. It implies that treasure may be found, thus encouraging search. It also puts a high premium on silence in case of success. When the harbor was dredged, several doubloons were said to have been scooped up.

But all this involved digging and scooping, and while we kept right on implicitly believing there might be treasure buried on the Cay, we remembered that there was other gold in the offing—$30,000,000 worth in every cubic mile of sea water.

Promptly we enlisted the aid of our guest, Carl Page, a very scientific young man. In due time he appeared with an odd contraption, a couple of bushels of charcoal enclosed in a wire fish trap. He had worked out an exact formula for treating this charcoal so as to precipitate a maximum amount of gold in solution. What more perfect spot for collecting gold by this method than our Cut? Four times a day, twice in and twice out, the tide rushes through the narrow channel. Untold millions of gallons of sea water would wash over the suspended charcoal every twenty-four hours. When the charcoal became sufficiently gold-plated, all we needed do was to scrape off a nice mess of gold and set the bait again. Supposing we worked only five cubic miles of sea water a season, there would be a tidy $150,000,000. But even if we got only, say, half that, it would be well worth our while, a gratifying return for the capital invested, an occasional barrel of charcoal and whatever dope Carl used for treating it.

But something happened—I forget just what—to divert us, so we still have our hope and anticipation unimpaired, and these are very nearly as satisfactory as realization. At least they generally last longer.

There *is* a buried treasure story that I can vouch for. A Pirate Picnic was given for the benefit of local charities, under the auspices of the governor. One feature was to be a treasure hunt and I was appointed the committee to bury the treasure and make out a chart, like an old one, indicating the approximate location. There were in fact two treasures, one a twenty-dollar gold piece, the other a stout canvas bag, suitably "aged" with dirt and stains, containing 500 English pennies. Each treasure was placed in a small wooden chest carefully painted in imitation of an old one, and buried on Paradise Beach. Many people dug. The gold piece was found, the pennies were not.

So, next day, Alfred Hamill and I went over to Hog Island to retrieve them. The beach was crowded; a cruise ship had come in; it was the fashionable bathing hour. Where I had buried the pennies, a couple were lying on the sand. The young lady's head was resting on the little mound that marked the spot. We started digging near by; they looked annoyed. I said we were digging for buried treasure. It was plain to be seen they thought me crazy.

"Excuse me," I said, hat in hand. "Would you mind moving? We wish to dig here."

With difficulty they restrained their indignation and grudgingly shifted their positions. I then dug furiously, and I could feel their resentment boring into my back.

"Ah!" I exclaimed when I struck the chest. With Alfred's help I pulled it up. I lifted the lid and raised the bag of clinking coins. We carefully refilled the hole, raised our hats a second time with an apology for disturbing them, and staggered off with our burden, leaving them to their thoughts.

Although we failed to realize any actual treasure from the many hours on the beach or in the hammocks dreaming, this special year was not without its reward. Shawie McCutcheon came along in October, and when we again migrated southward, he assumed Jackie's old place in the triangular knotted blanket.

## ~ 50 ~

## Sammy's Party

THE old *Alice* was finally retired from active service and ended up in the lagoon as an interesting piece of scenery, becoming more picturesquely wrecklike year by year and affording the little boys endless diversion.

My method of buying boats has been criticized by my nautical friends, but having been so successful in buying an island sight unseen I tried the same system in procuring a new boat. From the various offerings by mail of the yacht brokers, I selected one that pleased me both in price and specifications. She lay in Fort Lauderdale where an artist friend of mine lived, Frederic Clay Bartlett. I wired him to inspect her. He wired back: "Don't know anything about boats but her lines are good." Forthwith I bought her.

She was a shoal-draft Crosby yawl, thirty-eight feet over-all, painted white. We chistened her *Lucaya*, the name given the Bahama Islands on the earliest charts, and we loved her dearly from the first.

The morning the captain brought her over to the Island for the first time was a red-letter day. She looked trim and graceful. Captain Sweeting was bursting with pride. By purest chance this happened also to be the day of Sammy's party.

When Sammy had asked if he might have a party, I inquired, "What kind?"

"Oh, 'bout twelve-fifteen people, frien's o' mine. Dey kin dance on de tennis cou't."

The idea appealed to me and I gave my consent.

We, too, had guests at the time, Clarice and Alfred Hamill. Alfred and I decided to make the trip to town on the new boat, to see how she behaved, and return with Sammy's friends in the evening. It was agreed that we should start back from Rawson Square at six o'clock.

When the captain came across the Square from the Pipe of Peace about five-thirty, he told me afterward he had to push through a crowd of people. "Somebuddy axed me 'vere dese people goin'?' 'I dunno,' I says."

Alfred and I did not arrive until some minutes after the appointed time. A crowd jammed the landing. Above their heads we could see the spars of the *Lucaya*. Elbowing our way through, we reached the edge of the steps and looked upon a sight that made me gasp. The boat was solid black with people. The cabin deck and scuppers were full. Thirteen brunette belles sat in the small cockpit. There were twenty-six below in the cabin, I learned later. Two dusky gents bestrode the bowsprit. The numbers clinging on behind the jigger mast reminded me of the steps of a streetcar on Christmas Eve.

When I caught my breath after the shock, I asked the captain, "Is it safe? Can she carry them?"

"No!" moaned the most worried individual I ever saw. "Nossah, Boss. I mean ter say, Boss, she sinkin' a'ready!" He indicated the water trickling into the cockpit through the self-bailers which had got below the water line.

"Can't you make some of them get off?" I said, more than ever regretting my lack of the masterful qualities. The captain rolled his eyes to heaven. Sammy was frantic but helpless. At his appeals a few stepped off, but the rest sat solemnly in their places, everybody waiting for somebody else to move.

Wind and sea being quiet, it was decided to set forth. Owing to the low visibility caused by a band sitting in a row on the main boom, the captain had to stand up and steer with his toe.

It seems that fifteen or twenty people had really been invited, but word had spread about Grants Town that a picnic was afoot, with dancing, so everybody decided to come. There was no way of discouraging those good-natured people, short of calling a gendarme.

Thus it came about that I found myself wending a grandiloquent way down the harbor to the strains of a brass band, with 126 people aboard my new yawl. All along the water front other people stopped to gape.

It was dusk when we passed through the Narrows. The biggest yellowest moon arose. The sea continued smooth, else certainly we would have been swamped.

When we reached the Custom House, Alfred and I were put ashore at once. Unloading the rest by the single dinghy took some time. There was only one mishap. A large lady in pink satin slipped and fell into the sea. But the contretemps did not dampen her spirits. She danced herself dry. When everyone was landed, the half-mile march to the tennis court began.

Evelyn and Clarice were waiting for us, by candlelight, over a long-delayed supper. Suddenly out of the quiet the blare of the band broke on the night and reverberated through the groves. The thud of feet came up the path. Louder and louder, nearer and nearer; scuffle, scuffle, couple after couple passed the foot of the hill. Our wives gazed at each other thunderstruck, unable to speak. Gladys, the waitress, was the first to break the spell. Gliding out of the noisy shadows, she approached Evelyn, her shoulders drooping, her fingers twisting her skirt.

"Too many people, mum!" she murmured ruefully.

When I arrived at the house, I summoned Sammy who was subdued almost to the point of tears. He proposed that his cousin, a member of the Nassau police force, be put in charge to see that there was no drinking or disorder. As evidence of good faith, the cousin produced a large bottle from his hip pocket and deposited it with me.

From a row of chairs on the outskirts of the festivity, we commanded a scene of matchless beauty. Never before or since has the Island seen such a magnolious night. The cocoanut palms sparkled silver, and their shadows were outlined in jet on the gleaming court, across which the gaily dressed dancers swirled to and fro. Here and there a paper lantern added a carnival effect.

Sammy brought many of his friends up to speak to us. The native Bahamian voices are soft and their patois with its Cockney slant and local inflection has great charm though it is often hard to understand. Aside from a slight miscalculation about refreshment—two cakes and a couple of dozen bottles of pop which disappeared almost at once— the party was a knockout.

About ten-thirty the last lantern flickered out. Sammy struck on the ship's bell the signal for departure. An hour later he came up to say good night. I inquired after the boat. Sammy was optimistic.

"Boss, de las' I see o' her, she still goin' 'long!"

The captain was a little late next morning, but presently the *Lucaya* rounded the point, jib and jigger set, engine purring. We sighed with relief when he reported that the homeward passage had been effected safely and no harm done.

"Yassuh, Boss, we got home a'right. I mean ter say, I had to steer wid my toe, but dey behave dereselfs, yassuh, Boss."

The *Lucaya's* maiden voyage was the high point of her whole career. About six years later she ended up with a characteristic Nassau flourish.

We were dawdling cheerfully over the debris around the breakfast table. Laura and Lawrence Houghteling were with us this time. Evelyn had gone in to give the latest baby, George Barr McCutcheon II, his bath in the same large dishpan that had served his brothers, when suddenly we heard the drone of a plane. The sound was by no means the familiar one it is today. At that hour in the morning it was even more unusual. It came nearer. It was coming down outside the Cut. It could only mean news of some kind, probably bad. Listening nervously inside, Evelyn let the baby slip clear under the water.

The rest of us hurried down to the lagoon. Jackie and Shawie sculled out with Ronald in the skiff. When they reappeared, we recognized the captain standing between them. As they drew nearer, we could see that he was dripping wet, his face twisted with grief. A hundred possibilities flashed through my mind, none of them near the truth.

When he came close enough, he raised his eyes and hands to heaven and shouted, "*Lucaya* done blow up!"

Thus he broke the news. I had nerved myself for something serious from home. My reaction was ludicrously relieved. "Was anyone hurt?" I called.

"Nossah, Boss. Roy blow 'way up, but he come down in de sea. He ain't hurt."

The captain came up the steps, salt water dripping from his suit, tears of emotion running down his cheeks.

"Boss, I wuz drivin' up Bay Street in a hack wid de mail an' de hice. Jus' as I come in sight, I hear de noise of de 'splosion an' see Roy fly hup in de hair. Boss, I done hop out o' dat cab an run! I grab a hax layin' by a woodpile an' I jump right in de sea to scuttle her. But, Boss, hit wuz too deep! Dey had to fetch me hout." He paused for breath and to wipe his tears.

"Den dis gemman come alongside in his hairplane an' hax me if I want to let you-all know."

"You've never flown before, have you?"

"Nossah, Boss. I bin too scared to go hup. I ain't never wanted to try."

"Were you frightened now?"

"Well, sah, Boss, I bin so hupset 'bout de *Lucaya,* I didn' rightly know how I come over here. All I wanted wuz to git hout here quick's I kin."

The captain's sense of duty had overcome his natural fear and we could not help admiring him for that, although after he had departed once more for Nassau on the plane, and the Island had regained something of its normal tranquillity, sober judgment told us that it would have been wiser of him to bring the mail and ice out in a launch, even though it delayed the bad news another hour. This opinion was sustained 100 per cent when I received a bill for plane hire.

When we went over next day to inspect her, the *Lucaya* looked from the outside much as usual. But one glance into the cockpit and cabin showed how seriously the flames had gutted her. She was sold at auction by the insurance company to an outislander who used her as a fishing smack until she went down in the hurricane of 1929.

# ~ 51 ~

# The Papuan Chief

Up to the time I was eighteen, my record as a globe trotter was not calculated to surfeit my thirst for travel. I had not yet been outside the state of Indiana. The main drawback, in the late eighties, was lack of necessary funds, and as I saw no imminent likelihood of any in the near future, I began to buy chances in the Louisiana Lottery.

By investing a dollar a month I enjoyed the pleasant possibility of winning $15,000, one twentieth of the Capital Prize. For thirty days I dreamed of what I would do with the money—one third to my mother, one third laid away, and one third to explore the world! For that one dollar I had thirty days of hope and anticipation and only one day of disappointment. It seemed like a good investment.

Since then I have covered much ground, indulging an appetite that has never diminished. At first I willingly risked my job every time an opportunity to go anywhere presented itself. During war years it was possible to combine my newspaper work with my wanderlust.

Later I solved the problem in still another way. In each succeeding contract with the *Tribune*, I reserved the right to take four months' leave every year, if I wished. These leaves required a month's notice so that the paper could make other arrangements to fill my place, and were to be without pay except for the customary two weeks.

For some years after the First World War, the sea of matrimony—and the Island—provided sufficient adventure, but there came a time when I was once more tempted.

Midnight supper was being served at a ball at the Blackstone. Across the table sat Barney Goodspeed. He and his wife were inveterate travelers.

Barney called across to me, "John, I've got a grand trip for next year. Go to New Guinea by way of New Zealand and Australia; then from Peking cross the Gobi Desert and come home by way of Siberia." Most of these places were new to me. "Why don't you and Evelyn come along?"

Thus it happened that in early January of 1925 the four of us set sail through the Golden Gate. We were prepared for certain hardships but none so great as when we waved good-by to our two small sons, aged seven and three, parked under the watchful eyes of the grandparents. Furthermore, I had drawn so many cartoons ahead that my right hand and arm were acutely painful. But Barney, being a man of large and understanding heart as well as of an inventive turn of mind, skillfully diverted our attention as he cut up my food for me. When the sea was smooth he invented many things.

"What the Orient needs," he proclaimed, "is synthetic bird's-nest soup. This soup is the favorite Chinese delicacy, but at present there isn't enough to go round. If a company should be organized to supply

400,000,000 Chinese with synthetic bird's-nest soup, and if each Chinese spent only a dollar a year, you'd have an annual income of $400,-000,000! The soup could be piped across the ocean, and served hot!"

A good part of our subsequent mealtime discussions was devoted to elaborating this glittering project.

For us the magic lamp of Hawaiian hospitality was rubbed by Louise and Walter Dillingham. Fifteen years earlier I had addressed a letter to "Miss Louise Gaylord, young American lady traveling in Japan." She answered it to "John McCutcheon, American gentleman hunting in East Africa." Both letters reached their destination.

After Hawaii we made brief stays in Fiji and New Zealand. Just as Kamchatka has always connoted for me everything remote, so the Fiji Islands meant everything that was savage and wild. Even in 1925 I approached these islands with fear, not for my safety, but for my illusions. How many of the boys in our service in the South Pacific brought home any suspicion of the romance the mere mention of its atolls engendered in my mind? I suspect the bewildering panoply of modern warfare will have wrought incalculable damage other than that incident to war. Fiji's beauty, at least, remained intact.

When Maui, the legendary hero of Polynesia, cast into the sea a fishhook made of his grandmother's jawbone, and hauled up the Islands of New Zealand, he made a catch which later fishermen have never equaled. The tourist is handed an unlimited menu of scenery from which he can choose any kind he hankers to see, from deep tropic jungles to thermal wonders or mountain fjords.

The great island of New Guinea sits like a huge ungainly bird on the northernmost pinnacle of the map of Australia. A single inter-island trading steamer, once a month, constituted Papua's sole connection with the outside world.

The man in charge of the line operating this steamer was Captain Green, a merry-eyed keen-witted little Welshman who had been in the South Pacific trade for fifty years. Barney and I spent hours with him and the men who were to be found in his Sydney office, bronzed captains, pilots and shipfolk in general, each one full of salty yarns. When the cigars and pipes were lighted, that smoky room had all the flavor of a Louis Becke story.

When we boarded the little steamer and headed out along the Great Barrier Reef, I knew that I had once again left the tourist track. With the exception of us, the passengers were all traders, planters, mining prospectors, scientists or government officials. An old missionary with a long white beard was taking a hive of bees back to a remote corner where he had been shepherd to a little flock of natives for over twenty years. With infinite pains he had translated the New Testament into a dialect spoken by fewer than 5,000 souls.

There was talk of gold, oil and copra; reefs and fevers; tribal wars, native treachery, cannibalism and exploration. From the bar at all hours came husky choruses of he-men about to say good-by to civilization.

Two of its most persistent habitués were a pair of tall, middle-aged Scots. Each owned a flourishing cocoanut plantation in Papua, had made good money in the course of years and had resolved to take a long-delayed vacation back to Scotland. Arrived in Sydney and somewhat exalted by the prospect, they embarked on an extensive and prolonged drunk, during which one of them awakened one morning to find himself married to a waitress who hailed from near his home town. The other, not wishing to go on alone, found a second accommodating Scotch waitress. The quartet were now on our steamer, bound back to New Guinea.

The two brides kept to one cabin, which they insisted on having to themselves. Only at night when the raucous phonograph invited dancing, would they appear on deck, and dance gaily with other men, while the two grooms glowered in resentment. The brides then determined to leave the ship—and their spouses—at Cairns. The atmosphere seethed with conspiracy. But when we sailed from Cairns after a broiling day, the girls were still on board. They had not been able to figure out a way to get their new trousseaux ashore without detection.

It took eight days to reach Port Moresby, a little patch of semi-civilization clinging to the mysterious hinterland of the Owen-Stanley ranges. Beatrice Grimshaw, who lived there at the time while writing her South Sea stories, called it "the sink of the Pacific." The curious forked sails of native proas dotted the harbor, and naked bushy-haired Papuans thronged the jetty.

The hotel was a gaunt frame building at the head of a dusty lane. Our unvarying meals of tasteless beef or mutton and mashed potatoes were served by natives with gay red hibiscus blossoms in their hair which stuck out a foot all around. Their ramies, or breechcloths, were their only concession to convention. One sort of traveler's appetite was satisfied, at any rate.

An outside stairway led to the second-floor bedrooms which were open to the shadowy rafters and planking of the roof. A wide veranda screened by heavy jalousies imparted a cool half-light to this region. Soon we understood why. They kept out much of the rain which came in sheets driven almost horizontally. The sudden but brief wind and rain squalls that come down from the mountains are called gubus. They sweep down with almost hurricane strength and inside of ten minutes are gone, leaving a drenching trail.

The brides and grooms had rooms adjoining ours. During the day the men spent much of their time in the long canvas chairs on the veranda, with bottles and glasses beside them. The hotel held the town's only liquor license. At night there was no way to avoid eavesdropping except to go to sleep, which was difficult, partly because of the enormous cockroaches which roamed the floors and walls.

The stormy adjustment of the newlyweds was the main feature of our visit in Port Moresby. It was complicated by the arrival of a third Scot, a fiery, red-faced little man who had spent thirty-two years in Papua. One day, possibly inadvertently, he reminded his friends of the feud between their ancestral clans, based on cattle stealing some hundreds of years before. That started things. For the rest of the week it was necessary for us to peek cautiously around the corner each time we left our rooms, to see whether we were in direct line of a bottle hurtling through the air.

We had come here with no definite plan for getting away again other than the long trip back to Australia, which we did not want to make. Now Barney and I were able to charter a tiny coastwise steamer, the *Papuan Chief*, to take us around the Gulf of Papua to Thursday Island, where the northbound steamers touched. The four cramped cabins were occupied by our party, a genial Englishman whom we picked up and some French missionaries who thumbed a ride. As the deck outside the cabins was only three feet wide, the rain drenched our bunks nightly before we could shut the door. When it was too hot to sleep, Evelyn took her flashlight and star book out onto the bowsprit above where the prow cut silently among the pale sea snakes floating on the glassy surface. A naked native family slept on the hatch, the Chinese cook on the dining table.

We had offered to give one of the Scotch couples a lift to their plantation which was on our way. The bride wore the same light-blue satin dress she had worn for the past sixteen days, and as she climbed over the rail and down the rope ladder into the dinghy she said, "Gie me an hour to make things tidy, and I'll gie ye some tea."

After a while we walked up the black sand beach and through the cathedrallike aisles of the enormous cocoanut palms to where their house stood in a clearing. It was perched eight feet off the ground, made of split bamboo, and divided into three rooms. One was almost filled by a double bed under a mosquito-netting canopy; the living room had tables and chairs and books; the kitchen offered little to make a housewife's eye sparkle. But to our astonishment and admiration, the bride had taken hold with equanimity and good cheer. She served refreshment with real hospitality.

Toward sunset we walked away through the majestic groves. Our last glimpse behind us showed the bridegroom seated on his stilted balcony, playing new records on his phonograph and carrying on in native dialect what was evidently a most pungent exchange of comments about his new status with a couple of dozen stark-naked savages who squatted on the ground below and rocked with laughter.

We had been told that this was one of the finest and best-run plantations on the island. The owner never drank when at home, and was far more popular and successful with certain of the neighboring tribes than the government officials.

Each time the *Papuan Chief* stopped along the Gulf Coast, she was immediately surrounded by swarms of dugouts and outriggers. Whenever we went ashore, we were carried through the surf from the dinghy

by two grinning gentlemen, shiny with cocoanut oil and wearing only shell necklaces. Swarms of small-boned people surrounded us, and our course through their decorative villages was a huge procession. Our wives, because they were white, I suppose, were permitted to enter one of the long-houses or men's clubs, into which a native woman may not go, under penalty of death.

The lonely traders welcomed this unexpected advent of white visitors with pathetic eagerness. One white couple lived alone with 10,000 natives. Here they had brought up a daughter. We had not the heart to refuse their invitation to supper. As we walked toward the house through the tall grass there was a sudden commotion behind us. We turned in time to see a man catch the head of a black python in the

fork of a long pole. Wrapping the fourteen-foot body around the pole, he brandished it at the shrieking crowd. But some were shrieking with delight; they belonged to a tribe who regarded snakes as delectable food, or kai-kai. Presently, when its captor had tired of playing with it, he sold it to them for a stick of tobacco, and they roasted it in a big bonfire on the beach while we watched from the trader's porch.

The evening was stiflingly hot. The mosquitoes seemed almost as large as the full moon. When we finally said good night and started for the boat, Evelyn handed me her shoes and plunged into the surf. There was an outcry but she paid no heed and reached the dinghy, dripping but refreshed. It seems the shallow water near the river mouths was infested with crocodiles, and we had failed to notice that beaters always flanked our landing parties.

Thursday Island, in the Torres Strait, was where the big ships dropped or took on pilots for the Great Barrier Reef. It was also a center for pearl buyers, but we knew too little about pearls to risk temptation.

One night we attended a movie in an outdoor enclosure. It was *The Sidewalks of New York*. The impression of our country conveyed by our films to the remoter parts of the world must be anything

but uplifting. It seems to me we have thrown away a valuable opportunity for favorable propaganda. We were told that scenes of violence
in movies were always expurgated for these so-called savage audiences,
but the recent exhibition of violence staged by the so-called civilized
races far surpassed anything primitive peoples ever thought of. It was
a gorgeous night. Along about the middle of the show a couple of
people went out. At once there was a general exodus, almost a stampede. By the time we realized the import of the situation, the gubu
was upon us and we were drenched.

After six days the *St. Albans* arrived and bore us north via Borneo
and Manila to Hong Kong and Japan. I woke Evelyn at dawn to stand
on deck as we passed Corregidor, and described to her my earlier entry
into Manila Bay. In Hong Kong, for some reason, I happened to think
of the long hot walk to the Custom House on Treasure Island, and
thereupon had an inspiration. Acting on it immediately, I found the
address of a ricksha manufacturer and, with an interpreter, hastened
to his tiny workshop in a narrow lane. I selected a handsome model-T
style, picked out color and trimmings, gave him the Island address,
and paid him the cost—I think it was $55 gold. After that we could
only hope that all had been understood clearly and trust to the in-
trinsic reliability of the Chinese. My experience has been that they
will try to skin you on a bargain, but after an agreement has been
reached, they will keep their word.

Months after our return home we received an astonished letter
from Mr. Solomon announcing the arrival of the cumbersome case.
We held our breaths at first, until we found whether the wheel base
fitted the narrow stone paths. There was a six-inch leeway on either
side. Whoever pulls it must take careful aim where he runs. Ronald,
the fisherman, generally doubled as ricksha coolie, and many a guest
has been agreeably surprised at our unexpected transportation system.

To that part of the McCutcheon family traveling around the world,
the word "belly," while not ordinarily one of our choicest words, had
a most beautiful sound, ranking with tourmaline and frangipani.
There were often times when we were completely out of contact with
the homefolks, and after such gaps we looked with sharpened eagerness for the latest news. Cablegrams are rarely loquacious. We didn't
look for anything chatty. All we wanted was one word—BELLY. At
sight of it, reposing alone in the midst of an otherwise empty cable
blank, our spirits soared. This was the current Western Union code
meaning all is well at home, everybody fine, stay as long as you like.

"Are we almost there, Are we almost there?"
Cried the dying maid, as she drew near her home,
"Are them the slippery ellums that rare
Their proud green for-ums 'neath heav'ns blue dome?"

When the way is long and weary and the destination far, this song is obviously appropriate. It has the distinction of having been sung, among countless other places, in the box cars during the French retreat from the Strumnitza in the Balkans. Bill Shepherd and Jimmy Hare helped sing it under many trying conditions. Now Bobsy and Barney Goodspeed and we found solace in its troubled measures all the way around the world. Chauffeurs, ship stewards, railway porters, fellow passengers and what not, especially in New Guinea and Siberia, were always tremendously intrigued by this song.

Eventually, the four of us arrived in Peking.

# — 52 —

# Across the Gobi Desert

THE way to Urga lies northwest from Peking, through the triple loops of the Great Wall, over the passes of Nankow and Wanchuan, and thence for 700 miles across the Gobi desert, following the ancient routes of the caravans. When those caravans were coming from Iraq and Samarkand and the Roof of the World, and from Sarai on the Volga, which was the capital of the Golden Horde, the desert of Gobi was known as "the abode of many evil spirits which amuse travelers to their destruction." Tales were told of its treacheries that have not yet lost their potency.

Tales are still told to venturesome travelers who follow the old routes! Nearly everybody in Peking was of the opinion that it was impossible to make this trip. General Feng at Kalgan discouraged it on account of the prevalence of bandits along the route. He notified the Chinese Foreign Office, who notified the American Legation, who in turn sent us an official document of an unenthusiastic nature. There were also war rumors in the area: Feng Yü-hsiang and Chang Tso-lin were about to clash at any moment. Old-timers in Peking agreed that it was absurd for Barney and me to take our wives on such a trip and lent us revolvers. The prospect looked dark; nevertheless we started.

In Kalgan we were met by Bob Williams, our chauffeur-guide, a tall clean-cut American Hotspur of twenty-nine who had played football on the Wisconsin team and learned to fly, and was now running a freight transport service to Urga. Kalgan means "barrier" and from the compound wall we counted, on the bare brown hills, seventeen of the ancient watchtowers to guard against the Turanian hosts who followed Genghis Khan. It is true that there were many soldiers about, and bands were exercising at frequent intervals, but we suffered no hardships unless one assumes a Chinese band to be one. Bob seemed concerned only about whether we had enough lipsticks to guard against the fierce dry winds of the desert. The American consul was the only other person we had met who said it was safe to go on. However, we lay low, avoiding the Christian general. A personal request from him not to venture into the bandit region would have spoiled everything.

In the darkness of very early morning we slipped out and across the pass into Mongolia. Our tense nerves relaxed a little more after passing each of three control stops, especially the one where an American had been shot recently when he started his car a moment too soon; but evidently Bob had all the correct papers.

Our open Dodge car had reinforced axles and was padded on the outside to protect it from the 1,400 pounds of gasoline, bedrolls, food, water, shovels and other luggage which were lashed onto the running boards. We had to climb over all this impedimenta to reach the seats, something of a feat when we had on three coats and the top was up! Articles likely to be needed were evenly distributed over everyone's feet.

The first twenty-five miles took us three hours. Then we descended into the province of Chahar where we stuck in the mud for two hours. After that we hurried on past a number of ruined walled towns.

"Now," said Bob, "we're in the bandit belt for the next fifty miles. I had hoped to be through here before their business hours, eleven to three. They jumped out of that compound and held up five cars awhile back."

We reached Chap Sur safely at six o'clock, our first Mongolian "station." The chief, Bob whispered to us, was probably in league with the hunghutzes, although nothing ever happened in his domain. He was a slant-eyed old Mongol with drooping chin whiskers. His women, in beautiful headdresses of silver and coral, were friendly and offered us lukewarm tea with rancid butter, served in bowls which they carefully wiped out with the extra length of their sleeves. Although we had not eaten for twelve hours, we waited for our own supper. In a small odoriferous room—merely an aisle between two rows of k'angs or raised wooden platforms which are used as beds—with five or six curious Mongols crowding in at either door, we had the first meal of what turned out to be our main diet: instant coffee, crackers, cheese and raisins. We had brought various other things with us which we seldom had time to prepare.

"Now," said Bob, "we ought to see a lot of wolves. They are traveling in packs of fifteen or twenty this year."

After sunset we went on and on into the darkness. The headlights threw the sides of the trail into such shadow that when, at midnight, we drove through the lanterned gate of the next compound, we felt as if we had emerged from a dense forest.

Pangkiang, about 200 miles from Kalgan, consisted of two mud houses and three yurts inside the usual wall. A yurt is a rounded felt tent, ten or twelve feet across. The yard was full of cars—at least we suspected that cars were beneath those mountains of freight. We were taken into a little room which had a fire, but the k'ang already contained several sleepers humped under blankets and the air was close and foul. Luckily a yurt was vacant, and without even wondering what might be in there, we spread our sheepskin sleeping bags and all five of us were asleep in as many minutes. At four-thirty when Bob woke us, it was snowing. Dressing consisted of putting on our shoes and our hats. We breakfasted on coffee, bread and bacon in the warm room with the still slumbering humps, and were loaded and on our way in an hour.

Presently the low hills leveled off and we were in the Gobi at last—"the windy, wild wastes of the Desert of Gobi." Hummocks of sage and a few blue iris sprinkled the sand. The dips and rises of the dunes were hardly noticeable, and the horizon was veiled with mirages, blue lakes, misty islands, sometimes forests of tall trees. The ruins of Chandu, the fabulous Xanadu of Coleridge's poem, were not far away; and where a ridge of curious formation dipped sharply lay the fossil fields where Roy Chapman Andrews found his dinosaur eggs. Andrews was even then somewhere about. It was warm in the middle of the day; the way was marked by camel carcasses in all stages, and sick camels waited to die.

Skirting treacherous quicksands, we dipped again to the lower level of the salt lake beyond which the Lamasery of EhrLien glittered in the sun, and stopped in the compound for tiffin. We simply stood about and cut cheese on top of the dusty luggage, which was the cleanest place in sight.

The afternoon ride was hot and rough, for we wanted to make Ude by five o'clock. In a rocky river bed, where a caravan was encamped, with the camels' loads of fur piled high beside the indigo tents, an old chief came forward in his wine-red coat, yellow sash and peaked cap, to raise his thumb over his forehead in ceremonious salutation, and then squat to watch us out of sight. Antelope made targets of themselves everywhere. Immigrants from Shansi walked by their blue ox-carts. A heavily laden car with a broken axle had been delayed for at least five days, providentially near water. We passed the boundary between Inner and Outer Mongolia, a rocky gap with a lonely shrine ringed with little stone prayer piles.

Ude was the main Soviet border control station and crucial point for us. This was where we might be turned back. It was an unusually extensive metropolis, having two mud compounds and eight or ten yurts at the base of a shiplike scarp. In the sunset the pink and gold desert rolled around us like a sea. Below on the farther side was the ruined fort where, five years before, the Mongols under Baron Ungern von Sternberg had killed 13,000 Chinese.

Again a yurt was cleared for us and many Mongols in salmon and amber and mauve and green brocaded silk pushed in through the four-foot door while we unpacked and made supper—hot tomato soup, baked beans and tinned peaches. The perpetual mystery of why we needed five separate basins of water in which to wash interested them far more than a trader outside who was displaying silks of such hue and quality as made us marvel. Since the monarchy fell, the imperial storehouses which contained the hoardings of centuries of tribute to the Dragon Throne were being tapped for the markets. When our guests were firmly ousted, the door barricaded ten minutes before the dogs were loosed for the night, and we had crawled into our narrow bags, some kindly intentioned soul pulled the cover over the smoke hole above us, our only ventilation. We whooped in unison but it required a lot of explaining to get it open again.

Red tape, next morning, detained us until nine but we were glad to be able to go on at all. Dust devils scurried ahead of us.

"Is this where you have sandstorms?" asked Evelyn.

The desert heard her, and with one accord the sands of the Gobi arose and came upon us! For an hour and a half we combated what must have been a seventy-mile wind and a stinging yellow fog that seeped into everything, even scarring the glass of the windshield. Then the carburetor became clogged. For another two hours Bob worked over it while we tried to protect him with our coats, but to no avail. Remembering that we had passed a nomad camp about a mile back, we tugged the car around, intending to push it back to the camp. But Evelyn and Bobsy, who were in the car, braced themselves and with some difficulty managed to hold up one of the sheepskin shubas or greatcoats. The added sail area was all the wind needed to take the car right away from us. We had to run to keep up with the girls as they sailed gaily across the Gobi!

Dimly the yurts of Sainossu huddled beneath the storm. Two Chinese cars were already parked near by. Goggled riders beat against the gale to shelter, and a ghostly herd of ponies stood patiently, heads down, tails to the wind. The chief took us into his yurt where we shook ourselves out, cold-creamed our faces and had lunch, with the usual audience who finished the scraps. The oldest, a high lama, wore a vivid scarlet coat edged with azure and lined with white astrakhan. His purple cap had a crown of gold brocade. He was pleased when I made a sketch of him. Another wore a mauve coat, orange pants and a cap of sable. The colors of their padded garments were still splendid beneath countless layers of filth and grease; they carried embroidered bags with silver buttons and wore stiff, high turned-up boots; their long, loose sleeves often hung down over their hands, and all who were not lamas smoked thin, painted pipes of villainous tobacco. They persisted in bringing brass pots of buttered tea, and spitting and blowing their noses into the fire, which was of camel dung. Bob fixed the carburetor in the yurt, thereby adding a choice mixture of grease and gasoline to the already well-flavored interior.

There were guns around the walls, a red and gold lacquer shrine, and four low k'angs covered with felt and fur; an iron brazier in the center, and a box of desert fuel. The sand blew through the smoke hole, and the leather door flapped. The old fellow took snuff from a carnelian bottle with a coral top.

Their curiosity was intense and naïve but always civil. Bob, who spoke Chinese and Mongolian as well as Russian, interpreted when necessary, but Barney just strung words along together, successfully as usual, added a "ski" here and there and made many friends through the long afternoon.

After supper the storm stopped and the sun sank abruptly into the sand. We packed up, wrapped up and started on once more. Each of us had on a sweater, a topcoat, an army raincoat and a sheepskin shuba. Over us we piled one of the sleeping bags and a heavy dogskin robe. It was below freezing and the wind still had a terrific knife in it. Bobsy, Evelyn and I were wedged in so tightly on the back seat we couldn't turn, and the triple coat collars supported our necks like stocks. Evelyn was in the middle and fell asleep, behind her veil and goggles, while listening for Marco Polo's Singing Sands. "Marvelous indeed and almost passing belief are the stories related of these spirits of the desert, which are said at times to fill the air with the sounds of all kinds of musical instruments, and also of drums and the clash of arms." She flopped over sideways when I got out to help with a flat tire.

At four-thirty our headlights outlined the Tuerrin station doorway against a paling sky. A Russian couple in charge sleepily cleared some Mongols out of the telegraph office for us, and the next thing we knew Bob was calling "Seven o'clock!"

That fourth day we drove for seven hours with scarcely a stop. The weird outcroppings of rock behind Tuerrin cast strange silhouettes against the deep-blue desert. A lamasery was perched on the crags. Later we came to rolling wind-swept flats where we could make a good forty miles an hour. There was seldom any sort of road. A single wire clung to the telegraph poles—Peking to Paris—which roughly marked the route. Occasionally we were close beside them, more often miles away. Animal life was more active: gazelle, antelope, bustards, cranes; hundreds of marmots flapped their heavy flat tails as they galumphed to their holes; a lone wolf stopped to watch us, and eagles sat solemnly on the camel carcasses not ten feet from the car. The only stop we made was out of deference to a gentleman in a mulberry coat who leveled a rifle at us. He simply wanted a "look-see" at our papers. Bob was intent on making the Urga Customs before it closed, so we sped on, eating our cheese and raisins as we went. Just before five we circled the base of the Bogdo-ol or Sacred Mountain, crossed the Tola in its willowy valley and looked on Urga.

At the control yurt we shipped a hard-looking Mongol with a rifle; we drove through the stockaded streets of Maimachen, the Chinese trading town a mile from Urga; we crossed the waste to where the white, Russian-style houses of the Soviet officials stood, with red flags flying. We passed the famous prison behind its pointed double stockade of tree trunks; and a deep-belled camel caravan preceded us through the gates of the customs compound.

Here, true to form, the officials turned everything out on the ground among the manure. They tasted every one of a dozen bottles of boiled water and took a large swig of vinegar which they spat out disgruntled. They held up and gazed at both sides of everything. They were civil enough but curious. Every time a mangy dog walked through our belongings, they stopped to play with it. Most of the non-Russian whites in town assembled to cheer us. There was Larsen who for thirty years had sold Mongolian ponies and *objets d'art* to China, and mechanical toys to the Living Buddha. There was a handsome Danish Hamlet who wore a belted blue blouse, high-buttoned collar and black boots laced with thongs. He was about to start with his trading caravan on the tedious six weeks' trail to Uliassutai, although he was no stranger to the ballrooms of Shanghai and Harbin. These and others stood around, sympathetic but helpless. We just sat and laughed. One critical or angry word, we all knew, would complicate matters immeasurably. The customs took our films, our revolvers (we never had any ammunition!) and our two books, Marco Polo and a history of Genghis Khan. We recovered the films next day, the books when we left, but the revolvers—never!

This ordeal over, we threw everything into the back of the car, climbed on top and rode through the unpaved streets to Bob's business branch. The gates swung open, the chained dog barked viciously, and we were at last at home in Urga.

Urga, for so long the Sacred City of the Living Buddha, second only to Lhasa in mystery, was the capital of Outer Mongolia. That we had arrived and put ourselves within its clutches was incredibly a fact.

We were practically prisoners—if only to uncertainty and helplessness—in the house of Bob's Urga manager, Gregor Ivanovitch Andronovitch, who deserves a decoration for the way he behaved during those six days when Bob's first, and possibly last, "tourist party" was parked on him! Interpreters and permits were needed for everything we did, and the many humorously hectic hours we spent in that house impressed its homely details indelibly on our memories. Through the glazed entry-porch, where Bob slept, we entered the combination living and dining room. It was square, high and bare-floored with one window and five doors. Three Russian tile stoves were set in the walls. A kerosene lamp on the center table did little to enliven the pallid wallpaper, or to define the confusion on the desk which served as the general dump. The only other thing in the room, besides stiff chairs, was a red and gold lacquer chest, invariably buried beneath our coats. There were two small bedrooms. Andronovitch slept in the kitchen.

After we got used to the snarling dogs of Urga, we could walk the streets; the dusty lanes in front of the open meat-market counters; the dustier wide main street full of antediluvian droshkies with high-arched wooden horse collars; the narrow alleys of the Chinese part where jewelers worked in obscure alcoves; the stockaded streets of the lama cities, dominated by the gold-leaf roofs of the temples; and the churning, droning spellbinding aisles of the Mongolian bazaars. Here were Russians and Chinese, Mongols and Tartars, Buriats and Kalmucks, Tibetans and Kirghiz, and many more representatives of the interior of Asia. Most of them were clad in priceless tribute silk, of which the open stalls were full; the women wore fantastic headdresses of gold and silver and coral and turquoise and sable.

Urga, its name now changed to Ulan Bator, had even then come under the influence of the Bolsheviks, and there was no more a Living Buddha. The poor old Bogdo Khan and his wife had died rather suddenly a few years before, and the Soviets did not allow him to be replaced. Instead they were making a start, we were told, at "educating" the swarms of lamas remaining in the city. Only two of the government offices were occupied by Russians, but they stood invisibly at the shoulders of the acting Buriats and other puppets, who were like children with a complicated mechanism they did not understand. Mongol official mentality was notably illogical and inconsistent.

Our object, after once getting into Urga, was to take some photographs and then get out. It sounded simple enough. The "sights" of the city require perhaps a day. We had allowed four. Andronovitch opined that it would be ten before we got away; no foreigners had ever been permitted to depart in less. We did it in six, which amazed everybody.

Our most pressing concern was to obtain passes to leave. What held up the game was why in the world we had come there in the first place, even though permission for us to come had issued from this same headquarters. Nobody seemed able to grasp the idea of a tourist, especially the female of the species, and it was necessary to go before the G.P.U., successor of the dread Cheka.

"One at a time!" Bobsy, who was nearest, followed Bob up the narrow stairway. What sort of third degree was this? We waited in attitudes of assumed indifference, casting furtive glances up the stairs.

The minutes dragged. What were they doing to Bobsy? We remembered the mad baron's short shrift with dubious persons, possibly in this very house. We wondered if we looked suspicious, and at this our attitudes of nonchalance became positively painful to see.

But pretty soon Bob called and we all filed into a small room where a solemn little Buriat sat behind a large oak desk, while near by sat his secretary with bobbed hair and high-heeled patent-leather slippers! He might have the power of life and death, but for all that, I felt exactly like the Cowardly Lion when the screen tipped over and revealed the real Wizard of Oz. He and Bob talked in Russian, the usual questions about our political sympathies and whether we had ever been in jail. Later we found that Bob had conveyed the impression that Barney was in the motor-transport business and that I was his assistant!

Three days of negotiations were required for permission to take photographs, with a soldier escort, and to find a Chinese to develop and *print* them. Poor Andronovitch spent most of his time translating and retranslating requests and explanations into Russian and Mongolian.

Then came the little matter of the revolvers, which we had not wanted to bring in the first place and for which we had no permits. Permission for their return was not forthcoming.

"Very well," we said. "We'll go without them."

But not at all. We would be stopped at the first control if all details of this sort were not definitely settled and signed one way or another.

"Can't we make a present of them to the Mongolian Government?" suggested Barney. By no means. The committee had to sit upon the matter, and the committee chose to stand until Monday. Besides, the customhouse did not operate on Sunday, even if we could have arranged everything else.

Meanwhile we saw Urga. We saw the embryo museum mainly contributed by Roy Chapman Andrews, whose expedition was due any day. We saw the giant, almost eight feet tall, who amiably posed with his arm extended well over Barney's six-foot-two. We saw the Mongolian fire brigade in action, four men pumping from a barrel while the imperial five-toed dragon writhed all over their silken backs. Northward we drove across the roadless waste toward the range of mountains that go back and back to the fastnesses where Genghis Khan was born. The golden roofs of Michijarasik glittered against the bare hills, the monastery where the Living Buddha was educated. The students, a cheerful, red-robed pungent lot, crowded close in their endeavor to peer into our cameras.

Not so old as this, but far more majestic on its hill, with the stockades and schools and yurts of its lama city around its base, the Gan Dan lords it over the landscape, over the bazaars and the Chinese town and the Russian quarter, over the three barbaric palaces crouched a mile away, over the gullies full of bones, and the yak and camel caravans on the plains.

Its topmost balcony was on a level with the enormous face of the seventy-foot Buddha. The railings of the steep stairs to each balcony were hung with lama paintings; the space between the rails and the figure was so full of pendant gorgeousness that it was impossible to get a complete perspective of the colossal figure, draped from shoulder to heel, over the original gold leaf, in sumptuous yellow silk—shades from saffron to sand that folded into one another like sunset clouds. To the touch all was unclean, to the smell unsavory. Through the eyes alone the senses were enthralled. Ironically it was not able to achieve the purpose for which it was built: to preserve the Bogdo Khan's eyesight.

On Saturday night we went to the theater. The ponies tethered in the courtyard, the bare square interior, the primitive curtain and footlights, gave much the impression of any frontier town. A huge hammer and sickle framed the proscenium. Two modern one-act comedies were given with the usual Russian histrionic skill. Afterward the floor was cleared for dancing. We found ourselves seated conspicuously in front while the whole crowd stared us out of countenance. Our Buriat friend with the power of life and death was there, and the handsome Russian head of the secret service, and the commander in chief of the Mongolian Army. We joined the dizzy Russian waltz until we were winded; then we watched the plump pretty girls with full swinging skirts and little curls drawn forward over their ears, and the tall, lithe young men in riding boots and belted blouses, who kept going faster and faster until our eyes blurred with the motion and tobacco smoke, and our ears dinned with the army band of eighteen pieces of brass. So we came out into the zero starlight, and drove home through the streets empty of all save the howling dogs.

Sunday we wakened to find that a regular Siberian blizzard had buried everything and was still falling. Our spirits were dampened. Once, Bob told us, he had been held up three weeks before he could dig his car out.

When one of the Danes arrived to say that Mrs. Marshall asked us for tiffin, we accepted thankfully. Mrs. Marshall was the only English-speaking woman in Urga. Her husband was an English trader. We had dined with them on our second night, when eight separate nationalities were represented at table, with amusing linguistic complications!

When the snow stopped, we drove home through the slush by way of the Hill of the Dead, our last remaining "sight." It is considered, in Mongolia, a respectful finish for the rich and great to be laid in the open back of a cart and driven at top speed far out from the city over rough ground, while the driver never looks back. In this way no one will later be perturbed by a disgruntled spirit. Ordinary mortals end near by on the Hill of the Dead, where the dogs leave only the skulls. Andronovitch was particularly annoyed—for him—by this latest whimsy of the "tourists."

On our return to the cheerless room where we had killed so much time, we had sat down to supper when there came a knock at the door. The Chinese cook went, and returned and whispered to Bob, whose face turned ashen. "The secret service," he whispered and went out. We sat stunned, unable to eat, trying to think what we had done that might be considered suspect. But the Chinese boy had got it wrong; it was only the Minister of War, wanting a drink.

Monday morning all the knots unraveled at once. Our pictures came, properly O.K.'d; word came that the committee would not sit until next day but we could go without the revolvers; our permits to depart arrived. We loaded the car immediately and ate a hasty lunch. In the customs compound we were delayed from twelve-thirty until two, almost a record for brevity. It was very cold. The Goodspeeds had to undo the magnificent Mongolian woman's costume they had bought for the Field Museum three separate times for inspection by three different officials. With the sky clear and the coast clear, we passed the last control stop beyond Maimachen, crossed the Tola and were *out* of Urga!

Ahead the hills were snow-covered and the going was hard. At eight o'clock we stuck fast. In cold discomfort we tried to sleep while the wolves howled. At midnight a headlight came over the hill. Rescued! But just before they reached us, they stuck, too. Five jolly Russians, escorting a carload of silver to pay Mongol soldiers, came and pushed us out. It was more of a job with their car, but in time we went on together, while they sang Russian songs in the night behind us. Thirty miles from the nearest "station" we stuck again, both cars. So it went, through the night.

The hundred miles from Tuerrin to Sainossu were perhaps the loveliest of the trip. Ahead, the Gobi lay mauve and amethyst under storm clouds. Like a deep sea it was and imperceptibly we entered it, for around us was only sunshine on the colored stones beneath our wheels, blue and red and lavender, with white patches like recent hail. Across the plain where last week we had met the sandstorm now marched a thick gray curtain of rain. We raised the top in time, but in ten minutes the sun was out again. Then the way, although hard and good, was full of small lakes which sprayed out on one side of us into filmy white peacocks' tails, and on the other side were arched by the wind back into the car! Thousands of gazelles and antelopes raced with us thirty or forty miles an hour, herd after herd. Plodding caravans stood out in unnatural relief and the yurts of Sainossu looked calm and snug within the curve of a double rainbow.

Bob woke us at four. Storm clouds circled about, but we stuck only once just before reaching Ude. Would the quicksands beyond be possible after the rain? By circuitous detours for another hundred miles Bob brought us out onto solid ground just at sunset. Then for seventy more miles, like the silver thread of the fairy tale, the telegraph wire—Paris to Peking—led on unswervingly to Pangkiang, and I am sure the wind in that wire sang far more eerily than Marco Polo's Singing Sands.

The last morning Bob made us eat beans and sausage for breakfast because the 200-mile run to Kalgan—if we made it at all—would be hard. It was! We dodged and slithered between cloudbursts all day. With our hearts in our mouths and our heads battering the canvas hood, we came at last to the river. Bob waded across twice to make sure; a heavily loaded car on the other side waited our luck. How that engine pulled, and how we pushed with the muscles of our toes! We got across, but the other car turned back.

After thirteen hours of jolting, with never a stop for food, we were all but in. The last control took our worn, torn papers for the last time and motioned us to proceed into Kalgan. As Bob said, we saw "the whole works." Cold, wet, hungry, sleepy, worried, but tireless and cheerful, he had piloted us safely across the Gobi, and if, on that last afternoon, some nice, polite bandits had appropriated our superfluous luggage, the trip could have been only a degree more memorable than it was. At the end of sixteen days we returned to laugh at the false prophets in Peking.

At the Indiana Society Banquet, 1946.

At home.

FOUR McCUTCHEONS

1912                                  1938

1948

JTM: THREE AGES OF MAN

Nevertheless, I may admit, at this late date, that it was a foolish risk to have taken.

After this, our eight-day journey on the Trans-Siberian railway from Mukden to Moscow seemed relatively luxurious, even though the water gave out and the food gave out and the track was partly washed away and the engine broke down. We had had considerable difficulty in getting permission to enter Russia, largely, no doubt, because the paper for which I worked was definitely *non grata* with the Reds. We were informed that we were the first Americans to have crossed from east to west since the Bolsheviks took over.

Our eventual emergence into Scandinavia would have ended the adventurous part of the trip, had it not been for my decision, on a sudden impulse, to fly from Copenhagen to Paris. Evelyn had never been up. I wanted her to share my enthusiasm. This single day's flight seemed a safe one to start with, and we arranged to meet the Goodspeeds for dinner in Paris on the night of our arrival.

My hope and illusion were short-lived. The three-passenger jitney plane which took us across the Kattegat to Malmö, Sweden, showed immediate signs of fatigue. The engine hesitated and sputtered and choked in obvious agony. It nearly died half a dozen times and I wondered if Evelyn was feeling the same way. Fortunately the trip lasted only fifteen minutes. Our relief on boarding a shiny Swedish Junker, bound for Brussels, was also temporary. Fog rolled in. We could not follow the strip map very well, and neither, it was evident, could the pilot. Pretty soon we landed in a pasture full of inhospitable-looking bulls, and had to wait in the plane for an hour or so until a Schleswig-Holstein farmer arrived to liberate us.

After a train trip to Hamburg, where we spent the first night, a two-hour flight through more fog next morning landed us—back in Hamburg! On a third attempt we reached Brussels, where we were transferred into a big French Farman. By this time Evelyn was becoming somewhat skeptical about the pleasure of flying, and it was necessary for me to use diplomacy in urging her to give aviation another chance. I spoke too soon.

We were planted most politely in the very nose of the ship, in a sort of bay window of isinglass, a feature of those old Farmans. An engine thundered behind each shoulder; the vibration of the fuselage put our legs to sleep. We ran into a storm. Lightning zigzagged ahead of us; sheets of rain drove through the cracks in the isinglass and drenched us from the waist down. Periodically the pilot and the *mécanicien* engaged in long and acrobatic consultations, their gestures indicating that all was not well.

Off to our right, shafts of gold from the setting sun of the second day rayed out from under the storm clouds. Presently we realized that they were on our *left*—we must be returning to Brussels! But no. After another morale-shaking conference the pilot started to come down. He landed with the wind on what had been a small military field. The Farman took it in one bounce. Plunging through a fence, which draped the wings with wire, we sped on through another field and another fence. Ahead loomed a barn. With some idea, I presume, of stopping the plane, Evelyn and I instinctively put out our hands and feet. However, we came to rest in a potato patch just short of it.

We were dazed and speechless. Before even the pilot had adjusted himself to being still alive, a businesslike little man, drawing on the sleeves of an official blue coat, trotted across the field and stuck his head in the door.

"*Quel bonheur, messieurs!*" he announced. "*Je suis le douanier.*" (I am the customs inspector.) He made us open our bags in his cowshed.

From Valenciennes, near by, we notified the Goodspeeds that they needn't hold dinner any longer, and we arrived in Paris on the third morning by train after all.

# ∼ 53 ∼

# I Make Two Moves

FOR some ten years before my marriage I had been living at 39 East Schiller Street. Cheerfully I took my bride there and enjoyed seven more years in the friendly old-fashioned apartment on the top floor overlooking Lake Michigan and the lawns and brownstone turrets of the Potter Palmer castle.

Then we moved to a new co-operative apartment at the corner of Lakeview Avenue and Arlington Place. This one looked across Lincoln Park to the lagoon, it was near the Francis Parker School where the children went, and it had a den for me and a jolly playroom

papered with giraffes and elephants and porcupines and other things
equally suitable for small boys or the president of a zoo. Howard
Shaw designed the building, and to make way for it a handsome gray
stone house had to be torn down. This house, we were informed, belonged to one Christopher Columbus Crabb, and had been occupied
by his business partner, Lizzie Allen, until her death in 1896. Lizzie
was the notorious queen of the red-light district and owner of what
subsequently became the Everleigh Club. As I eat my breakfast, I
still look out at what used to be her stable, a drab reminder of those
gay nineties.

After I had adjusted myself to my new domicile and learned not to
get off the bus too soon of an evening, I had to change another habit
and get off the morning bus much sooner.

I was invited to move my studio from the Fine Arts Building to the
new Tribune Tower by the river. This time I was torn by sentimental
emotions of a different caliber. Many considerations entered into my
decision to accept, among which was the usual one of expediency.
There would be no rent to pay—mine had doubled from $45 to $90 a
month—and it was much more convenient to my new home. Even
more compelling was the fact that Colonel McCormick wanted me
to attend the editorial conference held daily in his office. This could
not very well be done from the old studio.

As further inducement I was offered my choice of a number of loca-

tions, to be partitioned off as I wished. I selected the thirty-first floor,
up among the flying buttresses, with fine north light, and on clear days
a wide view over the lake and the city roofs. Four hundred feet below,
the boulevard traffic came up to me as only a faint hum. My segment

of the "lantern" which rises ten stories above the main body of the tower, had nice possibilities as a studio. It was forty feet long and paneled in warm brown oak. The arched windows were on the floor level, leaving the upper half of the room in the romantic dimness I enjoy. From the fourteen-foot ceiling I hung the red-tasseled horn lanterns I had bought in Peking. The narrow woven runner from Turkestan, designed to fit round and round the interior of a Turkoman's kibitka, fitted nicely the length of the long wall. My other trophies were duly installed.

Near my desk I hung a bronze plaque of Evelyn, done by Alfeo Faggi before we were married. I like it because it emphasizes the long clear line of her profile and throat. Faggi married an old friend of mine, Beatrice Butler. Once at a party she extemporized on the piano musical portraits of us which were instantly recognizable. Another time I figured in portrait work as party of the second part was in Peking. At one of Lucy Calhoun's dinners in her converted temple dwelling a Chinese artist did a figure of me in colored bread crumbs, amazingly recognizable considering the material.

My most recent posing was done for my sister-in-law, Sylvia Shaw Judson, in her studio down the lane at Ragdale. It used to startle Sylvia a good deal to look up from her work and find the gaunt, pinched features of John D. Rockefeller or a smiling Semitic countenance focused on her. I've always been able to do things with my face. At other times I would part and comb my hair differently and for a moment she would look from her work to her model in bewilderment. These protean changes amused her, and, as they were brief, her work was not delayed. Bronze being under priority rating during the war, we had recourse to my studio where we found a large bronze vase of overlapping elephant faces and ears, which was metamorphosed into me.

Sometimes we gave parties in the new studio. I entertained the Wayfarers, and Evelyn served box lunches to that group of Chicago ladies who call themselves the Scribblers and whose programs are not always intended for mixed audiences. Winston Churchill came up to see me when he was in Chicago; I think Hazel Lavery asked him to. But the tempo of life no longer permits people to drop in for a friendly chat. Gaar Williams and Carey Orr also worked on the thirty-first floor. When Gaar died, the two smaller rooms were thrown together to make Carey a scrumptious studio with a fine view of the river and the Loop skyscrapers. Carey's style is vigorous and forthright, and its apparent simplicity shows a profound understanding of the art of cartooning. He was the cheeriest kind of neighbor, genial, kindly and obliging. However, the two of us were not always there at the same time. There was a detached atmosphere up among the wind-wrapped buttresses quite unlike the camaraderie of the noisy Fine Arts Building.

In my early days in Chicago, when I seemed to have endless energy to spare, I used to take on almost any outside work that came along. I never refused a paying job if it was along lines that I liked. When the first cafeteria started in the Y.M.C.A. building on LaSalle Street I did the chalk drawings that often hung in the doorway to lure the sidewalk trade to the feast within. For those large sketches, dashed off quickly, I received fifty cents apiece, and thought it easy money. When Morgan and Wright started *Wheel Talk* to stimulate the newly developing automobile industry, Schmedtgen and I did scores of drawings which amplified our modest salaries. We also did work for McQuilken in the *Inland Printer*, then one of the most artistic exponents of the printer's art. I did World's Fair sketches for the *New York Herald* at five or ten dollars apiece. In retrospect the remuneration for these outside jobs seems small, but I never felt that I was underpaid. My whole perspective in the matter of money was gauged on the basis of $25 a week.

Perhaps the first taste of big money was when Harry Selfridge, then a partner of Marshall Field, paid me $500 for a half-page drawing, the first, I think, of that size to be used in newspaper advertising. It was a view of the central court of the store with many little figures busily shopping. I probably thought it part of the day's work at a princely price.

For many years, there seemed always time to sandwich in a little extra work. When Norman Hapgood was editing *Collier's*, I did political cartoons during the Progressive period. For Trumbull White of *Appleton's*, for James Whigham in the *Metropolitan*, for Ray Long in the *Cosmopolitan*, for the *Saturday Evening Post*, *Hearst's International* and for others I did many illustrated articles or cartoons.

As time went on I began to limit myself to this class of outside work. The pressure reached a point where I had to choose between the magazine and the advertising fields. I could not do both, so I selected the one I preferred although it paid less.

It came to pass that this decision was to face a mighty test.

In the late twenties the representative of an Eastern advertising company called at my studio, a very agreeable gentleman with the dynamic go-getter approach then pervading business. This was shortly before the chilling blast of the '29 crash withered the world of industry. The young man asked me to do a weekly cartoon advertising a certain brand of cigarette.

"I'm sorry," I said, "but I have not been doing any advertising work for a long time, and besides, I don't smoke cigarettes."

The young man said that made no difference, that no one cared whether the artist smoked or didn't, and offered me $40,000 for one cartoon a week for one year. Again I demurred, but he was not impressed. He had risen to the top by getting things done.

"How about two cartoons a week for $80,000?"

It was a most flattering offer and I owed him consideration and courtesy. The fact that I was disinclined to undertake advertising work could not but seem to him a case of blind heresy. To soften the blow I said I would speak to Colonel McCormick. I did. I told Bert of the offer. I also told him I had no intention of accepting the job even if he were willing. He said he did not like the idea of my doing any sort of cartoons which would appear in other newspapers.

At my next meeting with the determined New Yorker, I reported the colonel's sentiments. I added that the increased pressure of another regular job might prove a physical strain too great for me to assume.

The young man continued unimpressed. He thought it only a matter of reaching a price. There followed an amazing crescendo of offers.

He asked if I would do two cartoons a week for $100,000. When I refused, very politely of course, he asked if I would do the cartoons if they provided the ideas. When I once more refused, he asked if I would accept if they provided not only the ideas but a ghost artist to do the drawing. My only contribution would be to allow the use of my name. Once more, and finally I refused.

I suppose I was dramatizing again. I was refusing $100,000—and enjoying it!

I was refusing partly because I didn't smoke cigarettes, and partly because in those days I felt there was something slightly—just slightly—infra dig about advertising. Probably the main reason was that I stood in no great need of money.

One time it was not I but my friends who received an unusual caller. An imposter went around to them saying he represented me, that I was drawing portraits for a book at a cost of $250 apiece, and would they do me the honor of posing and subscribing? A number of people paid. Only by accident, Judge Calhoun telephoned me to know where to send the check. I was horrified. I told him to make an appointment with the man and then had an officer there to arrest him. When the case came up in the old Harrison Street station, I testified, and it was proved that he had forged my name. But there was some loophole by which he squirmed out.

Another time a man in Texas passed himself off as me. He was hospitably entertained, put up at clubs, signed chits, borrowed money, and lived for some time on this misrepresentation. By chance I happened to read a newspaper notice about myself attending all these functions in Austin with persons I had never heard of. I wrote down there at once to disillusion the chief of police.

Ordinarily the serenity of my studio was disturbed only by the telephone, a device whereby much valuable time is swallowed up. Many a cartoon was finished before the deadline, with the receiver in my other hand, and many people might be piqued to know how little attention their words were receiving.

Mail was a problem I never satisfactorily solved. The tables and chairs were heaped high with things I meant to answer or had saved for reference. Every once in a while Evelyn conducted an archaeological expedition, excavated me from the accumulation and brought my correspondence up to date. She was amused when she found expired financial rights and warrants in the pile, and mystified by papers blackened with pencil marks. I spent a lot of time and pencil lead making these, my own mediums for tracing cartoon outlines. Sometimes by mistake I made them on my scalp.

"Why don't you put the ones already made in this drawer where you can find them when you need them?" she would ask.

"That would be contrary to my whole scheme of life, Evelino," I would tell her.

A man likes to have a place where he can leave things around, things that are full for him of all sorts of associations. These things are not apt to fit in well with the home scheme of decoration. My wife adjusted herself to a dining room that contained African animal heads, an enormous Japanese gong over 300 years old in which the children rejoiced, and a gigantic ironbound chest once used by the governor of Puerto Rico to hold customs collections after undoubtedly more dramatic piratical services. Finally it had found its way to the Chicago

Art Institute. Probably they had said, "My, my! We haven't any room for this! Let's send it up to John McCutcheon." Anyhow, one day we found it in the front hall.

The fact of the matter is, I had a couple of overflow studios, also decorated in the Afro-Indiana period. My den in the apartment is full. In a letter to Evelyn I told about getting around to cleaning out a desk. "It was not a great achievement," I wrote with modesty. "Perhaps I should say that not all the credit was mine. Clara [the maid] did the purely manual part. She emptied the desk and carried the contents into the den where she placed them in the closet. Later I emptied them all over the floor to make them harmonize with the rest of the room. I am glad to give Clara all the credit, but it was my idea."

When we built a house overlooking the meadow at Ragdale, we converted an ex-cowshed into another repository for such things as my Philippine saddle with the bullet hole in it, and my screened African hunting bed, which in point of decorative value is surpassed by almost everything I have ever seen. Most of the summer I worked out there.

So, for all its architectural distinction and dramatic setting, with all the old treasures around me, somehow the new studio lacked the spirit of the old one, although I had it nearly as long. The heart of my life had shifted to my home and family.

That I was not to be found more often in the studio was not, however, always my fault. Early in 1936, at a reception, my hand was shaken by a large earnest man who represented the League of Nations; he used all the pressure of his 200 pounds. I could hardly keep from crying out. Next day I made the horrendous discovery that I could not use my hand. I was unable even to put on my clothes, much less write or draw. It was eight long months before I could once more close my fingers comfortably around a pen.

# 54

# A Peculiar Form of Art

THE manual labor of drawing a cartoon is one of the few things that has not changed much in the last half century. Nor is there much mystery left to it. The equipment is usually only a bottle of ink and a pen, a piece of cardboard, an eraser—and sometimes an idea.

After I had settled on this last item, I blocked it out roughly on scratch paper so that I would know where I was going to place the major figures. Then I transferred it, either freehand or by tracing, onto a cardboard about sixteen inches wide, and went over it with black drawing ink, altering, cutting out, adding. If the subject happened to be a good one, there was no little pleasure in elaborating it. If I found I needed refreshment of memory as to faces or detail not supplied by illustrations in the current magazines or my own library, I telephoned down to the *Tribune* morgue, presided over by August Bartz, and told him what I wanted and which view of it would be most useful; in a few minutes these accessories would be on my desk.

I used to think I could not draw a cartoon unless I had two cigars on the desk beside me. When I evolved an idea, after more or less intensive concentration, I lighted Number One and began the process of transferring the idea to paper.

While my right hand labored assiduously, my left hand carried the cigar to and from my lips. It was constantly going out so that much time was spent in relighting it. Number Two followed. There was more motion up and down than there was smoking. But the cigar and the motion had a psychological effect with a precedent of many years to back it up.

I began smoking when I was twelve. Every Saturday night in Elston my pal Julius and I scrubbed out Johnston Brothers saloon, and we were paid in five-cent cigars, seventy-five cents' worth of Pride of the Weas. My mother suspected there was dirty work at the crossroads, but she reasoned that I would get sick and cure the situation that way. I did—but not for fifty years.

Then along came a warning tap from old Anno Domini. A bronchial condition collided with a duodenal ulcer, and Dr. George Dick prescribed Arizona for the winter. He added in the slow reflective way that made his ultimatums sound so casual, "I believe I'd cut out alcohol, if I were you—" pause—"and I don't think I'd do any more smoking."

While I had always enjoyed a cocktail, particularly our Treasure Island brand of Bacardi sour, I felt I could kiss the Demon Rum good-by without wearing crepe. But smoking! That was a major calamity!

It worked out differently. When Dr. Dick's ukase struck with its reverberating clunk, I wasn't feeling very well. I wasn't feeling at all like smoking. The first few months passed without a wrench. Finally I emerged into circulation again and a moment arrived when the Corona Coronas were being passed.

Can I resist those long brown sleek beauties? I asked myself in panic. I could and did. Thousands of cigars have passed since then but I never wavered.

I have only one other characteristic when drawing that may be un-

SKEPTICISM     STUPIDITY     WRATH     SURPRISED AMUSEMENT     AMUSEMENT     INCREDULITY     ANXIETY

usual. When I seek to express a certain emotion—joy, anger, incredulity, anything—I unconsciously register that emotion on my own face. Perhaps it makes me more *en rapport* with my subject. Sometimes when I have been drawing in a room with other people, I have gradually become aware of the cessation of all other activity, of a suspicious stillness, and upon looking up I have found everybody regarding me with merriment.

For the major part of my more than fifty years of cartooning, I produced one every day. Each one presented a new problem. By the very nature of the job, it could not become routine. I tried to vary the subject matter, to keep changing the form and nature of my cartoons to provide as great diversity as possible.

My first attempt at novelty was the Bird Center Series. At intervals of several years, other serials followed, in weekly installments with a picture and several hundred words of text. I never had the faintest idea where the next installment would wind up! But I was careful to end each one at a moment of suspended interest; consequently they proved effective circulation builders. "The Heir at Large" was especially lucky in striking the public fancy, and each time I began to draw the threads together for a suitable ending, the *Tribune* would stop me. This necessitated continual mental agility in reshaping the plot, introducing new characters, holding up the love interest, giving it a start in a new direction. It ran for nearly two years. Even then Joe Patterson remained adamant: he wanted me to continue, and to continue with the hero unmarried! For a week or two I conceded in spite of the universal opinion of my friends that enough was plenty. Finally, not wishing to go on yet scarcely daring to finish it off, I wrote an ambiguous sort of installment announcing the hero's engagement.

The following Monday, 1,500 calls came in to the *Tribune* wanting to know why there was no "Heir at Large." Dick Little made enormous fun of the whole affair in his Line o' Type and pressure from the paper was such that I was obliged to start a new one which ran almost as long.

Late in 1927 the *Tribune* planned to raise the price of the Sunday paper from seven to ten cents. In an effort to prevent the discontinuance of subscriptions which they feared might follow, they asked me to start a Sunday serial six weeks before the change. It was called "The Master of the World" and was the one I most enjoyed writing. It concerned a young scientist who solved the mystery of the cosmic ray. In view of the fact that this story antedated the magical results of splitting the atom by more than ten years, I have always considered it one of my more successful prophetic attempts.

Whenever I finished a cartoon which I considered good, there was a delightful glow that made the whole world seem warm and friendly. No ordinary everyday happiness is so satisfying as that which comes from something one has done, and done well, with one's own hands and brain. Long afterward one is conscious of the glow.

On the other hand, there were times when not a single cartoon seemed to have merit. A deep blanket of despondency enveloped me. Each time I struck such a sterile streak, it seemed to last longer than usual, and I became very blue. I thought my cartooning days must be over. I dreaded the mornings. If I noticed a streetcar reader looking at the cartoon, I averted my eyes so that I would not see the tired resignation settle over his face.

The merit of my work seemed to go in waves. There was no use trying to analyze them. It helped a lot when kindly folk wrote in expressing approbation. The day was brightened. But the old self-critical censor still stood guard to keep me from being too satisfied.

There were two noticeable peculiarities about these moods of self-commiseration. One was that when time had passed and I looked back with fresh eyes at the work I had been so gloomy about, I discovered to my surprise that it was not so bad after all. Many of the cartoons I have heard most about were drawn in those periods.

Also, oddly enough, I myself was not invariably able to judge what was good or, rather, what the newspaper public would consider good.

In 1904 when T.R. was swept into office by a huge majority, there was an opportunity to draw an amusing cartoon of the landslide. I went to the studio early and worked diligently on an elaborate one supposed to rise to the occasion. The deadline was nearing before I finished it. I had just started to roll it up preparatory to sending it over to the paper by messenger from the Auditorium Hotel next door, when Jim Keeley called up.

"John," he said, "the late returns show Missouri has gone Republican. Thought maybe you might want to do something on that."

I thanked him and hung up. How futile, I thought, to draw another cartoon after completing such a masterpiece! However, we find it wise to humor the managing editor, so I sat down again and drew a cartoon on the Missouri situation. I represented Missouri, frock-coated, with a broad-brimmed hat, having left the ranks of the Solid South and gone over to join the Republican states, while the Solid South looked on dismayed and thunderstruck. I couldn't spend much time on it, just hurried it off in less than half an hour and forgot to give it a caption. Then I sent the two cartoons over to the *Tribune*, confidently expecting to see the masterpiece on the front page. This rosy expectation was 100 per cent unfulfilled. It was tucked away in the back behind pages of election returns, and to this day no one has ever referred to it. The Missouri cartoon was on the front page, and because I had drawn the figure of Missouri like that of the mysterious stranger in Bird Center, Keeley had given it as caption the simple phrase "The Mysterious Stranger," a stroke of genius. It drew an instant flood of letters and has retained its place among my better-known cartoons.

Even after many years of experience I continued to be surprised by the inconsequential things that help to strike the popular fancy, or by the details that unexpectedly arouse comment.

One Christmastime in showing a crowded street with much movement and activity, I drew a streetcar turning a corner. To heighten the sense of motion and make it more amusing, I drew the car itself bending in crescent form as it made the curve. A deluge of letters descended on me. In the utmost seriousness I was assured that a car did *not bend* when turning a corner; it remained stiff and straight.

After that at reasonable intervals I again curled my streetcars around corners, and in no case did there fail to come the reminders of my indifference to physical laws. Sometimes I have felt that if the readers

were always as vigilant in defending their vested rights as they are the habits of streetcars, the nation need have no fear for the future.

Occasionally a cartoon which I thought would bring no special re-action stirred a hornets' nest. Such was the one I drew during the summer of 1931, suggesting that as the steel business was languishing, possibly they could revive activity by constructing steel and glass houses, durable and easily moved. I never realized I had so many friends in the lumber business! The first indignant letters were doubt-less spontaneous; after that, many communications from widely sepa-rated sources were phrased in so nearly the same language that it became evident an organized pressure was being brought to bear on the paper.

One December night the telephone rang alarmingly, long after midnight. It was near vacationtime; the boys might be driving or even flying home. My wife was out of bed in an instant. An angry lady representing the League of Irish Women Voters demanded an im-mediate explanation of the next morning's cartoon. Evelyn soothed her as best she could.

"What in the world did you do to the Irish?" she asked as she came back to bed and reported the irate lady.

The Irish? There was nothing about the Irish in the cartoon I had sent in that afternoon. Hold on a minute, though! I fetched the telephone and called Don Maxwell at the office. "Don," I said, "is there still time to make a little change in the cartoon?"

"Sure. Time for the last edition. What do you want?" I explained about the aroused Irish. "Oh, don't let that bother you!" he interrupted.

But I went on: "It occurs to me they are disturbed about the two words at the bottom of South America, *Pat* and *Terry*. You'd better rout 'em out. Of course they only stand for Patagonia and Tierra del Fuego, but they have no connection with the significance of the cartoon, and if they're going to be taken as a slur, they might as well come out."

When the lady looked at her paper next day she saw every nation in Central and South America represented by a face, and at the tip she saw the two little faces, Patagonia and Tierra del Fuego—who could have resisted giving Pat and Terry an Irish cast of countenance?—but in the morning light their names were mysteriously absent!

If they touch on controversial subjects, cartoons will usually have an immediate response. It has been significant of the wide diversity of taste in the reading public that again and again I received bitter denunciation and ardent approbation about one and the same cartoon. In the great majority of cases, letters reviling me were scrawled in pencil and showed ignorance. But there were occasions when persons of obvious intelligence appeared to be sincerely distressed. These were harder to take.

In general, I speedily knew when I had made a hit. The elevator man greeted me with gratifying approval; the doorman spoke of it, and the barber. From various sources I would receive favorable comments until the more distant quarters were heard from.

Whenever the news of the day was uninspiring, or I had run into one of those unhappy streaks and found myself pressed for an idea, I used to tide over the doldrums with one of my reserves. These were not drawn ahead of time; they were simply types of cartoon not dependent on news. I had half a dozen of these features ready to be drafted at a pinch.

One was captioned "Mr. Lugubrious Blue and Mr. Smiley Gladd Discuss the Situation." To emphasize his ultra-pessimistic attitude, I showed Mr. Blue, crushed by despair, about to jump off a high bridge or throw himself under a train, while Mr. Gladd points out on all sides evidences of cheer. These two philosophers began airing their views back in 1902. After that they debated most of the controversial issues which tore the nation, expressing extremes of opinion with a freedom which in many cases might not have been acceptable in the columns of the paper unless attributed to imaginary persons like Mr. Blue and Mr. Gladd.

Another reserve type which acquired a lot of service stripes introduced a character named J. Raglan Patchmore. He was a man who "never recovered from the depression of 1893 when he lost his whole fortune of $3.70"—a cheerful city bum who depended for sustenance on his wits and never on work. His bright eyes peered out from a sunburst of whiskers and his clothing was ancient and air-conditioned. The pattern for this cartoon was a newspaper office. A crisis faces the nation. The city editor summons his star financial reporter and bids him seek Mr. Patchmore. The resulting interview was run as a news article, illustrated by several one-column or half-column cuts.

I am pleased to feel that Mr. Patchmore made many friends. At critical times, when "all the world's ajangle and ajar," readers have asked to know what this Apostle of Inertia thought about things.

A third form of cartoon that I depended on was "The Changing World." This was a framework in which things of the past might be compared favorably or otherwise with things of the present. It permitted a wide range of subjects—artistic, international, athletic, educational, military—in fact nearly everything that had a past and a present. I used this first in 1913.

In 1919 my synthetic reputation as a devotee of flying was still of news value. In my constant lookout for novelty I decided to sketch the Dempsey-Willard fight in person, then fly back from Toledo that same afternoon with the sketches.

It was 112 degrees on the wooden benches of the enclosing saucer. The gigantic Willard was knocked to the floor seven separate times during the first round. The bell started ringing the count; the referee held up Dempsey's hand. He was carried away on the shoulders of the crowd, buffeted among friends. But something had happened; I think the bell got jammed and had not rung the count of eight! So Dempsey was called back and re-entered the ring far more tired than when he left it, with the added disappointment of losing $110,000 by not finishing in the first round.

As soon as the fight was over, I hurried off through the confusion.

Groping my way out among the upright timbers of the understructure, I came upon Willard, his face battered and bleeding, apparently lost and alone. There were only curiosity and pitying contempt on the faces of others who recognized him. But I couldn't stop. It was already after six when I reached the golf course where the plane waited. The menacing trees at the end of the fairway grew higher and higher; we cleared them by inches. The pilot had no strip map; he flew west by compass as long as the light held. Then, without radio beams or beacons or lighted airports, he dared go no farther and landed in a pasture near Goshen, Indiana.

I had made my sketches at the ringside. I had tried to finish them more carefully as we flew. However, since my mind was distracted by the uncertainty of our position and the oncoming darkness, I fear they were inadequate; naturally they were too late for the morning paper.

Another time I tried to take advantage of the newly publicized mechanism for sending photographs by wire. It might be possible to send drawings too. Congress was in session, the Fall-Doheny trial in progress. No photographing or sketching was permitted in court, but the *Tribune* arranged for me to take one of its seats for an hour. Doheny was being examined by his attorney; Secretary Fall sat within a few feet of me, slouched in his chair. As I listened, I studied every line of their features, their expressions, their attitudes and costumes. As soon as I left the building, while these impressions were still fresh, I made my sketches. They were rushed to Philadelphia where the nearest machine for sending was located. Thus, the following morning, the *Tribune* contained the only pictures of the Teapot Dome trial.

A third unusual transmission of pictures occurred early in 1929. King George V became gravely ill in December 1928, and his life was considered in danger. The Prince of Wales was hunting in Africa. With unusual speed he made the return trip to his father's bedside. The interest of the world was centered on this poignant situation. I drew a cartoon captioned by the familiar quotation, "Home is the Hunter." It showed the façade of Buckingham Palace. In the foreground in heavy silhouette was the massive gateway, through which a car was entering between lines of anxious subjects. The whole effect was shadowed except for a single light in the king's window. The editor of the *Seattle Post-Intelligencer* happened to be in Chicago and was impressed with the cartoon. Not wishing to wait until it could be sent out, he asked

ON THE ISLAND

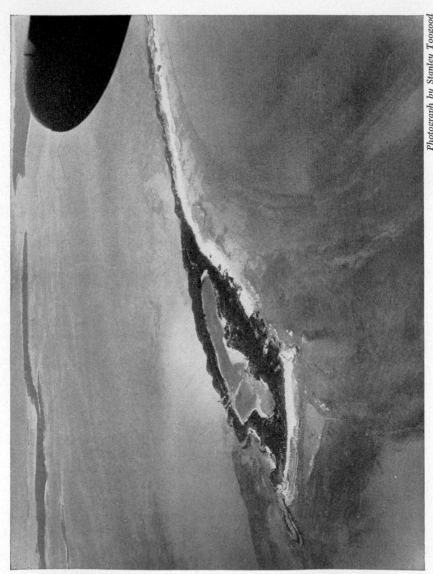

Photograph by Stanley Toogood

TREASURE ISLAND FROM THE AIR

if he might let his artist reproduce it from telephonic description. Of course I consented and waited with interest to see how nearly the result might resemble the original. The method of treatment differed but the general effect was fairly similar.

I am afraid the point of dramatic interest in these early efforts at speedy delivery or transmission has been largely lost.

Color is another development with which we experimented years ago. The first time we tried color on the front page was in a caricature of Mark Twain I made in September 1903, not long after I went to work for the *Tribune*. Soon it was used again in a cartoon of the Chicago fire. Different tints of red were used for flesh tones, dog's tongues, hair ribbons, and Jersey cows. In 1905 yellow and blue were used, each separately with black. Thirty-two years later my cartoon of "The Rivals," spring and summer, was printed in four colors. As I recall, the preliminary work for this unusual achievement required several days. Another five years, and the process was sufficiently simplified to use every day. While I appreciated the appeal of color, I never felt that it helped my own cartoons. Perhaps I had come to rely too much on detail which was apt to be submerged. Or perhaps the change came when I was no longer flexible enough to adapt myself to it.

Certain cartoons lend themselves to repeated reproduction in later years in their original form. These are seasonal ones like "Injun Summer," "Jack Frost" and the "Hunter's Moon."

There is much truth in the belief that men who write or draw are apt to be proudest of their achievements in the branch they do less well. When I drew a combination cartoon entailing a good deal of writing, I read it over and over, as pleased as though it were the first accepted endeavor of a hopeful amateur.

The composition of the "Ballad of Beautiful Words" entailed almost a word-by-word study of a dictionary, with euphony and melodiousness the sole consideration. Meaning was secondary. Then I linked the chosen words together into verses with rhyme but without reason except such as came from a sequence of impressions.

"The Rhyme of the Restless Rover" was consecrated to the Wanderlust. I spent a long time on this one, tabulating from an atlas the names of places which stirred the imagination and conjured up visions of adventure and romance. Then I assembled in rhyme 250 such names, every one capable of making a homebody dissatisfied. If I have a favorite among all my cartoons, it is this one. Professional pride mingled with paternal solicitude when I once came upon my second son Shaw, miserable with mumps, memorizing the thirty-six stanzas of the Rhyme with the aid of a guitar and a stop watch.

In my efforts to give variety in form and substance to my cartoons I tried poetry and tabloid fiction. I tried dialogue, monologue, oratory and dialect. I tried woodcut drawing, McGuffey Reader style, Egyptian style, modernism, and silhouette.

On some I never heard a syllable of comment, kindly or otherwise; for some there were friendly words; and for some I took the javelins in my breast.

## ~ 55 ~

## The Watch Tower

IT SOMETIMES seems to me that the interest in islands is well-nigh universal. Down the procession of the centuries the known world has been dotted with the activities of these geographical entities. There was a good deal of activity on *my* little dot during the winter of 1926.

For a long time the wooden tower that stood by the Cut had been in precarious condition. I asked Howard Shaw to design a stone one to replace it and to provide a setting for the second of the old guns which he had brought over when he mounted its mate in Fort Canopus, and which had been lying in the lagoon for seven years.

As the whole family was on hand, this seemed an opportune moment to carry out the project. The old tower was pushed over into the sea with a kaslumptious splash. Stone and masons were once more imported from Nassau. Week by week the new tower rose. Into the lower courses were embedded stones from the three Nassau forts, Charlotte, Fincastle and Montagu. There was a stone from the Vendue House on Bay Street where the slave market used to be held, and one from Blackbeard's Tower.

We needed something from the sloop *John B.*, immortalized in one of our favorite local songs.

"We come on de sloop *John B.*,
My gran'fadder an' me.
Roun' Nassau town we did roam.
Drinkin' all night,
We got in a fight—
I feel so break-up
I wanna go home!"

We knew the remains of this historic craft lay half buried on a beach on the island of Eleuthera, sixty miles away. While construction was in progress, Evelyn and I determined to fetch something from it and forthwith set sail.

Captain Sweeting was a Carib. He couldn't read or write but he could sing, and he could dance anywhere, even on the wheelbox. Uncle Charlie delighted his soul by providing gold stripes for his sleeve, one for every five years of Island service. He had seven when he died. He had tremendous pride in his ship, in his job and in the family—our family.

He doubled as Island painter, and on occasion Evelyn used to help him. This made him very nervous at first, something like a Jonah aboard—a white woman doing that sort of thing. But he got used to it after a while and accompanied the brushwork with stories.

Most of this work, however, he did during the summers. One time we left orders for the house to be painted. We returned to find our creamy yellow walls a bright strawberry pink. We had always suspected the captain of being color-blind, now we knew it. Too late but never mind! In order not to hurt his feelings, we let it stay, and in time it faded to a soft warm color, not inappropriate.

The captain had been urging us for a long time to visit his home in Gregory Town, in the Cove, on Eleuthera, as Mr. Van Winkle had once done, so he was pleased with our plan for a cruise. We started out soon after daybreak and reached Harbor Island that night. Next day we sailed back around the Devil's Backbone and arrived at the Cove wet with spray. The captain's wife gave us a warm welcome and supper in the clean bare kitchen, and Evelyn dried her hair by the wood stove while the captain told us about his father, who tended the drums for the Masonic band. One time his father was delegated by the sheriff to keep watch over a wreck. By day he kept the local vandals in abeyance; by night he carried away loot.

"Well, sah, Boss," continued the captain, "dat night he didn't do a t'ing but take de heads off dese-here drums he wuz keepin' fer de

S'ciety, an' he fill 'em full—de deep bass drum full wid glassware, an' de tenor drum full wid lots o' dem big roun' yaller cheeses. Den wot he done, he put a rope t'rough de rafter in his kitchen an' tie dese drums 'way up 'igh. Course de gov'ment give a search, in de mo'nin' dey notice several t'ings missin', an' dey search ev'ry house, ye-es, Madam. An' jus' de night aftah dey finish searchin', an' de sheriff wuz settin' in de kitchen wid my fadder, dose drumheads done bursted an' ever't'ing wuz scattered all ovah de place, ye-es, Madam!"

Another time there was a wreck near Dunmore Town, a molasses boat. "Ever'body went out dere! My fadder, he want to git dere too to git some o' dat molasses. Now wot he done, he tie a demijohn roun' his neck to he'p float him hout, but dat demijohn didn' have no cork—he wuz so hurried he didn' stop to look. An' dat demijohn began to fill, yessah, Boss, an' he had a trouble to git hit hoff afore he drown!"

The captain's guest room was reserved only for white folks—the owner of Salt Cay who visits the Cove every quarter century, and the Bishop who comes somewhat oftener. This guest room contained a double bed. But the room and the bed were so similar in size that the only method of getting into either was to take a running jump and dive over the footboard.

By daylight we noted that the captain's house was a tone poem symbolic of the Island. The yellow of our walls, the red of the roofs, the blues and greens of the furniture, the coral of the *Lucaya*'s decks—each and every one did its bit to make the captain's house the pride of the town.

Sailing out of the Cove, we proceeded to Governor's Harbour where we found the remains of the sloop *John B.* and extracted from her a ringbolt and a fine knee of horseflesh, the local hardwood. With these and a crate of oranges we started for home.

For some mysterious reason the "hengine" wouldn't work, but there was a quartering breeze and we made most of the sixty miles in good time. Already we had sighted the tips of our own palms above the horizon. Our mouths were watering for supper not two hours ahead. Evelyn was at the wheel.

As far as we could see, nothing in sea or sky had altered, but with a sudden violent exclamation the captain leaped to the mainsheet. Hardly in time. Before the sail was fully lowered, a "hurricane gust" struck us and heeled us over until the sail lay on the water. We ourselves were stretched prone across the cockpit seat, yet appeared to be standing upright, so great was the angle of the deck.

There was a ghastly moment. Then slowly the *Lucaya* righted and we tore down the sails. The sky had become overcast in no time, the wind was dead ahead. It was impossible to make any headway without the engine. It was equally impossible to allow ourselves to be blown out to sea before the wind, the nearest haven in that direction being Portugal. It was too deep to anchor; we were just off the lee shore of the farther end of Rose Island. Two courses were open to us. We could beach the boat over the reef; we would be safe but almost certainly at the cost of the *Lucaya*. Or we could try to make our way back around the end of Rose Island to where there was a tiny harbor a few miles up the coast. With two hours of daylight left, the latter plan seemed preferable. But between wind and rain and tide, with the small amount of canvas it was safe to expose, it took us five hours to round the point. By then it was too dark to pick our way among the coral heads into the little cove even if we could have reached it. We had exchanged the danger of being blown out to sea for that of being dashed against the jagged overhang of the windward shore. The captain decided to drop both anchors and pray that they would hold.

There ensued a most harrowing night.

Enormous seas raised the dinghy far above the stern as they passed under us, then jerked it down almost onto our heads. The cockpit was flooded. Early in the evening the two sailor boys became too terrified to be of any use. They said we'd all be drowned before morning, and with characteristic fatalism lay down on the floor in the water among the tangled sheets and slept. There was more than a foot of water in the cabin. The oranges broke loose from the flimsy crate and sloshed back and forth; the knee of horseflesh pitched about dangerously.

Every now and then the captain went forward to wrap the anchor hawser with another bath towel to keep it from wearing through. Each time, as he clung there, he was plunged through green seas. The rest of the night he sat bolt upright by the wheel, motionless, faithful, his eyes glued to the dim outline of the unfriendly shore to see that we were not drifting upon it.

We had no food except oranges, but we did have the traditional bottle of rum and it was a lifesaver. We passed it around just often enough to take off some of the penetrating chill, as we sang Island songs. It seemed impossible that any night could be so long. There was never a moment when we felt free from dread lest the next moment bring disaster.

We tried to divert each other by recalling other such nights. There was the time I could not resist a visit to Robinson Crusoe's island, Tobago, although the only way we could make it from Port of Spain in the time at our disposal was by chartering a Royal Mail tugboat. Through a long nervous night we skirted the mountainous coast of Trinidad through seas that were equally mountainous; we shipped such green ones that fish were tossed aboard and slithered to and fro on the deck under our Army cots.

Then there was the eleventh annual Mackinac race in 1911, my only yacht race. Jim Heyworth invited George Ade and me to go along on his big sloop, *Polaris*. It turned out to be the most dramatic and exhausting race in the annals of Lake Michigan yachting. Only six boats finished, many dropped out, three were wrecked when they were swept ashore. For thirty hours the *Polaris* battled the gale with bare spars almost horizontal. Heyworth never relaxed his grip on the helm. There was the added peril of being run down by the regular lake steamers fighting their own way through the stormy night. With disaster just around the corner, so to speak, George Ade chose this moment to get off one of his most famous lines:

"I'm every inch a sailor except about four inches amidships."

Of all my nervous nights at sea, that one on the *Lucaya* seemed the longest, perhaps because she was the smallest ship.

With dawn the wind dropped from steady pressure to gusty puffs. We could raise the triple-reefed smaller sails for a moment or two, always standing ready to drop them on the instant. Bit by bit we worked our way down the long curve of Rose Island. About noon, wet and bedraggled, we landed on the Cay where the family, having sighted us, were awaiting. They had been only moderately concerned about us, since we had given no definite time for our return.

Presently thereafter the Watch Tower was completed. Then the man power of the Island was mustered to mount the gun. It was hoisted onto a riding sled, a block and tackle were rigged, the captain rose to the occasion with a chantey, "Mary Lately Got Religion." At the refrain "O Mary, O gal!" everybody heaved on the rope and the heavy gun was raised to its destined mount, from which it commands the Cut in a most imposing manner.

A day was set for the formal dedication. The sea co-operated, a dozen boats lay at anchor, a gay crowd sat expectantly below the Tower. There were speeches—His Excellency the Governor, the Speaker of the Bahamas House, the American consul and I.

It was during the governor's speech that there came swaggering up the slope a most fearsome-looking pirate. His attire was correct even to the patch over one eye. A little pigtail curved up behind his tricorne hat. He held a cutlass in his hand; a brace of pistols and a bottle were thrust in his sash. He glowered at the crowd and approached the governor with menacing mien. At that moment I sprang upon him from behind, overpowered him without mussing up my best clothes, and clapped him into the Tower. There was a clanking of chains, some profane howling, then silence. The program was resumed.

At the conclusion of the speeches, flags were unfurled—the Union Jack from the flagpole, the Stars and Stripes from the crenelated battlements. As the crowd gazed aloft at the brave display of color, the body of the pirate swung out on a gibbet. Limply he hung at the end of the rope before the uplifted eyes of the startled guests. For an instant the illusion was striking. Certainly the costume was the same.

Then Knowlton Ames, Jr., emerged from the Tower in his own clothes, followed by certain smiling conspirators, Jackie and his grandmother. Howard had made the framework about Ames's size and the clothes had been hastily transferred.

The culmination of the afternoon was to be daytime fireworks. I had gone to considerable trouble about this. Since they could not be carried by passenger steamer, they had been sent by freighter, and I had given up hope of their arrival. Too late but never mind. To my joy they turned up with some early guests.

It is not clear why Captain Sweeting was detailed to take charge of the display; he had never seen any fireworks. However, he was established on the opposite side of the Cut, and carefully I arranged with him the signal to fire. But the captain was a conscientious cuss; overanxious to acquaint himself with his duties, he decided a little practice would help. In the middle of the first speech the crowd was nearly knocked off their seats by a terrific explosion. Looking hastily in the direction of the sound, we beheld the captain turning a back somersault down among the rocks. Thereafter, entranced, he continued to set off the fireworks, regardless of my frantic gesticulations. The rest of the program was punctuated with ear-splitting thunderclaps. Gradually the sky became cluttered with paper fish, elephants and sundry other forms parachuting gently down into the puzzled sea.

The last of our guests sailed homeward by sunset; a few days later we and the Shaws followed them, on our way north, with a grateful feeling that the building of the Watch Tower and its dedication had been tremendous successes.

Earlier in the winter Howard had declined the presidency of the American Institute of Architects on account of his health. It was hoped the beneficial effect of the Nassau climate would enable him to attend the convention in Washington in May to receive in person the award of the Gold Medal of the Institute for his distinguished work. As the time of the meeting approached, however, it was evident that he would be unable to attend. He died on the eve of his fifty-seventh birthday.

The next winter we took with us to the Island a granite tablet carved with the words:

> This tower was completed March 26, 1926.
> It was the last work of Howard Van Doren Shaw.

We set it into the face of the Watch Tower which seems a fitting monument to one whose imagination, enthusiasm and whimsical humor put him in such complete sympathy with the spirit of our little Island kingdom.

# ～ 56 ～

## Too Late But Never Mind

A DYNASTY ended on the Island when Sammy was replaced. While we were in residence on the Cay, Sammy was satisfactory and picturesque beyond words, and his tears at our annual departure were flattering. But it did not take Sammy long to discover that one of us at least was very easygoing. When he found that excuses were accepted with good-natured indulgence, Sammy became an escapist, and after that his picturesqueness began to outweigh his usefulness.

The process of getting rid of Sammy took three or four years. Although he had *not* planted any new cocoanuts and had *not* deepened the fish crawl and had *not* mended the canoe and a hundred other deficiencies, yet he had carried all our babies with tenderness, had watched the growing boys with affectionate care and had contributed much to our diversion and pleasure.

The final severing of home ties was a heart-rending occasion. Sammy wept, Evelyn wept and I am sure I wept. I think everybody in Nassau, including Sammy himself, wondered why we had put up with him so long. He has since found life on shore more demanding than on the little Cay. Recently he has been selling salt from a pushcart. Our relations, I am happy to say, continue good, so good, in fact, that each time I go ashore Sammy is generally waiting at the dock. Occasionally he appears on the Island of a morning with the captain. I want to think it is because he likes us, but possibly a square meal has something to do with it. He borrows the guitar and plays again for us, a chord here, a chord there, a word now and then, soft minor cadences with no insistent strumming.

"Any new songs, Sammy?"

"Ain't caught none o' dose good yet. Gettin' old. Not too much o' brains. Ain't been pickin' de guitar lately."

"No," I said, "Sammy's been practicing the harp, haven't you, Sammy?"

"Dass right. Cyant git to Heab'n les'n you kin play de ha'p."

Sammy's successor, Levi, had the quiet, assured air of a sea captain and the general appearance of Genghis Khan. Also, he carried a long knife in his belt. Once in the heat of argument he drew it on the captain. True, the Island lost something of its earlier *sans-gêne*, but almost at once things were accomplished, things which had been on Sammy's list for years. We were in a constant state of gratified amazement at the efficiency and dispatch with which our wishes were carried out. Levi was very religious. Each year we found a new prayer tacked up in the Custom House. In addition to his useful accomplishments, he had two ornamental ones. He beat the drum and played the mouth organ, preferably simultaneously.

His daughter Helen kept house for him. Most of her early life she spent within the confines of the Island. Perched on the tanktop by the drawbridge, brown eyes shaded by a huge cocoanut straw hat, brown toes curling over the wooden edge, Helen watched for the *Windrift*, or else just watched the sea. A dark speck far down on the north beach, her lop-eared spotted hound at heel, Helen gathered shells to sell to the makers of native souvenirs. Eyes sparkling, white teeth gleaming in a broad smile, Helen sculled swiftly down the lagoon to the Tower where, silhouetted against the evening sky, she waited by the gun for her father to return from his biweekly trip to town. And sometimes we found her capering in the Custom House by moonlight. She was a gay laughing little sprite, a native Miranda, with a taste for literature. She used to keep a log for us, away up in the cold north, about Island doings.

Sometimes it be's lonely for there is no friends, but if you think a flower or a wild bird is a friend, you enjoys being alone. I rather be's by myself for then I study more. Of course too much of studying makes my head ache, because it hurts my brains, they being young.

Short be's our visits to town always. It was bleaky weather today and after we weighed anchor we were caught between a heavy gust from the northwest and a stiff ebbtide. Tossing and dipping, plunging and shaking, she mash the waves so hard—but who was sorry? None—except the cook. Very seldom he stir a pot. We had to treble reef her and she wash water inside. We found the island a green cool of trees.

Helen was happiest, however, when we were in residence. Then there was more going on.

The carpenter who repairs places here is a colored man named Mr. Demeritte. He has a short moustache and a tall thin body. He is very courteous and kind. No matter how many questions you asks, there is always a pleasant reply. Wise people always enjoys being questioned.

To the island this year was a visitor by the name of Mr. Bruce Rogers. He has both fame and a jolly way. He gave the figure-head woman a new make-up. She has been moved under a palm-tree. I brings pink conchs to decorate her pathway.

Her father was very strict with Helen. Sometimes she was nowhere. Days passed and we caught no glimpse of her smile. Then we knew that he was displeased with something and had ordered her to stay at home in the small bungalow among the thickest of the palms at the far end of the lagoon.

At Sunday supper Levi played his harmonica for us. Levi loved his harmonica and the sound it made. He played it with flourish and enthusiasm. Sometimes he moved close to the chimes and accompanied himself with an impressive if somewhat deafening second part. But we willingly gave up a little table conversation in order that Levi might indulge himself. As far as we knew it was his only outlet.

After supper was cleared away, the whole population assembled on the porch or in the grove for the singing. Levi moved to a chair in the path of light from the living-room door, where in his upright Sunday clothes he assumed a rigidity of attention that would do credit to a guard at Buckingham Palace. His family sat near by. Josephas, who was then second man, and his family brought up chairs. One after another the girls came from the kitchen in their floppy shoes and hats. They always wear hats after dark. The youngest children sat in front, swinging their fat little legs. Ronald hung back in the shadows.

Josephas picked a few preliminary chords. "Now then, let 'er go!" A nudge, a giggle, and they began. "When the Saints Go Marching Home," "Beulah Land," "My Cup Runnin' over with Joy," "Don't You Grieve after Me," "The Old-Time Religion," "I Don't Want to Be a Gambler."

> I vant to know . . . if I be velcome up dere. . . .
> I do not vant . . . to be denied. . . .

and many many more. Gladys generally led with her strong soprano. The cook carried the harmony, and sometimes ran away with it.

"I'm gonna set dis vorld on fire von o' dese days." Ronald's deep bass came out suddenly on the *Hallelujah*. Everybody giggled. Nodding their heads and tapping their feet, the whole group was silhouetted against the lantern, carried away as the hour passed by the rhythm they loved so well.

Curled each in a wicker armchair, Jackie and Shawie—and later Barr—sometimes called for favorites, and afterward handed cigars to the men. Once in a while, when they were little, one would have to be carried to bed, sound asleep.

We found that many of these songs were not in print, and many were far too appealing to be entrusted only to our memories. So our next great constructive work was the compiling of an *Island Song Book*. In addition to the local songs, there were others that we wanted to put in permanent and available form, the kind that we were always forgetting and wishing we knew where to look for. The Admiral of the High Seas Fleet, who in his role as Poet Laureate also doubled on the banjo, was relieved from the more pressing of his duties, and for some weeks did detached duty assembling material. We hummed the songs to him. When memory languished, we improvised here and there, but we hoped these lapses would not unduly offend the *cognoscenti* of the musical world. I made a number of drawings and there were liberal footnotes. From an ancient history of "pyrates," we copied the form of the title page. We had a limited edition of this little book printed and copies were handed to anyone we thought might be tempted to burst into song.

Very early in our Island days, we were introduced to a song, the refrain of which ran:

> Too late but never mind!
> All my trials, Lord, soon be over.

It soon became vividly apparent that the thought expressed in those few words—too late but never mind!—could not be improved on as an Island motto. When vital necessities, and even guests, were forgotten on the wharf; when rages prevented the catching of any fish for a chowder party; when the boat blew up and the bathhouse blew down, and in many more periods of crisis we have been sustained by this comforting laissez-faire policy.

Too Late But Never Mind.

The temperamental *Alice* was almost always "too late." As season after season passed, her habits became still more uncertain. She used to bring out most of our guests, and we never could guess within an hour or more when she would disembark her passengers.

For this reason it became necessary to plan a menu which would be adaptable. Frances, the cook, rose to the occasion. She produced a grouper chowder, like a rich stew, with a definitely nonteetotal sauce. The longer it simmered, the tastier it grew. As many potfuls as seemed advisable could simmer together. A salad bowl was easy, and a velvety ice cream made from the milk of our own cocoanuts had equal advantage as a dessert. These three items provided all the elasticity necessitated by the vagaries of boats or weather, and Evelyn was thereby unharassed by the usual anxieties of a hostess.

We evolved, too, a system of setting the tables for our chowder parties. Since our invitations were phrased to include new arrivals in the way of relatives or house guests, and since if a cloud passed over the sun or a vagrant breeze ruffled the water, many people sent a note instead, it was seldom possible to know how many were coming. Therefore, the moment the boat arrived, a census was taken and a runner dispatched to the kitchen; a suitable table or tables were then set up, in whichever porch or grove the prevailing wind indicated, and quickly covered with the Island lace or the long cloths I bought in Madagascar in 1900, with their big circular designs in red and black.

Many of our most distinguished guests have been unexpected. Often Evelyn and I had to compare notes behind the scenes as to whom we had with us. When Cardinal Hayes came over, we hastily received the party with the dignity befitting the occasion. In fact, there was dignity three feet deep over the entire place—until Shawie came upon the scene.

With his cheeriest grin he demanded, "Why do you wear that bathrobe?"

The formality being happily disposed of, hand in hand Shawie and His Eminence inspected the Fort, and we all fell under the spell of his kindly smile. He left a blessing on the Cay.

It always surprises me to think that a King of England has strolled through my kitchen, courteously to thank the cook. Our Guest Book would prove very revealing if we could decipher more of it.

Fortunately Bruce Rogers' penmanship is of a delicate clarity.

Well, here I yam once more on Treasure Island,
The very upper crust of turtle-pie-land,
Swimming in soporific, sapphire seas
Where groupers group and grunts grunt as they please.
Pa-paws a little while in these *cabañas*
While all your days are spent plantain *mañanas*.

Sweeten your tea with *dolce-far-niente,*
Let *tempus fugit*—here are peace and plenty.
Concher that silly urge for storm and strife
And lead the sapodillatory life;
Eat lotos till your belt won't stand the strain;
Too soon, alas, we'll all Bahamagain.

                                        Nassaull.
                                          B.R.

In addition to the Guest Book, the Island library boasts four home-made cases, the lower shelves of which provide a solid foundation of Dickens and Thackeray, here since Van Winkle time. The rest are full of pirate history and story, adventure, travel and seafaring yarns, with plenty of W. W. Jacobs. Mr. Chalk has always been my favorite character in fiction—he's so much like me.

Barr's ability to read the Island literature at an early age had signal results: you were a "low-lived bum" if you sent him to bed, and his hat and bucket were apt to be "God knows where!"

Above the bookcases are several ship models, rickety now, and hollowed by termites; in the corner hangs a stuffed porcupine fish—we found him there, and there he has remained. The wall covering, faded to the warm brown of a cocoanut and stained with many leaks, makes a pleasing background for the things we have found to hang on it—star maps, dried sea horses and a set of Guy Arnoux prints of a whaling voyage.

Above a yellowed chart of these waters hangs an ancient pistol and a cutlass or "snickersnee." They go with my pirate costume—the one I had constructed to wear at the Butchers' and Bakers' Twelfth Night ball when Evelyn and I were engaged. It was correct in every detail, from the tricorne hat, the pigtailed wig, the black patch and drooping mustachios to the skirted gold-buttoned coat, baggy red breeches and boots with flaring turned-down tops.

Once every year, on the occasion of Evelyn's birthday party, I take the weapons down and don the pirate costume. The first time I stole quietly around to the kitchen where the staff were idling by lantern light over supper and a guitar. I made not a sound but suddenly one looked up and there in the doorway I stood glowering. Panic ensued. The women and children shrieked, the captain fell over backward off his stool. It was a long moment before they recognized me.

This party was always a costume ball, and for the last hour of daylight there was a frantic rush and a calling for "Mommie" to help with this or that. Jackie liked to be a ghost in a sheet. Shawie used to make

a fine old seafaring beard out of seaweed. Barr twirled a hula skirt
and paper leis. Once Barney Goodspeed squeezed himself into the
laundress' white dress, a starched one with ruffles. He fairly popped
out of it, and had little bows tied all over his head. As darkness came,
we would all fall in and march around past the kitchen and the Fort,
singing, "Hail, hail, the gang's all here."

If there was a moon, guests were always invited out from town. Once
I was walking back from the Tower when I came upon a goat tethered
in a well-hidden spot beside the path. Hm! I thought, remembering
the time Sammy raised hogs; but I won't speak of it now. It might spoil
the party. So I came home and dressed up and soon the revelers were
assembling amid great hilarity. Then up the path came none other
than Gandhi in his spectacles and diapers, leading his goat! It was
young Langhorne Washburne, who had with some difficulty brought
the animal out earlier in the day.

Another time we were all dressed and waiting, the chowder ready,
the family hungry. Where were the guests? Was it a case of too late
but never mind? As we peered anxiously down the path toward the
Custom House there came a shouting and clanking from the opposite
direction. Purposely waiting for dark, a rival pirate crew, headed by
His Excellency the Governor, Sir William Murphy, had landed at a
different place and "boarded" us unawares.

The long table was set on the north porch, the Chinese lanterns
lighted, the full Island orchestra ranged along the railing. Josephas
played the guitar, Wilfred put real verve into the triangle, the children
shook the maracas we had brought from Cartagena; and as a special
treat Levi favored us with his drum. Every now and then he would
disappear to warm it over a small bonfire. Young and old, everybody
else on the Cay came to sing and dance where we could look on. Before
they were three years old, the twins, Gladys' grandchildren, swung their
small hips in and out among the shuffling feet.

The chief feature of the evening used to be Henry Lee, one of the
sailors. He had a squint eye and he had been around. His smile and
his disposition endeared him to us, and also his engaging ability to
dance with a bottle or a full glass of water on his head. One and all,
we clapped in unison to "Ballymena" or "Flatfoot Floozie" while he
executed the most remarkable steps, never spilling a drop.

Once he disappointed us—he'd just had a haircut!

After Captain Sweeting died, Wilfred succeeded his "honcle" as
captain of the Island boat. Gentle and courteous, a pillar of the church
in Gregory Town, he carries on in most pleasing fashion, and, like his

uncle's, his dancing has a style and swing that sets all the girls rocking with glee.

The first year he was captain, his wife had a son, the next year a daughter, both born at his home in Gregory Town on Eleuthera while Wilfred was with us. The secrets of maternity were in danger of remaining for him forever a mystery.

The secrets of boats are one of the mysteries of life with which I am not overly familiar. I am not a practical sailor, nor a practical anything else, I am afraid, and I have difficulty in buying a suit of sails or an engine. What's the use of my asking anybody's advice? What's the beam? they ask. I have to confess I don't know.

"What's the power of your present engine?"

"I don't know."

"What size propeller have you?"

"I don't know."

There may be just some little nut or screw missing, and I spend large sums for a whole engine. But after all the boat is laid away up in Hatchet Bay where nobody can look at it; the current engine has served us well enough even though it's pretty old and sat at the bottom of the sea a good while during the last blow, and was put in shape again by somebody who knew little about engines. Too late—but never mind.

Neither am I much of a fisherman. When we sailed of an afternoon, the little boys would be everywhere from the bowsprit to the dinghy. Sometimes they had the patience to hold the trolling line. More often not—unless I had a bite. Then Shawie would leap to the line and haul in his catch with enthusiasm. Also, more often than not the catch was only a silvery barracuda which we threw back. Anyhow, we had a fisherman.

One year we found an addition to the Island population not of the usual variety. Ronald, a giant of a Negro, some distant relative of Sammy's, came out self-invited and attached himself to our staff. He was good-hearted and likable. He had been a sponger over on Andros, was an expert fisherman and wielder of the harpoon. He started out spearing a few lobster for us now and then. Nothing was ever said about compensation, nothing was ever said about his coming again. But there he was year after year, and gradually he wormed his way into usefulness and into our affections and there was nothing for it but to put him on the pay roll.

On every calm morning he could be seen, sometimes close inshore, sometimes far out on the reef, rhythmically swinging his left arm as he sculled powerfully with his right. He set his baited fish traps and, without any visible means of marking the spots, could take you to the exact hole in the reef where each lay.

He kept the crawl full of gay turbot and jacks and big striped grouper. There was a story that in Van Winkle time a bell rope used to dangle into a corner of the crawl. When the tide rose to a certain height, the fish were able to nibble at the rope which rang the bell. If the black buttons whose duty it was to feed the fish was not on the spot pronto with their dinner, Mr. Van Winkle became very wroth. Mr. Van, we suspected, had been something of a martinet.

We left all this to Ronald. He fed the fish with conch; speared and cleaned them when the cook required; collected whelk for soup off the reef at low tide, often accompanied by the entire kitchen staff; produced for our edification other strange creatures from the sea—porcupine fish, which he stuffed, and morays from whose dried skin he made belts. He sculled us and our guests out along the reef where, through the glass bottom, we could survey the finest of the sea gardens; he turned the ice-cream freezer, made humming kites which soared aloft droning like a distant plane, pulled the ricksha, sang a fine bass and was a hero in the eyes of the children.

None of us was ever able to understand much of what he said, but whatever it was, he always said it cheerfully.

One year we missed his amiable smile. Upon inquiry we elicited the information that Ronald was languishing in jail.

"Good gracious! Whatever for?" I exclaimed.

"Oh, he *stob* a lady," we were told.

## 57

# Hazards over the Andes

ONE evening as we sat by the fire in our apartment, I looked over the top of the paper at my wife.

"I heard somewhere," I began tentatively, "there's some sort of air hookup over the Andes to the Amazon. I've been thinking I might write to the Pan American Union to find out what they know about it."

Evelyn always says that one reason she married me was because I took such interesting trips. She says she was lured by the siren echo of tomtoms in Africa and musketry in the Khyber Pass, of caravan bells in Turkestan, of hostile silences in Sulu, and surf on the reefs of pirate isles.

She still heard the siren echoes, but she heard other things, too: "Mommie, why can't *I* go?"

On the trip I had in mind—up over the Andes from the Pacific, across the jungle to the headwaters of the Amazon, and down that river to the Atlantic—the travel bureaus of that winter were entirely unable to assist me. From the *Tribune* correspondent on the spot I learned that an American, Jasper Grow, then in charge of Peruvian aviation for President Leguía, had recently instituted a service from the end of rail and motor roads in the high Andes to Iquitos on the Amazon, in order to connect Lima more closely with eastern Peru. Her Brazilian and Colombian borders were thus—with a certain amount of luck!—brought within three days of the capital instead of from seventeen to twenty-seven as formerly, by mule and canoe over the ancient Pichis Trail.

This flight covered a distance of about 800 miles and was broken into two legs. The first of these hops paralleled, more or less, the route of the old trail for 250 miles over a series of razor-back ridges and canyons and torrents, where the construction of landing fields was still only being talked about. Even in the driest season the occasional sand bars in the rivers were not adequate for an emergency landing. This part was done by landplane. The second hop, nearly 600 miles by seaplane, followed the Ucayali River across the hinterland of Brazil.

I was able to find only one person, Mr. Cleland of Omaha, who had made this crossing from ocean to ocean. Because of delays in connections it had taken him forty-four days. He kindly gave me what information he could. But after months of correspondence and cable the details and connections were still nebulous; it was impossible for me to get any definite information from either end.

Ultimately the trip, as we planned it, resolved itself into a stimulating succession of uncertainties and hazards.

There was the tremendous altitude of the Cordillera; there was the Tarma Road, described by Mr. Cleland as the most dangerous road in the world; there was the seaplane flight across virgin jungle to the

Amazon; and there was the 2,300-mile voyage down the Amazon itself with its perils, real or imaginary.

As we contemplated our maps in front of our fire beforehand, one of the hazards struck Evelyn as a trifle sporting for the parents of three children. That was the flight in a single-motored landplane over the easternmost ranges of the Andes. Her hesitancy doubtless stemmed from the memory of her one and only previous experience in the air which had landed her unceremoniously in a potato patch. It was possible to avoid this flight by taking to mules, of whose landing facilities there was less uncertainty. We compromised on this exchange of hazards. I was never much of a mule rider, but we compromised; otherwise the trip might have collapsed into a conventional cruise photographing llamas.

Our expedition of two departed hopefully on the twelfth of February, 1929. We knew we would be taking another chance—the weather in the rainy season. But it was necessary for me to go at that time. Besides, the alternatives were no better. There were, as elsewhere, four seasons, but they were named differently. They were the rainy season, the windy season, the foggy season and the season of electrical storms.

We had to carry thin clothes for the tropics, warm clothes for the mountains, evening clothes for social emergencies, camping clothes for the trail, waterproofs for the rainy season, mosquitoproofs for the jungle, medicine kits and camera supplies. The chief requisite was that we had to travel light for flying.

A Grace liner, the *Santa Maria*, took us through the Canal. As preparation, we spent a couple of weeks in southern Peru, ascending the Andes on the installment plan, in order to accustom ourselves to the altitude, of which there was a great deal. We scrambled on foot 2,000 feet, the height of five Tribune Towers, perpendicularly up from the canyon of the angry Urubamba to Machu Picchu. These Inca ruins, discovered in 1912 among the most inaccessible fastnesses of the Andes, had been largely swallowed again by the jungle. In no part of the world have I seen so much overwhelmingly impressive scenery in such a short time. We made the seventy-mile trip from Cuzco to the base of the fortress in an autocarril—a Ford in disguise on rail trucks— and we slept in a split-bamboo shack at an Indian construction camp at the railhead.

Then the main trip commenced.

We left Lima before breakfast one morning to go "up the hill" on the highest broad-gauge railway in the world. In six hours it ascended from sea level to nearly 16,000 feet. There were over sixty tunnels and an equal number of switchbacks. The scenery was titanic. Oxygen tanks and an attentive doctor made us very nervous, but the minute the summit at Ticlio was passed, we ordered a generous lunch.

Next came the drive from Tarma to San Ramón. For much of the way this road was scarcely eight feet wide, a mere shelf hewed out of the sheer mountainside, an old mule trail widened a little. It was a one-way road. Traffic came up one day, down the next; they told us they counted on losing a car a month over the edge. It was also a patch-work of repairs. Either the top of the mountain descends upon you, or the roadbed slithers out from under you into the river gorge a thousand feet below. Often these landslides or *derrumbes* blocked the road for days. This, in fact, was the condition we found. We came up against the end of a long line of thirty or more *camiónes* or trucks which had been held up for four days. They were full of Indian women and children and supplies for the interior. Ahead the road made a sharp curve, so we found ourselves directly opposite the land-slide across a deep cleft. A road gang was working feverishly, while on our side a man with a whistle watched the face of the cliff. Every few minutes a fresh slide of rocks was loosened and there came a sharp blast of warning. The men with shovels scattered to either side. As soon as possible they commenced work afresh until there was another whistle and another rush to safety.

For several hours we watched this drama, and were adjusting our minds to spending the night in the car when they signaled to let the first truck through. Warily it started. We held our breath. The heavy wheels sank into the outer shoulder; a few rocks fell. It got over. Then the next truck, and the next. One by one they crept across, jolting perilously over the insecure foundation. Finally our turn came. We ran ahead of the car, squeezing as far from the precipice as we could.

Then we resumed our exciting ride. At times our wheels were within three inches of the edge. Most of the hairpin turns were made at a steeply descending angle. Our fender swung out over space. Some-times it was necessary to back a little in order to make the turn at all. It was no place for a scenery lover. With muscles tensed, I tried to keep my eyes off the brink and worked overtime in an effort to appear at ease.

After this, we thought, the perils of the Pichis Trail would not worry us. But upon arrival, after dark, in the single street of San

Ramón, the local governor gave us the bad news. The trail was *"Malo! Malo! Malo!"* which, in Spanish, means bad multiplied three times. Everything that could happen to a jungle path in torrential rains seemed to have happened, and the muleteers would provide no beasts— certainly not until the next mail pack was due to leave in more than a week's time.

Here was a complication. We were suddenly confronted with the choice of waiting for the mules or of making the flight in the land-plane. Just as we were contemplating the Grand Hotel doubtfully, came a telegram from Commander Grow saying that word had arrived that a boat was leaving Iquitos the following week and that he had reserved a cabin for us. To catch this river boat meant that we must fly all the way. To miss it meant that we might have perhaps a month in which to enjoy the scenery of Iquitos, which rhymed with mosquitoes, and where, from all reports, there wasn't enough scenery to last that long. Circumstances made the decision to fly almost imperative.

Evelyn was sorry. She said we were all dressed, packed, primed for the trail. Seven days of spectacular mountain riding; picturesque Indian tambos at night; the thrill of crawling over a *San Luis Rey* sort of bridge on all fours, maybe. Rare orchids decking our bridles, butterflies as big as your hat, rainbows from peak to peak. Then seven more days of being paddled by Indians silently along the upper tributaries of the Amazon; shooting rapids; possibly seeing an anaconda coiled around an overhanging branch, and alligators by our camp at night. To give up that two weeks of intimacy with the jungle, the fragrance, the shadows, the sounds, the live, vivid, elemental romance of such a trail—for what? For two and a half hours of tense, roaring nerve strain; for the vague, terrified impression of 250 miles of singularly inhospitable terrain—and three children at home!

I wasn't so sorry when I looked at the other side of the picture: the drenching rains, the morasses and landslides; the evening chill of the mountains, and the probably minus quantity of dryness, rest and refreshment at an Indian tambo after twelve hours a day in a saddle; and on the rivers, the prostrating heat and assorted bugs. To exchange two weeks of violent discomfort for a couple of hours of clean, cool flying toward a sure connection for our return home didn't seem to me a bad bargain.

Anyhow Evelyn's objections faltered against the fact that San Ramón was the jumping-off place for the planes as well as the mules, and the pilots lived right there in the Grand Hotel, where the bedrooms were papered with newsprint.

Lieutenant Wayne Carleton, an ex-U. S. Navy flier, had been one of the mechanics who prepared the NC3 for the first attempt at an Atlantic crossing in 1919. He was a cheerful citizen. To him flying over impossible country was all in the day's work. The Indians in the district traversed by this service were not friendly. Several times, after flying low, Carleton had found poisoned arrows in his lower wings. Survivors of a forced landing, assuming there were any, would not be able to make their way out through the morass of tangled vegetation that extended for hundreds of miles in every direction.

These were the little items of interest on which we reflected in our eight-by-ten room that night, to the accompaniment of guitars and mestizo love songs.

On the other hand, Wright Whirlwind engines were not in the habit of stopping at awkward moments. We cheered ourselves with this thought on the way across the swinging bridge to the hangar next morning. We had paid our hotel bill and hoped to have the ordeal over within a few hours.

The plane was wheeled out, our baggage stowed away. Then the weather began to thicken. After waiting around awhile with a conspicuous absence of that buoyance of anticipation which should accompany a trip anywhere, we all went back to the hotel for lunch. Immediately after it we returned to the field. Conditions had not greatly improved, but apparently conditions were never completely satisfactory; we were told to climb in. It was a little Keystone biplane, an open, flimsy, unhandy affair judged by modern standards. There was a small double seat forward, with a windshield. Evelyn and I crowded into this. Just behind us was a single seat for the pilot.

Our movies, which revive these memories so poignantly, show Carleton telling us, with a broad forward gesture, that we were going to have dinner with him in Masisea—a grave piece of misinformation. Evelyn hopes they do not also show that she has had at this crisis several very heartening cocktails.

When our helmets and goggles and belts had been adjusted, we took off, leaving the ground just short of where the tiny field dropped abruptly down into the river gorge; thus happily avoiding being catapulted into space.

The chief danger zone, we had been told, was the approach to the pass. After half an hour we reached the vicinity of this last high range. It was called The Hump. It was disconcertingly invisible. The clouds enveloped the plane also, swirling ones that chilled us. We went up to 10,000 feet in a vain effort to see something. Then Carleton left the valley of the Chanchamayo and turned up the valley of the Perené as far as Pichinaki, in a futile attempt to get through by that longer and more difficult pass. Finally he gave up his search for a hole in the clouds and swung the plane back toward San Ramón where we disembarked with relief. We had been up well over an hour and covered the worst of the Montaña *twice*, going and coming!

That night we slept again at the hotel, although our baggage was still in the plane.

Next day was worse. Rain poured down. The town itself was buried in low fog. We played a good deal of dice golf with the pilots in the combination dining-room-poolroom-bar. That evening a Peruvian colonel arrived, en route to Iquitos to take command of that department. As he had been booked for the regular weekly flight before we had, we feared we might have to yield him the precedence. The matter was settled by using the two planes quartered at San Ramón.

The third morning dawned, if it can be called dawning, with no sun and no sky. Once more we went out to the field and tried to appear unconcerned. We had a picnic lunch with the pilots, Carleton and Alvariño, a Peruvian. At two o'clock they said, "Fine! Let's go!" although we could see little difference in the view. As soon as we were in the air it was astonishing how the way seemed to open up. There were still clouds, but they were fluffy and separate this time.

It was companionable having the other plane along; sometimes it seemed almost within chatting distance.

Carleton had told me he would slow the motor whenever he wished to say something to me, but I had urged him not to do this. How was I to know that he was slowing the engine? Might it not be the engine's own idea? Besides, as long as a good motor is behaving, why disturb it? So, instead, he pounded and prodded us in the shoulder blades, sometimes holding up both hands to show how well the plane could run itself; sometimes indicating over the side the route of the Pichis Trail, along which we might have been plodding. Soon we were crossing the territory of the Cochibas whence Carleton had received the poisoned arrows.

We traveled at about ninety-five miles per hour, swooped through the pass at 10,000 feet like giant condors and left the Andes behind to fade again into their blue haze. The sun came out. Far below, thin shreds of cloud, like broken bits of rainbow, drifted over the upper Amazonian jungle. After two hours and fourteen minutes Carleton made a neat landing on the miserable little clearing at Masisea.

Next day we celebrated Evelyn's birthday, weather-bound again. A "Sadie Thompson" sort of rain kept up, at times so thick we could not see across the Ucayali, at times so driving we had to shut the blinds and leave ourselves in the dark. It seeped under the door halfway across the concrete floor. The three or four large airy bedrooms in this aviation headquarters were screened but had no chairs; the bathrooms were genuinely modern, but the beds were of solid boards with mattresses of humpy straw.

The hangar next door was also very grand, like a prefabricated garage, with Numbers 5 and 6, the landplanes, kissing each other in the center. A runway led down to the river, where the two little seaplanes, Numbers 3 and 4, were hitched, with their noses tied up in waterproof bags, looking patient and docile.

The only other building that we could discover in this metropolis was the thatched, stilted split-palm residence of the Indian caretaker, where we had our meals on an open porch. The four fliers, two for each set of planes, the colonel in a natty uniform, Evelyn and I amused ourselves by playing still more dice golf, while a victrola ground out "Ramona." Green and cobalt macaws punctuated the music with screams. On one side of us was the cane corral where boa constrictors came to get the chickens; on the other a sort of pasture from which the jaguars stole young lambs on moonlight nights. Close behind was virgin jungle. The five-year-old daughter of our host used the hardshell stomach of an alligator as a sled across the mud.

The following day Carleton turned us over to a young Peruvian pilot, Lieutenant Cornejo, for the remaining flight to Iquitos. He was very nice, except that he was having a bad digestive upset and was in considerable distress. So were we. We flew from seven-thirty in the morning until four-thirty in the afternoon, with three stops, but no lunch. Nobody ever thought of it. Probably Cornejo wasn't hungry.

On taking off that gray misty morning, we plunged at once into an opaque fog, banked steeply to avoid a tall tree, and lost sight of the other plane.

After that we flew just below the fog, from fifty to a hundred feet above the jungle, across which we drew a compass course. For the first time we realized that this seaplane flight, which we had anticipated as only mildly venturesome, was no better than the other. Below us were poisonous green swamps, tree ferns, brilliant blossoms and birds. White egrets watched us from the tops of towering palms. Flocks of gaudy butterflies, panic-stricken, scattered beside us. Occasionally we saw reed-covered balsas on the river and, hidden a little inland, thatched huts around a clearing and Indian children looking up. Sometimes wisps of mist dangled down to the treetops like smoking campfires; sometimes fog rushed at us in one thick curtain after another, as we almost stumbled over the ghostly outlines of the taller trees. Whenever we crossed the tortuous bends of the Ucayali, hot air currents rising from the water seemed like solid stone walls. The plane bucked and lurched. We learned to brace ourselves.

But the chief difference between this and other early air routes was the thought that, had we been forced down a little off our course, we might easily have found ourselves among the tribe who, not a month before, had massacred all the men of a small white settlement and carried off the women and children.

Once we had to land at a small trading post, Santa Isabel, to wait a couple of hours for a too-low thunderstorm to pass. The river, empty on our arrival, swarmed suddenly with dugouts full of Indians, who, like the cholos of the Cordillera, all chewed coco leaves, that combination dope and stimulant which dulls them to heat or cold, hunger or fatigue. The other plane caught up with us. Twice we came down to refuel, at Contamana and at Requena.

After the last stop we slithered under a final storm cloud and came out into bright sunlight. We were almost sorry to leave the exciting neighborhood of the treetops, but more excitement lay ahead. We cut off larger and larger bends of the Ucayali. Beyond the foamy clouds and the great black shadow patches Cornejo pointed out the snaky silver course of the Marañon. The Ucayali on our right and the Marañon, coming in on our left, were about to join. Ahead we could see the point of land between them. Nearer and nearer it came until we were directly over the junction of the two rivers that form the mighty Amazon. It was the big moment of the trip.

Then we rose to 3,000 feet. The jungle looked as smooth as a lawn. Our shadow trailed across it steadily. Below to the side the other plane sparkled like a flying fish.

Forty-five miles farther lay Iquitos. After our days in the hinterland this port of the Putumayo district looked impressive, with Good Friday crowds thronging the water front, watching us. We curved in formation and circled the opposite bank—two shadows on the Amazon—

then landed in a by-water and were soon being pulled ashore by a ground crew.

Iquitos was a mushroom town dating from the rubber boom. Its population had shrunk from 60,000 to 12,000. After the processions dispersed and the city resumed its normal aspect, we saw that the streets were full of grass and open sewers. The houses were built mostly of Spanish tile of a pale bathroom species, arousing unfulfilled hopes. But we had a nice hexagonal room with a balcony overlooking the river and were very happy. In fact we took out the children's pictures for the first time.

It pleased me to reflect that my wife was the first American woman to make this flight unless possibly Mrs. Grow had accompanied her pioneering husband. The weather and terrain compelled great admiration for the courage and efficiency of the pilot personnel. This particular hazard was very soon to be brought sharply home to us. In Pará a brief newspaper notice was called to our attention: "An accident has been reported on the San Ramón-Iquitos Air Service." When we reached home, we found a letter telling of the crash of our plane, the IR4, on just such a foggy day as we had had. Cornejo and an Englishman were killed.

We had to wait only three days for the little stern-wheeler *Victoria*. Neither the captain nor any of the cabin passengers spoke English, but that only increased the tranquil pleasure of our trip down the "turbid Amazon."

It was a cool, comfortable open-air life. The cabins were screened, but there were neither mosquitoes nor bedding! We ate at a long table on deck, which was often set with orchids. The food was fair. We spent long days in canvas chairs watching the passing jungle. Like the sea it was hypnotically unwearisome; there was no need to do anything but watch it, dense and mysterious and clamorous with bird life. The boat crept along quietly at its ten miles per hour. For eleven days we swung from green wall to green wall, following the vagaries of the channel. When gray sheets of rain masked the jungle, the *Victoria* had to turn and mark time in the current until they passed.

Many hours a day or night were spent tied to the reedy bank, loading wood for the engine, or other cargo, all carried by hand over narrow planks shoved out from the lower deck. Open all around and almost at water level, it was piled high with firewood, crates of balata or rubber, vegetable ivory, huge mahogany logs five feet across, bundles of salted fish, bales of jaguar hides. Twenty or thirty assorted monkeys roamed around loose, and as many strange birds and parrots screeched and preened themselves. Cattle and turtles were fastened beside wild turkeys and caged tapirs. We had to tie up to the bank every so often to cut fodder for the zoo! Above, among the birds and bananas, were slung the hammocks of the twenty-three deck passengers. There were two young men, an Austrian and a Parsee from Bombay, who were bicycling around the world. There was also a disillusioned old Californian who had lost all his money. From Pará I was able to help him to a passage home.

We went a night's journey up the Javarí to a place called Remate de Males, or Culmination of Evils. Explorers like to jump off from here. We reached it in a torrential rain and saw the stilted shacks only by lightning flashes. A few flickering lanterns in open doorways showed women's bright-colored skirts. From eleven until three in the morning the men balanced in endless procession over the slippery planks and bounced the great rubber eggs into the cavernous hold, one by one, while the supercargo droned the count.

Other river life was scarce—only dolphins and manatees, and an occasional canoe. Fruit boats came out to us from the towns, propelled by half-naked men with queer heart-shaped paddles. By night, candles in their bows made weird glancing shadows. We saw only one Indian in the historic garb that accounted for the name Amazon. He wore long hair and a rose-colored grass skirt. Like Pizarro's brother, we could hardly believe it wasn't a woman.

They are happy memories, those long lazy days spent sliding down the vast reaches of the Amazon. We read some, we napped some; most of the time we were content just to observe the slow-moving jungle walls or the sunsets, gorgeous beyond description; and by night, fireflies, bullfrogs, the rustle of the bow against the bank, and the hoarse whistle for the "hombres" to come carry a couple of thousand chunks of wood for the insatiable engine.

We made a record trip of twenty-one days from Lima to Pará, yet scarcely felt as if we had been rushed!

At Pará we found ourselves in luck again. A small freighter was sailing the next evening for Barbados with a cargo of Brazil nuts, and we learned for the first time that they are spontaneously combustible. The whole 800 tons had to be turned and shoveled and aired constantly.

All the other hazards of the trip dwindled in comparison to the devastating prospect of being blown up by Brazil nuts on the way home!

## ～ 58 ～

## Hurricane

In 1920 the people, bitterly disillusioned, voted their resentment against the war, against the League, against the vast expenses. They voted against Cox rather than for Harding, one of the old group from whom no much-needed adjustments in the national welfare could be expected.

I voted for Harding, notwithstanding my lack of enthusiasm. His position, promising extrication from our involvement in Europe against a Democratic platform avowedly favoring it, was so completely in accord with my convictions, and what I conceived to be the convictions of most Americans at that time, that I was bound to support him for this reason if for no other. I recall visiting Harding in the White House with General Dawes and James E. Gorman. The lunch table was set for four. Cocktails were passed. The President mentioned that eight cases of beer, sent by a loyal follower, were waiting to be picked up at a railway station. Apparently he did not see anything out of the way in getting his liquor supplies in this manner, even though prohibition, as a law of his country, was in force. Equally characteristic of him were graciousness and affability. He was a mixer, far more at home with his poker-playing cronies and good cigars than with the Mellon-Hughes-Hoover wing of his Cabinet.

In spite of some misgivings about the Republican party under Harding I cheerfully voted for Coolidge, the unresponsive Vermonter, who concealed his views—or lack of views—in an enigmatical silence which could be interpreted as the reserve of wisdom, even though it presented difficulties on social occasions. At Postmaster New's Cabinet dinner, Mrs. New, bridging an awkward lull, was talking across the table to Mrs. Coolidge about books. The rest of us were listening sympathetically. *John Brown's Body* was under discussion. The First Lady, apparently interested, charmingly animated, was doing her best to help.

"You really must read it, Mrs. Coolidge," contributed another guest.

"Yes, I want to," she answered cordially.

"I shall do myself the honor of sending it to you in the morning," said the Postmaster.

From the shirt front at the opposite end of the table, where the President's chin seemed permanently sunk, came the uncompromising assertion: "We hev it."

After Coolidge had been in office more than half his term, I had the disappointed impression that an analysis of the administration revealed no special betterment of the fundamental conditions of the country. Hoover, too, while clearly wise and able himself, seemed hampered by Republican inertia.

Sincere efforts at amelioration of farm troubles were invariably amended to the point where the needed legislation would be emasculated. I don't think I ever made any cartoons unsympathetic to the problems of the farmer. Similarly, helpful labor legislation always encountered the same sort of effective opposition. Few of their gains, until recently, came without strife. I have drawn few cartoons that have not indicated a friendly attitude toward the problems of those who do the nation's work. These were usually in support of official action necessary to the preservation of peace and the resumption of normal work. It is important to remember that we all belong to the same Union.

Prosperity, whether healthy or not, ordinarily came, I had observed, during Republican administrations. The Democrats seemed to have a genius for gumming things up; if they didn't fight among themselves, they did other ill-advised things to neutralize any advantage their administration might have had. However, the questions I had begun asking myself became steadily more insistent as the Republican party moved along its complacent way toward the now famous crash, guided by old landmarks, some of which had been showing evidence of dry rot for some time.

It is easy to make predictions after events have pointed the way, but whoever cares to look may trace such warnings in my cartoons throughout the twenties.

A year before the crash, in October 1928, I drew a cartoon representing Speculation as an Amazonian figure proceeding down Wall Street under full sail. She was entitled "Stock Prices." Far behind her, a harried little husband was lagging. He was entitled "Stock Dividends." The caption read: "She had better not get too far ahead of her meal ticket!" Unexpectedly the New York Stock Exchange asked for the original to place in their private gallery.

Simultaneously with the stock crash came another blow delivered by nature, as though she had become disgusted with the extravagance and wastefulness of humanity, or the decay of ideals and standards, or for some other reason—possibly sunspots.

During our first ten years on the Island the West Indian hurricane season had been a remote, mythical goblins-will-get-you sort of threat. The local boosters dated the last major blow back in 1866. But in the autumn of 1929 a genuine hurricane was reported heading for the Bahama Islands. For three anxious days Nassau cable connections were interrupted. Then we received a message from Mr. Solomon: "Hurricane blew away Custom House, bathhouse, summerhouses, drawbridge. Many trees down. Main buildings and cottages stood well. No lives lost."

Eagerly we awaited Levi's communiqué. His letters had become family classics.

Dear Sir Mr. McCutcheon,

I write you these few lines to let you know the wonderful works what the Lord has done.

First we had a great hurricane and it last three days and four nights and after that calm off then comes down a heavy rage.

This one done lots of damage to the island. The sea has it for a sunking rock. I see the sea-cap on the North Cottage top myself. The house I am live in, the water running cross and cross, but while during the hurricane I was up to the big house and the water leak down in all directions.

I hate to write you all what happen but I just have to do it that is my duty. Now, sir, be of good cheer.

Tennis court some of that wash away, and one corner of the dock wash down and some of the fish-crall wall also wash down, and other places in the wall lots of it.

All of the board breakwater wash away and the two thatch shelter to the north barthing beach they all but gone.

The road is all buried with sand rock log trash no end. And about one hundred cocoanut trees is destroy more or lest.

I was walking and looking to see what has been done—a very heavy sea come—I have to run up in a cocoanut tree two time.

So that is that.

So I hope you won't get discouraged as it is all of God's doing.

So give my best respects to the Madam and the Boys,

Yours sinecely
Levi
at Salt Cay
where the high waves run
Amen

The Custom House was scattered all over the landscape. Our design for a new one grew out of a rough sketch by her father on the back of an envelope which Evelyn had saved. I replaced the murals. On either side of the north door I set two heavy stanchions—they were part of the frigate *Old Ironsides* which I bought when she underwent reconstruction. The bathhouse, too, being demolished, I dreamed of replacing it with the balustraded poop of an old galleon, complete with deckhouse, crow's-nest and all. But this proved impracticable.

While hurricanes may be the penalty Nature exacts for her lavish gift of favors to these tropic isles, yet she is quick to repair the damage. A few years after this hurricane—as destructive in its way as the financial one had been—the scars were gone.

# ~ 59 ~

# General Dawes

IT HAS been my good fortune to be included on several hunting and fishing trips with General Dawes.

Once he arranged to take a lot of us out to the camp of Mark and George Woods in northern Nebraska. General Pershing was one of the party. When we reached Lincoln it seemed as if the whole town had turned out to meet the two generals, with all the trimmings.

That was where Dawes had gone as a very young man, to work on the outer fringes of a bank. He was engaged to a girl in Cincinnati. One day he went to the president of the bank and announced that he would have just enough to bring her out to marry him if the president would lend him $100!

Meanwhile he had been eating at a place run by one Don Cameron, a miserable little sidewalk affair. He and a young math instructor used to eat together there for about fifteen cents apiece. The instructor's name was John J. Pershing.

In France in 1918 they were both guests at a dinner given by Morgan Harjes. It was an impressive occasion, with many notables. During a lull in the table talk, General Dawes called out, "Hey, John, does this remind you any of Don Cameron's?"

They told many such stories on themselves at the big luncheon given in their honor that day in Lincoln.

On this particular hunting trip the general brought along a gun for me. I had only lion and elephant equipment, and had never tried to hit anything as dinky as a duck.

Each day the huntsmen would radiate by automobile to the various hunting spots, sometimes with a canoe on a trailer. One day the general and I started out in the rear seat of a little open Ford. The driver, Heinmarsh, was a famous shot of those parts. He was a garrulous soul and talked most of the time, often glancing back, more often letting his words of wisdom shoot back over his shoulder with the wind. Unfortunately he was a tobacco chewer. He was undoubtedly a goodhearted man and I have nothing against him, but his aim was certainly open to criticism. Dawes sat in the most exposed position and all the spray and spindrift were whipped back into his face. I urged him to change places with me, because, I reasoned, if anybody was spat on, it was not fitting that it should be the Vice-President of the United States. He refused to do this, and also he declined to remonstrate. Those who picture him as a highly explosive person with a tendency to sharp invective will be interested to hear that the harried general spent the time watching carefully and dodging briskly. He got a lot of "ducks" that day.

I first met Dawes soon after his return from Washington, where he had been Comptroller of the Currency under McKinley. As manager of McKinley's campaign in Illinois in '96, he was given credit for having carried the state for the Republicans and thus to a great degree won the Presidency for McKinley. He reached this influential position at thirty years of age.

Once in a reflective mood he said to me, "Civic service provides the only sort of reputation that is enduring."

The general used to come up to my studio in the Fine Arts Building, and sit and talk while I drew my cartoons. In spite of the fact that we differed on many political matters, it never seemed to make any difference in our personal relations. I drew cartoons savagely attacking the old standpat element in Congress, most of whom were his close personal friends. He was conservative, I was progressive. In the political upheaval of 1912, when Medill McCormick, an ardent advocate of Theodore Roosevelt, threw the great weight of the _Tribune_ in support of the Progressive Party, I found this most congenial. Dawes frankly disliked the colonel.

When Dawes himself had become a virile and forceful figure of international importance, I found much in him that was reminiscent of Theodore Roosevelt. Not since T.R. dominated our national stage has there been an American in public life who combined so many of his picturesque qualities, and this despite their many divergences of character and outlook. They were too much alike to be friends.

Many kinds of people were always waiting to see the general at his bank, scholars, musicians, financial giants, old schoolmates from Marietta, farmers from Nebraska, political acquaintances from all over the country, an assortment as varied as visited the White House when the first Roosevelt was President. Whoever was there at lunchtime went along with him to Rector's basement restaurant where the orchestral din pleased the general and explained his partiality for the place.

He advised me in my modest financial investments—not, it is true, always for the best—and I saw evidence on every side of the support he was giving to young men who were struggling to get a start in life. He was able to run a bank without becoming hard-boiled. One old fellow, to whom misfortune was chronic, would talk interminably about matters of no importance before winding up with the inevitable touch. The general came to know this routine and made a compact with him whereby he should come to the bank when in need and stand in a certain spot, but should never utter a word. Often on the way to luncheon I have seen the general suddenly stop, produce a dollar bill and hand it to the silent figure, who would then bow ceremoniously and depart. Neither said a word—it was part of the compact.

The general has a youthfully eager and inquiring mind, a catholicity of taste and a memory that enables him to retain the essentials of a very wide range of reading, both light and serious.

Yet with all the variety of his intellectual and public life, he has a less complex side. He lives quietly and has none of the showy indulgences which he could easily afford if his tastes were so inclined. His general lack of formality is the despair of those of his admirers who care about such things.

It was at a family dinner at his house in Evanston that I handed across the table to Evelyn her diamond ring. I think I did it for the dramatic effect of surprising the general—it was the way I announced to him my engagement.

When he found that he smoked less tobacco in a pipe than in a cigar, he switched over to the famous underslung pipe, which he spends ten minutes in relighting to one of actual smoking. My small boys were always highly edified by the little woodpile of matchsticks beside his seat.

As Vice-President, he was not the colorless automaton precedent had led the country to expect in that chair. He had a joyous lack of

*The man who couldn't be pigeonholed in the Vice Presidency, the one real personality in Washington*

deference for the sacrosanct fogyisms of the U. S. Senate. But his fairness of decision and his striking ability won him first a grudging respect and later genuine admiration from the Senate as a whole, irrespective of party.

There was a time when I used to play golf on Saturdays. General Dawes was my favorite partner. His only preparation for the game was to take off his stiff collar and put on an old-fashioned white stock. Shoes didn't make any difference to him. Once he played around in patent leathers. He had no conception of form—he simply hauled off and hit the ball, using irons entirely. One he called his slap-stick, another his high-stick. Curiously enough, he got remarkably long, straight balls. Characteristically also, he observed none of the rules of etiquette whether in our friendly foursomes, which most often included Judge Landis and "Uncle Charlie" Atkinson, or at a Commercial Club tournament. The general didn't take the game seriously and refused to allow any of his companions to do so.

In 1937 my wife and two younger sons and I went out to visit him at the Humphreys' Lodge near Wagon Wheel Gap in Colorado.

We did a good deal of fishing and riding, our nine-year-old Barr usually galloping ahead until one day his saddle slipped and spilled him off, so he was careful for a couple of hours.

In my luggage were various unnecessary articles of wearing apparel, some of which I had used in my African hunting nearly thirty years before. That shows how I have retained my girlish figure. I had with me my mosquito boots, but not the original pair. These are thin suede things that come two thirds up to the knee. Their entire motif is comfort. When you return from your hunt, after tramping all day in heavy hunting boots, and get into your mosquito boots, you can just hear your tired doggies purr. I had taken my African ones on a trip with the general to Waite Phillips' ranch a few years before and Phillips wanted them so much that I simply couldn't deny myself the pleasure of giving them to him although it was like cutting off two or three of my most valuable toes to part with them. I bought another pair from Selfridge's in London, and by ignoring pointed hints and in-nuendoes, I still have them in my possession.

I had also my ten-gallon hat and a pair of those ornamental high-heeled boots, relics of the winter I spent with my family in Tucson, and a lot of other fancy articles which the general jeered at a good deal. Whenever I try to put over any studied sartorial effect, the gen-eral takes mischievous pleasure in deflating me. He says no matter how much I spend on my clothes, nor from what high-grade tailor I buy them, there is always something of Bird Center about me. Once—for that winter in Arizona—I bought a complete jodhpur outfit, intending to look like a young Oxonian out riding on the estate of his friend the Maharajah. It had long skirts to the coat, boots that cost $18, and a special kind of hat with a rakish tilt. I never wore this outfit but once and that was to have Evelyn take my picture in it. When I saw the photograph I knew the general was right.

Perhaps the most colorful experience for which we are grateful to General and Mrs. Dawes was our visit to the American Embassy when he was Ambassador to the Court of St. James's. Together with the Tiffany Blakes and our eldest son Jackie, we went over on the *Majestic* in May 1930.

The London of that year was happily not bomb-scarred. I was glad that Evelyn could see the pomp and circumstance and color of British public life at its best at the first Diplomatic Court of the season. That was the evening, you may remember, which Tiffany and I spent in Whitechapel.

As there were many plans made for us that could not include a twelve-year-old, we turned Jackie over to a most astonishing and praiseworthy institution called Universal Aunts, Inc. You simply called up and asked for an aunt for the day.

"What would you like her to do?"

"Take him up the river to Eton and Windsor."

A most charming young lady arrived, daughter-in-law to a master at Eton; she took Jackie up for luncheon with the boys at school. On other days, equally pleasant and well-informed ladies supplemented his English history with carefully planned trips around London.

Evelyn was responsible, however, for his most outstanding experience. Her story is that she was dancing with the Lord Mayor of London, Sir William Waterlow, at a ball at the Persian Ministry. She thinks she must have been having hard sledding conversationally, else why would she have been talking about Jackie?

"Would he like to ride in my coach?" the Lord Mayor asked.

Evelyn's dancing suffered a momentary collapse. As they stood in the middle of the ballroom, His Honor turned back layer after layer of white lace until he arrived at his starched shirt cuff.

"What is your telephone number?" Evelyn told him and he wrote it on his cuff.

Thinking she must have been dreaming—certainly that the shirt had gone to the wash—Evelyn did not mention this to anyone.

But a day or two later, while we were all at luncheon, with the general's usual assortment of guests, one of the four footmen announced: "His Honor the Lord Mayor of London wishes to speak with Mrs. McCutcheon on the telephone."

Amid a salvo of exclamations Evelyn went out.

Next day was the Lord Mayor's Day, the annual show of the City of London when the Lord Mayor rides in state from the Mansion House to the Guildhall.

According to instructions we delivered Jackie at the door of the Mansion House punctually at a quarter before one and left him among the gold plate in the reception hall.

"Don't wear your overcoat unless you need it," were our parting injunctions. "It's an awful old thing!"

Then we betook ourselves on foot to the Guildhall. The streets between had been cleared by police, and we ranged ourselves on the sidewalk with the crowd. Presently three coaches arrived. The first was drawn by six horses. Within the resplendent red and gold equipage, right beside His Honor in all his magnificence, sat Jackie in his old overcoat. Facing them, with their backs to the horses, sat the two other dignitaries who hold the emblems of office. Jackie was grinning at the crowd.

The coach drew up before the Guildhall, His Honor alighted and assisted Jackie to the sidewalk, shook hands with him and turned him over to us with a friendly nod.

"How did you get along? What did you talk about? What did you call him?" Simultaneously Evelyn and I popped our questions.

With his usual serenity Jackie answered, "Oh, fine. He told me to call him Bill."

## ～ 60 ～

# The Brookfield Zoo

As I was sitting unsuspectingly under a palm tree down on the Island in the early weeks of 1921, there came a letter from Charles L. Hutchinson, long president of the Art Institute and one of Chicago's most valuable citizens. He explained the formation of the Chicago Zoological Society and asked me to accept the presidency.

This society stemmed from a typical American combination of civic devotion, philanthropy, high taxes and dull times. The possibility of the expansion of the excellent Lincoln Park Zoo was so limited that even as far back as 1909 the need for a new modern park adequate to the importance of the city was recognized by Daniel H. Burnham in his plan for the future Chicago. It was not until 1920 that his recommendation received the definite impetus that resulted in action.

In a way this impetus was due to a slump in real estate, which in turn activated the generous impulse of a rich and civic-minded lady. Mrs. Edith Rockefeller McCormick was the owner of a large tract of subdivided land in Brookfield, fourteen miles west of the Chicago Loop. A few folks bought lots but the customers weren't standing in line. It began to look as though omnivorous taxes would eat up the whole subdivision. Mrs. McCormick was also interested in the open barless method of exhibiting animals adopted by the Hagenbecks. She therefore offered 105 acres of her land to the Commissioners of the Forest Preserve District of Cook County on condition that they be used for a zoological park, and that the commissioners assume the back taxes. They accepted the gift and decided that the best way of carrying out the plan was to delegate the construction, maintenance and management of the park to a citizens' committee, entirely free from politics, which should operate subject to the support and approval of the commissioners. Thus the Chicago Zoological Society was incorporated, following the general form of the New York Zoological Society which manages the Bronx Zoo.

At this point it became necessary to select a president, and somebody remembered my book on Africa.

If I had missed that Wayfarers' dinner in 1909 I would never have been asked to join the Akeley expedition; and if I had not gone with him to Africa I could not have written about such a wide range of animals; and if I had not done that, I doubt if it would have occurred to anybody that I was qualified to be president of a zoo!

As I look back, I am quite aware that I had few of the qualifications necessary for the executive management of a project involving millions of dollars.

In his letter Mr. Hutchinson had assured me that the other members of the society would help in every way. With this assurance, I accepted, and was duly elected president at a meeting of the society held on February 1, 1921. While I do not now recall the process of reasoning which led to my acceptance, I suspect two motives, one above criticism, the other natural but not so noble. This latter reason was doubtless the gratification of my vanity; the more virtuous one was the feeling that men who benefit from their citizenship should be willing to serve in civic affairs. Here seemed a chance to do something for the city which had done so much for me.

If I have played any real part in creating the park at Brookfield, it was wholly due to the splendid way the members fulfilled Mr. Hutchinson's assurance of helpful support. I was thrown into frequent association with Chicago's most public-spirited citizens, and these relationships, I now realize, have been among the most prized perquisites of my position. From a reservoir of able charter members, committees were drawn. My one valuable quality as president, as I see it, was that I did not try to act like one all the time. After committees had been appointed to do certain things that they were eminently fitted to do, I did not interfere with them. Perhaps for this reason there was constant unity and harmony in the society through-out the 28 years I held office.

Perhaps, too, the greatest credit for our success should go to Stanley Field, chairman of the Building and Operating Committee. Nowhere else could the Zoo have found, for any consideration, a man of like experience. For many years the advice and support of James Simpson, Ezra Warner and John Pirie were valuable to us. The head of the Animal Committee, a difficult but glamorous position, was occupied by Herbert Bradley whose experience and acquaintance in the hunting fields of Asia and Africa made his appointment especially fitting. In the early days Lester Falk and in more recent years Clay Judson steered us through the legal reefs. It always gave me a sense of security to know that Solomon A. Smith was taking care of our money.

The first five years were beset with discouragements.

At one time the project seemed to be breathing its last. Since it involved a tax levy to be disbursed by a citizens' committee, it had to be approved by a referendum of the voters of Cook County. I took active part in this campaign. There were naturally many good things to say about the benefits of a good zoo, all of which have since been demonstrated. I forget how many speeches I made—perhaps I made too many. At any rate the zoological proposal was defeated and there we were with a lot of land, a society and a program, but no money to build a zoo! My cartoon the day after defeat helped, I hoped, to remove any sting left by the bitterness of certain phases of the campaign.

With the approval of the project by the voters at a second referendum two years later, the actual work of construction was begun with the first tax funds available in 1927. Under the direction of Stanley Field, the architect Edwin Clark swiftly wrought amazing changes in the Brookfield meadows. The tremendous advantage of starting from scratch became apparent to all. Most zoos, as well as cities, unfortunately, are a conglomerate result of years of evolution. Our design was adopted after the study of the best existing zoos in the world. The best features of each were adopted and in many cases improved on. Many acres of native woodland were added by the Forest Preserve. When finally completed, the park will be a carefully conceived, harmonious whole.

As rapidly as accommodations were ready, the animals began to arrive. Edward H. Bean, a zoologist of many years' experience, and his son Robert became hosts, as director and assistant director, to 5,000 specimens of wild life.

We had hoped to show a finished product when the zoo was finally opened, but those hopes had been born during the days when, like many others, we aimed our arrow at a star. Certain things affected our aim, and we had to be content with much less than a bull's-eye. On June 30, 1934, the Chicago Zoological Park was opened officially at a preview attended by over 2,000 invited guests. There were speeches, music and a lot of sight-seeing. It was my privilege and honor to preside at this memorable event.

"If he should see more elephants than donkeys," I said in introducing Governor Horner of Illinois, "I hasten to assure him there is no political significance. The donkey is not wild, at least not so wild as he was three or four years ago, whereas the elephant is now much wilder."

It was a beautiful day and, in classic Indiana words, a lovely time was had by all.

Since that day many millions of people have visited the park. The weather is the most important factor in zoo attendance. It is watched as closely as a ship captain watches his barometer. A rainy Sunday will quarter the crowd. And we can't use brilliant lights to attract, like so many other exhibitions, for ours is not a night entertainment. Our exhibits almost all go to sleep at sundown. But the love of children for animals is one of the eternal verities, so we feel safe in counting on human nature as our ally in maintaining the park.

When it came time to turn the lions and tigers loose in their barless enclosures, we all wanted to be on hand. We did not really believe they could negotiate the deep and more or less invisible pits which separated them from observers, but still we were a little uncertain. I drove my car to a strategic position opposite, and the ladies stood on the far running board, peering over the top. Mr. Bean, Robert, Herbert Bradley and John Wentworth stood near the pits, their guns poised. I had brought my elephant gun. When all was set, the doors of the inside cages were opened and we waited in suspense.

One by one the beasts ambled out and looked around curiously. Then they yawned, found spots in the warm spring sunshine and went to sleep.

Impending obstetrical events are full of interest. Once there was excitement about a blessed event in the elephant quarters. Nancy was figuratively knitting little garments in preparation for a bouncing 250-pound baby. If the period of gestation is only nineteen months, it will be a girl. It takes a little longer to manufacture a boy. But twenty months passed, and the two-year mark; then we all got discouraged. Wisecracks came in from all over the country. What Nancy put over on us, I still don't know.

Once in the small hours of night our telephone rang. This is never a pleasant sound. Brookfield was calling.

"There's a baby rhino!" came Robert Bean's excited voice. "It's hardly twenty minutes old. There's never been one born in captivity before. I want to tell the committee!"

Indeed I was quite as pleased as Robert, but I told him I thought he had better go back and see that the baby was really doing well before reporting to the rest of the members in the morning.

Once I managed to carry an ostrich egg safely home—and we had to eat omelet for days.

Then there was the time an elderly relative took our Lake Forest house for the winter. The morning after she moved in, she was shattered by a telegram announcing, "Hippopotamus being delivered tomorrow. Please have space prepared."

Of course Su-Lin was our triumph, our first—and the world's first—giant panda, brought from China near the Tibetan border. Her popularity as an exhibit was instantaneous and surpassed our wildest hopes. Shirley Temple has her autograph, an inky footprint with several seals of certification. This was obtained for her collection in 1938 by Jackie after he had taken her out to pay a special call on the panda.

*The Platypus with Zoo Consideration*

In the routine operation of a zoo, human nature sometimes shows up to great disadvantage. Animals have died in agony, and an autopsy has revealed many pounds of such things as bottle caps and broken

glass in their stomachs. The person who is so thoughtless or so wan-
tonly cruel as to hurt the creatures who are kept for his pleasure and
entertainment is easily entitled to the honor I have conferred on him
in several cartoons: "The World's Most Ornery Pest."

We have had some tragedies in the collection of animals. I think
especially of the eleven magnificent Emperor penguins brought by
Admiral Byrd from the Antarctic with the object of selling them for
the benefit of his men. Our zoo bought them and they were shipped
out in a refrigerated car. They too were the first of their kind in
captivity and nobody knew just what care they needed. Their arrival
was followed by two harrowing weeks. One of them died. A hurried
autopsy was made in the hope of locating the trouble, thus saving the
others. Great blocks of ice were put in their quarters. Another died.
Some were put out in the winter cold; others in an air-conditioned
cold room. But the tragedies could not be averted. Doctors skilled
in bird treatment did what they could but every one of those splendid
penguins died. A fungus growth in their lungs was the only trace of
trouble that could be found. The assumption was either that they
had picked up some infection from the hay used in their quarters on
shipboard, or else that they lacked resistance to accommodate themselves to any air less pure than that of the Antarctic which contains no
particle of dirt or vegetable matter whatsoever. Now they form a
handsome group in the Chicago Natural History Museum.

## ～ 61 ～

## Aboard the Graf Zeppelin

WHEN one flew in the early days something always happened—or
nearly happened. This feeling was still strong when the *Graf Zeppelin*
started its first regular crossings of the South Atlantic. I wanted to
make the trip at once, but it did not strike the happy, responsive chord
in my wife that I had hoped.

For a couple of years I presented the idea in various circumstances,
always without noticeable success. In the spring of 1935 I approached
from a different angle. Jackie was about to graduate from Milton
Academy. Already he was writing home to know what was going to

happen in the summer. I suggested that we should give him a trip as a reward for good scholarship. I added that it should be something interesting and unusual and thoroughly modern—like flying around South America to Rio, crossing to Germany on the *Graf Zeppelin* and sailing home on the *Normandie,* then about to be launched. I was pleased to note that instead of a definite dismissal of the project, there was now a tendency to reflect and consider. Evelyn still felt there were some arguments in favor of her staying at home with the two younger boys, but came to the conclusion that she would rather take active part in any disaster than read about it in the papers. In the end I made our reservations and the initial payments, and so we were committed.

After we had once spread the news, there was no turning back, but our flying began long before the appointed date—flights of fancy. Night was the favorite "qualming-time" when the fate of the *Akron* and the *Macon* came to mind, and the *Shenandoah,* buckling in a thunderstorm; when the splendid record of safety of the Pan American Airways and the reassuring regularity of the Zeppelin's comings and goings carried much less weight.

The problem of baggage was as usual a major one. On trips longer than 2,000 miles Pan American allowed fifty-five pounds per passenger, but that is not much in which to squeeze clothes for all possible occasions in all possible climates.

The day of departure drew near. We had our passports, letters, credentials, health and police certificates, the full set of fingerprints required by Chile—oh, a lot of things. About this time there was an accident in Colombia. A trimotored Ford passenger plane crashed. And one morning there was a brief notice in the paper: "The *Graf Zeppelin* is reported in difficulty tonight off Morocco."

Just at this awkward moment Jackie was very thoroughly exposed to the mumps!

In face of these disturbing circumstances, on a broiling July night the three of us left home with a minimum of ado. One last arrangement had been made. Colonel McCormick, himself greatly interested in flying, suggested that I send a short daily dispatch to the *Tribune,* chronicling the course of the trip. Hence it came about that many of our friends had the latest news of our progress dished up to them with breakfast.

This little item on the front page became for our family at home the important matter of the day. It does not take much imagination to picture the suspense with which they reached for the folded paper and looked in the accustomed place for the little headline: McCUTCH-EON IN THE AIR.

The presence of a small baby among the passengers made it difficult to feel heroic, but it was fun to share with the home folks our daily doings hot off the griddle. Like the White Queen, Evelyn found that she had done all her worrying beforehand. She brought home a package of sleeping pills entirely intact.

In Cristobal we looked up an old friend of honeymoon days, Captain Fenton. In 1917 he had taken us through the locks in the freighter *Acajutla*.

Captain Fenton listened with interest to our plans.

"The Zeppelin?" he exclaimed. "Why, there were a couple here a while back who were going over on that! Name of Leeds. Yes, sir, I believe it's the same trip you're going on. Nice people. He'd been wanting to do it for a long time and she said she guessed she might as well get it over."

Evelyn grinned at me.

Just before we landed at Buenaventura among the steaming Colombian jungles, the pilot told us he expected to pick up two Americans. Full of curiosity, we climbed through the hatch and there on the floating pier was Burton Holmes. I tapped him on the shoulder and he was properly astounded. Certainly it was not a place where one expected to be meeting friends. The usually impeccable Mr. Holmes was *very* hot. The other American was Hudson Strode, author and professor of English at the University of Alabama. He was gathering notes for his *South by Thunderbird*.

In the coolness of the upper air we settled down to some jovial rivalry over who was going to steal whose thunder, Holmes's new lecture, Strode's book or my dispatches.

We liked Peru especially, perhaps because of the prominence of the buried treasure motif.

Dr. Albert Giesecke took us to the Ancón burying ground and after poking around a bit among the bones and skulls, we had the unusual experience of disinterring a pre-Inca gentleman over a thousand years old. Inca princesses are more profitable digging.

In Lima, too, Jackie and I went on a quest for golden doubloons. We clinked them knowingly and compared designs. When we returned to the hotel a slim young man with compelling eyes cornered me. He told me that, in return for some favor, an old man had revealed to him the location of a cave in the mountainside, where as a boy he had seen with his own eyes twelve jars, the size of a small man—full of gold! So far, the young man went on, he had spent over $30,000 digging, but all he had found were the bodies of twenty Inca priests with their heads cut off. Then his money and his digging concession ran out. And somehow or other he must have found out that I was the kind of fellow who, back in 1929, had cabled home to buy Chile copper!

We liked the upward splash of color that was Valparaiso on its hillside, with little funiculars up and down, and the world's shipping in the blue bay at its feet. Our heads were full of romance and sailors' yarns, but a Swiss waiter disillusioned us.

"I haf been four year in Valpo," he said. "Dat iss t'ree year too long. Dere iss notink at all happens here. Next year I go to Miami Beach!"

During the four days in Chile our prospective flight over the sheer wall to the eastward, almost four miles high, occupied much of our thoughts. When we finally made it, that hop over the Andes, through the pass below Aconcagua at 14,000 feet, over the Lago del Inca and the statue of Christ, was for me one of the most outstanding of my flying experiences. Dizzily we dropped and tipped and bucked, just skimming the sawtooth ridges. Our wing tips seemed almost to scrape the scarps. The gigantic peaks glistened with the pink and gold of the sunrise, then disappeared as we started the slow descent to Mendoza through a couple of miles of thick white cloud.

In Rio the *Tribune* had arranged for me to broadcast at midnight— 10:00 P.M. New York time—under the auspices of the Rio IT&T. The idea of talking across such vast spaces to an advertised coast-to-coast audience seemed to me formidable. I found myself swamped amid a mess of paper, selecting, cutting, copying. My hand ached. Evelyn took up the copying while I dictated. Together we worked until we suddenly realized it was nearly eleven and we had forgotten dinner. Promptly at eleven-thirty we were called for and driven through dark back streets to a mysterious little doorway which opened on the short-wave station of IT&T.

A voice seemed to come from nowhere: "Hello, Rio, this is New York."

They put me in a small, enclosed cubicle, in front of a microphone to test the reception of my voice and find out what my last sentence was to be. Minute by minute the time passed. At 11:58 came the voice: "Hello, Rio, two minutes to go."

Then dead silence. And on the stroke of midnight: "Hello, Rio. Go ahead."

For fifteen minutes I covered the high spots of the last three weeks, and ended with a few words about the Zeppelin. Evelyn handed me the pages and speeded me up toward the end. In the outer office Jackie and the others listened to my words as they came *back* to Rio from New York, having covered the intervening 6,000 miles twice. Seven-year-old Barr was waked by his grandmother to listen in Lake Forest, and Shaw heard me from an automobile on a ranch in Wyoming.

Late in the afternoon of our last day in Rio the *Tribune* correspondent silently handed me a news release. It reported the death of Will Rogers and Wiley Post. He wanted a statement from me. We were inexpressibly shocked. But by some mental quirk that plane crash in Alaska seemed to have nothing to do with commercial aviation in South America. Rogers' own South American flight two years before had done much to inspire our present trip. Now we had been soothed into a sort of confidence by the courtesy, efficiency and apparent dependability of Panagra and Panair service. It had become just a convenience, hardly an adventure.

This ended the first phase of our trip. It then became necessary to shift our mental focus from Brazil to Germany, and to reduce our luggage by thirty pounds, both difficult operations.

The departure of the *Graf Zeppelin* was to take place from a great plain called Santa Cruz, fifty miles south of Rio.

The accustomed telephone call awakened us on Saturday morning, August 17, at a little after three o'clock. Breakfast followed almost at once. But somehow it was quarter to four before we knew it, and the office called again. Hastily we collected our things and went down. A taxi was waiting. The streets were empty, every door and window closed with an iron shutter.

The station seemed more alive. Guards with formal yellow sleeve bands marked "Graf Zeppelin" conducted us to a special train. Since there were three cars full of people, it was impossible to distinguish our prospective fellow passengers from their friends and relatives. Promptly at 4:10 the train left Rio and circled southward around the moonlit hills. Externally all was quiet, even sleepy. But internally a tide of excitement kept rising in us.

Shortly before six o'clock the train stopped by the side of a tremendous gaunt steel skeleton, the new hangar in process of construction. There were motors for those who wished, but most people walked down a rough lane between fenced fields toward a gate.

Small pink clouds drifting over the rim of peaks gave rise to continual false alarms. The wind was strong and cold, the crowd was jittery. Mounted police guarded the gates.

Six-fifteen—there she is! Long, slim, silver, rounding a hill from the east. Unmistakable. Ten minutes later the sun came over the same hill and the big moon began to pale.

Another fifteen minutes and the *Graf* was almost over the field. Tremendous! Incredible! Everyone seemed calmer—destiny seemed to be upon us. It was rather surprising to consider that the people on board must be excited too. Very slowly, serenely, she approached, came lower. A steward in a white suit stood in the door of the gondola.

She settled gradually. Ropes were cast down and the ground crew maneuvered the giant craft into position. She steadied, then came to a stop, and steps were lowered from the doorway. It was just seven o'clock, and bright sunlight.

At that moment the gates were opened and the crowd surrounded the airship. People disembarked, bags were lowered from windows. There was a shout: "Passengers on board!" We hurried up the ladder.

Inside, the cabin seemed small and close and crowded. Almost at once the door was closed. Outside there was a shouted command and the ground crew let go, then up we rose. In a breath the people and the field were too distant to distinguish, and ahead of us lay the sea. It all happened so silently, so suddenly, we were left in a daze.

Breakfast was served while we followed the coast back up to Rio, but the steward took away all our cameras.

There were twenty passengers, sixteen men and four women. Six of us were United States citizens, ourselves, Robert Menapace and Mr. and Mrs. Walter S. Leeds. This was quite a record as previously there had been only fourteen other North Americans in three years, according to the register. In addition, there were Werner Kraus and his wife Maria Bard, distinguished German dramatic artists; the wife of a German sea captain; two German professors. Most of the rest were German-Brazilian businessmen.

At first the cabins, which had not yet been cleaned after the hasty departure of their last occupants, seemed stuffy and uninviting, but the stewards scrubbed them up directly and the breeze soon had everything fresh and airy. There were ten little cabins in a row, five on each side, about the size of sleeping-car compartments, with our names over the doors. Jackie roomed with Mr. Menapace, who complained of claustrophobia. The two berths were narrow but soft. There was a shallow wardrobe and a table by the queer, slanting window. If you looked *up* out of those windows, you could see the great gray over-hang of the balloon. Evelyn felt that it reminded her of her where-abouts with insufficient tact.

Aft of the cabins were the conveniences. Three washrooms for the Herren and one toilet. One washroom and one toilet for the Damen. The washroom signs were removable and varied with the proportion of passengers. On an earlier passage an Argentine friend had crossed with nineteen men and one woman who very nearly got thrown over-board. Those washrooms of the air—both plane and Zeppelin—were commodious enough, once you got adjusted to the architecture which had to adapt itself to the exterior of the craft. Sometimes you had to lean awkwardly and even curve about a bit. Sometimes, as on the Zeppelin, nothing seemed at right angles to anything else to steady your sense of equilibrium, and the outer wall sloped *out* so alarmingly.

The thin duralumin walls of the cabins were covered with heavy flowered silk and *gave* to the touch. When our neighbors sat against them, they *bulged*, and when we leaned back, we *bulged*. In fact, everything *gave*. The ceilings puffed in and out. The little isinglass windows did not fit snugly; there was a draft through every crack, and sometimes a slight smell of gas. The washbasins were of celluloid; there was not much water. Everything was for *lightness*; even the sheets were of the finest percale.

Ahead of the cabins was the combination lounge and dining room, about seventeen feet square. Here was centered all the communal activity of the passengers. The walls and wide window sills were covered with maps and charts. There were six small tables at which we were assigned regular seats. We pushed our books and writing materials up onto the window sill when the steward set the table for meals. The meals were prompt, hot and adequate. You could have breakfast whenever you wanted, up to ten o'clock; lunch at twelve-thirty, tea at four and supper at seven. But it always gave us a shock to look at the clock, they set it ahead so often. We were going east so much faster than train or boat. Nowadays it is probably possible to land at a place before you've left home! Each of us had a cloth napkin in a self-addressed envelope which appeared at every meal for five days.

Forward of this salon were the kitchen, with electric stove, the radio room, and the control cabin, which was decorated with flags of all nations, and men were posted at each of the different rudder and elevator wheels.

Rumor had it that this was the one-hundredth trip across the South Atlantic. Thoughts of the Wonderful One-Hoss Shay came into our heads, but it turned out to be only the ninety-sixth.

All day we followed up the coast of Brazil, about a thousand feet above the miles and miles of beaches with their lacelike surf and an occasional wreck being battered to pieces. A head wind kept our progress down to forty miles per hour. At nine o'clock we passed over the lights of Bahía, our powerful searchlight illuminating a huge circle directly beneath us while the moon rose theatrically from the ocean. Every leaf and blade of grass sparkled and glittered with raindrops. With all my flying, it was, strangely enough, the first time I had ever been in the air after dark, and I found it a very wonderful spectacle. We all slept soundly on our first night, possibly as a result of starting the day at three in the morning.

At dawn we arrived at Recife. A ragged ground force of two hundred caught the ropes and were reaching for the handrail when a gust of wind struck us. We lunged suddenly downward and the bottom of the gondola bumped against the ground. Simultaneously, tons of water ballast were released and we shot up fifty feet. They dragged us back, maneuvered the airship into position, hung blocks of concrete on the rails and secured her to the tall mooring mast, where she spent the entire day refueling. We dismounted as casually as if we always traveled in Zeppelins, and spent the day in town.

At eight o'clock that night we said good-by to South America and headed out through the darkness over the Atlantic Ocean toward the westernmost bulge of Africa, about 2,000 miles away. We passed over the great rock of Fernando de Noronha, and later over St. Paul's and its lonely lighthouse. Jackie commented in his journal: "A grand feeling of loneliness to think of this cabin of twenty people amid miles and miles of black space."

At breakfast Monday morning the chart on the wall showed us already halfway over to Africa. We had just crossed the Equator. As we sat leisurely over our coffee, the chief steward sprayed each of us with an atomizer. We began hastily wondering what we had been exposed to. It turned out to be an equatorial baptism with essence of tannenbaum from the Black Forest, and we each received an engraved certificate from Neptune signifying membership in the Order of Zeppelin Equator Crossers.

Life was lazy on the Zeppelin. Passengers read, wrote, played cards or took naps. There was no room for the brisk walk which people enjoy on shipboard. There was one walk which we took, but it could not be recommended for exercise purposes. This was the 700-foot stretch down the length of the interior of the huge balloon, on an eight-inch catwalk with the ocean 600 feet below, screened only by the thin fabric casing. Without the screen it would have been like walking from the top of the Tribune Tower to the top of the Wrigley Building on a narrow plank, the same not being appealing to the average pedestrian.

There was only a rope or a wire strut now and then to steady one. With luck, if you lost your grip and your balance, you might pitch sideways into the tentlike coops where the crew slept, or into their dining alcoves, or into a fruit cage or an icebox, or a group of gasoline drums, or a heavy rubber ballast sack full of water, or a bin of spare parts. Otherwise there was only a sheet of isinglass, or a piece of wire screening, or a thin much worn-looking cloth between you and the water below. Once our guide pulled a cord and an entire section of the bottom yawned open.

All of those things were placed alternately along the sides of the catwalk with an amazing conservation of space and weight. Nothing was beyond reach from the plank. The heaviest single piece, the generator, was just aft of the gondola. This great mysterious space above the passenger quarters was full of surprises. It was a hundred feet high. Only ten feet along the bottom was allowed for equipment. The other ninety feet was occupied by the gas bags. Above us those enormous sacks of hydrogen hung against crosses of rope giving a tremendous quilted feather-bed effect.

There was one long sack of illuminating gas which they used as fuel when the buoyancy was just right and they wanted to conserve gasoline. The weight of the gasoline had always to be taken into consideration. Illuminating gas, although it has no buoyancy, weighs nothing. There were extra controls in the rudder, in case of trouble in the control room. Much of the refrigeration was done with dry ice. By letting out all the water, gasoline, supplies, furniture and luggage, they could probably make a slow-enough descent in case of leakage of hydrogen. But we didn't especially want to prove it.

When the walk was over, I asked the guide what would happen if a rifle ball were fired through a gas cell. He replied that several bullet holes had been found after crossing Siberia. I also asked what would happen if lightning struck. He replied that the ship was once struck, but that the bolt passed through on the radio aerials without damage. We looked up along queer slanting ladders to the four side gondola entrances where four of the engines were housed, and down through open space to the underslung fifth one where an engineer in a flier's cap was connected with civilization only by a ladder that collapsed sideways to reduce wind resistance. The officers' quarters were just above the control room. They also were tentlike affairs with just enough solid flooring to step on in front of a cot. The crew numbered forty-two. Their clothing hung here and there along the catwalk looking startlingly alive. There was a dumb-waiter from the kitchen to the catwalk, and whoever corresponded to the kitchenmaid must have had to sprint maybe a quarter of a mile down and back to get the cook an extra can of sauerkraut. Evelyn was the only one of the ladies who took this very diverting promenade.

The radio operator accepted my press dispatches collect. I sent them daily. At lunchtime the steward returned our cameras, there being nothing in sight save a few ships, whose passengers waved and cheered.

There was no motion on the *Graf*. They told us no one was ever seasick. Not that it didn't roll or maybe pitch, but there was no lurching or hesitation on the downward swing as on a ship. It was so gentle you didn't notice unless you were watching the horizon line across the window sill. There was hardly any vibration. The muffled roar of the five engines was much less noisy than a train. They were a couple of hundred feet behind and the sound was carried astern. The sound of water along a ship's side was replaced by the whishing air.

By Tuesday the Atlantic had been safely crossed and we cruised evenly off the coast of Senegal, but she was more coy than most gals, and modestly hid behind a veil. It was raining. We could see the water trickling down the curve of the balloon. A strong head wind was holding us back to only thirty-eight miles an hour. Perhaps we would pass Gibraltar at night! Or not reach Friedrichshafen until Friday? Rumors were plentiful. The sea was rough, but the *Graf* was smooth and steady.

At supper I asked, "What does the *Graf* do in a terrible wind?" "Why, you have had one."

We awoke on the fourth morning to find Morocco spread beneath us—Mogador with its fort, Mazagan, Rabat. Inland the red desert stretched away to the Atlas Mountains, scene of Riff warfare and tales of the French Foreign Legion. Cattle grazed on the slopes. Caravans plodded the roads. We could look directly and without invitation into the blue-tiled courtyards of mosque and harem. As the huge dirigible roared overhead, chickens and donkeys and camels fled in terror. Its long cigar-shaped shadow trailed mysteriously over the market places. It was low enough for us to hear the people cheering on the roofs. Evelyn lost an earring leaning out of the open window.

Soon after lunch we reached Tangier and cruised out over the Straits. Tarifa lay at the foot of the mountains on the opposite shore. From here the old-time pirates sallied forth exacting tribute from passing ships; hence the word "tariff," which some quarters still regard as a form of piracy. The Mediterranean was properly blue and full of porpoises and ships. Crowds at the rails hailed us noisily. Gibraltar gleamed in the bright sunlight. We passed close to its southern tip. I had last seen it from the revenue cutter *McCulloch* thirty-seven years before.

On we went, at ninety miles an hour now, up along the Spanish coast with its bare brown mountains capped by little medieval watch-towers. Time leaped ahead by bounds. I thought I came out to breakfast at nine but the clock said ten. We started supper at seven, a simple three-course affair, served quickly—and finished at quarter of nine! Our brains were in a whirl. With the lights of Valencia fading astern and those of Barcelona twinkling ahead, it was difficult to believe we had wakened at Mogador and lunched over Rabat. Far into the night the passengers worked, marking passage charts, making out tip lists and filling out forms—like so many examination papers.

Nobody slept much that night—there was too much excitement. The *Graf* flew higher than usual in a light fog, but the brilliant downward-pointing searchlight revealed it to be of uneven thickness and often France showed through. Before dawn it cleared and we came low again. We moved our pillows to the window end of the bunk to watch the Rhone Valley slip by underneath—wooded hills, vineyards, red-roofed towns clustered along streams, tree-lined roads, now and then a château.

Everyone was up about six and breakfasted successively at the center tables. The other tables had been let down to make more room by the windows. From Lyons to Besançon we glided, then east to Basle. The Rhone gave way to the Saône, the Saône to the Rhine. Over France the Zeppelin was permitted a five-mile strip. If she so much as poked her nose over its edge, she must immediately radio an explanation to the Air Ministry in Paris.

Soon after nine we could see Friedrichshafen, the home port of the *Graf*. About the middle of the lake the engines were cut out. In complete silence we glided along, a wonderful sensation. Except for the passing show beneath, we could not feel that we were moving. The excitement aloft was intense, especially among the home-coming officers. But down along the beaches of the Boden See, in all the gardens, on all the rooftops and boat decks, there was pandemonium. The shouting and cheering drowned out our own voices.

Our shadow grew larger and larger. The engines purred again and we nosed down toward the field—lower—lower. The crowd waved and yelled. But just as we were opposite Dr. Eckener's windows, there was a lurch and a swerve—and on and up we went. The wind had shifted at the crucial moment. We made a big circle over the town and approached from the opposite direction. The white markers and the gray uniformed ground crew (so different from those of Brazil!) had moved to the other end of the field.

We slid over silently. It seemed too high. It seemed too fast. Just over the markers the thick coils of rope were dropped and our nose was pulled down at a sharp angle. One wondered how those small creatures could halt such a monster. But it was so light it settled down very meekly. A hundred pairs of hands seized the rail to steady it— and we were down.

The crowd, hitherto restrained by police cordons, rushed forward. Still gently the *Graf* was propelled into a hangar where the human weights were replaced once more by concrete blocks. The mass of people was so dense about the steps that it was hard to get off.

Across in the other hangar we met Hugo Eckener, a sturdy old man who spoke fair English and who showed us through the new airship still under construction. The framework was only half covered at that time. It was 750 feet long, with a two-story passenger compartment in the belly of the ship. This was the ill-fated *Hindenburg*. When she made her first round trip, Jackie went from Harvard to Lakehurst to greet her. On her second arrival in Lakehurst she burst into flames.

This finished the second phase of our summer's outing. We spent six days in Europe seeing zoos—in my capacity as president of the Chicago Zoological Society, I inspected Munich, Berlin, Hamburg and Paris.

The *Normandie* seemed a good deal of a contrast to the *Graf*—there was so much elbowroom, and everything was so heavy instead of so frail. But when we had climbed the seven decks from our cabin to see if there was an ocean anywhere about, the sea and sky looked much as they had from the *Graf*.

# ~VI~
## DRAWING TO A CLOSE

# 62

# War Effort on the Island

IN A LARGE measure Franklin Roosevelt was the man to see the handwriting on the wall that had been so persistently overlooked by previous administrations. I speak of the F.D.R. of 1933 to 1937. He went into office full of vitality, with the nation behind him. Most people wanted action, quick and effective. They got it. The New Deal became the vehicle for a saturnalia of spending; it scattered the golden flood into every county in the nation, with or without reason.

Much of this early activity was essential; much of it was well-intentioned; much of it was necessarily experimental. I suspected that perhaps enormous operations were being attempted too quickly, that there were undoubted waste and false motion. But I hoped that out of all the alphabetical whirlpools, solid results might emerge.

This second Roosevelt, too, seemed at first sincerely trying to benefit the large majority of the people. Whether or not his methods were sound is another question. There were many editorial comparisons of the two Roosevelts, but they neglected to say that Theodore had been hated by exactly the same people who were hating Franklin. The reactionaries of the former period were the reactionaries of the early thirties.

This was one of the two great issues on which the *Tribune* has felt most strongly and fought most determinedly, but on which I never made a cartoon in support of its policy—neither during the fourteen years of prohibition, nor during the first four and a half years of Franklin Roosevelt's administration. This did not mean that I was satisfied with the evils of the former—I was never a prohibitionist—or that I was wholly supporting F.D.R.'s program. I simply felt that both great experiments should be given a fair chance.

Then the New Deal began to slip; people began to doubt. The attempt to "pack" the Supreme Court with sympathetic judges stirred the nation to such poignant criticism that possibly the President felt he had to divert attention from his home policies. Whatever his reason, he struck an alarming note. In the Chicago Bridge speech, in October 1937, Franklin Roosevelt, by a single sentence, turned the current of public opinion from home affairs to foreign affairs, and by inference beyond that—to war.

From being a fairly friendly partisan, I changed in that moment to profound opposition. I believed beyond a doubt—and I said so in my cartoons in every way that I could think of—that the President intended, by every means in his power, to seek to involve the United States in war. From there on I could not but regard him as committed to a course which I felt was overwhelmingly counter to the best interests of his own country. Step by step, I tried to call attention, in my cartoons, to the way he was following the Wilsonian road to war. For two years before it came, he had made it inevitable, while conveying to the nation the impression that by some prestidigitation of statesmanship, at the eleventh hour, it would be averted. The people trusted him; he got his election—and he got his war.

I could not stir up much patriotic feeling about either of the great wars. I felt that both were wars into which America had been drawn to protect and serve other nations. I could not see that an American objective was involved. I could not see that failure to support certain elements in Europe or Asia would result in a war fought singlehanded, close at hand. That is something no one knew in 1914; no one knew in 1939; and no one knows today.

SHE DREADS A RETURN OF HIS OLD WEAKNESS

After the trend toward war became evident, I did not find it easy to be light and gay in my work. In a cartoon sense there is not much fun to be had out of war, although Bruce Bairnsfather managed it fairly well, a couple of wars ago; his pictures of Old Bill were a welcome relief.

I loved to forgather with the correspondents whenever I had a chance, but war is a hard thing to enjoy from the side lines. My two older boys went into uniform at once. And to my surprise, I was able to be of vicarious service in a third way.

My deeds of possession to the Island, which descend through four owners in direct line from the original crown grant in 1875, make one proviso: The British Government reserves the right to occupy it if, in case of war, it is deemed necessary.

Late in 1943 Jackie was serving at the Naval Air Station in New Orleans. In addition to his naval duties he had assumed those of husband and father. We went down there to meet our first grandchild, Miss Pandy, a captivating young lady who looked much as her grandmother had when I first met her not too many years before, and who rated a glowing *umslopagus* 88. While I was admiring her, I received a message: a commander from the British Admiralty was flying down from Washington to see me. Immediately Evelyn and I had identical presentiments—the Island!

Sure enough. The commander explained that the Admiralty desired to rent it for war purposes of a very secret nature. I was unenthusiastic. I explained that we loved the Island dearly, that everything on it was old and infirm, like me, but to us irreplaceable, and that, on my doctor's orders, I planned to go there myself.

The commander was charmingly suave. "Yes," he said, "I have been there. I can readily understand. We will try to take care of things. Of course we hoped to make an arrangement agreeable to you on your terms. There is no place else so suitable for this special purpose. If we have to requisition it——" The commander won at a walk.

The Island was leased to the British for a year on very fair terms, but we were given not one single hint as to what might happen there. Our caretaker was retained. When Levi finally retired to his farm on one of the Exuma Cays, Josephas had taken over his duties. Josephas is trim and smart with a smileful of superlative white teeth, and an admirable wife, Lineth. But he was under strict orders and his letters to us were entirely about the weather and the planting of cocoanuts. The sea round about was "restricted area"; even the fishermen were kept at a distance. There was curious and excited speculation. What part was our beloved little Island playing in the war effort?

It was strange to think that while our own boys were serving their country in distant parts—Jackie spent the next two years on a Navy oiler with the task forces in the western Pacific; Shaw passed the same period with the Eighth Air Force in England—other boys were serving on Treasure Island!

The lease was not renewed. We made our plans to return with eagerness and apprehension. To our intense relief there appeared to have been no serious damage. Squatting by the flagpole at sunset, Josephas answered questions, and over at Government House the Duke of Windsor provided further details, so that we were able to picture with more or less accuracy the unusual activities on the Cay during 1944.

It had been used for the successive training of three large groups called Undersea Demolition Squads. These were a species of seagoing commando, the rigor of whose drill in and under water was stupendous. It was a preparation for dangerous work. Each group numbered fifty; the first was composed of British and Empire recruits, including many veterans of Dunkerque; the other two groups were mainly American, who qualified as expert swimmers.

They lived on the mainland and came over each morning in a landing barge. Classes were held in navigation and the use of undersea gear. Often the boys were too hasty with the diving helmets and had to be revived. When they made the circuit of the Island, nearly eight miles, on paddle boards, Josephas told us exhausted boys would come ashore all along the North Beach. Once there was trouble with a jellyfish; for a time it was feared the boy's windpipe might have to be opened to enable him to breathe. He was in acute pain for some days and disabled for weeks. We had heard of such encounters, but have seen only a few small samples of the blue balloonlike sails of the poisonous man-of-war stranded on the beach. In the course of training frequent heavy charges were set off, which were heard in Nassau. The vibration broke windows and loosened the upper course of the Tower. Twice a week, with full equipment, the group swam back through the Narrows to their headquarters.

Each night three different men were left on guard duty and discipline appears to have been relaxed. Among other pastimes, they used to drop more depth charges off the cliff, or sit on the porch shooting the red shingles off the Lookout less than fifty feet away.

When the time came for the last group to leave, vast piles of mattresses, paddles, canvas canoes and much other useful equipment were burned while Josephas looked on aghast.

After a thorough cleaning and fresh paint, inside and out, the Island appeared little worse for its experience. But there was a sequel.

On our usual morning inspection of what's doing, we noticed a small crack in the stone path to the Lookout. After breakfast, to our dismay, it had widened to a couple of inches, and a fissure had appeared in the sand at the left. An hour later another fissure had opened on the right. We realized that a major catastrophe was about to occur. The Lookout was sloughing off! With an odd feeling in the pit of our stomachs we watched while the crack widened and deepened to a foot, two feet, three feet; while the front wall of the Lookout dropped off; while the retaining walls below bulged outward, then buckled. Gradually the whole segment settled until it hung precariously over space, held only by the interlacing roots of the sturdy casuarinas and beach plums. It seemed about to take flight, yet clung to the roots with a sort of desperation that wrung our hearts.

During the day, by means of ropes and daring volunteers we managed to salvage much of the timber of the little shelter where we had sat so often and so happily to watch the bluefish and the bluer streaks in the sea. But though we hung about with cameras poised, above and below, and hesitated even to go for a swim for fear of missing the denouement, it was not until the storms of the hurricane season that the rest of it fell. A third of our front yard went along with it. Now the brink drops away a scant thirty feet from the porch.

Experienced geological and engineering inspection convinced us that the responsibility for the disaster lay with the steady firing, especially the depth charges which had cracked the surrounding flat reefs like china plates. With the idea of collecting only enough to cover new retaining bulwarks, we set the vast machinery of diplomacy and the law in ponderous action—McCutcheon *versus* Rex, Rex being, I suspect, a euphemism for Uncle Sam via lend-lease. But nothing came of it.

Anyhow we were glad that the Island had been of some service to the Colony of which we felt so much a part. We sought to follow up the records of the squads, but found only one report. In the *Weekly War Notes* of the British Information Service, dated February 22, 1945, was a paragraph called "Landing Craft, Human."

The 33rd Corps of the Fourteenth Army has established a bridgehead on the south bank of the Irrawaddy against which the enemy is launching repeated counterattacks.

The assault was preceded by a squad of champion swimmers.

These were led by an ex-Irish Guardsman, Captain Michael Muldoon, who, in the darkness, slipped naked into the Irrawaddy and, gaining the sandbank in the middle of the swiftly flowing stream which was half a mile wide, stood breast high in the water, guiding the first wave of British, Indian and Gurkha infantry with red and green beacons.

Captain Muldoon's comrades, picked from the toughest men in the corps, included Captain Jock Elder, formerly in the Black Watch, and Lieutenant Barry Kimmins. Night after night, they had rehearsed under the noses of the Japanese, once barely escaping the enemy patrol boats by floating downstream on their backs.

Josephas proudly claimed friendship with all three.

# 63

## Slowed to a Ramble

HERE where I sit by the lagoon in a long canvas chair which accommodates itself gratefully to the curves of my back, it is all quiet. The palms are not tall enough to feel the trade wind that is blowing the crests off the waves on the northern beaches. For today I have had enough of that clamor and tumult. Pearly clouds are piled behind the Tower, whose warm color in the late afternoon sun is reflected in the smooth water; so is the stone wall of the pier. There is sunlight, too, on the mast of the fishing sloop *Guanahani* where she lies careened well up the beach. Every ninth wave rolls in through the Cut and fans out into a white collar of foam.

Above the fish crawls there's a highlight on Gremore. I think I have not yet explained Gremore. Beyond the last tree and bit of beach, the eastern tip of the Island had once needed something architectural on it to balance the Tower and the Custom House. It *needed* an old pirate ruin. But for some dozen years all I ever did was to talk about it at breakfast. One morning we missed the little boys, and again on several mornings. Finally they led us to the point. With infinite difficulty they had hacked and cleared a space out of the bush, and even more laboriously had hauled a circle of big stones to the spot. The

foundations were laid for my pirate ruin! Course by course it rose—
with some assistance of a dusky nature, it is true—until it capped the
rise, a small replica of Blackbeard's Tower, complete with gaping
window and topless doorway. Our favorite song at that period being:

> Benancy's dead an' gone, O Gremore, Gremore;
> Eat up de peas an' corn, O Gremore!

and the name having a most obviously bleak and sinister connotation,
we forthwith christened the ruin Gremore; and the boys still grin
broadly when visitors ask its history.

We have just watched the *Windrift* sail away toward Nassau with
a chowder party, the fair breeze pushing her along with easy speed.
Evelyn pulled me back here in the ricksha and left me with a stack of
new papers—newly arrived, that is; they are about ten days old.

"You're a nice girl, Evelino," I told her. "If I were not married to
you, I'd go right out and sing under your window."

Her father used the ricksha with great comfort and convenience;
then Charlie Atkinson. Now it's my turn. I find it a pleasant means
of locomotion. It is far less demanding than the all-day bicycle picnics
I used to attend from Chicago as far out in the country as the Saddle
and Cycle Club. It's not much slower than that early "horseless carriage" race in 1895, from Jackson Park to Evanston and back, a distance of about fifty miles, when the winner crossed the line in ten
hours and twenty-three minutes. And it is conducive to all sorts of
retrospective ramblings.

I bought my first automobile in 1916, a Studebaker, and I was allotted number nineteen, a number that has come so often into my
life that it really means something to me. On the nineteenth of August I was first asked to go around the world; I left Chicago on the
nineteenth of December, and on the same day, three years later, I
was taken seriously ill. Many other times the number has persisted in
marking big epochs in my life. So I was happy to have it on my car.
I never drove very dashingly. My attention was always rigidly fixed
on the wheel and the road with the result that I could not be as entertaining a companion as I would have wished. I did my most skillful
driving in Kansas or Texas.

Once when we were driving home across country from Arizona
I was able, through the kindness of Waite Phillips, to play an Arabian

Nights trick on my family. Purposely I dallied in Taos, so that we got
a late start up toward the Raton Pass. Chill shadows began to deepen
over the wild inhospitable country. Evelyn became concerned about
where we were to spend the night. The boys were restless and hungry.
We had passed no signs of life for hours. Surreptitiously I had been
consulting directions, camouflaged by a road map. I directed a right
turn; the road became rougher; then another right turn. "Oh, we'll
find some place to stop," I said with assurance, hoping that in the
darkness no one would notice that the left turns marked the regular
route. Suddenly we passed under a wrought-iron gate; an avenue
widened ahead to where a light glimmered. We drew up to the portico
of the handsome Spanish palace which passes for the Phillips' ranch.
We were expected. A delicious dinner was served in style before a
friendly fire. We slept in splendor. Although the Phillips family were
not at home, my own were highly impressed by my skill with Alad-
din's lamp.

That was the first winter we spent in Tucson on doctor's orders.
Again in 1941 we took a house in the Catalina foothills, an ascetic
country that seems to come alive only after four o'clock and then
conjures up all sorts of enchantments with color and shadow and
afterglow. We used to go for a drive every afternoon, stopping at a
certain cheerful road stand where ice-cream sodas were served to us
in the car.

In addition to sodas and fried chicken, I am partial to caramels. In
a way they were responsible for my most recent trip to foreign parts.

When we took Jackie on the Zeppelin as a reward for satisfactory
behavior and scholarship, we inadvertently started a precedent. Four
years later his younger brother presented the same qualifications and
we noticed an expectant look on his face.

I made tentative plans for the China Clipper, but conditions in
the Far East and the outbreak of war in Europe made it inadvisable
to go. The next year was no better. We settled down to a quiet
summer at home, but along in August Nora and Edward Ryerson
started for Rio the long way round. "Why don't you meet us there?"
they urged.

Well, why not? Shaw deserved the trip; no place else was open to
travel.

There was another cogent reason. Last time I was there I had
found some delicious caramels—chocolate caramels—in Petrópolis, the

lovely hill station back of Rio. I had commissioned a couple of other delegations to get me more, but for some reason or other they had failed to bring home the goods. There seemed only one thing to do— go and get them myself.

I admit this reason wouldn't get very far on an expense account, but as I didn't have such an account, it didn't greatly matter.

Scarcely a week later we boarded a plane for Miami, but not without a major crisis. About six o'clock on the preceding evening Shawie developed a badly infected knee. The local doctor advised a week in bed! Evelyn telephoned me just as I was leaving the studio. "Johnnie," she said, "I'm afraid the trip is off."

"*What?*" I exclaimed, clapping my hand tenderly on the paid-for tickets in my pocket.

But the doctor had also suggested that we consult a surgeon, so Evelyn and Shaw started from Lake Forest, and I from the *Tribune*, and we met on the doorstep of Dr. Vernon David in Evanston. He looked at the knee long and silently. We braced ourselves for disappointment. Finally he turned to me.

"Well," he said, "I know how you feel. I guess we've both got a bit of the gambler in us. If he were my son, I'd take him."

There were three anxious days and nights, however, before the knee justified his faith and began to improve.

That part of the trip from Miami to Puerto Rico was made in a new stratoliner, its first flight with pay passengers, and the first time I had been in a pressurized cabin. Half an hour out, we were three miles up in the air over Andros. I could not recognize the reefs I had so casually crossed in the *Sundog*, but forty miles away to the northeast we saw New Providence, and beyond it the tiny blob that was our Island! Through glasses the glint of the sun on the Tower was as clearly visible as it is to me now. We imagined the astonishment of the staff, could they have known that we were looking down on them from such a height and such a distance.

All the way to Rio Madam Elisabeth Rethberg, the singer, was a fellow passenger. On the sixth day of arising at four in the morning, she looked fresher than ever in her third hat. Landing almost on the minute, we saw the Ryersons waving.

"Look!" we cried. "There are the friends from Chicago we've come here to meet."

Madam Rethberg looked at us, not at them. "But would it not have been easier," she asked, "to see them at home?"

Easier and a lot cheaper but not half so much fun. We couldn't
have followed Shaw around the fine Gavea golf course, or watched
him dive from the thirty-foot platform into the Copacabana pool,
which had been so highly recommended by his brother.

On my return to Chicago sixteen days after leaving it, in my usual
report on the trip in cartoon form I was guilty of a slight oversight.

Promptly the letters and telegrams began coming in. "Just read
your story. Did you get the caramels? Answer quick. Cannot stand
the suspense!"

I hastened to relieve their minds. I *did* get the caramels. Unerringly I nosed my way to the exact shop in Petrópolis by the canal,
where the horse-drawn victorias were lined up beneath the traveler
palm. But somehow, in the picture Evelyn took of me doing some
experimental chewing, I look sort of dubious.

Here on the Island, when the wanderlust strikes us and variety is
deemed desirable, we make occasional contact with the gayer doings
in Nassau.

The ceremonies of proroguing Parliament are formal and full of
color, with wigs, silk stockings, buckles and mace bearers. It is also
interesting to drop into the courthouse for a few minutes, where curious crowds lean through the open windows to watch while the judge
leisurely takes down the testimony in longhand. The octagonal public
library used to be the gaol. Pie-shaped cells are now book-lined and
each alcove is a cool retreat with a rocking chair.

Fish hauls are always fun. At these functions scores of guests wade
up a small tidal creek beyond Old Fort, and man long seines across
the channel, where, at turn of tide, hundreds of fish are caught on
their way to open sea. Following close on the heels of the seine hold-
ers, all the way up and down, come two natty butlers, natty at least
above the water line, pushing and pulling a skiff equipped as a bar.
Even the fish have cocktails.

A shark hunt is different. For this sport, two or three barrels of
blood and entrails are secured from the slaughterhouse and dumped
into the ebbing tide at the harbor entrance near the Lighthouse. The
keen scent of the shark is supposed to attract him at once to the
vicinity whereupon he will be harpooned with great dexterity. Unfortunately, on my several hours' wait in the tossing boat, everyone did
his part nobly except the shark who not only did not attend but did
not even send regrets.

Less than an hour away are these and many more sophisticated perquisites of civilization such as formal dinners and dancing, gambling and golf. Yet with the drawbridge hauled up, our sense of isolation is enjoyably complete. We settle down tranquilly to our evenings of reading aloud or anagrams; of dice golf or poker patience, where there are no age limits one way or the other.

There was a time when I played real poker—or tried to.

I belonged to a club within a club—Room 6 at the Chicago Athletic Club—where a number of men met once a week to play. A steward named William was part of the institution. He circulated behind our chairs, and I think he really tried to help me; however, I found the companionship well worth my regular losses.

Here comes Tara, our Irish terrier, wagging several inches of hair off her tail, which seems entirely recovered from the severe strain caused awhile back by the arrival of Miss Pandy and her parents. All three of our boys are with us now, the first time in eight years that it has been possible for us to be here together, a notable reunion. And there are more of us than there used to be.

Tara was given to me by Ruth Hanna McCormick Simms when I stopped over in Albuquerque on my return from the coast in 1937. I had been invited to make the maiden trip of the Santa Fe's new Chief, along with General Dawes and some other friends. At one point, on a curve, everything on the dinner table slid off into the aisle. There was immediate official action to slow down.

Tara's pedigree kennel name was Sheila. Without further explanation I wired Evelyn: "Sheila and I arriving tomorrow in time for dinner." Until then I amused myself picturing her expression when she should open the door to find the puppy's long hind legs and sprawling toes dangling down from under my arm. Reckoning one dog year as equal to seven of our years, as they say, Tara is older than I, but she is a good deal livelier.

Evelyn follows her down the path.

"Will you be finished with the paper pretty soon, Johnnie?" she asks.

"Just going down the stretch," I tell her, folding up the latest *Tribune*. "Now, what is it you have in mind, Evelino? A little snooze? How about a little *New York Daily Snews*?"

Once in my white tie and tails I had to ride a small donkey through just such winding jungle paths as these, full of much more startling animals and birds—all stuffed—on the way to my seat in the Red

Lacquer Room of the Palmer House. That was during the golden age of banqueting when the Indiana Society took note of my return from the Amazon. These splendiferous annual affairs of the Indiana Society are really pageants involving much expense and large casts of professionals.

The greatness of another series of banquets, the Gridiron dinners, is due to two other considerations. Conducted and performed entirely by the Washington correspondents of various American papers, who have demonstrated their ability and cleverness through years of experience, no similar body in the United States has such a reserve of intelligence on which to draw for entertainment. A second reason for their distinction is due to the fact that Washington has such a vast majority of the nation's great to draw on as guests. Through the kindness of William E. Curtis, Clifford Berryman, Cal O'Laughlin and Arthur Henning, I have been privileged to attend many of these dinners. At one of my first, in 1903, I recall the awe I felt when I looked up into the piercing eyes above the bulbous nose of J. Pierpont Morgan. At my most recent Gridiron dinner in the spring of 1947 I was piloted by Arthur Henning in and out of the throng of distinguished gentlemen on the way to my seat. I was proud to have the virile backing of the *Chicago Tribune* on this journey among the notables. Another cause for pride was that a cartoonist, Harold Talburt, was president of the club.

It is a pity the good-fellowship of the Gridirons cannot be permanently extended beyond the banquet hall. In many of my cartoons I have tried to suggest that if all rivals and competitors could sit down together and give and take one another's criticisms in the same spirit of amity and good will, their various antagonistic interests might be harmonized. However, I could more wholeheartedly endorse such plans as a United Nations, had my years and experience led me to a condition of mind where I could have more confidence in mankind as ruled by present-day manipulators. Sometimes I feel as if I were a Victorian or person of an earlier age transplanted into a world of new moral values, especially in respect to business and diplomatic integrity.

It is not only a fast changing world, as I have shown so often in my cartoons, but a fiercely contentious one, where the clash of opinion and belief is confusing as well as disturbing. In the *New York Daily News*, for a time, Joe Patterson used to run parallel columns giving both sides as fairly as possible, commending that part of each which was commendable. To present only one side of an issue weakens a paper editorially. It is reassuring to feel that increasing numbers of young people bring both education and experience to bear in judging which is the grain and which the chaff in these controversial whirl-winds.

There are no arguments on the Island. There are no traffic jams for the ricksha to get snarled up in. No telephones or deadlines or other harassments. Not even a radio, until Josephas acquired one. Some of our kerosene lamps date from Van Winkle time. It amuses us to imagine that, like Rip, he might pop in some day and be amazed at how *little* the Island has changed. We have tried to keep it as simple as we found it, especially in spirit.

## ~ 64 ~

## I Draw to a Close

IN MY albums I find many cartoons about jobs and opportunity. Real success, and it need not be financial, seems to depend pretty much on the efforts of the individual, regardless of his start in life, if he knows where he wants to go and bends every effort upon that one objective.

When I spoke at Jackie's graduation from Milton, I asked several successful men of my acquaintance to give me a sentence to quote. Major General W. D. Connor, at that time superintendent of West Point, sent me this one: "In these get-rich-quick days, when so many are seeking short cuts to their desired goals, I feel that the saying of the wise Mogul Emperor Akbar can hardly be improved upon. Said Akbar the Emperor, 'I have lived a long time, but I have yet to see a man lost on a straight road.' "

Sometimes success thrives on adverse conditions which sharpen the wits as well as the appetites. Sometimes one is led to believe the lucky breaks are essential.

That I became an editorial cartoonist seems to have been as fortui-tous as many other things that happened to me. When, thanks perhaps to the friendliness engendered by the little dog, I had got a fair start as a cartoonist, chance turned me into a foreign correspondent. Since I enjoyed the work tremendously, I might easily have made this my permanent career. Happily it turned out that I was enabled to combine my two lines, which doubtless helped to give variety both to me and to my work.

As I look back, I seem to see many inconsistencies in my life, many wide and striking divergences from the code commonly prescribed for success.

There are instances of glaring deficiency in the manners of my childhood. Take the time Emma, the hired girl, came out to the Elston barn to call me for dinner—"Yonnie! Yonnie! Come!" There being no answer she stepped up the ladder toward my lofty retreat. On the third rung a brick fell on her head and knocked her flat. It was rigged for especial protection against Injun Joe, as I recall.

Are qualities of ability indicated to readers who find that, alone in a big city and presumably intent on serious pursuits, I used to blow myself to a cake of Lubin's heliotrope soap whenever I was particularly flush? Will the fact that when I was older and undoubtedly wiser, I used to buy Manila cigars a thousand at a time and smoke twenty a day teach economy and self-restraint?

What may be got out of this biography of a cartoonist, I am not certain. Since there have been few disappointments in my life to act as a spur, the lion's share of any credit must go to chance, to the number of lucky breaks that have come my way.

Very lately General Dawes and I sat opposite each other in our easy chairs, reminiscing about the bank moratorium in 1933, when the only bright and thoroughly solvent thing in the world seemed to be his Century of Progress Exposition. Evelyn and I were caught, en route from Tucson to Los Angeles to visit Ed Harden, with only $11 in cash. It was no unusual thing for Ed to find me broke; however, this time he was able to help out. We fared very well on our restricted funds, enjoyed our visit, and were in the underpass of the station leading to the return train when the big earthquake struck that wrecked Long Beach. It was like being in one of those trick rooms where the floor rolls under your feet. Our knees went out of control and we braced each other against the wall.

"We got back to Tucson next morning," I told the general, "and when we saw the papers, we were disappointed to find what we'd missed."

"Yeah, the darn fool!" exploded the general to my wife. "That's been

Jawn's life. He was only disappointed when he *got there,* when nothing happened!"

At any rate, it has all been quite kaslosterous, to say the least, and I am happy to feel that I can look back with a smile, and trace hereditary tendencies in my sons. I am unable to explain why they are good at algebra. Still it is handy always to have someone around who knows what *x* equals.

With a warm feeling of pleasure I followed Jackie through his apprenticeship at the City Press and on to the *Tribune.*

Almost fifty years to the day after I sailed from New Orleans with that cargo of mules for the Spanish Army in Havana, Barr sailed from the same port with a cargo of horses bound for Trieste as UNRRA aid. He called himself the "meadow-muffin magnate" and said his job was to dump dung through the dung bung. Since the animals were seasick, it didn't much matter at which end he worked.

When I galloped into Elston with those sizable sums for Cad Bell, I wonder whether he felt the same way I did when I caught sight of Shawie, at a most undependable age, paddling down the lagoon with $15,000 worth of newsreel equipment in the canoe, "so the man wouldn't have to carry it." Much later I was glad to cooperate with him when he borrowed the lionskin from my studio floor at Ragdale and draped it over a log down the lane near the Skokie. Then, with a flashlight, he took a young lady for a walk. Presumably she retreated into his arms.

All the boys went to Harvard, doubtless poetic justice. I must have crowed too loud back in 1927 when for the first time our hayseed football team was invited Down East, and Harvard spelled it P-E-R-D-U-E. They learned better, though, when we licked 'em 19 to 0, even though they may continue to associate us with the French spelling.

After the war we gave a party to welcome two daughters-in-law. I didn't stand in the receiving line. Instead I played invalid in my den where, to my surprise, all the guests came to greet me. I never kissed so many ladies in my life, and I was glad to note that I had not lost the knack of it.

For nearly forty years my regular job, when I was at home, had been to draw seven cartoons a week. Prompted by pats on the shoulder from old Anno Domini which couldn't be laughed off, these were gradually reduced to six and then to three. Outside demands kept pressing, too; charity programs, speeches, favors—the usual lot. Evelyn was stern with me: "Johnnie, you didn't accept?"

"Well, I told him I didn't think so, that I was under doctor's orders and—— No, no, Evelino, I think it's all right. I was *almost* firm."

Finally, in 1944, through the generosity of both Colonel McCormick and Carey Orr, another evidence of kindness of which I have had so much, it was arranged for me to do only the Sunday cartoon. I could not have wished for a more satisfactory adjustment. It left me still one of the *Tribune* family, sharing its prosperity and its vicissitudes; but since the Sunday cartoon could be drawn well in advance, I could draw it wherever I happened to be. My health, to say nothing of the state of the world, encouraging fewer and fewer trips, it came about that we spent longer and longer winters in that part of the world abaft the Tropic of Cancer.

Here we have been working spasmodically, Evelino and I, to get these rambling memoirs in shape—a most gosh-awful job. Time passes unbelievably fast on the Island. It is a great place for noble resolutions, but a poor one for execution. It stimulates the imagination, but not the energies. If only a Burbank could cross them, the result would be a valuable blend. It would be a splendid place for work if it were not for the bathing, sailing, loafing and procrastinating.

Now I have reached an age when I am frequently referred to as the dean of American cartoonists. This simply means that I have managed to survive the various hazards of peace and war and that my aging contemporaries have either died or found a better way to spend their time.

If one can look back such a long way, it suggests that one cannot look ahead so very far. Whenever I find myself lamenting that I am getting old—or older, as I prefer to call it—I also find myself unwilling to part with a single year of those I've lived. If I were asked to sacrifice the experiences of any five or ten of them in order to be that much sprier now, I don't believe I would be able to give them up, even to be young and handsome.

For me the end of the nineteenth century was linked with the Lawson papers. Since 1903, the twentieth century has been linked with the *Tribune*, which, in spite of the buffets of the winds of opinion, seems to stand invincible on its chosen path of Americanism. I am deeply grateful for the associations I have enjoyed in both these cherished relationships.

Many things have happened on this trip down the years from the seventies of the last century to the seventies into which I have moved slowly and somewhat creakingly.

Since I left the banks of the Wabash to seek my fortune in the city, I have been on hand for the greatest boom, the greatest depression and the greatest wars the world has ever known, and the greatest period of scientific discovery. I have been on the reception committee to greet the arrival of electric light, the telephone, the automobile, the airplane, radio, television, and now atomic fission.

Nowadays explorations no longer seem to be in remote places. They are close at hand in the fields of science, economy and sociology. All over the world men seem to be groping for new answers to old problems. Doubtless some of the old charts and pilots that have stood the test of time can never be improved on, but we may be in a transition between one historic epoch and another, the nature of which only the perspective of years and experience can reveal and appraise. The world and I are engaged in overlapping serial dramas, each new installment of which has always left me with a feeling of suspense and unsatisfied curiosity. Just now the plot of the world's story seems unusually tangled, but I'm hoping for a happy ending. For my own, too . . .

And so I draw to a close—perhaps my most successful drawing.

The end of our annual Island visit is at hand.

The bags are packed. All day we have wandered about in that aimless, nostalgic fashion, looking last long looks at the views, sitting for restless moments in each hammock, dipping—some of us—at each beach.

Once more we walk down the alley between the casuarinas, each of whose needles is already tipped with its bead of dew, toward the last sunset. Now it goes down far out in the ocean instead of behind Fort Charlotte. At bedtime Orion will have one foot in the sea and Scorpio will be halfway up. Josephas lowers the flag ceremoniously.

Our favorite dishes are served at supper. The candlelight sheds a special luster on the yellow flowers of the tablecloth, on the blue Syrian honey jar with its fragrance of oleander blossoms.

Into the deepening dusk along the porch comes the staff to join in the well-loved songs.

> My Boss, you goin' to leave us.
> God Almighty goin' to bless you.
> I hope you res' wid Jesus,
> For you is goin' home.
>
> Shake you' han' in de good-by.
> God Almighty goin' to bless you.
> Shake yo' han' in de good-by,
> For you is goin' home.

*My Madam, you goin' to leave us.* Master Jackie, Master Shawie, Master Barr, Little Pandy and the rest, we are all going to leave them with full hearts. The bond with the old retainers who have year after year shared the daily doings of the family, who have seen each new baby come and grow, is truly strong and genuine. For the last time we all stand for the warm, affectionate farewell: "God be with us till we meet again!"

Till we meet again. What sort of white rabbit will Fate pull out of her hat this year? One of the first sacrifices we have had to make in the current world of uncertainties is the luxury of living in the future. Next year we will cruise along the Exuma Cays . . . next year we will deepen the lagoon channel . . . Some day we will . . .

But we always allow ourselves to think with gratitude and humility that there are worse places than a tropical island in which to try to forget, if only for a little, the grim realities of depression days or world war clouds.

Tomorrow from the Pan American Clipper we will watch the Island fade, first its lizard length, then its crown of palms, and last the tip of the Watch Tower gleaming in the afternoon sun. Over the rim of the world they will sink, to become a mirage that beckons us through another year.

With real appreciation we fall back on another old favorite:

> Spare me one more year, O Lord.
> Spare my one more year, O Lord;
> Take me to Havana, feed me a banana.
> Spare me one more year, O Lord!

*The Banks of the Wabash.*

# ACKNOWLEDGMENT

SOME of this material was condensed from my newspaper correspondence to the *Chicago Record,* ancestor of the *Chicago Daily News,* and the *Chicago Tribune.* Some was adapted from articles published twenty-five or more years ago in such magazines as *Brush and Pencil, Collier's Weekly, The Cosmopolitan, Hearst's International* and *Saturday Evening Post.* Acknowledgment is hereby gratefully made.